HEREFORDSHIRE MILITIA
ASSESSMENTS OF 1663

HEREFORDSHIRE MILITIA ASSESSMENTS OF 1663

edited for the Royal Historical Society
by
M. A. FARADAY

CAMDEN FOURTH SERIES
VOLUME 10

LONDON
OFFICES OF THE ROYAL HISTORICAL SOCIETY
UNIVERSITY COLLEGE LONDON, GOWER STREET, W.C.1
1972

ISBN 0 901050 08 3

Printed in Great Britain by Butler & Tanner Ltd
Frome and London

CONTENTS

TABLES

PREFACE

The estate valuations which form the subject of this volume are a remarkable and valuable survival. Despite some imperfections, they are a record of great interest, not only for Herefordshire, a relatively ill-documented county, but for England as a whole. Their context is the fiscal and military needs of seventeenth-century government, but they give an insight into the social and economic structure of a rural county before the agrarian changes of the eighteenth century. I know of no comparable document for any other county. The listings are also of value to the genealogist and family historian for they indicate individuals' local connexions which may not otherwise be known.

The background to the valuations is briefly discussed in the accompanying Introduction and some of the uses to which they may be put are also briefly indicated. Tables are used to save lengthy narrative.

I acknowledge with gratitude the permission of the Trustees of the British Museum to publish the document (Harleian MS 6766), and its acceptance for publication by the Council of the Royal Historical Society. I owe a particular debt of gratitude to Mr Keith Thomas, Joint Literary Director of the Society, for his advice and help. That this edition has achieved publication is largely due to the help and generosity of Professor G. E. Aylmer; for this and for his encouragement and advice at every stage it is difficult adequately to express my gratitude. I am much indebted to Mr E. J. Cole for allowing me to use his transcripts of material from the Hereford diocesan archives and for giving me on many occasions the benefit of his great knowledge of the history and families of Herefordshire. I should also like to thank the Hon. Editor of the *Transactions of the Woolhope Naturalists' Field Club* for permission to cite published articles, Captain T. R. Dunne for permission to quote from the Gatley Park MSS, Miss E. M. Jancey, the Herefordshire Archivist, for help on frequent occasions, Mr A. T. Milne for permission to consult material in the library of the Institute of Historical Research, and also my colleagues, Mr G. O. Lawton and Mr J. M. Thomas, for advice and information.

Transcripts of Crown-copyright records in the Public Record Office appear by permission of the Controller of H.M. Stationery Office.

I thank my wife for accepting with good humour the disruption of domestic priorities over a long period by the work of preparing this volume, which has been very much a spare-time occupation.

M. A. Faraday

ABBREVIATIONS

Acts and Ordinances	*Acts and Ordinances of the Interregnum*, ed. C. H. Firth and R. S. Rait (1911).
Add. 11050–4	British Museum, Additional MSS: Scudamore Papers: Herefordshire military and taxation papers.
Add. 19678	British Museum, Additional MSS: Returns of Traitors' Estates, 1649.
Add. 36452, fo. 190	British Museum, Additional MSS: Aston Papers: Petition on behalf of loyal Herefordshire Catholics under Punishment, 1684.
Assizes 2	Public Record Office, Clerks of Assize Records: Oxford Circuit, Crown Books.
Baronetage	*Complete Baronetage*, ed. G. E. Cokayne (1900–1904).
CCC	*Calendar of the Proceedings of the Committee for Compounding.*
CJ	*Journals of the House of Commons.*
C.6	Public Record Office, Chancery Proceedings: Collins Division.
DL	Deputy Lieutenant (from Public Record Office, S.P. 29/11, fo. 62: Herefordshire Lieutenants, 1660).
DNB	*Dictionary of National Biography.*
E.179	Public Record Office, Lay Subsidy Rolls etc.
E.182	Public Record Office, Receivers' Accounts of Land and Assessed Taxes: Subsidiary Documents.
FP 1661	Public Record Office, E.179/248/11 and E.179/32/223 (Herefordshire returns for the Free and Voluntary Present, 1661–2, Lay and Clerical).
Harl. 911	British Museum, Harleian MSS: R. Symonds, Diary of the Marches of the Royal Army, 1645: estimates of the wealth of Herefordshire gentry.
Harl. 6726	British Museum, Harleian MSS: Silas Taylor's collections for a topography of Herefordshire, *c.* 1659.

Harl. 6766	British Museum, Harleian MSS: Herefordshire estate valuations for the tax at 2s in the pound; and Silas Taylor's collections for a History of Herefordshire.
Hereford	Wills proved at Hereford (National Library of Wales, Probate Records of the Hereford Episcopal Consistory).
Hereford City Lib.	Hereford City Library.
Hereford CRO	Hereford County Record Office.
HT 1664	Public Record Office, E.179/119/492: Herefordshire Hearth Tax Duplicate, Lady Day 1664.
HT 1665	Public Record Office, E.179/119/486: Herefordshire Hearth Tax Duplicate, Lady Day 1665.
JP q	Justice of the Peace; member of the quorum (from Public Record Office, Petty Bag Office: Commission of the Peace for Herefordshire, 1660, C.220/9/4; and S.P. 18/95/72(ii): Herefordshire Justices, 1655).
LJ	*Journals of the House of Lords.*
Loan 29	British Museum, Portland MSS: Harley Papers, particularly Loan 29/49 (Herefordshire Militia Papers etc.).
MP	Member of Parliament; from *Return of Members of Parliament, Part I, Parliaments of England, 1213–1702*, House of Commons Sessional Papers, lxii (1878).
PCC	Public Record Office, Probate Records of the Prerogative Court of Canterbury, Prob. 11.
PC 2	Public Record Office, Privy Council Registers.
PRO 30/53	Public Record Office, Powis Papers.
Robinson	C. J. Robinson, *A History of the Mansions and Manors of Herefordshire* (Hereford, 1873).
Shaw	W. A. Shaw, *Knights of England*, ii (1906).
Sheriff	Public Record Office, *Lists and Indexes N°. 9*: Sheriffs, Herefordshire.
S.P. 12	Public Record Office, State Papers Domestic, Elizabeth I.
S.P. 16	Public Record Office, State Papers Domestic, Charles I.
S.P. 18	Public Record Office, State Papers Domestic, Interregnum.

S.P. 28   Public Record Office, Commonwealth Ex-
               chequer Papers.
S.P. 29   Public Record Office, State Papers Domestic,
               Charles II.
Sta. Cha. 8   Public Record Office, Star Chamber Proceedings,
               James I.
Subs. 1663   Public Record Office, E.179/119/484 and
               E.179/300 (Lay Subsidy Returns, 1663, for
               Wigmore and Wormilow Hundreds).
TWC   *Transactions of the Woolhope Naturalists' Field
               Club.*

HEREFORDSHIRE 1663

1. WALFORD
2. PEYTO, STANWAY AND GRANGE
3. STRETFORD
4. LETTON
5. HURSTLEY
6. WILLERSLEY
7. BROBURY
8. KENCHESTER
9. EDVIN LOACH (WORCS)
10. BROMYARD
11. ROWDEN
12. STANFORD KINGS
13. MORTON JEFFERIES
14. LIVERS OCLE
15. WESTON BEGGARD
16. EGGLETON
17. LLANDINABO
18. HAREWOOD
19. HOARWITHY
20. LLANHITHOCK

Del. M.A.F. 1971

INTRODUCTION

(i) The Militia Acts

The Restoration settlement depended upon its military arrangements. The Civil War and the overthrow of the monarchy were the consequences of the king losing his monopoly of control of the military forces. His son's advisers learned from this experience. Nevertheless even a strongly royalist parliament would not accept the institution of a standing army; both political and economic realities required that the government depend upon the militia. The requirement was for a force of large numbers of adequately trained men, capable of rapid mobilisation, and officered by loyal men with a stake in the society they were defending. The expected enemy was within the country. The lieutenants were instructed to 'be very vigilant over those of the Republican party, there being too much reason to believe that there is a design among men of desperate fortunes to make some sudden insurrection'.[1] The purpose of the militia was both to put down plots and risings and to harass the disaffected in order to keep them disorganised, disarmed and leaderless. In this task it was successful. Given that the militia had to exist, it was vital that the royal government should maintain control of it.[2] Temporary measures were enacted immediately after the Restoration, but the government achieved what was intended as a permanent military settlement with the Militia Acts of 1662 and 1663.[3] This legislation affirmed that the command of the militia was the royal prerogative rather than a parliamentary right,[4] and permitted the king to appoint lord lieutenants and deputy lieutenants for each county to commission officers, to lead musters and to conduct military operations.[5] It required the lieutenancies, according to statutory rules, to charge property-owners with providing horse and foot-soldiers, arms, ammunition, cartage and supplies,[6] and it gave them wide powers of summary and appellate jurisdiction over militia matters.[7]

[1] *Calendar of State Papers Domestic, 1661–1662*, p. 442 (17 July 1662).
[2] J. R. Western, *The English Militia in the Eighteenth Century* (London, 1965), pp. 3–51, gives a full account of the Restoration militia arrangements.
[3] 13/14 Car. II, c. 2, received the royal assent 19 May 1662; *LJ*, xi, p. 472. The second Act, 15 Car. II, c. 4, was found within a year to be necessary, being introduced in the Commons on 3 April 1663 (*CJ*, viii, p. 464); it did not, however, receive the royal assent until 27 July 1663; *LJ*, xi, p. 578. [4] Militia Act 1662, s. 1.
[5] *Ibid.*, s. 2. In later references I have followed Professor Western (*supra*, note 2), in terming the lord lieutenant and his deputies the 'lieutenancy'.
[6] *Ibid.*, s. 3 *et al.*; Militia Act 1663, s. 18.
[7] Militia Act 1662, ss. 9–11; Militia Act 1663, ss. 3, 5, 16.

1

At a time when the more important direct taxes were levied by county quota, it is curious that the militia was not similarly raised. The number of men to be maintained was to be proportionate to the annual value of property in the county, and the respective numbers of horsemen and foot-soldiers were to be determined by the social distribution of that property.

Estates worth less than £50 a year were only specifically brought into charge by the 1663 Act, but, as this was chiefly an explanatory measure, it is likely that this had been intended in the previous Act.[8] Certainly the Herefordshire assessment, which antedates the 1663 Act, implies that no property was exempt. The valuations indicate that nearly two-thirds of the property in the county was held in estates of less than £50.[9]

Three taxing provisions were contained in this legislation. First, the king was given an enabling power to raise, in case of apparent danger, in each of three years a sum equal to the county monthly quota under the 18 months assessment of 1661, which for Herefordshire was £1,166 13s 4d.[10] Owing to 'the plots and conspiracies of last year', which required 'the often summoning of the militia', this sum was in fact levied for 1662, 1663 and 1664.[11] Sir Edward Harley feared that 'the country will be left naked on account of dislike of the charges'.[12] Secondly, the lieutenants were given powers to rate their counties up to a quarter of a month's quota under the 18 months assessment to pay for ammunition etc.[13] Herefordshire could therefore have been charged up to £291 13s. 4d a year. Thirdly, the lieutenants were empowered to charge all property-owners with providing horsemen, foot-soldiers, horses, arms and furniture. The 1663 Act laid down that only the small estates were to be charged by parish rates, but Herefordshire seems to have rated all estates in this way.[14] The statutory rules for determining the liabilities for finding horse and foot are set out in Table 1. The estate valuations contained in this edition were made under these provisions.

The strict rules of the 1662 Act would have been scarcely workable because many people had property in more than one parish and the business of grouping liabilities would have been both lengthy and contentious. The 1663 Act amended these procedures.[15] An unintended effect was that relating the units of liability to the parish instead of the

---

[8] Militia Act 1663, s. 4.
[9] See Table 1.
[10] 13 Car. II (2), c. 3.
[11] *Calendar of State Papers Domestic, 1663–1664*, p. 458 (29 Jan. 1664).
[12] *Ibid.*, 26 June 1664.
[13] Militia Act 1662, s. 7.
[14] Militia Act 1663, s. 4.
[15] *Supra*, note 14.

TABLE 1: *Statutory Rules for Determining Liability to Provide Horse and Foot*

ALTERNATIVE BASES OF CHARGE (*whichever larger*)					Liability
Revenue		Capital			
Amount	Subject	Amount	Subject		
Above £500	Land in possession	Above £6,000	Goods or money except house furniture		To find more than one horse
£500	,, ,, ,,	£6,000	,, ,, ,,		To find one horse
£200–£500	—	£2,400–£6,000	—		To contribute to horse (1662). Not to contribute to foot (1663)
£200	Estate	£2,400	Personal estate		To find ...
£100–£200	,,	£1,200–£2,400	,, ,,		To contribute to horse (1662). To be charged to foot or horse (1663)
£100	In possession in lands tenements hereditaments leaseholds copyholds	£1,200	—		
£50–£100	—	£600–£1,200	—		Not to contribute to horse, but to contribute to more than one foot-soldier
£50	In possession	£600	Personal estate in goods money except stock on the ground		To find one foot-soldier
Up to £50	—	Up to £600	—		Not to find one foot-soldier, but implicitly to contribute (1662). To contribute by parish (1663)

county reduced the average burden; fewer estates would have been grouped to find horse. It is likely, however, that the second Act merely ratified what was already a common practice.

The 1662 Act provided for the charge on non-resident landowners to be sent to them or to be laid on their resident managers or, if their estates were leased, on their most sufficient tenants, who, if their leases did not gainsay it, had a statutory right of recovery from their rents.[16] As Table 1 shows, there was no standard description of the kinds of property charged, but it is likely that the most specific description— 'lands, tenements, hereditaments, leaseholds and copihold'—was intended wherever 'revenue yearly' or 'revenue in possession' or similar expressions were used.[17]

There were no specific exemptions from charge, although peers' estates were to be assessed separately by a panel of five out of twelve peers commissioned under the great seal.[18] Cottagers, tenants at will, and tenants paying a rack-rent were not properly within the scope of the Acts, since they either had no income from land or had no legal estate in the land. The 'tenants at rack' who appear in the valuations were probably charged for their absent landlords. The yearly value of estates was charged and it was possible for landlord and leaseholder each to be charged on their respective increments from the same land, although it may be doubted how often the assessors were able to determine these.

The concept of yearly value was a familiar one, as church and poor rates and previous direct taxes had often been based on it. It was nevertheless ill-defined. One of the earliest satisfactory statutory defini- tions was given in the 1670 Subsidy Act,[19] which defined it as the value 'by the year which the said messuage . . . (is) now worth to be leased if the same were truly and bona fide leased or demised at a rack rent and according to the full true real and clear yearly value thereof without any respect had to the present rents therefore reserved if the same have been reserved upon such leases or estates made for which any fine or income hath been paid or secured . . .'

The principles embodied here are implicit in the Militia Acts. Where the liabilities of rich men were to be assessed exactitude mattered little, for marginal inequalities were easily borne, but where the charge fell on poorer people the assessors had to be both reasonably exact and demonstrably fair. To this end the principles had to be well understood. A rates dispute at Lyonshall in 1684 indicates both the extent and the limits of this understanding; the wardens claimed that a property was let

[16] Militia Act 1662, ss. 16, 17, 29.   [17] *Ibid.* s. 5.   [18] *Ibid.*, s. 18.
[19] 22/23 Car. II, c. 3.

at less than a rack-rent and should be charged at a greater sum, although the valuation they tried to substitute was a stereotyped valuation of 1636.[20]

Personal wealth formed the alternative subject of charge. The given definitions varied. It may be that no distinctions were intended or that the value of household contents was deemed important only in the houses of persons chargeable to horse on other grounds.[21] Liability was implicitly attached to whichever was the larger of landed or personal wealth, just as the subsidies were assessed on lands or on goods. As the 1662 Act forbade a charge to both horse and foot, an individual with both land and personalty would have been charged on only part of his wealth.[22]

The greater families of the county had considerable personal wealth, as their wills often demonstrate. This escaped charge entirely. In the towns mercantile fortunes also escaped. Francis Hall of Ledbury was charged to foot on landed income of £163, yet in his will he left not only this property but also over £1,300 in cash legacies.[23] It is likely that he properly qualified to be charged on his personal estate. Many urban merchants either inherited or invested in land and so are represented in the valuations by this instead of their mercantile fortunes. Even in Herefordshire a great deal of personal wealth may have escaped assessment through the operation of the statutory rules against aggregation and also because the proper alternative charge was almost entirely ignored.

There is no valuation for the city of Hereford and the only references to personal wealth in the county are to two estates in Lyonshall and to an iron-mill in Burrington; it is doubtful whether this last was properly classified as personalty.

(ii) The Herefordshire Militia

Although the Herefordshire militia was called out several times there is no evidence that the county itself had special insurrectionary problems, real or imaginary, or that its lieutenancy was marked by especial zeal. Herefordshire was comparatively mild in its treatment of dissenters, certainly by comparison with Gloucestershire; it reserved its more unpleasant persecutions intermittently for the catholics.[24]

---

[20] Hereford CRO, Hereford Diocesan Archives, Court Papers, I. and O.P., Box 5, bundle 27, Churchwardens of Lyonshall v. Powell, 1684. Detailed assessments for 1636, 1642, 1643, 1645, 1646, 1656 and 1673 were adduced in evidence.

[21] See Table 1.

[22] Militia Act 1662, s. 4.

[23] Proved 23 October 1668 (PCC).

[24] E.g. the arrest and execution of the priest John Kemble in 1678–9; Assizes 2/1.

What therefore was the militia establishment maintained by Herefordshire property-owners? Three troops of horse and nine companies of foot-soldiers were maintained between 1662 and 1667. Thomas Price, James Scudamore and Roger Vaughan commanded the former; John Pitt, Sir Edward Hopton, Humphrey Cornwall, Bennett Prior, John Booth of Hereford, John Booth of Breinton, John Skipp, Thomas Wigmore and Rudhall Gwillym commanded the latter.[25] The militia accounts for 1664 also include the cost of repairs to three drums belonging to 'the Lord Lieutenant's Company'.[26] This company still existed in 1677, for the Harley Papers include a calculation of the pay of its inferior officers.[27] The lord lieutenant was Lord Herbert of Raglan, who combined the office with that for Gloucestershire; this company may have belonged to the latter.[28] The valuations refer to the estates of Captains Elton and Millard, both of Ledbury, and of Captain John Hanbury of Little Marcle, but they did not hold Herefordshire militia commissions; Hanbury's rank, for instance, related to his Civil War career. The accounts show that each of the nine units was mustered for the statutory fourteen days training in 1662-3, 1663-4 and 1664-5. Later evidence is scanty, although disbursements for general militia purposes, including inferior officers' pay, remained considerable. Roger Vaughan's troop served its fourteen days in 1666; his officers were paid £17 10s by William Penrice from the 1664 month's tax.[29]

The exact size of these units is not known. The cost of furnishing one hundred and two hundred troopers respectively for fourteen days, together with commissioned and inferior officers, was reckoned at £55 13s for officers, £10 10s for inferior officers and £175 for one hundred troopers.[30] But this is far from proving actual manning at this level. The Indigent Officers Relief Act[31] provided aid for those who had captained troops of not fewer than thirty horse or companies of not fewer than forty soldiers; by implication normal manning was above this. In 1646 Birch's regiment consisted of eight troops with an average of sixty-nine men each and twenty-three companies with an average of seventy men each.[32] In 1692 regular cavalry troops were to be manned at fifty men each.[33] The militia in 1663 would not have exceeded wartime

---

[25] Militia Accounts, 1662-8, Loan 29/49, pf. 4, no. 69.
[26] *Ibid.* This company was guarding Hereford city in October, 1663; *Cal. State Papers Domestic, 1663-1664*, p. 295.
[27] Loan 29/182, fo. 252.
[28] There were precedents for linking the two counties in military matters; see S.P. 28/229.
[29] Loan 29/49, pf. 4, no. 69/16.
[30] *Ibid.*
[31] 15 Car. II, c. 3.
[32] Loan 29/15, pf. 2 and 3.   [33] Powis Papers, PRO 30/53/9, 10.

levels of manning; so it seems reasonable to estimate a force of over one hundred troopers and six hundred foot-soldiers.

As we have seen, the theoretical manning of the militia was determined statutorily by the distribution of wealth.[34] It may have made administrative sense in seventeenth-century terms to fasten particular obligations firmly on individuals, but it could only have been a military nonsense to determine manning in this way. Herefordshire, a sparsely populated rural county, needed for its defence cavalry rather than infantry; strictly followed, the statute would have provided the opposite.

In the whole county estates totalling no more than £14,000 in value were marked to provide horse. At the statutory rates this would have produced three troops of nine men each, which is unlikely. Either those persons marked for horse bore three and a half times their statutory burden or the annotations of the schedules did not include all those eventually charged and liability was extended to smaller incomes than allowed by law. An establishment of something over one hundred horse and six hundred foot would have required the support of estates of some £50,000 to £60,000 and £30,000 respectively. Although crude, these estimates are consistent with a county militia valuation of £88,000 as shown in Table 7.

The Militia Acts gave the deputy lieutenants considerable military, fiscal, administrative and judicial powers. They derived from their offices greater prestige and influence even than that of the justices. The prerequisites were wealth, vigour and proven loyalty to the government. The duties however were unpaid and onerous. The time and travelling involved is suggested by the details of their circuit of meetings to hear grievances in October 1677, when they met successively at three- or four-day intervals at the Sun Tavern, Hereford, at the Unicorn, Leominster, at the King's Arms, Weobley, at the King's Head, Ross, at the King's Head, Ledbury, and finally at the Sun, Hereford, for a general county meeting.[35]

The county militia was nevertheless run on a shoestring. Both the month's tax and the week's tax remained constantly in arrears. Over 11% of the former for 1663 and 1664 was uncollected in 1668. The week's tax was worse. The funds were in deficit by 1667 and, of the £1,167 due for 1662–5, 44% was outstanding in September 1668.

The cost of the annual fortnight's duty was about £55 and £120 for commissioned officers of horse and foot respectively and £23 and £30 for their inferior officers. This, together with the cost of drums and ammunition, was charged to the special militia tax funds. The pay of troopers and foot-soldiers, about £175 and £420 respectively, and their

---

[34] *Supra*, p. 3.   [35] Loan 29/182, fo. 252.

armour, weapons and horses, fell on the charged estates. This came to about £1,000, increased to as much as £1,500 if the militia were called out frequently, although insufficient evidence exists to quantify this.

About 18% only of the month's tax appears to have been spent on officers' pay by 1668. Perhaps 30% of the funds were remitted to London. The accounts were described in 1668 by the justices as 'so ravelled and perplexed' that they could not understand them. The passage of time has not made them more comprehensible. Until 1666 Philpotts, the treasurer, disbursed sums directly to unit commanders; thereafter he made over funds to Marshal John Hill who then distributed the inferior officers' pay. Commissioned officers were paid directly from funds held by individual month's tax collectors, usually by John Smith. Doubtless this helped to disorder these accounts.

Philpotts kept better accounts of the week's tax, which can be summarised:

	£	s	d	£	s	d
Total Charge 1662–5				1,166	17	3
Uncollected arrears in 1668				512	4	8
Total collected				654	12	7
Constables' salaries	4	13	4			
Ammunition and powder	210	0	0			
Inferior officers' pay	324	16	6			
Drums	45	6	4			
Other militia expenses	38	9	0			
				623	5	2
				31	7	5
Claimed by Philpotts as reward for his pains				32	14	6

Militia activity may have slackened after 1668 for the week's tax was not levied in full every year. Sir Edward Harley thought that making up the shortfall would be illegal, prejudicial to the king's revenue and a grievous burden on all their estates.[36]

(iii) **Methods of Valuation**

The raters were usually chosen from the more substantial farmers, who could have estimated adequately the incomes of others of their

---

[36] Loan 29/49, pf. 4, no. 69. Letter to Herbert Awbrey junior, 5 Dec. 1671, *ibid.*

own class. Their estimates of the income of the gentry would have been less accurate for they would not have had access to farm or rent accounts. There was no statutory liability for persons to declare their incomes, and, while the deputy lieutenants could take some evidence under oath, they were prohibited from taking such evidence from the charged persons themselves.

Much of the property of the gentry was subject to complicated family arrangements whereby widows and other kin held life and other interests. Village raters would have had little idea of its value. In assessing their superiors the raters would rarely have shown great zeal for accuracy. Even if they were meticulous in this regard they were unlikely to have found the evidence obtainable from the servants or tenants of the gentry completely reliable.

In practice such difficulties were partly overcome by methods like those employed by the Leinthall Earls raters for the additional aid of 1666:

> . . . we used our best skill not only by view but also by comparing tenements of unknown value with those we found at rack, and ballancing their proportions with the rates amongst themselves agreed upon, and by all other meanes which we judged conducible to the finding out the true value . . .

Having been refused admittance to Gatley Park and suspecting the motives of the owner, the raters

> . . . tooke the advantage of a foote path through the middle of the parke from one side to the other. And also rounded a great part of the park on the outside of the Pale where we observed the nature of the turfe and soyle. We have also enquired into the management of the estate by those imploy'd in the service and we have received a good account of the number of acres . . .

They also obtained details of crops and stock at Gatley Park:

> . . . from divers of the Inhabitants of Lenthall Earles who are ready (yf required) to make good this theyr Testimony upon oath. Wee have allsoe received Information from the same hands concerning the quantity of Gatley Parke that it hath been allways reputed 900 accres which at iiis per Acre amounteth unto £135.[37]

The Leinthall Earls survey adopted a valuation of 3s an acre for tillage, although the returned parish valuation implies 3s 10½d. There is some understatement in the militia valuation, which comes to 2s 7½d

[37] Hereford CRO, Gatley Park MSS, also published in *TWC*, xxxiv (1952).

an acre. That for Lyonshall may have been based on a survey made for shipmoney in 1636; it was stated in 1684 that all taxes since then had been based on it, but the militia charges were not mentioned as one of them.[38] These examples provide insufficient evidence of substantial or general understatement or obsolescence in the militia valuations as methods of compiling the returns probably varied across the county.

How far were the gross valuations affected by partiality? Men were not lacking in public spirit, but the community to which they acknowledged obligations varied with their social rank and geographical horizons. Fiscal legislation often ineffectually attempted to curb the partiality of commissioners and others. The collection of taxes, for instance, was hastened by allowing collectors a poundage salary, but local assessors received no such incentive. Some inaccuracy and understatement was inevitable, but it is likely to have been distributed randomly unless commissioners for particular hundreds acted in concert to confound the purposes of the statute or to unload their burdens onto other hundreds. Since their own property was often scattered across the county, only party factionalism could have provided them with adequate motive, but in 1663 the only real opposition, the republicans, scarcely existed as a party and were excluded from office; furthermore the deputy lieutenants, being by definition politically reliable and responsible for the spending as well as the raising of militia resources, had no apparent reason to connive at general undervaluations.

There may have been some understatement of large estates and personal wealth was almost entirely omitted, but there was probably no concerted attempt to distort the valuations. They may therefore be used to gain an impression of the social and geographical distribution of landed wealth.[39]

(iv) The Quota Taxes

The summary schedules for each hundred which precede the parish militia valuation schedules in the MS show in the right-hand columns charges which in magnitude come between the hundred quotas under the 18 months' assessment (1661/2)[40] and the royal aid (1664/5).[41] The reconstructed totals of these columns are given in Table 3 (fifth column). The dating of the document suggests that the militia valuations were used as a means of re-allocating the altered county quota

[38] *Supra*, p. 5.
[39] See Table 5. The grouping of the 59 subsidy commissioners in 1663 was typical: 29 served for more than two hundreds (3 for six hundreds); this mitigated parochial partiality; Add. 11051, fo. 82.
[40] 13 Car. II, c. 2.
[41] 16/17 Car. II, c. 1.

TABLE 2: *Herefordshire Direct Tax Quotas, 1527–1702*

Reference	Year	Authority	Description	Total Charge England & Wales (£ s d)	Quota (£ s d)	Quota as % of Charge	Notes
Statutes of the Realm S.P. 12/287 fo. 8	1527	19 Hen. VIII, c. 32	Aid	31,648 0 9	363 14 1½	1·149	Herefordshire did not include the marcher lordships
	1602	Privy Council	Charge for fleet against the Dunkirk pirates	—	250 0 0		Total charge of £8,732 on southern and south-western counties
PC 2/45 fo. 77	1635	Privy Council	Shipmoney	217,500 0 0	4,000 0 0	1·839	The total and county quotas varied in successive years
Statutes of the Realm	1640	16 Car. I, c. 32		400,000 0 0	7,146 4 6	1·786	
Acts and Ordinances	1642/3	24 Feb.	Weekly Assessment	33,333 p.w.	437 10 0	1·312	
"	1647	23 June	Monthly Assessment	60,000 p.m.	868 2 3	1·447	Because of 'unequal rating' the quotas were revised for the 2nd quarter of the tax
"	1647/8	16 Feb.	"	20,000 p.m.	289 7 5	1·447	
"	1649	7 Apr.	"	90,000 p.m.	1,302 3 4½	1·447	
"	1650	26 Nov.	"	90,000 p.m.	1,500 0 0	1·667	repeated in 12 Car. II, c. 20; 12 Car. II, c. 27; 13 Car. II (2), c. 3
"	1654/5	8 Feb.	"	120,000 p.m.	2,000 0 0	1·667	
"	1657	26 June	"	60,000 p.m.	1,000 0 0	1·667	
"	1659/60	26 Jan.	"	35,000 p.m.	583 6 8	1·667	
Statutes of the Realm	1662	14 Car. II, c. 3	Militia Act	70,000 p.a.	1,166 13 4	1·667	'Month's Tax' for 1662–4 'Week's Tax'; permanent Quotas re-computed according to the 'Medium' less abatement
"	1664	16/17 Car. II, c. 1	Royal Aid (3 years)	68,819 9 0 p.m.	291 13 4 / 1,131 13 4	— / 1·644	
"	1665	17 Car. II, c. 1	Additional Aid (2 years)	52,083 6 8 p.m.	856 8 1¾	1·644	Added to Royal Aid quota
"	1665	17 Car. II, c. 9	1 Month's Assessment	120,902 15 8 p.m.	1,988 1 5¼	1·644	
"	1673	25 Car. II, c. 1	18 Months' Assessment	68,819 9 0 p.m.	1,131 13 4	1·644	repeated in 18/19 Car. II, c. 13
"	1677	29 Car. II, c. 1	17 Months' Assessment	34,410 9 6¼ p.m.	565 16 8	1·644	repeated 30 Car. II, c. 1 and 31 Car. II, c. 1
"	1689	1 Gul. & Mar., c. 3	General Aid	68,820 19 1 p.m.	1,131 13 4	1·644	
"	1690	2 Gul. & Mar. (2), c. 1	General Aid	137,641 18 2 p.m.	2,263 6 8	1·644	repeated 3 Gul. & Mar. c. 5
"	1697	9 Gul. III, c. 10	Land Tax	1,484,015 1 11¼	15,307 0 0	1·031	repeated 10 Gul. III, c. 9; and 12/13 Gul. III, c. 10.
"	1699	11 Gul. III, c. 2	Land Tax	989,965 19 6¼	10,204 13 4	1·031	
"	1702	1 Ann., c. 6	Land Tax	1,979,931 19 1	20,409 6 8	1·031	

TABLE 3: *Comparison of Hundred Quotas*

Hundreds		1636 Shipmoney	c. 1647 Army Assessment	1648 Army Assessment	1662 Militia Month's Tax
Broxash	£ %	417 11 10 12·73	152 14 6½ 12·73	142 8 7 12·72	142 7 8 12·71
Ewias Lacy	£ %	149 3 9 4·55	54 10 11 4·55	51 1 6 4·56	50 17 2 4·54
Greytree	£ %	298 3 1 9·09	109 1 10 9·09	102 6 6 9·14	101 12 5 9·07
Grimsworth	£ %	313 0 2 9·54	100 0 0 8·33	93 5 2 8·33	93 4 7 8·32
Huntington	£ %	178 18 8 5·46	65 9 1 5·45	60 19 6 5·44	61 0 4 5·45
Radlow	£ %	417 11 0 12·73	152 14 6½ 12·73	142 8 7 12·72	142 7 9 12·71
Stretford	£ %	313 0 8 9·54	114 11 2 9·54	106 18 1 9·54	106 19 9 9·55
Webtree	£ %	268 8 1 8·18	98 3 4 8·18	91 11 3 8·18	92 6 8 8·24
Wigmore	£ %	239 6 3 7·29	87 5 6 7·27	81 8 1 7·27	81 5 10 7·26
Wolphey Leominster Borough	£ % £ %	373 16 10⎫ 11·40 44 0 0⎬ 1·34⎭	£152 14 6½ %12·73	£142 8 7 %12·72	£142 3 10 %12·70
Wormilow	£ %	268 8 2 8·19	112 14 10 9·40	105 4 2 9·39	105 17 11 9·45
County except Hereford City	£ %	3,280 0 0 100·00	1,200 0 3½ 100·00	1,120 0 0 100·00	1,120 3 11 100·00
City of Hereford	£ %	220 0 0 6·71		80 0 0 7·14	46 13 4 4·17
County Quota	£	3,500 0 0 (Year)	(4 weeks)	1,200 0 0 (12 weeks)	1,166 17 3 (Month)
Source		S.P. 16/346 fo. 61	Loan 29/15 pf. 3	S.P. 28/229	Loan 29/49

in Assessments, 1636–1698

1664 'Contribution'	1664 Royal Aid	1665 Royal Aid	1672 Assessment	1677 Assessment	1690 Aid	1698 Land Tax '3s'
1,708 15 6 12·77	414 5 3 12·71	419 4 3 12·71	419 4 3 12·71	209 15 3 12·71	3,353 14 0 12·71	1,704 18 0 11·57
621 12 4 4·64	147 19 0 4·54	149 14 3 4·54	149 14 3 4·54	74 17 1½ 4·54	1,197 15 4 4·54	403 10 9 2·74
1,219 4 8 9·11	295 17 0 9·08	299 7 9 9·08	299 7 9 9·08	149 14 9 9·08	2,395 2 0 9·08	1,575 9 3 10·69
1,126 19 8 8·42	271 4 9 8·32	274 9 8 8·32	274 9 8 8·32	136 18 2½ 8·30	2,199 17 4 8·34	1,232 8 0 8·36
732 4 0 5·47	177 7 3 5·44	179 19 7 5·44	179 19 6 5·44	89 14 9 5·44	1,435 16 0 5·44	591 1 7¼ 4·01
1,732 13 3 12·94	414 5 0 12·71	419 4 0 12·71	419 4 0 12·71	209 11 7 12·71	3,353 12 0 12·71	2,159 9 9 14·66
1,261 8 4 9·43	311 5 6 9·55	314 19 10 9·55	314 19 10 9·55	157 9 11 9·55	2,519 18 8 9·55	1,319 15 6 8·96
1,107 15 0 8·28	268 13 0 8·24	271 17 2 8·24	271 17 2 8·24	136 8 6 8·27	2,174 17 4 8·24	1,181 8 3 8·02
981 2 0 7·32	236 10 0 7·26	239 6 6 7·26	239 6 6 7·26	119 13 3 7·26	1,914 12 0 7·26	604 5 3 4·10
{ 1,525 8 0 11·39 99 12 0 0·74 }	£413 17 3 %12·70	£418 16 2 %12·70	£418 16 2 %12·70	{ 196 19 10 11·95 12 8 5½ 0·75 }	3,151 14 0 11·94 198 15 4 0·76	1,909 6 6 12·96 250 6 9 1·70
1,268 6 0 9·48	308 12 0 9·45	311 15 8 9·45	311 15 8 9·45	155 17 10 9·45	2,494 5 4 9·45	1,802 2 6 12·23
13,385 0 9 100·00	3,259 6 0 100·00	3,298 4 10 100·00	3,298 4 9 100·00	1,649 7 4½ 100·00	26,389 19 4 100·00	14,734 2 1¼ 100·00
	135 15 3 4·17	96 15 3 2·93	96 15 3 2·93	48 2 7½ 2·92	770 2 0 2·92	572 18 0 3·89
(Year)	3,395 1 3 (Quarter)	3,395 0 1 (Quarter)	3,395 0 0 (Quarter)	1,697 10 0 (Quarter)	27,160 1 4 (Year)	15,307 0 1¼ (Year)
Harl. 6766	Add. 11051 fo. 87	Add. 11051 fo. 121	Loan 29/50	E.179/119/490	E.182/378	E.182/378

under the latter, although the final assessments may well have been different. Sir Edward Harley was both a deputy lieutenant and a royal aid commissioner; this may explain a conjunction of the two purposes in the document. The schedules refer to the 'contribution at 2s per pound per annum'. This cannot be the 2s aid of 1689,[42] but early Restoration assessments were widely regarded as taxes notionally at 2s in the pound.[43]

Taxing by means of county quotas had a long if discontinuous history. Table 2 sets out some of the more notable of these taxes as they were charged on Herefordshire. It must be allowed largely to speak for itself. There were at least two deliberate attempts to alter county quotas to more realistic figures, one in 1649[44] and the other in 1664. The use of Commonwealth quotas was evidently a source of embarrassment and the royal aid quotas were calculated from the 'medium' of the county quotas for shipmoney in 1639, the 18 months' assessment of 1661 and the subsidy returns of 1641. Some counties received an abatement after this calculation; Herefordshire was abated £43 17s 1d, bringing its monthly quota to £1,131 13s 4d. The nature and weight of the county's claims is not known, for the abatement was specifically passed without a division.[45]

Table 3 gives a selection of hundred quotas for some of these taxes. The city of Hereford appears to have gained most from the reduction in the county quota in 1664; after the first quarterly charge for the royal aid the hundred quotas were adjusted in its favour. It was probably very much under-assessed. Between 1636 and 1664 changes in the county quota were very largely changes in the city of Hereford's quota.

The Privy Council prescribed the shares of the shipmoney county quota to be levied on the boroughs, but left to the sheriffs the allocation of shares to the hundreds. In Herefordshire these shares bore the same proportions to the county charge as had the hundred shares of the county purveyance composition quota two decades earlier.[46] The

---

[42] 1 Gul. & Mar. (2), c. 1. The hundred and parish quotas allocated in March 1664/5 were revised in May 1665 on the grounds that the city of Hereford had been overcharged by £39 in the first quarter; see Table 3; Add. 11051, fos. 87–121, *passim*. The Wigmore royal aid schedule summarised in the footnote on p. 133 lists the unrevised parish quotas; Loan 29/49, pf. 4, no. 69/14.

[43] C. D. Chandaman, 'The English Public Revenue, 1660–1688' (unpublished Ph.D. thesis, London, 1954), p. 412.

[44] *Acts and Ordinances*, 7 April 1649.

[45] Chandaman, *op. cit.*, p. 416; *CJ*, viii, p. 582.

[46] Add. 11051, fo. 11. The purveyance proportions were also explicitly followed by the justices in fixing the hundred quotas for the relief of the Ross plague victims in 1637; Add. 11054, fos. 33–4. The precedent provided by coat and conduct money hundred quotas, in 1627 for example, was not followed in allocating later quota taxes; Add. 11050, fo. 190.

TABLE 4: *Distribution of Tax Charges on the Townships of Lugharnes, 1636–1698*

Townships	1636 Ship-money (Quota) %	1640 Subsidy %	1663 Subsidy %	1663 Militia Valuation %	1664 Hearth Tax %	1665 Royal Aid (Quota) %	1666 Poll Tax %	1677 Assessment (Quota) %	1689 Aid %	1690 Assessment (Quota) %	1693 Aid %	1698 Land Tax (Quota) %
Combe and Byton	13·6	12·1	12·2	8·5	12·5	13·3	9·0	13·2	8·3	13·2	7·8	8·4
Knill and Harton	8·3	13·7	9·7	12·7	7·7	9·5	17·4	9·5	16·3	9·5	15·1	15·9
Litton and Cascob	7·9	4·5	5·2	4·3	7·0	7·3	4·7	8·0	3·3	8·0	3·2	3·8
Mowley, Waples Eves and Over Staunton	13·6	12·9	15·7	18·9	14·0	13·3	13·3	13·2	16·1	13·2	14·8	13·7
Over and Nether Kinsham	9·8	13·7	10·6	8·9	10·8	10·0	6·7	9·9	7·2	9·9	7·0	7·6
Rodd, Nash and Little Brampton	13·6	12·1	14·6	11·3	12·0	13·3	11·9	13·2	15·8	13·2	18·2	15·1
Stepleton and Frogstreet	9·8	9·0	10·6	14·0	11·5	10·0	16·6	9·9	10·3	9·9	11·9	12·8
Titley	13·6	11·4	12·3	14·9	15·1	13·3	10·8	13·2	15·0	13·2	14·7	14·2
Willey	9·8	10·6	9·7	6·5	9·4	10·0	9·6	9·9	7·7	9·9	7·3	8·5
Total Lugharnes	100·0	100·0	100·0	100·0	100·0	100·0	100·0	100·0	100·0	100·0	100·0	100·0
Lugharnes as % of Wigmore Hundred	40·5	38·4	37·9	38·2	33·3	40·2	28·5	40·2	26·0	40·2	27·0	25·8
Lugharnes as % of County except Hereford	3·0	—	—	2·6	2·7	—	2·8	2·9	—	2·9	1·1	1·1
Sources	PRO S.P.16/346,fo.61	PRO E.179/237/45	PRO E.179/119/484	B.M. Harl. 6766	PRO E.179/119/492	B.M. Loan 29/49, pf.4,no.69/40	PRO E.179/119/488	PRO E.179/119/490	PRO E.182/1310	PRO E.182/378		

hundred allocations of subsequent quota taxes were generally made by named commissioners whom the statutes normally required to meet to determine hundred quotas and later, in groups, to determine parish allocations within hundreds. These meetings would have afforded some opportunity for local pressures to assert themselves, but in Herefordshire there was often a striking similarity from one tax to another between the amounts and relative proportions of both hundred and parish quotas. Changes in hundred quotas were infrequent and small; between 1665 and 1691 even parish quotas changed little and often to a pattern.[47] The inertia of precedent inhibited even statutory opportunities for change.

The distribution of tax charges on the townships of Lugharnes is given in Table 4.[48] The relative valuations and charges of 1663, 1689 and 1693 show that the pre-land tax quotas became progressively unrepresentative of the actual distribution of wealth. The Lugharnes quotas were allocated on a conventional basis and similar practices were followed to a lesser extent elsewhere in the county. The southern townships were allocated just over 62% of the Lugharnes quota; of this a variable proportion was allocated to Knill and the remainder was equally divided. A similar system prevailed in northern Lugharnes. This suggests that a body of local precedents and conventions rapidly developed for the allocation of quotas.

(v) The Wealth of the County

The valuations show that the mean annual value of land in the county, excluding the city of Hereford, but otherwise including the whole land-surface, was only 3s 4d an acre.[49] There were, however, wide variations, from Litton and Cascob at 10d an acre to Ledbury borough at 32s an acre. The lowest mean values (under 3s an acre) were in the hilly areas around Bromyard and Woolhope, western Wormilow, parts of Wigmore, and in Huntington and Ewias Lacy. Values were highest, above 5s an acre, in the towns and along the Wye west of Hereford and near Ross and in parts of the Frome and Lugg valleys. Land values do not appear to have been higher around the smaller boroughs, whose populations and economic activity were probably insufficient to stimulate neighbouring agriculture.

The hearth tax return for Lady Day 1664 provides, for want of a

[47] See Tables 3 and 4.
[48] The southern division of Wigmore hundred was formerly the lordship of Stepleton or Lugharnes.
[49] These calculations are based on measurements from Ordnance Survey maps with adjustments for boundary changes. Exactitude is not claimed.

more certain figure, totals of households in each parish. It is therefore possible to estimate the distribution of wealth in relation to the population.[50] A significant proportion of the property in many parishes was owned by outdwellers[51] or was tenanted, and there were fewer owners than holdings. The mean annual income per household in the county (apart from the city of Hereford) was £7 2s. The highest averages (of over £13) were in the Wye valley west of Hereford and around Ross and in the Frome and Lugg valleys. The lowest averages (under £8) were in the towns and in the rural areas of Ewias Lacy, Webtree ,western Wormilow, north-eastern Broxash, northern Wigmore, Stretford and in the Woolhope hills. This is not a measure of the geographical distribution of income, but more an indirect measure of the relative productivity of manpower. Figures are highest around the towns, but lower in the towns themselves because income from trade is not included (although its existence supported rental values).

In 1663 only 2% of the property in Herefordshire was owned by peers; the proportion was to rise considerably during the next century. In this county the gentry were a class of no precise limits or identity and the description 'gentleman' must be taken to reflect social standing according to several criteria, rather than wealth alone, for many farmers in other parts of England were richer than most Herefordshire gentry. Taking as gentry that wide class which included both baronets and gentlemen of no great account outside their own villages, we find that not less than 45% of property was owned by them, the proportion being highest in Webtree and lowest in Ewias Lacy. Where land was poor or far from markets yeomen rarely became rich and there was less incentive for outsiders to buy land for investment.[52]

Few of the greater landowners derived their wealth from single estates; accumulation made for wealth and influence. Many owned land in other counties so their wealth in Herefordshire was not a true measure of their social superiority. Nevertheless, with the exception of the lord lieutenant himself, the standing and influence of Herefordshire notables depended largely on the magnitude of their estates in the county. Most of the larger estates were owned by Herefordshire residents. Lord Scudamore seems to have been the most considerable landowner in the county; he and twenty-five other landowners with £300 a

---

[50] See Table 6. Gregory King's figures associating hearth tax charges with household size are not appropriate to Herefordshire without adjustments. Here the analysis is related to households rather than heads.
[51] See Table 5; the proportions are obtained by comparing hearth tax returns with the valuations.
[52] See Table 5.

year or more together owned one-eighth of the property.[53] The deputy lieutenants and justices included most of these larger landowners together with some others, owning in total 12% of the county. There were few of these whose families had not been prominent in Herefordshire for at least a hundred and fifty years, a characteristic of the county aristocracy which was to change greatly in the next century.

TABLE 5: *Social Distribution of Wealth in 1663*

Hundreds / Distributions	Broxash	Ewias Lacy	Greytree	Grimsworth	Huntington	Radlow	Stretford	Webtree	Wigmore	Wolphey	Wormilow	County except Hereford City
Proportion of Wealth owned by various Social Classes	%	%	%	%	%	%	%	%	%	%	%	%
Owned by Peers	2	1	4	—	—	1	3	6	2	3	1	2
Owned by Knights and Baronets	3	—	6	7	6	5	3	2	9	3	16	5
Owned by Esquires	14	3	14	18	20	16	18	22	8	23	15	17
Owned by other Gentry	26	22	19	23	19	26	23	31	22	13	25	23
Owned by Others	55	74	57	52	55	52	53	39	59	58	43	53
Proportion of Land owned in Holdings of various Magnitudes	%	%	%	%	%	%	%	%	%	%	%	%
£500 and more	—	—	—	—	—	—	—	6	—	—	—	1
£200–£499	—	—	8	8	8	8	17	11	—	13	—	7
£100–£199	8	—	18	6	21	12	9	15	8	6	16	11
£50–£99	12	2	11	20	14	20	16	13	21	10	14	15
£11–£49	51	54	42	52	40	46	38	38	40	46	44	41
£10 and less	29	44	21	14	17	14	20	17	31	25	26	25
Other Distributions												
Assessed to Horse in Harl. 6766	—	—	—	—	4	5	17	47	22	37	34	16
Owned by J.P.s and Deputy Lieuts.	4	5	13	9	5	9	9	19	9	14	24	12
Owned by Outdwellers	41	30	45	48	43	43	33	47	33	39	45	42
Owned by Residents	59	70	55	52	57	57	67	53	67	61	55	58

An estimate can be made of the relative preponderance within each parish of its chief landowner. It was usual for the largest estate to comprise between 10% and 30% of a parish. Only in Ewias Lacy was it less. The dominance of the relatively larger estates was most marked in the central river valleys. Wigmore hundred differed from the other two

[53] During the next two centuries large estates became even larger. In 1873 the twenty-six largest landowners owned 22% of the county valuation (including the city of Hereford); House of Commons Sessional Papers, *Return of Owners of Land 1873, England and Wales*, lxxii (1874).

border hundreds because of the relative and absolute wealth of the Harleys. Their primacy, not only within certain parishes, but over the whole of north-west Herefordshire and northern Radnorshire, made them in normal times politically influential whatever the complexion of the government. This territorial base gave them greater weight nationally than many richer families elsewhere.[54]

Small landowners, that is freeholders, leaseholders and copyholders, were still well represented in the county. 25% of the valuation was held in holdings of £10 or less, but only in a minority of parishes did they own more than 30% of the parish valuation. These were mostly in areas of low land values, such as Ewias Lacy, Wigmore and parts of Broxash and Wormilow. This heterogeneous class comprised urban artisans, hill-farmers and also yeomen and husbandmen in lowland areas where great estates were being formed and the social structure polarised in consequence.

Only 206 properties of less than £1 in value are listed, mostly in Broxash and Wormilow. Although the Lyonshall assessment for 1656 included several charges of 1s 6d or less on persons who were not in the 1663 valuation there is no evidence that these were freeholders.[55] The county militia valuations were probably only slightly understated, if at all, on this account.

It is likely that in most parishes tithes appear under nominal descriptions only; they are specifically valued in only sixty-seven schedules, occasionally together with glebes. These amount to 8% of the value of those parishes. This was probably typical. In many years this would have exceeded the direct taxation of the state and would have been a great burden on the resources of productive farmers.

Since the fairness of the land tax quotas was disputed at the time,[56] it is worth comparing the 1693 valuations, upon which they were based, with those of 1663 and with the 1677 quotas. In 1693 the county, apart from the city of Hereford, was valued at £98,000.[57] This expressly excluded the estates of persons who had less than £1 a year, but only a minor adjustment to the 1663 figures is necessary to enable a comparison to be made.[58] The overall increase was 11%. This conceals wide variations within the county; in the west values decreased, but in the south and north, particularly in Wolphey, Wormilow, Greytree, parts

---

[54] See Table 5.
[55] *Supra*, note 20. The 1656 assessment on Lyonshall is closer to the hearth tax return of 1664 in numbers of names than it is to the 1663 militia valuation.
[56] W. R. Ward, *The English Land Tax in the Eighteenth Century* (1953), p. 8 *et seq.*
[57] 4 Gul. & Mar., c. 1. The city of Hereford was valued at *circa* £3,800 in 1693.
[58] See p. 23.

C

of Radlow, eastern Broxash and western Stretford, there were increases of over 40%. At the least this does not suggest that whole counties as such were advantaged by the new quotas being out of line with relative taxable capacity. In Herefordshire the changes do not seem to correlate with the political colour of districts or families and must in part be ascribed to changes in the agrarian economy of the county.[59]

The parish quotas changed considerably between 1677 and 1702.[60] The total charge on England and Wales was £412,926 in 1677 and £1,979,932 in 1702. Herefordshire's share of this fell by over a third from 1·644% to 1·031%, but some parishes actually suffered relative increases in their shares of the national charge. Increases, and decreases of below 22%, were suffered in the Teme valley, eastern Broxash, southern Radlow, parts of Greytree and south-eastern Wormilow, together with Leominster and Hereford city. Generally the west of the county gained the most from the re-allocations.

(vi) Comparison with the Hearth Tax Returns

Few sets of valuations of wealth have survived which are as comprehensive as the Herefordshire militia valuations. Within their limitations, chiefly that they measure income from only one source, they may therefore usefully be compared with other available measures. In particular they may be used to assess the adequacy of hearth tax returns in estimating the social and geographical distribution of wealth. The two are not wholly comparable however, because the valuations measure beneficial interests in land, whereas the hearth tax was charged on occupiers rather than owners.

The hearth tax returns were intended to include, as charges or exemptions, every household with a hearth, and for most individuals a charge represented the whole of a man's wealth wherever situated. As measures of this wealth, however, the returns have defects. The tax was regarded by contemporaries as an excise tax, since it fell on items of expenditure, hearths being chosen as a rough and ready yardstick of taxable capacity. Nevertheless expenditure has never provided a wholly accurate measure of income. Indeed the tax itself probably had a

---

[59] See E. L. Jones, 'Agricultural Conditions and Changes in Herefordshire, 1660–1815', *TWC*, xxxvii (1961), p. 32, and J. N. Jackson, 'Some Observations upon the Herefordshire Environment of the 17th and 18th Centuries', *TWC*, xxxvi (1958), p. 28. Some of the factors leading to change are described in these articles, which together represent almost the only published work covering the rural economy of Herefordshire in the late 17th century.

[60] 29 Car. II, c. 1, and 1 Ann., c. 6. The 1677 assessment, at half the royal aid rate, is the only one for the period 1660–88 for which a full set of parish quotas is available; E.179/119/490.

TABLE 6: *Herefordshire Hearth Tax, Lady Day 1664*

Hundreds and Boroughs	Hearth Tax 1664						Valuation 1663*	
	Charged Hearths	Charged Houses	Exempt Hearths	Exempt Houses	Exempt Houses as % of all Houses	Hearths per Exempt House	£ per Charged Hearth	£ per House
Broxash								
Bromyard	232	74	114	90	55	1·27	0·6	0·9
Remainder	1,510	756	353	352	32	1·00	5·5	7·6
Ewias Lacy	568	381	300	300	44	1·00	5·3	4·4
Greytree								
Ross Borough	396	164	67	62	27	1·08	0·8	1·5
Remainder	1,212	657	388	380	37	1·04	7·1	8·3
Grimsworth	1,123	504	396	391	44	1·01	8·0	10·0
Huntington								
Kington	323	168	38	36	18	1·06	4·2	6·8
Remainder	476	265	178	171	39	1·04	8·5	9·3
Radlow								
Ledbury Borough	291	95	146	132	58	1·11	2·6	3·4
Remainder**	1,583	776	378	377	33	1·00	8·3	11·3
Stretford								
Pembridge	214	105	106	98	48	1·08	3·7	3·9
Weobley	142	62	71	64	51	1·11	4·9	5·5
Remainder	754	414	395	384	48	1·03	7·2	6·8
Webtree	1,340	690	602	591	46	1·02	6·5	6·8
Wigmore	1,264	659	260	261	28	1·00	4·6	6·3
Wolphey								
Leominster Borough	579	217	260	229	51	1·14	1·5	2·0
Remainder	1,551	734	497	480	40	1·04	5·7	7·2
Wormilow	1,700	852	423	412	33	1·03	5·0	6·7
City of Hereford***	1,230	361	498	357	50	1·40	—	—
County*****	16,488	7,934	5,470	5,167	39	1·06	5·8	7·1

Notes: * The valuations used are those returned for the militia, adjusted arithmetically where necessary (see Table 7, col. 1).
    ** For Bosbury and Eastnor the 1665 Hearth Tax figures have been used.
  *** The College of Vicars Choral (48 hearths) and Coningsby's Hospital (19 hearths), respectively charged and exempted, are treated here as single houses.
 **** Hearth and household valuations are based on figures for the county except the City of Hereford.

considerable distorting effect on the incidence of hearths; this and deliberate avoidance diminished the numbers returned.

Expenditure on hearths represented fashions in standards of comfort
and display, which were less advanced away from towns and from
London. A lower incidence of hearths would not necessarily be a
measure of relative poverty. Patterns of personal expenditure would
similarly have varied from one social class to another.

A comparison of the hearth tax return for Lady Day 1664 with the
militia valuations shows that in the rural areas the annual income per
hearth (obtained by dividing the militia valuation by the number of
charged hearths) varied from an average of £4 12s in Wigmore hundred
to £8 8s in rural Radlow;[61] in the boroughs without rural foreigns the
variation was from 12s to £2 12s.[62]

There is a fair degree of association between the parish valuations
and the parish returns of chargeable hearths. The coefficient of correlation between the two has been calculated for each of several hundreds.
A very significant degree of correlation of over 0·80 is shown by each
of Huntington, Ewias Lacy, Stretford, Grimsworth and Webtree
hundreds. A lower degree of correlation of between 0·50 and 0·60,
which is still significant, is exhibited by Wormilow and Wolphey. Even
smaller coefficients obtain for Wigmore and Greytree (each between
0·40 and 0·50); for Greytree this is not even significant. Some of these
less satisfactory results may be the consequence of non-homogeneous
data, for example the figures relating to towns. The four towns for which
figures can be isolated from those for their rural foreigns, that is Bromyard, Ledbury, Leominster and Ross, show a correlation of nearly
0·70, which, because of the very small number of examples, falls short
of significance.[63]

[61] See Table 6.

[62] In these lists only these boroughs are given separate valuations from those parts
of their parishes which constituted the manors foreign (in the strict sense) or other
rural manors. Kington, Pembridge and Weobley, perhaps even Kingsland, were
boroughs or small urban areas whose valuations are amalgamated here with the
more considerable rural parts of their parishes.

[63] The product moment coefficient of correlation for each of these hundreds has
been calculated thus:

$$r = \frac{\left(\Sigma\, hv - \dfrac{\Sigma\, h . \Sigma\, v}{n} \right)}{\sqrt{\left(\Sigma\, h^2 - \dfrac{(\Sigma\, h)^2}{n} \right)\left(\Sigma\, v^2 - \dfrac{(\Sigma\, v)^2}{n} \right)}}$$

where r = coefficient of correlation, with value from 0 to 1,
and h = the number of charged hearths in each parish in the hundred,
and v = the total valuation of each parish in the hundred,
and n = the number of parishes in the hundred as given in the militia valuations.
$r = 1$ would show perfect linear correlation and a functional relationship; $r =$

These figures suggest that if hearth tax returns are used as measures of either gross or relative wealth a deal of caution is necessary; only socially similar and, if possible, internally homogeneous populations should be compared. The larger the area or class under examination the more dependable the hearth taxes will be, but probably the less useful will be the results.

There is nevertheless considerable value in comparing a hearth tax return with the militia valuations. In all the comparisons in this edition the hearth tax return for Lady Day 1664 has been used, for this is both fairly close to the date of the militia valuations and the most detailed return available, particularly as it distinguishes exemptions in a systematic manner. (It wants, however, returns for Bosbury and Eastnor, figures for which have here been supplied from the 1665 return.)

TABLE 7: *Valuations, 1663–1693*

Hundreds	Valuations			
	1. 1663 Militia	2. 1663	3. 1664 Royal Aid	4. 1693
Broxash	8,505	15,765	17,088	11,366
Ewias Lacy	2,984	5,620	6,216	2,690
Greytree	8,888	10,880	12,192	10,503
Grimsworth	8,963	11,304	11,269	8,216
Huntington	5,433	6,577	7,322	3,940
Radlow	13,859	17,731	17,327	14,397
Stretford	6,909	14,516	12,614	8,798
Webtree	8,729	11,023	11,077	7,876
Wigmore	5,800	9,274	9,811	4,028
Wolphey	9,653	16,052	16,250	14,392
Wormilow	8,488	12,161	12,683	12,014
County except Hereford City	88,211	130,908	133,850	98,227

1. Col. 1: The totals of the original returned valuations arithmetically corrected where necessary.
2. Col. 2: The totals in col. 1 adjusted for the marginal uplifting factors (or estimates for these where they are imprecise) in the MS returns.
3. Col. 3: The totals of the middle columns of the hundred schedules in the MS returns.
4. Valuations taken for the first Land Tax.

would show a complete absence of linear correlation; $r =$ a fraction would show a correlation of some predictive value. The fewer the parishes in the hundred the higher would be the value of r necessary to establish a significant correlation, that is, a value which could not be the result of chance.

Reasons of space prevent the inclusion here of a full transcript of this hearth tax return, which contains 13,101 names. As an illustration of what can be done, however, transcripts of the returns for each of the townships of the Lugharnes division of Wigmore hundred have been given in footnotes to the militia valuations for those townships. In addition, for the Wigmore division of that hundred and for each of the other hundreds tabular statements of the hearth tax charges of each magnitude, together with exemptions, in each township have been given in footnotes to the hundred schedules. These provide useful pictures of the social structure of communities for which the militia valuations are evidence of the distribution of landed wealth.[64]

(vii) **The Document**

The valuations are contained in a bound volume, Harleian MS 6766, fos 1^r–188^r, in the British Museum. They carry no formal title or date, although they can be ascribed to the early months of 1663 (New Style). Numerous footnotes have been included in this edition which together provide evidence for this dating. The valuations post-date, for example, the knighting of Sir Thomas Tomkins of Monington on 2 January 1661/2, the consecration on 9 February 1661/2 of Herbert Croft as bishop of Hereford, and the death in January 1661/2 of Sir Henry Lingen, whose widow, Lady Alice Lingen, appears several times. They antedate the death of Sampson Wise of Hampton Court, whose will was proved on 30 October 1663. The valuation for Pembridge does not include Richard Tomkins, who died in August 1662, but does include Thomas Tomkins, his executor, son and heir. Even stronger evidence appears in an annotation to the parish schedule for Hope, Hampton and Winsley giving the date of the review as 21 March 1663. Only clergymen admitted to their benefices in and before January 1663 (New Style) appear in the appropriate parish valuations and only those admitted after December 1662 do not appear; this indicates that many valuations were made in January 1663 (New Style).[65] It should not necessarily be assumed that all the valuations are adequately dated by the dating of some of them; nevertheless the textual evidence, taken

---

[64] A similar analysis for Hereford City shows: exemptions: 357 (including 12 void); single hearth houses: 73; 2 hearths: 96; 3 hearths: 66; 4 hearths: 50; 5 hearths: 29; 6 hearths: 12; 7 hearths: 11; 8 hearths: 10; 9 hearths: 6; 10 hearths: 3; 11 hearths: 3; 28 hearths: 1; 48 hearths: 1. The 1664 return may understate the number of households in the county by 1,500; the Michaelmas 1671 return records over one tenth more households in each of 32% of the parishes and over one tenth fewer in each of 22%, there being 20,123 charged hearths and c. 13,800 households charged and exempt; E. 179/248/14 (and E. 179/331 for Hereford exemptions).

[65] P.R.O., E. 331, Institution Books, Series B, i.

together, is sufficient to identify the valuations as having been made by the authority of the Militia Act of 1662.

The valuations present numerous problems of interpretation; conjecture must play a large part in any discussion of them. A proper identification of the document has failed to be made in the past because of undue significance being read into the presence on several folios of a collection of materials for a history of Herefordshire by Silas Taylor, the antiquarian and sequestrator for the county. The opening page is noted in pencil '1652 Nov 24'. This too has misled.

The dating of the valuations indicates that they post-date Taylor's departure from Herefordshire. At the Restoration he joined Sir Edward Harley's staff at Dunkirk and later obtained a post in the Customs at Harwich. His various collections on Herefordshire were left at Brampton Bryan in the Harley archives.[66] The collections in Harl. 6726, in the same hand as those in Harl. 6766, were written in 1658–9;[67] Taylor's handwriting had not changed when he wrote to Harley in 1677[68] and was totally unlike that in the militia valuation schedules. Indeed the latter bears a striking resemblance to the writing of Sir Edward Harley himself in his personal letters,[69] although there is no reason to suppose that so busy a man would have engaged himself in so tedious an activity. A reasonable explanation might be that Taylor bought the paper in the 1650s, wrote his notes on it, left it at Brampton Bryan in 1660, and that someone else used the blank pages to copy the valuations.

Most, but not all, of the earlier schedules have been written on either side of the folios of the MS; after fo. 71, however, all versos are blank. The schedules are all in one hand and are presumably copies of originals made in the parishes, which may account for transcription errors. Alternative versions of personal and place-names are given in this edition.

Each hundred schedule includes a column heading: 'The value horse being taken out'. The object appears to have been to take the valuation returned by the raters and add to it the value of estates charged to provide horse, on the assumption that they were not returned in the parish totals. These columns in fact contain no detail, for in practice it seems that the raters' returns usually included all estates.

There are several omissions and apparent errors in the columns of figures in the hundred schedules. Those in the middle and right-hand columns are often capable of substitution or correction by comparisons

---

[66] Domville, *alias* Taylor, Silas (*DNB*).
[67] Taylor lists the sheriffs up to 1658/9.
[68] Loan 29/49, pf. 4, no. 67/1.
[69] Loan 29/182 *et seq.*

with the 1677 assessments. Where the charge in the right-hand column is not one-tenth of the value in the middle column it has usually been possible by making these comparisons to determine which of the two figures requires correction.

The majority of the parish schedules contain marginal annotations requiring additions to the valuations. These additions vary from one-tenth to three times the returned amount, but some are too imprecise to be quantifiable. Some refer to 'the Table of the Contribution Rate (or Rule)', while that for Richard's Castle suggests that the valuation should be doubled because the estates were paying little more than a shilling in the pound to the contribution. It is likely that the factors were determined by the royal aid quotas, at least at hundred level, and not that the distribution of the quotas was determined by these factors. The analyses given in this Introduction are therefore based on the more realistic and reliable original returned valuations.[70]

The parish schedules themselves have been totalled and where the arithmetical totals differ from those given in the MS they have been written in by the present editor. It is left to the reader to determine whether the copyist's error in any particular case arose from mistotalling or from miscopying either the total or one of the individual estate valuations; there is no evidence available other than that in the transcript itself. In the Tables accompanying this Introduction the present editor has necessarily taken his own view.

The chief omission from the valuations is the city of Hereford. There are however some others, most of which are listed by the copyist at the end. Other apparent omissions may be embodied in other parish schedules; these are discussed in footnotes.

Editorial Practice

The printed text follows the original MS in Harl. 6766 with only a few exceptions. To conserve space, marginal annotations in the MS have been printed in bold between the nominal or narrative items and the columns of figures or at the end of the parish schedules. Each parish schedule in the MS is headed 'The Valuation returned by the Raters'; in this edition this heading has been used once only. Where no ambiguity results some capital letters in the MS which are not required by modern usage have been rendered in lower case. The original spelling of place-names has been maintained in the text, but the modern spelling has been used in the editorial comment. All editorial additions to the text itself appear in italics within square brackets. In the original MS most of the valuations are in the form: '010 00 00'; this is here rendered

[70] See Table 7 for a comparison.

'10 0 0'. For the purposes of indexing, each parish schedule has been given an alphabetical code indicating the hundred, and a numerical suffix. These are shown at the head of each schedule (see p. v).

Footnotes have been added to throw light on the dating of the returns and on the identification of individuals and their wealth and standing within their communities. Details of the largest charge to hearth tax on Lady Day 1664 in each parish are also given in footnotes, even where there is no estate valuation for a person so charged, as an indication of the social pre-eminence or otherwise of particular individuals in their own parishes. Thus, if, for example, the largest charge is on seven hearths, the note will read 'HT 1664 (7)'. For Wormilow and Wigmore hundreds the largest 'valuations' for the 1663 subsidy are also given in footnotes. They provide a rough measure of the lack of reality in the subsidy book valuations, which, moreover, were meant to represent the whole of a person's real or personal estate, not merely his property in that place.[71] These notes are in the form: 'Subs. 1663 (lands £3)'. The larger offers and donations to the Free and Voluntary Present are shown since these too are well-documented contemporary evidence of disposable wealth and also an indication of sympathy with the government. These are shown in the form: 'FP 1661 (£2 paid)', taking the date of the Act authorising the subscriptions, although the collections were made in 1662 and 1663.

The map of Herefordshire in 1663 printed on p. xiv has been compiled from Ordnance Survey maps, the *Topographical Dictionary of England* by S. Lewis (London, 1831), the *Index Villaris* by J. Adams (1680), and numerous seventeenth-century tax schedules.

Note on the Indexes

Entries in the estate valuations have been indexed separately under *Persons* and *Places*. The further *Index of Editorial Matter* includes all references to persons, places and subjects mentioned in the Introduction and the notes.

---

[71] In Wigmore and Wormilow the subsidy charged estates whose militia valuations totalled, respectively, only 70% and 35% of all real property in the hundred. Individual estate valuations for the subsidy averaged one-seventeenth of the respective militia valuations.

THE MILITIA ASSESSMENTS

Broxash Hundred[1]

	Value Returned by the Rators		The Value Horse Being Taken out	Value according to the contribution			The whole years contribution at 2s per pound per ann' for the particular parishes in this Hundred		
	£		£	£	s	d	£	s	d
1.	383	Avenbury & Hopton Solers		764	15	0	76	9	6
2.	845	Bodenham & Livers Ocle		1892	0	0	189	4	0
3.	74	Bridenbury & Wigton		102	1	8	10	4	2
4.	144	Bromyard Burrough		508	1	8	50	16	2
5.	155	Collington, Hampton & Harton		398	8	4	39	16	10
6.	683	Cowharne Magna		1342	13	4	134	5	4
7.	220	Felton		427	6	8	42	14	8
8.	184	Grendon Bishop		366	5	0	36	12	6
9.	248	Linton Towneship		463	5	0	46	6	6
10.	963	Marden & Amberley		1892	0	0	189	4	0
11.	368	Norton Towneship		463	5	0	46	6	6
12.	279	Ocle Pitchard		569	6	8	56	18	8
13.	486	Pencombe cum Ham'		895	6	8	89	10	8
14.	325	Sapie Perry & Hide		418	0	0	41	16	0
15.	120	Stamford Bishop		356	8	4	35	12	10
16.	163	Stamford Regis Township		274	18	4	27	9	10
17.	63	Stoake Bliss		125	18	4	12	11	10
18.	309	Stoake Lacie		549	12	6	54	19	3
19.	450	Sutton		854	10	10	85	9	1
20.	127	Tedston Delameere		255	8	4	25	10	10
21.	40	Tedston Wafer		125	18	4	12	11	10
22.	214	Thornebury & Rowden		418	1	8	41	16	2
23.	189	Ullingswick & Cowhorn Parva		488	3	4	48	16	4
24.	78	Wacton		147	15	0	14	15	6
25.	383	Whitbourne		764	13	4	76	9	4
26.	243	Winslow Township		463	5	0	46	6	6
27.	527	Withington & Preston Wyn		1342	13	4	134	5	4
28.	245	Wolferlow		417	13	4	41	15	4

[*Total £1708 15s 6d*]

1. In several cases the proportion of the hundred charge represented by particular parish charges is the same as, while others are close to, those of the 1677 assessment: E.179/119/490. [*Footnote continued on page 30.*

The Valuation of the Raters   (2r)

1. Avenbury and Hopton Solers [B1]

	£	s	d
John Browne gent or his Tenn't	24	0	0
Thomas Crowther for the Mills	12	0	0
Henry Pitt	21	0	0
John Conney [Cunney]	6	0	0
Edward Porter for Birchingfield	6	0	0
Anthony Rowndon [Rowden] gent or his Ten't	6	0	0
Alexander Gretton Esq or his Ten'ts	6	0	0
Phillip Bennett	3	0	0
William Sherriff for the Heath	21	0	0
John Michell for Burberies	12	0	0
John Ball gent or his Tennant	9	0	0
Richard Corbett	9	0	0

Footnote continued from page 29]

Hearth Tax return, Lady Day, 1664:

Broxash Hundred	Total Charged Hearths	Total Houses	More than 10 hearths*	10	9	8	7	6	5	4	3	2	1	Total Exempt Houses
Avenbury & Hopton Sollers	84	52			1	1			6	1	4	3	15	21
Bodenham	133	62	1 (14)					3	1	4	9	9	35	0
Bredenbury	23	17							1		2	2	8	4
Bromyard	232	164	1 (12)		1	2	3	2	6	10	10	23	16	90
Collington	37	29								1	3	3	18	4
Hampton Charles	18	24										2	14	8
Much Cowarne	89	77		1			1			3	9	3	27	33
Felton	28	23							1		2	2	13	5
Grendon Bishop	36	14			1				1	4	1	1	1	5
Linton	50	90							1		1	7	28	53
Marden	140	73	2 (15 & 12)							6	6	12	47	0
Amberley	17	8							1	1	1		5	0
Norton	76	71	1 (15)				1	3		1	3	6	11	45
Ocle Pitchard	27	20								1	1	1	4	7	6
Pencombe	99	43				1		1	4	5	7	3	18	4
Sapey, Perry & Hide	59	47							1	2	6	7	14	17
Stanford Bishop	35	34					1			1	3	4	7	18
Stanford Kings	23	10								2	1	5	2	0
Stoke Bliss	21	18								1	1	4	6	6
Stoke Lacy	40	31	1								1	5	17	7
Sutton	49	28				1				1	4	4	18	0
Tedstone Delamere	49	40							2	2	4	2	15	15
Tedstone Wafer	16	14									1	3	7	3
Thornbury & Rowden	64	36				1	1	1		2	1	8	16	6
Ullingswick & L. Cowarne	43	44						1		1	2	4	19	17
Wacton	14	17									3		5	9
Whitbourne	97	99	1 (11)						1	6	4	12	21	54
Winslow	47	32							5		1	1	17	8
Withington	58	38				1				1	3	5	28	0
Wolferlow	38	17					1		1	3	4	3		4
Total	**1,742**	**1,272**	**6**	2	4	5	9	12	32	57	96	149	458	**442**

* Actual charges shown in brackets.

Broxash: Avenbury and Hopton Solers continued

	£	s	d		£	s	d
John Hackett Esq for Gleabe and Tiethes	48	0	0	Roger Woodyatt	6	0	0
Edward Shepard for the Brookhouse	27	0	0	William Bennett	3	0	0
				Anne Corbett widow	3	0	0
Mr Stitch for the Lower Venn	27	0	0	Rowland Rea	1	10	0
				William Lucas	2	10	0
John Broome gent and his Tenn't William Sherriff	18	0	0	Gilbert Nicholetts Esq and his Tenn't[2]	36	0	0
Richard Handcox gent	6	0	0	John Browne gent de Hall Court[3]	3	0	0
John Pembridge gent and his Tenn'ts	18	0	0	Rich: Corbett or his Ten't George Gough	3	0	0
Mrs Katherine Selly [*Scilly*] widow	6	0	0	William Caldow [*Caldwall*]	2	0	0
Thomas Taylor	3	0	0				
John Farley gent for his brother Richards Lands	1	0	0	Charge	383	0	0
Robert Charlett gent	21	0	0				
John Farley for his bro[r] Wms Landes	12	0	0	Richard Corbett, Robert Charlett, Rich: Hancock. Assessors and Raters.			
John Love and John Pembridg gent	1	0	0	**This appears by the Table of the Contribucion Rule to be att halfe Value**			

---

2. Bodenham [*and Livers Ocle*]

(2v)

[B2]

	£	s	d		£	s	d
Michaell Moore Esq[4]	60	0	0	John Jenkins for Mr Halls And for the Lord Scudamores	7	0	0
Thomas Mayo gent	35	0	0				
And for Mr Halls Land **Inquire of this Blank**	—	—	—	Thomas Sandford for Davies Land	2	0	0
The Parsonage Farme	22	0	0	Thomas Sandford for Croones Land And for free Landes	1	0	0
Richard Winton for Mr Crowthers	3	0	0				
Richard Winton for Mr Halls **And this Blanke**	—	—	—	The widow Sinock		10	0
				Thomas Cheese for All	1	0	0
Thomas Coningsby gent	20	0	0	The widow Mason			
The widow Beck	2	10	0	**q this bl**	—	—	—
Humfrey Newton for All	18	0	0	Mr Adams	4	0	0
Richard Hill iun	7	10	0	Richard Hill Joyn[r]		10	0
For Mr Chrowthers Land	4	0	0	Mr Pember his Vicaridge	30	0	0
Walter Syncock [*Sinock*] for Wintons	4	10	0	His free Land	3	0	0
				John Bowker	1	0	0
For Mr Halls Land **q this bl**	—	—	—	Richard Morgan	1	10	0
John Seeth [*Leeth*]	2	0	0	Thomas Heare	3	0	0

---

2. Sheriff 1668; HT 1664 (9).
3. In Bishops Frome.
4. The largest HT charge in 1664 was on Anne Moore (14).

Broxash: Bodenham continued

	£	s	d
For Churchyard Land and for Mr Halls Land q this bl	—	—	—
Henry Prosser	12	0	0
For purchased Lands q this bl	—	—	—
The fifteene Acres	5	0	0
Mr Coningsbye's Copies	6	0	0
		(3r)	
Richard Simons	1	10	0
John Rogers	1	10	0
Thomas Baker	14	0	0
John Jones	3	0	0
John Hodges	2	0	0
Mr Smith		15	0
Phe: Reece	1	0	0
John Rainsford	22	0	0
John Hill	1	10	0
John Haines	15	0	0
William Reeves	7	0	0
The widow Bedowes	20	0	0
Her free Land	3	10	0
Richard Baker	12	0	0
The Byfields	10	0	0
John Baker	7	0	0
Thomas Mason	1	0	0
Henry Mason	1	10	0
Jeremy Birtcher	2	10	0
Richard Farmer	1	0	0
Henry Jay	1	0	0
The widow Baker	3	0	0
John Edwardes	28	0	0
James Mason	20	0	0
Howton's Tyth	1	10	0
John Winton	30	0	0
Phe: Pyvinch	18	0	0
Thomas Hare	22	0	0
The widow Hill	2	0	0
Francis Sayer	3	0	0
Richard Wolf	2	0	0
Richard Cooke	1	0	0
George Bowley	1	0	0
Mathew Meysey	2	10	0
		(3v)	
Johan Lewis Land	2	0	0
John Caldow	1	0	0
Thomas Rainsford	15	0	0
John Marshall	12	0	0
John Careles	47	10	0
John Plaine's Land	3	0	0

		£	s	d
Giles Caldow		3	0	0
John Morley		3	0	0
Christopher Andrewes		3	10	0
Thomas Toffey			15	0
George Burhop			15	0
Alexander Bowker	q bl	—	—	—
Mr Bridges Land		2	0	0
William Hope		3	0	0
Richard Hatch	q bl	—	—	—
John Hope			10	0
Mr Price for Livers Ocle		75	0	0
William Wattons Land		1	0	0
Richard Lovell			10	0
Henry Barton		4	0	0
Richard Hare		7	0	0
The widow Wathen		14	0	0
Henry Reighnolds		1	0	0
Evans Land		3	0	0
John Stansbury		2	10	0
Widow Bowley		4	0	0
Widow Ferrington		1	10	0
Richard Whetston		1	0	0
William Smith		1	10	0
James Bedowes		3	0	0
Richard Hare		1	10	0
Thomas Leeth	q bl	—	—	—
Thomas Jay		1	0	0
Lords Copies: Buck:				
Summorsett	Peere[5]	20	0	0
Thomas Higgins		4	10	0
Tieth Corne: Mr Coningesby		47	0	0
Mr Price for Broadfieldes Court		25	0	0
			(4r)	
Henry Lawford		1	0	0
Phe: White		1	10	0
John Careles for Rowbury & for other purchased Landes		8	10	0
Mathew Meyseyes free Land		1	5	0
		845	0	0
		[846	0	0]

This appears by the Table of the Contribution Rate to be almost double

John Rainsford, Hum: Newton, Tho: Baker, & John Winton. Assessors & Raters

5. George Villiers, 2nd duke of Buckingham, 1628–1687.

3. Bridenbury[6]

[B3]

	£	s	d		£	s	d
Richard Hopton Esq	2	0	0	William Morris	1	0	0
Gilbert Nicholets gent	15	3	4	Richard Corbett		15	0
Anne Rowdon widow	2	10	0				
John Saunders gent	20	0	0	Charge	74	8	4
Anthony Rowdon gent	3	5	0	[55	9	4]	
John Ball gent	1	10	0				
John Smith	3	6	0	**This appears by the Table of the Contri-**			
John James	2	0	0	**bution Rule that a third part is to be**			
Thomas Boyse	1	0	0	**added**			
Joyce Onions [Eynon]	1	0	0				
Peregrine Jones gent	1	0	0	Thomas Boyse, John James. Assessors			
Thomas Cowper	1	0	0	and Raters			

Wigton &c[7]

(4v

[There follows a blank three-quarter page]

---

4. Bromyard Burrough

[B4]

	£	s	d		£	s	d
John Clarke Vicar[8]	10	0	0	Thomas Hall gent	3	0	0
Phineas Jackson clark	2	10	0	Thomas Corbett	1	10	0
John Tomkins gent	16	0	0	Anthony Rowdon gent	1	10	0
John Beynham gent[9]	6	10	0	Christopher Capper senr &			
John Ball gent	5	10	0	iun	2	10	0
John Browne gent	3	0	0	James Jauncey	1	10	0
		(5r)		Mr Jaunsons	1	0	0
The Landholders of An: Ball				Thomas Partridge & John			
gent	7	10	0	Broy	1	10	0
John Barnaby Esq	8	0	0	The widow Bowley	1	10	0
Richard Hopton Esq	9	0	0	Edward Porter	1	10	0
Roger Wednestor gent	4	0	0	Roger Powles	1	10	0
John Williams gent	5	0	0	Mary Parsons	2	0	0
Gilbert Nicholets Esq	4	0	0	John Jenninges	1	10	0
The widow Bennett	3	10	0	John Langley	2	10	0
Humfrey Davies Tayler	3	0	0	Richard Perrins	1	10	0
John Goode	16	0	0				
The Heires of John Stan-					144	0	0
borne	1	10	0				
John Clark iunr	2	0	0	**This appeares by the Table of the Contri-**			
Elizabeth Yeates widow	2	0	0	**bution Rule that two thirds and halfe a**			
Gregory Collins	2	0	0	**third is to be added**			
Mr Philips	3	10	0				
William Sych [Souch]	1	10	0	John Baynam & Arthur Clarke. Asses-			
Richard Michell	2	0	0	sors and Raters.			
Joseph Adco'	1	10	0				

---

6. The largest HT charge in 1664 was on Margery Berington, widow (5).
7. It is likely that Wigton was normally taxed with another place.
8. James Cleark, vicar, is listed as having given £5 to the FP 1661.
9. HT 1664 (12).

(5v)

5. Collington &c   [*B5a*]

	£	s	d		£	s	d
Thomas Baskervile Esq[10]	30	0	0	James King	2	7	0
Richard Wood clerk[11]	15	0	0	George Ballard	2	2	6
Mathew Barrow gent[12]	15	0	0	John Whetston	2	11	6
John Hill	10	0	0	John King	2	12	6
John Perry	9	0	0	Thomas Grubb	4	0	0
William Holder	10	0	0	Thomas Coode [*Goode*]	1	11	6
Thomas Holloway	1	10	0			(6r)	
John Caldow	1	10	0	George & Nicho: Wood	1	10	0
William Wood	2	0	0	Jo: Pitt		9	0
Joyce Barrett widow	5	0	0	Jo: Cherry for Bickertons			
William Poole	1	10	0	Lands	2	0	0
Katherine Perkins widow	1	10	0				
				Charge	37	4	0
Charge	102	0	0				

This appeares by the Table of the Contribution Rule that this value is to be more than doubled

William Holder, John Caldo. Raters

Hampton Charles   [*B5b*]

	£	s	d
John Cherry	2	0	0
The widow Ballard	2	0	0
Roger Bray	9	5	0
Henry Hallard	1	10	0
George Jay	1	12	6
John Jay	1	12	6

Roger Bray. Rater

The proportion is to be doubled

Harton[13] [*B5c*]			
Harton Farme Mr White-breads	16	10	0

proportion to be doubled

Roger Wood. Rater

The Whole rate of Collington Hampton and Harton is	155	0	0

---

6. Cowhorne Magna   [*B6*]

	£	s	d		£	s	d
John Berrington Esq[14]	113	0	0	Hump: Davis	3	0	0
Edmond Taylor	14	0	0	Charles Lawrence	9	0	0
Thomas Freene [*Freane*]	14	0	0	Thomas Baker	7	10	0
Joseph Travell [*Travile*]	14	0	0	Phill: Miles	1	10	0
John Nutt or Mr Berrington	1	6	8	Evan Edwards		10	0
Barnaby Scull gent	9	6	8	Launcel' James	2	0	0
Anth: Lawrence	3	0	0	Rich: Mayfield	1	0	0

10. JP 1660 (C.220/9/4), although not so shown in the Brampton Bryan MS published in *TWC*, xxxiv (1954), p. 292.
11. Rector, FP 1661 (20s paid).
12. Will proved 18 May 1663 (PCC) by his heir Richard Barrow, who was charged for 4 hearths in 1664.
13. Probably Horton, now in Edvin Ralph parish.
14. In 1660 he paid to the Exchequer a rent of £58 for his own lands in Cowarne; PRO, Various Accounts, E.101/630/30.

Broxash: Cowhorne Magna continued

	£	s	d		£	s	d
Margery Smith widow	1	0	0	Richard Stallard	15	10	0
William Adams	1	0	0	William Winslow	1	3	0
Robert Shepheard	1	0	0	Tho: Hallinges	2	1	8
Rich: Clee	6	10	0	John Alcott [*Awkett*]	8	10	0
		(6v)		Thomas & John Clerke		9	0
Miles Gwin		10	0	John Perkins		6	8
Joseph Ward gen	65	5	0			(7r)	
John Oliver		5	0	John Jauncie	11	1	8
Francis Mayos [*Mayoes*]		10	0	William Babe		11	8
Nath: Gardiner gen	28	0	0	Anne South wid	5	15	0
William Bailies	1	10	0	Rich: Babe	1	5	0
John Smith	3	0	0	Evan Jones		15	0
Tho: Oliver	2	0	0	Johan Barnett wid		3	4
James Brompton	8	3	4	Rich: Clee	13	3	4
Tho: Clee		10	0	Rich: Rawlins	8	0	0
James Lawrence	19	0	0	Tho: Lingen Esq[15]	73	0	0
John Smith for the Witchen				Anne Hill wid	14	15	0
[*Witchend*]	23	0	0	Roger Watkins	1	10	0
Fortune South wid	5	10	0	Walter Hopton Esq	1	0	0
David Edwards & Tho:				Wm Aldren		6	8
Baker		15	0	Tho: Clee for Mr Davies	14	15	0
James Lawrence for Goods				John Snead	13	3	4
Lands	1	10	0	Miles Gwin	6	3	4
John Robinson & Georg				Johan Bundy wid	14	15	0
Bennett **q bl**	—	—	—	Edward Wheeler	9	13	4
Thomas Rawlins	12	17	0	Joseph Adcox	1	0	0
Guil: Nicholetts gen	8	10	0	William Mayfield		16	8
Tho: Hayling [*Haylins*]	6	3	0	Tho: Hill, Tho: Jauncey,			
Fra: Minton cler	8	0	0	Francis Badham	1	6	8
Tho: Clee	7	0	0				
William Rawlins	44	12	0	Charge	683	5	8
Tho: Taylor	2	3	0				
John Jauncie for Babes Land	3	0	0	Nath: Gardiner, Tho: Hayling, James			
Tho: Taylor iun	1	17	0	Lawrence, Tho: Clee. Raters			
John Jauncie	5	10	0				
William Nutt		15	0	**Valuation to be doubled**			

7. Felton

	£	s	d		£	s	d
William Maddox cler[16]	15	0	0	Anne Badham wid for Mr			
John Mason sen[r]	15	0	0	Seabornes farme	30	0	0
Henry Mason & his sonne	15	0	0			(7v)	
James Pitt for Lower Hope	20	0	0	Hugh Philpotts for Mr Prices			
James Pitt for Mr Wil-				farm	20	0	0
loughby's est:	20	0	0	John Evisham [*Evesham*]	10	0	0

15. HT 1664 (10).   16. Vicar, FP 1661 (20s paid).

D

Broxash: Felton continued

	£	s	d
Christopher Andrewes	5	0	0
Johan Mason for Westfields Mr Prices	5	0	0
Mich: Mason	2	10	0
John Hill for Buswall	2	10	0
Fabian Pyvinch	10	0	0
James Evisham for Mr Gwillims farme	15	0	0
James Evisham for Burtons	10	0	0

	£	s	d
Anne Pitt widow & John her sonn	10	0	0
Joyce Badham & John her sonne[17]	15	0	0
Charge	220	0	0

John Mason, Will: Hill, John Evisham. Raters

Proportion almost doubled

8. Grendon Bishop [B8]

	£	s	d
Edwyn Skrymsher gent[18]	64	0	0
Edmund Parlor	24	0	0
Mr Kinersley & Mr Pateshall	24	0	0
For Bachleys & New Inne	16	0	0
John Vaston	8	13	4
Charles Wyer	20	13	4
Phillip Sowth	18	13	4
Charge	184	0	0
	[176	0	0]

Charles Wyer, Phillip Sowth. Raters

Valuation doubled

9. Linton [*Towneship*] [B9]

	£	s	d
John Barnaby Esq	13	0	0
Ralph Hill gent	10	0	0
John Sanders gen	8	0	0
Paul Rumney gen	40	0	0
James Jauncey[19]	5	0	0
John Baynham gen	40	0	0
Mr Bridges & his Tenn'ts	2	0	0
William Bosworth	10	0	0
		(8r)	
William Wyer & John Michell	3	0	0
Henry Pitt	2	15	0
Will: Smith	10	0	0
Edm: Bennett gen	5	0	0
John Mason	9	0	0
William Sibles [*Sibbless*]	12	10	0
John Morris	5	0	0
George Browne	5	0	0
Rich: Browne	1	10	0
William Cooke & his Tenn'ts	3	0	0
John Cooke & his Tennants	2	10	0

	£	s	d
Roger Powles	1	0	0
John Watts gen	5	0	0
Rich: Beedle	10	0	0
Mr Wyer & John Such	30	0	0
John Such		10	0
John Ball gen	20	0	0
Mrs Grace Nicholletts	7	0	0
Hugh Parsons	3	0	0
Tho: Colley	1	5	0
Tho: Underwood, Mrs Bowley and the rest of her tenn'ts	5	0	0
Charge	248	0	0
	[269	15	0]

James Jauncey, Richard Beedell, Will: Sibles, Hugh Parsons. Raters

Valuation to be doubled

17. The largest HT charge in 1664 was on John Badham (5).
18. FP 1661 (£5 paid); HT 1664 (9).   19. HT 1664 (5).

10. Marden &c   [*B10a*]   per Ann'

	£	s	d
James Hathway Viccar	13	0	0
Phillip Baker	12	0	0
For the mortgaged Land	10	0	0
For the Lease Lands und' y: Lady Lingen out of which the one moitie fines to the Lady Lingen[20]	6	13	4
Tho: Sutton the 3 parte Walter Powells	8	10	0
John Gwill'ams Land	2	10	0
		(8v)	
Dinmores Tieth Ten't to Mrs Fastescue and for other landes of Mrs Fastescues [*Fortescue*]	6	0	0
Will: Wootton	42	0	0
The groves in his possession in the Close late widow Rices	8	0	0
Richard Lovell for John Wyles farme	4	0	0
Giles Hussey [*Hossey*]	3	13	4
Geo: Crumpe & for wid Brownes land	4	3	4
Arth: Preeces farme	2	3	4
John Wootton	8	3	4

Wisteston   [*B10b*]

	£	s	d
John Price Esq[21]	80	0	0
Wm Edwin & for Mr Tho: Williams land	18	0	0
And for Mr Chutes Land	2	0	0
Walter Mayos	9	16	8
John Cooke Tent to Mr Price	18	0	0
Arth: Loyd ten't to Mr Price	12	0	0
Tho: Turner & the severall purchacers of his farme	17	10	0
Walter Preece for his sev'all purchases	3	6	8
Mr Rogers Land	12	0	0

	£	s	d
Mr Symons Land	5	0	0
Tho: Mayos	2	0	0

Verne   [*B10c*]

	£	s	d
William Towne for ye Lord Scudamor's Land	73	6	8
The Tieth of the Venne and Verne	6	13	4
John Evans for his owne & the Lord Scudamore's & for purchased Lands	11	13	4
Rich: Evans	5	6	8
Will: Whooper	4	13	4
Rich: Cooke &c	7	10	0
William Daniell	2	13	4
Roger Bowker Ten't to Mr Price	2	0	0

Vau: [*The Vauld*]   [*B10d*]

	£	s	d
		(9r)	
Walter Phill: & James Reece	12	16	8
Tho: Williams & his sonne	15	12	0
Tho: Wootton for the Ld Scudamor's land	10	0	0
Rich: Williams Ten't to Hen: Barton	2	0	0
John Morley & John Pennell	5	10	0
Mr Adams for the same farme	5	10	0
Rich: Wotton for ye Lady Lingens land	14	0	0

Fromanton   [*B10e*]

	£	s	d
William Davies gen	44	0	0
Anne Hall wid	20	0	0
Thomas Wooton Ten't to Mr Price	6	0	0
The wid: Edwards	2	10	0
Amberley Tieth	2	10	0
The purchasers of Mr Smiths farme	5	6	8
Tho: Hussey	2	0	0

---

20. HT 1664 (15).
21. The real estate in the county of Thomas Price of Wistaston was valued at £243 a year in 1646 (Loan 29/15, pf. 2); he compounded at ⅙ of his estate, valued at £1200, but settled £50 a year from the tithes of Bartestree and Dormington on their ministers; *CCC*, iii, p. 1980. In 1646 John Price's estate was put at £30 a year; Loan 29/15, pf. 2. He was appointed JP q in 1660.

Broxash: Marden &c continued

	£	s	d
Will: Preece Ten't to Mr Powell	2	0	0
Will: Greene	6	13	4
Walter Mayos	4	0	0
James Squire	6	13	4

Sutton Freene   [*B10f*]

	£	s	d
William Emmett Ten't to ye Lady Lingen	120	0	0
Rich: Hoords ten't to the Lady Lingen for Kinges Mills[22]	20	0	0
James Dutson [*Dudson*]	6	0	0

	£	s	d
Roger Taylor	2	10	0

Amberley[23]   [*B10g*]

	£	s	d
Roger Berrington gent	33	0	0
Tho: Badham	7	15	0
The Demeasne lands	95	0	0
The Gleebe & Tieth	88	0	0
Charge of all	963	13	8

William Adams, Tho: Wootton, Phil: Daker [*Baker*], Tho: Williams. Raters

Valuation to be almost doubled

(9v)

11. Norton Towneship[24]   [*B11*]

	£	s	d		£	s	d
John Barneby Esq	100	0	0	Edward Winwood	8	0	0
Edward Freeman Esq[25]	12	0	0	Elizabeth Pillinger wid	9	0	0
William Watson gent for &c	45	0	0	Johan Lane wid	7	10	0
Wm Acton gent for &c	35	0	0	Sarah Hallard wid	7	10	0
Edmund Bennett	20	0	0	John Arden	3	10	0
Tho Broy &c for &c	15	0	0	Geo: Baylies for lands &c	1	10	0
John Strafford for &c	17	10	0	Tho: Gough	1	10	0
Richard Colley	12	0	0	John Baynham gent for lands &c	2	0	0
John Morris	12	0	0	Wm Hill gen	1	0	0
Tho: Tarbox	9	10	0	Will: Grubb	1	0	0
William Westfaling gen for &c	15	0	0				
Tho: Howman and his landlords	10	0	0	Charge	368	3	8
The Impropriate Tiethes	9	0	0				
Sarah Clements widow	6	13	8				
The lands late of Tho: Wood	7	0	0				

John Arden, Tho: Tarbox. Raters

A fowerth part to be added to the Valuation

---

12. Ocle Pitchard[26, 27]   [*B12*]

	£	s	d		£	s	d
John Pers Esq	20	0	0	Tho: Baker for his owne And for Mr Tomkins land	31	0	0
Reece Morris clerke	20	0	0				
Edward Chamberlen	35	0	0				
Tho: Phelpotts	18	0	0	Edward Watkins	9	10	0

---

22. In 1679 Kings Mills were valued at £30 a year; 'List of Herefordshire Mills Extracted from Herefordshire Quarter Sessions Papers', ed. C. C. Radcliffe Cooke, *TWC*, xxxii (1947), p. 154.
23. The largest HT charge in 1664 was on William Addams gent. (6).
24. The largest HT charge in 1664 was on Elizabeth Flacket widow (15).
25. JP 1662 (S.P. 29/59); royal aid commissioner.
26. Probably excluding Livers Ocle.
27. The largest HT charge in 1664 was on Thomas Freene (5).

Broxash: Ocle Pritchard continued

	£	s	d		£	s	d
Rich: Colley for his owne &				Johan Bayly wid	7	0	0
Joyners Land	13	0	0	John Knight	2	0	0
		(10r)		Rich: Hankins	7	0	0
Warncombe Carpenter for				John Chamberlen sen[r]	1	0	0
ye Tieth farme & other				John Deene		10	0
lands[28]	28	0	0	John Price Esq his Tieth	10	0	0
John Sombers [*Somers*]	13	0	0				
Rouland Taylor	13	0	0	Charge	279	0	0
John Chamberlen[29]	16	0	0	[*269 10 0*]			
Rich: Taylor	16	0	0				
Tho: Spencer	9	10	0	Tho: Philpotts, Edw: Watkins. Raters			
Edw: Taylor q bl	—	—	—				

13. Pencombe cum Hamlet[30, 31]   [*B13*]

	£	s	d		£	s	d
The Parsonage of Pencomb[32]	53	6	8	John Greene gen	20	0	0
Tho: Benson gen & John				Durston farme	18	13	4
Cornwall gen	36	0	0	Elizabeth Eaton wid	20	0	0
John Barnaby Esq & Tho:				Will: Andrewes	13	6	8
Stansbury	13	6	8	Edmond Gittoes	8	13	4
Tho: Benson gen & Wm				Tho: Andrewes	7	10	0
Jones	13	6	8	Tho: Downes	4	13	4
Henry Boyse	17	6	8	Tho: Lewis	5	6	8
Tho: Nichols & Henry Boyse	7	10	0	Solomon Parker	2	13	4
Mayfields lands	6	0	0	Sam: Smith	5	6	8
Tho: Hayward	16	0	0	Pencombs Mill	2	10	0
Tho: Mayo gen	14	0	0	The Court Lands of Grendon			
The Ten'ts of Mr Prices				Warr'	46	13	4
lands	8	0	0	The parsonage of Grendon	7	10	0
Tho: Higgins	7	13	4	Peter Dunne	2	10	0
Tho Hill	21	0	0	Grendon Mill	5	0	0
The Churchyard farme	20	0	0	Sam: Powell	1	13	4
Tho: Pitt	9	13	4				
		(10v)		Charge	486	0	0
Tho: Spencer gen	20	0	0				
Rich: Turnor	9	3	4	Tho: Hill, Tho: Andrewes. Raters			
Will: Spencer	12	13	4				
Will: Sirrell	16	13	4	**The Valuation to be doubled**			
Bitterley's Hide	12	13	4				

28. Month's tax collector for Radlow and Broxash; Loan 29/49, pf. 4, no. 69.
29. Chief constable of Broxash, 1663; Loan 29/49, pf. 4, no. 69/15.
30. Included Grendon Warren and Marston.
31. The largest HT charge in 1664 was on Ben. Coningsby (8).
32. Thomas Pooter, rector, paid £5 to the FP 1661.

14. Sapie cum Haml'[33]   [B14a]

	£	s	d		£	s	d
Tho: Childe Esq	19	0	0	John Nott	7	8	0
Will: Acton Esq	8	0	0	James Stedman	4	0	0
Tho: Wright Rector	16	0	0	Jane Mason	5	0	0
Edward King	19	0	0	John Crumpe	3	3	4
Edmund & John Hill	14	0	0	Wm Ingram	2	10	0
Tho: King	25	0	0	Wm Comby & John Uncles	2	10	0
Rowland Barnes	18	0	0	John Frizer	1	16	8
Edward Pritchett [Pritchard]	29	0	0				
	(11r)			**Perry & Hide** [B14b]			
Edmund Hill & Tho: Hill	13	0	0	Tho: Hill	25	0	0
Richard Lewis	11	0	0	Wm Smith	13	10	0
Humph: Hodnett [Hardnett]	7	0	0	Rich: Smith	9	0	0
Edw: Perkins	9	0	0	John Pitt	6	10	0
Walter Cook & for Sr Jo:				John Downes	2	10	0
Winfords la'd	11	2	0				
Francis Burrett [Barrett]	16	0	0	Charge	325	0	0
Will: Gibbins	9	10	0				
Edm: Comley [Comby]	9	0	0	Rowl: Barnes, Walter Cooke. Raters.			
Walt' Cook for Rich: Lewis							
Land	3	0	0	**Valuation a 4th part to be added**			
Will: Holloway	6	0	0				

15. Stanford Bishop[34]   [B15]

	£	s	d		£	s	d
Alexand' Hancox gen	15	0	0	Rich: Dimocke	8	0	0
Grace Nicholetts wid	30	0	0	Tho: Meadowcourt	2	0	0
	(11v)			Rich: Perry	1	0	0
Dr Langley	13	0	0				
Edw: Bennett gent	15	0	0	Charge	120	0	0
John Tomkins gen	18	0	0				
John Ballard	9	0	0	**Valuation 2 parts to be added**			
Eliz: Dimocke wid	9	0	0				

16. Stanford Regis   [B16]

	£	s	d		£	s	d
Richard Hopton Esq	19	10	0	John Williams	3	0	0
Henry Stich Esq	82	10	0	Humph: Acton gen	1	17	6
Wm Weobley gen[35]	29	15	0				
Seth Shepard	12	0	0	Charge	163	0	0
Mr Strowd	15	0	0				
				Rob: Parker, Geo: Unett. Raters			
				Valuation to be almost doubled			

33. The largest HT charge in 1664 was on Thomas Kinge (5).
34. The largest HT charge in 1664 was on Anne Giles widow (7).
35. The largest HT charges in 1664 were on William Weobley and John White (4 each).

17. Stoake Bliss [B17]

	£	s	d		£	s	d
Edw: Russell cler[36]	2	0	0	Roger Osland for Hitchcocks			
Tho: Holloway[37]	15	0	0	Land	2	0	0
Tho: Wich	10	0	0				
Mr Griffiths Land	10	0	0	Charge	63	0	0
		(12r)			[54	0	0]
Edward Holloway	5	0	0				
Rich: Brooke [Brock]	5	0	0	Tho: Holloway, Edw: Holloway. Raters			
Giles Browne	5	0	0	**Proportion to be doubled**			

18. Stoake Lacy [B18] per Ann'

	£	s	d		£	s	d
Leicester Viscount Hereford				Phill: Holt	3	0	0
&c **Peere**	41	14	0	John South	4	15	0
James Rodd Esq &c	60	0	0	Anth: Lawrence	2	10	0
Wm Cartwright Esq &c	60	0	0	Rich: Barnes	9	0	0
Tho: Taylor of Ocle Pitchard				Edw: Hill	2	10	0
gen	50	0	0	James Robins	5	0	0
Dorothy Winston wid[38]	30	0	0				
Francis Stedman cler[39]	30	0	0	Charge	309	0	0
John Rawlins gen	12	10	0		[354	9	0]
Joyce Baynham wid	9	0	0				
Walter Hawlins [Haylins]	9	0	0	Rich: Hallins, Rich: Barnes. Raters			
Humph: Davies	4	10	0				
Rich: Hawlins	9	0	0	**A 3rd part and half a 3rd pt is to be added**			
Phill: Bennett	9	0	0	**to the Valuation**			
Rich: Smith	3	0	0				

19. Sutton[40] (12v) [B19]

	£	s	d		£	s	d
The Lady Alice Lingen[41]	110	0	0	Benedict Hall Esq & his			
Walter Harries gen	30	0	0	tenn't[42]	20	0	0
John Watts cler	20	0	0	Jane Gibbons widow	20	0	0

36. Vicar, FP 1661 (30s paid).
37. HT 1664 (4).
38. HT 1664 (10).
39. Francis Stedman, junior, rector of Stoke Lacy, is to be distinguished from Francis Stedman, senior, of Yarkhill; FP 1661 (40s paid).
40. Included both Sutton St Nicholas and Sutton St Michael.
41. HT 1664 (15).
42. His estate in the county was valued in 1646 at £243 a year, of which £55 was in Llangarren, £14 in Ganarew, £14 in Whitchurch, £20 in St Weonards, £18 in Thruxton, £5 in Wormbridge, £35 in Wellington and £40 in Sutton; Loan 29/15, pf. 2. In 1660 his estate was rented from the Exchequer by Nathan Rogers for £70; PRO, Various Accounts, E.101/630/30.

Broxash: Sutton continued

	£	s	d
Will: Lingen gen	10	0	0
Geo: Burropp	9	0	0
Henry Gibbons for his Mothers farme	20	0	0
Henry Gibbons for Mr Coningesbys land	4	10	0
Philip Birt wid & Tho: Birt	15	0	0
Roger Spencer	9	0	0
Samuell Smith cler	4	10	0
John Spencer for his owne & Mr Walwyns	5	0	0
Jerome Addis gen	8	10	0
Rich: Baker	2	0	0
Mrs Anne Baker	2	0	0
Edw: Pitt	14	0	0
Mary Davies wid for Mr Coningsby's Mr Bakers Land & her owne	6	0	0
Tho: Guise	7	10	0
Alice Leech wid	4	0	0
Humphrey Walker	6	0	0
Anne Turner widow	4	10	0
Will'm Evett & his sister Elianor	2	16	0
Hugh Spencer	2	0	0
Will: Spencer yeom'	2	0	0
Phill: Higgs for Mr Rowses Land	6	10	0
John Carwardine for Tullies land	3	0	0
John Dawkes for his owne Mrs Walwyns & Mr Roger Lingen's Lands	12	0	0
The heires of Margarett Deeme wid deceased **q bl**	—	—	—
Elizeor Powell & John Dier	1	0	0
Tho: Williams & his Tenn't	4	10	0
Roger Beddoes	4	0	0
John William & Walter Wootton of Thingell for their lands in Sutton	1	0	0
Mrs Probert & Mrs Casson for Mr Roger Lingens farme	4	10	0
James Pitt for lands att Rosmands in the parish of Sutton St Nicholas[43]	18	0	0

	£	s	d
Mr Tho: Gibbons & his mother for Mr Jeffery's land	8	10	0
		(13r)	
Henry Hadland for Mathewes lands	2	10	0
William Spencer carpenter	1	10	0
Mrs Seaborne of Hereford for her lands in Lugg meadow in Sutton	1	0	0
Tho: Stead	1	10	0
James Bowen	1	0	0
Tho: Millard	3	0	0
James Squire	1	10	0
Mrs Acton of Shelwick Mill	2	0	0
Tho: Howells for lands in ye Wirgins	3	0	0
Tho: Hopley of Wyett	2	0	0
Tho: Careless gen	2	0	0
Tho: Hill of Lugwardine for lands in Sutton	1	0	0
George Burrop for Southalls lands	1	10	0
John Leech of Lyde	2	0	0
Mr Dickes Lande in the Wirgins	1	0	0
John Sirle	1	0	0
Tho: Williams of the Vale	1	10	0
Nathaniell Gardner	2	0	0
William Bridges for the Lds Orchard	1	0	0
Luke Lingen	1	10	0
John Smith of Thingell	2	0	0
Jo: Wooton & Mr Bell for Gunddy meadow	2	10	0
Jo: Deeme of Withington for Leonards Crosse	1	10	0

Charge 450 0 0
[*440 16 0*]

Tho: Gibbons, Edw: Pytt, John Dawkes. Raters.

This Rate is uncertaine. Proportion is to be almost doubled.

---

43. Rosemaund is now in Felton parish.

20. Tedston Delamer [B20]

	£	s	d		£	s	d
Mr James Parry Rector				Rich: Stallard	4	10	0
ibidem	12	0	0	Anne Pitts land	3	0	0
William Acton Esq	12	0	0	Rich: Hacklett [*Hackluitt*]	1	10	0
Robert Mason gen[44]	27	0	0	Simon Collins	1	0	0
Mr Salloways land	5	0	0	Tho: Lewis	1	0	0
John Batman gen	2	10	0	Antho: Lea jun[r]		15	0
		(13v)		Tho: Ingland		7	6
Geo: Lane	12	0	0	John Whiteing		7	6
John Barnes	4	10	0	Henry Norgrove		10	0
John Cooke	6	0	0	Katherine Cony		15	0
John Hill	2	10	0				
John Capper	4	10	0	Charge	127	0	0
Anne Lewis wid	2	10	0	[*124*	*15*	*0*]	
Rich: Hill	6	10	0				
James Batman	5	0	0	John Barnes, John Hill, John Mathewes.			
Eliz: Howlders land	4	10	0	Raters			
Will: Wynne	4	10	0				

21. Tedston Wafer [B21]

	£	s	d		£	s	d
Will: Hill & his sonne[45]	10	0	0	John Pitt	5	0	0
Mary Deikins wid	5	0	0				
Rich: Wood	5	0	0	Charge	40	0	0
John Hodges	5	0	0				
The widow Bayliffs land	5	0	0	Tho: Deikins, Morris Ricketts. Raters.			
John Lane	5	0	0				

(14r)
22. Thornebury &c [*and Rowden*] [B22]
per Ann'

	£	s	d		£	s	d
Anthony Rowdon gen[46]	28	0	0	Will: Norris	6	0	0
James Watkins gen	50	0	0	Rich: Holland	3	0	0
Geo: Baylies	18	0	0	John Goode	2	10	0
Job Winton	20	0	0	Rich: Mason gen	4	10	0
Tho: Greene gen	16	0	0	Will: Baylies	3	0	0
Edw: Collins	14	0	0	Morgan James	3	0	0
John Whittington gen[47]	14	0	0				
Geo: Fincher cler[48]	14	0	0	Charge	214	0	0
Tho: Goode	9	0	0				
Humph: Goode	9	0	0	Job Winton, Edw: Collins. Raters.			

44. HT 1664 (5). John Hall and Anne Hall together were also charged for 5 hearths.
45. HT 1664 (3).   46. HT 1664 (9).
47. He may have been rector of Pudleston in 1661; E.179/32/223.
48. Rector, FP 1661 (£3 paid).

23. Ullingswicke &c [*and Cowhorn Parva*][49]   [*B23*]

	£	s	d		£	s	d
Tho: Barkley cler[50]	24	0	0	John Bowley & the pur-			
Rog: Ensell	30	0	0	chasers	3	0	0
John Hill gen	13	10	0	Tho: Hill	12	0	0
Will: Bennett	4	10	0	Phineas Jackson	7	10	0
James Bowley	1	10	0	Stephen Hey		15	0
Tho: Tovey	7	10	0	John Seaborne		15	0
John Hill senr	10	10	0	John Hill gen	3	0	0
John Hill junr	4	0	0	Robt Vie	4	10	0
James Bowen	3	10	0	Edw: Bullock & Humph			
Mary Baddam	4	0	0	Burton	3	0	0
Tho: Holt & Tho: Davies	5	0	0	John Hill & James Bennett	9	0	0
John Meyricke	1	10	0	Walter Hawlings [*Hallings*]	3	0	0
		(14v)		Phineas Jackson		15	0
Robert Hill	15	0	0				
Eliz: Caldow	1	10	0	Charge	189	0	0
Tho: Love	6	5	0	[*181*	*15*	*0*]	
John Chamberlaine		15	0				
Robt Vie [*Vey*] & Evan				Rogr Ensoll, John Hill jun[r], John Hill			
Edwards	1	10	0	sen., Raters			

Valuation something more then doubled

---

24. Wackton   [*B24*]

	£	s	d		£	s	d
John Barnabie Esq	25	0	0	John Tomkins gen in Tiethes	5	0	0
Rich: Clarke[51]	15	0	0	James Clarke cler in privy			
Abraham Wykes [*Wyke*][52]	10	0	0	Tiethes	2	10	0
Henry Mace[53]	7	10	0				
John Brodford	3	15	0	Charge	78	0	0
Tho: Abrahall	3	15	0				
Roger Brasier	2	10	0	Henry Mace, Roger Brasier. Raters.			
The Relict of Tho: Elton							
clothier	3	15	0	**The Valuation to be doubled**			

---

49. The largest HT charge in 1664 was on Sim. Jacobb gent. (6).
50. Rector, FP 1661 (£3 paid).
51. HT 1664 (3).
52. HT 1664 (3).
53. HT 1664 (3).

25. Whitbourne (15r) [B25]

	£	s	d		£	s	d
John Birch Esq[54]	100	0	0	Wm Groome	4	0	0
John Cooke cler	32	0	0	John Davies	5	6	0
Tho: Martin gen	13	0	0	Dan: Andrewes	4	0	0
Wm Gardner	20	0	0	Robt Chappell	5	0	0
Roger Wall[55]	17	10	0	Will: Comby cler	2	10	0
Tho: Wood	15	0	0	Rich: Collyns	4	0	0
John Hucke	17	10	0	Margery Jewe	2	10	0
William Mason gen	13	0	0	John Moseley	2	10	0
Wm Barnes	10	0	0	Edw: Griffithes	2	10	0
Tho: Gardner	10	0	0	Peter Harvey	4	0	0
John Colly	9	15	0	Alice Wynn wid	9	15	0
Tho Pytt	9	15	0	Tho: Colly Cromolbury	4	0	0
Wm Wynn	9	15	0	Henry Ecle	2	0	0
Wm Done [*Dove*]	10	0	0				
Geo: Unitt	8	0	0	Charge 383	0	0	
Margery Collyns wid	8	5	0				
Jane Hill wid	7	15	0	Rog: Wall, William Hopkins. Raters.			
Rich: Hinchman [*Hincksman*]	7	10	0				
John Arden	8	10	0	**Valuation is to be doubled**			
Wm Hopkins	3	15	0				

26. Winslow [*Township*] (15v) [B26]

	£	s	d		£	s	d
John Barnaby Esq	3	0	0	John Baynham gen	5	0	0
Tho: Dubitott [*Dabitott*] gen[56]	13	0	0	Mrs Tomkins & Mrs Wednester	3	0	0
John Hardwick gen[57]	20	0	0	Henry Daunce	5	0	0
Phineas Jackson cler[58]	30	0	0	Humphrey Davies & his sonne	5	0	0
Tho: Benson gen[59]	20	0	0	Edw: Tyler	3	0	0
Pet[r] Harvey gen	15	0	0	Tho: Mayfield	3	0	0
Tho: Botfield[60]	15	0	0	James Slade	2	0	0
Hen: Penell	10	0	0	Mr Watson	1	0	0
Rich: Barnes	10	0	0	Mr Tomkins		10	0
Jo: Cony	15	0	0				
Christopher Coup[r]	10	0	0	Charge 243	0	0	
Will: Wilkes?	5	0	0	[*233 10 0*]			
Will: Morris	10	0	0				
Rich: Hopton Esq	5	0	0	Will: Wilkes, Barnaby Butler. Raters			
Tho: Williams & Jo: Baynam gen	10	0	0				
John Browne gen	5	0	0	**To be almost doubled in the valuation**			
Anthony Rowdon gen	10	0	0				

54. HT 1664 (11).
55. Chief constable of Broxash, 1663; Loan 29/49, pf. 4, no. 69/15.
56. HT 1664 (5).
57. HT 1664 (5).   58. HT 1664 (5).   59. HT 1664 (5).   60. HT 1664 (5).

27. Withington &c   [B27a]

	£	s	d
Humph: Taylor Esq for the Court[61]	30	0	0
John Parsons cler	8	0	0
		(16r)	
John Syrrell [Syrle]	16	0	0
Rich: Collas	10	0	0
John Deeme jun	8	0	0
Hen: Baylie	8	0	0
Anth: Franke	4	0	0
Katherine Bennis wid	3	0	0
Rouland Taylor	3	0	0
John Smith	2	0	0
Tho: Deeme	1	6	8
John Winter		15	0
Johan Tomkins wid		10	0

Thinghill   [B27b]

	£	s	d
Rich: Carwardine	14	10	0
John Carwardine	14	10	0
Walter Mayos	10	0	0
John Deeme senr	8	0	0
Mrs Church wid	8	0	0
Anthony Franke	4	0	0
Elinor Dale wid	8	0	0
John Hill	4	0	0
Rich: Baylie	4	0	0
Walter Davies	4	0	0
John Wotton	4	0	0
Edw: Chamberlen	4	0	0
John Smith	2	0	0

Ewithington and Nonington
[Eau Withington] [B27c]

	£	s	d
Grissell Burhill [Burghill] wid	30	0	0
Dan: Alderne gen	20	0	0
Will: Browne gen	40	0	0
Tho: Careless gen	22	0	0
Roger Powell gen	10	0	0
Anne Draper wid	4	0	0
Richard Carwardine of Bach	10	0	0
John Deeme sen	4	0	0
Tho: Deeme [The Dean] & Chapt[r] for ye Tyth	30	0	0
Tho: Tomkins	6	0	0
		(16v)	

	£	s	d
John Broome gen	4	0	0
Martha Baylies ten't	3	10	0
Kath: Smith & Rog[r] Powell gen	5	7	0
Henry Higgins	4	0	0
James Seaburne	5	0	0
James Norton		10	0
John Deeme the youngest	3	0	0
Wm Seaborne	1	10	0
Mrs Powell of Heref	3	0	0
Rich: Guy	1	10	0
Jo: Price Esq for ye tieth of Little Thinghill	4	0	0
John Clements gen	1	10	0
Mr Rodd		10	0
Mr Dancer	1	0	0
Mr Barkeley		10	0
Mr Philips		10	0
Mrs Price	1	0	0
Tho: Godwin gen		10	0
Mr Collins		10	0
Abell Eysham		10	0
Christopher Collins	1	10	0

Charge 402 18 8

Rich: Carwardine, Rogr Powell, Rich: Collas. Raters
Proportion to be doubled

Preston Win [in] Withington Parish
[B27d]

	£	s	d
Hump: Tayler Esq	22	0	0
Mrs Seaborne	32	0	0
Tho: Hodges	11	0	0
Rich: Mayos	10	10	0
Edw: Hodges	5	10	0
James Squire	5	10	0
Eliz: Farmer	5	10	0
Tho: Taylor gen	5	0	0
		(17r)	
John Wotton		15	0
Sam: Hill	1	7	0
Jo: Tomkins for the Deans Tieth	17	0	0

---

61. HT 1664 (7), probably for Thinghill Court.

Broxash: Withington &c: Preston Win continued

	£	s	d	
Phill: Mayos	1	0	0	Tho: Hodges rater.
Phil: Spencer	6	0	0	
Mr Helline	1	0	0	Withington Parish the whole charge
Jo: Spencer		18	0	£527
				Valuation to be doubled
Charge	125	0	0	

28. Wolferlow [*B28*]

	£	s	d		£	s	d
Tho: Child Esq[62]	120	0	0	Nichol' Powell	10	0	0
Giles Rawlins [*Rasell*] cler	20	0	0				
Tho: Griffiths gen	30	0	0	Charge	245	0	0
Mrs Ursula Awbrey & Math:							
Hall	30	0	0	John Broome, Math: Hall. Raters.			
Jo: Broome	15	0	0				
Jo: Russell	10	0	0	**Valuation to be doubled**			
Tho: Taylor	10	0	0				

62. HT 1664 (8).

Ewias Lacy Hundred[1]

	Value Returned by ye Raters		The Value Horse Being Taken Out	Value according to the contribution			The whole yeares contribution at 2s per pownd per ann' for each particular parish in the Hundred		
	£		£	s	d		£	s	d
1.	491	Creswall	711	0	0		71	2	0
2.	222	Cusopp	310	6	8		31	0	8
3.	226	Lancillo &c	821	13	4		8	3	8
							[82	3	4]
4.	316	Lanveynoe	711	0	0		71	2	0
5.	648	Longtowne	1415	6	8		141	10	8
6.	377	Michael Church Escley	790	3	4		79	0	4
7.	282	Newton	711	0	0		71	2	0
8.	315	Waterston	745	13	4		74	11	4

[*Total £621 12s 4d*]

1. The charge against Llancillo is an error, but it is not clear when it was made. The month's tax quota would have been very close to one twelfth of £82 rather than of £8, just as for the first three months of the royal aid Llancillo was charged £5 16s 2d a month; Add. 11051, fo. 94.

Hearth Tax return, Lady Day, 1664:

Ewias Lacy Hundred	Total Charged Hearths	Total Houses	Numbers of Charges of Each Magnitude					Total Exempt Houses
			Hearths					
			8	4	3	2	1	
Craswall	56	73			2	9	32	30
Cusop	34	34		2	1	5	13	13
Llancillo & Rowlston	58	53		1	4	10	22	16
Llanveynoe	58	76			1	13	29	33
Longtown	146	179	1	2	14	23	42	97
Michaelchurch Escley	70	76		1	2	11	38	24
Newton	67	102			3	16	26	57
Walterstone	69	78	1		3	8	36	30
Total	568	681	2	6	30	95	248	300

1. Creswall [*Craswall*]   (19r)   [*E1*]

	£	s	d		£	s	d
Walter Vaugham [*Vaughan*]				Tho: Lewis	1	10	0
gen	7	10	0	David Watkin	6	0	0
Tho: Hugh & Mr Carpenter	16	10	0	Zakery Guilbert	7	10	0
Phill: Lewis & Jo: Tho:				Wm Guilbert & Eliz: Guil-			
Griffithes	14	0	0	bert	11	0	0
the wid Guilbert	15	0	0	Robt Shaw	11	0	0
Wm Higgins	20	0	0	Edmund Price	7	0	0
Jenkin Miles	15	0	0	Phill: Powell[3]	23	0	0
Watkin David	25	0	0			(19v)	
James Nicholls iun	16	0	0	Watkin Jenkins	9	0	0
Roger Taylor	7	10	0	John Jenkins	11	0	0
Tho: Lewis	7	10	0	David Watkin Will'm	3	0	0
Tho: Rogers	14	0	0	Howell Phillipp	3	0	0
John James	7	10	0	Lewis Rice Harry		15	0
David Smith[2]	15	0	0	Thomas Watkins iun	3	0	0
Mary Powell & Lewis Powell	15	0	0	The Tieth of Wooll & Lambes			
Hugh Jones & Jo: Jones	7	10	0	Esq Arnolds ten't	4	10	0
Jo: Thomas	10	0	0	Cayr Daullwyth	1	0	0
Blanch Griffith	10	0	0	Kildare	1	10	0
Hugh Lord & Jo: David	11	0	0	Cayr Moody [*Maerdy*]	1	0	0
Tho: Watkins gen	45	0	0	John Perrotts Mill	6	0	0
Henry Griffith & Geo:				The late lands of Anne Jones	2	0	0
Jenkins	22	0	0				
Hugh Charles	7	10	0	Charge	491	0	0
David Nicholls	7	10	0				
The wid Shaw	6	0	0	No personall estate within the said			
James Goode	3	10	0	Towneshipp			
Will: Harry	3	10	0				
Eliz: Harry	9	0	0	Lewis Powell, James Nichol, Will:			
James Watkin	2	0	0	Guilbert, Rice Phillipps Perry, Will:			
Phill: Harry	5	10	0	Harry, David Watkin, David Nicholl.			
Geo: Jenkins q Bl:				Raters.			
Rich: Mapp & James Mapp	7	10	0				
Rice Phill: Harry	7	10	0	**A third part to be added to the valuation**			
James Nicholls sen	11	0	0				
Hugh Charles	6	0	0				

2. Cusopp   [*E2*]

	£	s	d		£	s	d
Mrs Elizabeth Loyd wid[4]	20	0	0	Rich: Davies	10	0	0
Mr John Rawlings cler	20	0	0	Mr Bruhine Dackomb gen			
Tho: Morgan	18	0	0	for free la[d]	15	0	0
Rich: Lewis	6	0	0	John Gunter gen	11	0	0
James Lewis	6	0	0	Eustance Thomas	8	0	0
Lewis Watkin Lewis	12	0	0	Rich: James	7	0	0

2. HT 1664 (3).   3. HT 1664 (3).   4. HT 1664 (4).

Ewias Lacy: Cusopp continued

	£	s	d
Walter Higgins	8	0	0
Tho: Morgan	8	0	0
		(20r)	
Rich: Probart	10	0	0
John Watkins	6	0	0
Lewis Watkins gen[5]	6	0	0
Leonard Higgins	6	0	0
Henry John ap John	6	0	0
Will: Watkins	6	0	0
Leonard Higgins & Rich: Morgan	5	0	0
David Goodduggan [*Cadugan*]	6	0	0
Bruine Duckombe gen for tieths	4	0	0
Evan Butler	1	0	0
Margery Jones wid	1	0	0
Tho: James		10	0
Roger Robert	1	0	0
Susan Leonard wid		10	0
Tho: Lewis and John James		10	0

	£	s	d
Eythan Lewis gen	6	0	0
Thomas Lewis gen	3	0	0
Will: Hay gen for free & lease lands	3	0	0
Will: Ravenhill for the like	2	10	0
Walter Lewis gen	2	10	0
John Traunter gen	1	0	0
David Jones gen	1	0	0
Tho: Pennogre [*Pennoyre*] gen	2	10	0
Simeon Brace gen	3	0	0
Walter Phillipps	2	10	0
James Bevan		15	0

Charge 222 0 0

[*236 5 0*]

Rich: James & Leonard Higgins, Raters.

Halfe a third part to be added to the valuation

3. Lancillo &c[6]   [E3]

Freeholders	£	s	d
James Scudamore gen[7]	16	0	0
Charles Powell	12	0	0
Lewis Guilbert	8	0	0
Charles Beynon	4	0	0
Tho: Jonnes	4	0	0
		(20v)	
Katherine Morgan wid	4	0	0
Phe: Pritchard	9	0	0
James Morgan	4	0	0
Reece Prosser	3	0	0
Jane Prosser wid	2	0	0
Elinor Landon wid	7	0	0
John Gwill'm	6	0	0
Anne Watkins wid	4	0	0
Rich: Pritchard	4	0	0
Eliz: Pritchard wid	4	0	0
Phe: Price	4	0	0
John Gabb gen	1	0	0

	£	s	d
Thomas Gwill'me gen	4	0	0
Landholders rack ten'ts & Jo: Scudamore Esq[8] **Bl:**			
Will: Hall Esq	30	0	0
Will: Wall	4	0	0
Jane Wall wid	15	0	0
Lewis Roberts	15	0	0
Katherine Morgan wid	10	0	0
Elinor Landen wid	5	0	0
Hugh Valentine	3	0	0
David Phe:	1	0	0
Howell Thomas	2	0	0
John Parry gen	8	0	0
Will: Protherough	8	0	0
John Price	5	0	0
Ten'ts to the Hospitall Land **q bl:**			
John Parry gen	7	0	0

5. HT 1664 (4) with Watkin Griffith.
6. Included Rowlston, normally taxed with it.
7. Chief constable of Ewias Lacy, 1663; Loan 29/49, pf. 4, no. 69/15.
8. The two blanks in this assessment were queried in error; they precede two lists of tenants.

Ewias Lacy: Lancillo &c. continued

	£	s	d		£	s	d
Walter Watkins	6	0	0	Giles Griffithes	11	0	0
Other Tenn'ts	8	0	0	John Phillipps	2	0	0
Abraham Mile [*Mille*]	—	—	—	David Christopher	5	0	0
Gronow Pritchard[9]	6	0	0	Walter Watkins	3	0	0
The occup'nts of John				Will: Johns	2	0	0
Sanders lands	10	0	0	Tho: Madox	2	0	0
Henry Howells	1	0	0	Jane Pritchard	3	0	0
Thomas Price	40	0	0				
Edward William	6	0	0	Charge	226	0	0
Jane Pritchard wid	3	0	0	[*329*	*0*	*0*]	
		(21r)					
Will: Sanders	1	0	0	Phil: Pritchard & Lewis Guilbert.			
John Lewis	1	0	0	Raters.			
The occupiers of Will:							
Mathews land	3	0	0	**Twoe parts to be added to the Valuation**			
Henry Price	3	0	0				

4. Lanveynoe [*E4*]

	£	s	d		£	s	d
Mrs Eliz: Wallbeef ten't to				Gwyn Thomas	5	0	0
Jo: Parry gen	10	0	0	Tho: Price & Geo: Griffith	5	0	0
Geo: Parry gen & his mother	15	0	0	Jon Robt ten't to John			
Will: Powell & his mother	12	0	0	Watkin gen	5	0	0
Howell Ychan & his mother				Jon Thomas ten't to the heirs			
in law[10]	13	0	0	of Wa: Willi'm	5	0	0
Charles Nicholls	14	0	0	Jon Wm Harry ten't to ye			
George Jenkin	12	0	0	coheirs of ye Ld Hopton[11]	3	0	0
Jo: Watkin & Howell Watkin				Charles Thomas ten't to			
ten'ts to Mrs Wallbeefe	12	0	0	Maud Ychan	5	0	0
Ben: Parry	10	0	0			(21v)	
Howell Nicholls	10	0	0	Will: Watkin ten't to Geo:			
David Lewis ten't to Rich:				Parry and &c	5	0	0
Francis	8	10	0	John Guilbert	5	0	0
Jo: Gilbt ten't to the heires				Miles Hunt and his Mother	5	0	0
of Tho: Gilbert	10	0	0	Tho: Rees Phillipp	5	0	0
Anne Wms wid ten't to How:				Howell Ychan and his			
Ychan &c	10	0	0	Mother	3	0	0
Jo: Thomas and Tho: John	9	0	0	Rees James ten't to David			
Jon Lewis and his mother	8	0	0	Smith gent & &c	5	0	0
The wid Morgan	8	0	0	Harry John William	5	0	0
The wid George	7	10	0	James Nicholls ten't to Geo:			
Lewis Rees Harry	7	10	0	Delahay	2	10	0
The wid Price ten't to Jo:				Lewis Guilb't	3	0	0
Price gen	7	0	0	Will: Thomas and the wid Hunt	2	0	0

9. HT 1664 (4).   10. HT 1664 (3).
11. The estates of Lord Hopton, who died in 1652, were inherited by his four sisters; *Complete Peerage*, ed. G. E. Cokayne (new edn., London, 1910–40), vi, p. 577n.

E

Ewias Lacy: Lanveynoe continued

	£	s	d		£	s	d
Katherine Walbeefe wid	2	0	0	Tho: Watkins iun gen	2	0	0
Tho: Powell	2	10	0	The ten't of Mr Braine for			
Evan Prosser ten't to Mr				wool & lambe	2	10	0
Booth	4	0	0	Beniamin Parry ten't to the			
John Watkin Will:	2	10	0	coheires of the Lord			
Phillip Harry	5	0	0	Hopton	2	0	0
The widow Rees Howell	2	0	0	Howell Ychan ten't to the sd			
Will: David ten't to Jon				heires	2	0	0
Will: Pritchard	2	0	0	Gwin Thomas ten't alsoe to			
Simon Jon Phillip	4	0	0	them	2	0	0
Hugh Charles	2	0	0	David Thomas ten't to the	1	10	0
The wid Lewis	2	0	0	Will: Powell ten't to themm	1	0	0
Harry Watkin	2	10	0				
For Tiethes				Charge 316 0 0			
Katherine Walbeefe wid	5	0	0	[307 10 0]			
James Nicholls gen	5	0	0	Geo: Parry, Tho: Jones, Rich: Charles.			
Tho: Watkin gen	2	0	0	Raters.			

5. Longtowne   (22r)   [E5]

	£	s	d		£	s	d
Mabell Parry wid	22	0	0	Jane Rees wid &c	8	0	0
Tho: Delahay gent ten't to				Sibbell Jenkins wid &c	3	0	0
Mr Jo: Parry	11	0	0	Tho: Watkins gen &c	5	0	0
Phillip David ten't to the				David Thomas gen &c ten't			
Coh: of ye Ld Hopton[12]	22	0	0	prd' Jo: Parry gen	8	10	0
Henry Guilb't & Eliz:				Will: Harry ten't prd Joh'is			
Guilb't wid ten't as				Parry	10	0	0
afores'd	18	0	0	Oliver Madocks ten: prd Jo:			
Henry Watkin ten't to the				Parry	5	0	0
sd coheires	3	0	0	John Price ten't prd Jo: Parry	3	10	0
Sam: Landon ten't as				Jo: Watkin Corvicer ten't			
aforesd	6	0	0	prd Joh'is Parry	6	0	0
Gabriell Griffith ten't to the				Henry Watkin ten: prd Jo:			
sd coheires	1	0	0	Parry	2	10	0
Marg: Watkin wid ten't as				Kath: Pritchard wid ten:			
aforesd	5	0	0	prd Jo: Parry	17	10	0
Tho: Prichard ten't as				Sibbell Webster wid ten: prd			
aforesd	17	0	0	Jo: Parry		10	0
Anne Pugh wid ten't as aforesd	1	0	0	Will: Pitts ten't prd Jo:			
Will: Edward &c[13]	5	0	0	Parry	3	10	0
Lewis Powell &c	2	10	0	Will: d'd tucker ten't prd			
Lewis Lucas &c	2	0	0	Jo: Parry	3	10	0
James Parry gent &c	1	0	0				
Walter Jenkins &c	3	0	0		60	10	0
Zachery Lewis &c	2	0	0				

12. HT 1664 (8).
13. '&c' is probably the copyist's abbreviation of the previous narrative descriptions repeated.

Ewias Lacy: Longtowne continued

	£	s	d
Will: Sandy &c	2	10	0
Marg: Watkins &c	8	0	0
Will: Meredith &c	8	0	0
Will: Read &c	8	0	0
Will: David &c	4	0	0
Will: Powell &c	2	0	0
Lodovicus Powell ten' Tho: Clarke de Civit: Hereff: gen	8	0	0
		(22v)	
Henry Howell ten't p'd Tho: Clarke	3	0	0
Phil: d'd &c	4	10	0
Humphrey George &c	3	0	0
idem Humfridus &c	2	0	0
Lewis Watkins &c	4	0	0
Idem Lod: Watkins &c	3	10	0
Walter Jenkins &c	2	10	0
Idem Walter &c	2	10	0
Watkin John d'd &c	7	10	0
Will: Pritchard &c	2	10	0
James Lucas &c	2	10	0
Lucas David &c	1	0	0
George Pritchard & Jacob Powell &c	22	0	0
Hugh Pritchard	3	0	0
Idem Hugh &c	2	10	0
Rowland Jennings &c	3	0	0
Will: Price &c	6	0	0
Hugh Button & Jo^n Watkin W^m	1	0	0
Freeholders			
John Jennings & Rouland Jenn^s	16	0	0
Willm Gwill'm	6	0	0
John George	2	0	0
Tho: Gwill'm gen	6	0	0
Rowland Watkins	6	0	0
Henry Watkins pred'	2	10	0
Will: Pitt	9	10	0
Will: Vaughan gen	3	0	0
Anne Jenkins wid	7	0	0
Will: John Watkins	8	0	0
Katherine Will'm spinster	2	0	0
Tho: Watkin Preece	2	10	0
Robert Barnes gen	17	10	0

	£	s	d
Maud Ycan wid	4	10	0
		(23r)	
Will: Bevan & John Bevan	6	0	0
Phil: John Thomas	7	0	0
Rees Thomas Pritchard	8	15	0
David Tho:	2	0	0
Eliz: Walbeefe wid	21	10	0
Marmaduke Lewis gen	13	0	0
Paul: Tho: gen	8	0	0
John Rogers	3	10	0
Will: Price	5	0	0
Lewis Powell	10	10	0
Lison David	7	0	0
John Jones	8	10	0
John Eustance	1	0	0
Katherine Wallbeefe wid	12	10	0
James Parry	8	10	0
Hugh Thomas	3	0	0
Ollif Phillip wid	2	10	0
Henry Powell	3	10	0
Henry Jo^n	5	0	0
John Jenkins	5	10	0
John Sim'ons [*Symonds*]	11	0	0
Michaell Morgan	13	0	0
Charles Jennings	2	0	0
Tho: Jenkins	7	0	0
Tho: John de Cage	2	0	0
Will: Powell	1	0	0
Howell Niccholl		10	0
Tho: de le Hay p^{r}d pro Gwrloe porth	2	10	0
Jo: De la hay cler	30	0	0
James Lucas pred'	1	0	0
Tho: Watkins &c for tyths	3	10	0
Johan Price wid &c pro tythes	10	0	0
James Powell	1	0	0
Hugh Button	1	0	0

Charge 648 0 0

[*634 15 0*]

Lewis Powell, Tho: Jenkins, Mar: Lewis, John George. Raters.

The valuation is to be doubled

6. Michaell Church Esclie   (23v)   [E6]

	£	s	d		£	s	d
Michaell Thomas & Edm: Tho: gen[14]	60	0	0	James Probert	6	0	0
Thomas Watkins of Craswall	20	0	0	Tho: Dav: Maddock & Jo: Maddock &c	11	0	0
David Smith of Craswall	14	0	0	Lewis Prichard & Jo: Parry gen	11	0	0
The Lds of the coh: of the late Ld Hopton	10	0	0	Mary David wid	7	0	0
Tho: Delahay gen	5	0	0	James Pitt &c	5	0	0
Alice Preece wid &c[15]	13	0	0	Will: David &c	5	0	0
John David &c	10	0	0	David Miles	4	0	0
John Will: Prichard	20	0	0	Reece Harbert	4	0	0
Phill: Price	25	0	0	Tho: Smith &c	5	0	0
Phill: James &c	12	0	0	Watkin Powell	4	0	0
Kath: Powell wid & Morgan Pow[11] gen	20	0	0	Howell Pritchard &c	6	0	0
Will: Exton	20	0	0	Rich: Powell &c	4	0	0
Henry Powell &c	11	0	0				
Alice Preece wid &c	12	0	0	Charge	377	0	0
Lison Bevan &c	10	0	0	[369	0	0]
Tho: Powell	10	0	0				
Tho: David iun	5	0	0	James Probert, Tho: Watkins. Raters.			
Tho: Watkins	20	0	0	**The valuation is to be doubled.**			

7. Newton[16]   (24r)   [E7]

	£	s	d		£	s	d
Humph: Haworth Esq	15	0	0	Walter Nicholas	4	10	0
Mrs Rachell Thomas	12	0	0	David James	4	10	0
Chestons lands	2	0	0	Tho: Prosser[17]	7	10	0
Mich: Thomas gent	13	0	0	Humph: Jones	7	10	0
The Coheires of the Lo: Hopton	5	0	0	Harry John Harry	8	0	0
				Harry Griffith	4	10	0
Treamori Thick [Tremorithic]	12	0	0	Tho: Jennings of Trecoed' [Trecadifor]	7	10	0
Lleendees Lands [Llyndu]	6	0	0	Will'm David	5	0	0
Wayn Herbert	6	0	0	Morgan Lewis	5	0	0
				John Harry Preece	5	10	0
Hospitall Lands				Tho: Bevan	5	0	0
Alexander Savaker	12	0	0	Johan Jennings	8	0	0
Rich: Will: James	5	0	0	James Nicholls	5	10	0
Walter Delehay gen	10	0	0	Charles Jennings	6	0	0
Griffith Jo[n] David	6	0	0	Tho: Morgan	5	10	0
Phillip Harrie	4	10	0	Quareleys Lands [Cwarelau]	8	0	0

14. HT 1664 (4).
15. '&c' may refer to Lord Hopton's coheirs.
16. Included St Margaret's.
17. Thomas Prosser of St Margaret's, nephew of Esay Prosser of Peterchurch, whose will was proved 1666 (PCC).

Ewias Lacy: Newton continued

	£	s	d		£	s	d
Henry Eustance	5	0	0	Will: Thomas	2	0	0
Edward Jones	8	10	0	Tho: Jennings of More-			
Wellingtons lands	8	10	0	hampton	1	10	0
Johan & Sarah Greeg	6	0	0	Jeremy Pritchard	2	0	0
Sibble Jennings wid & her							
sonne	18	0	0	Charge	282	0	0
		(24v)			[273	0	0]
Rich: Beavor	2	0	0				
Nicchols lands	2	0	0	Tho: Jennings, Tho: Prosser, Griffith Jo:			
Lewis Andrew	2	0	0	David. Raters.			
Newtons tieth within Clo-							
dock	6	0	0	**The Valuation is to be doubled and**			
Walter Phillipps	2	0	0	**something over.**[18]			
Friberies Lands	1	10	0				

8. Waterston[19]   [*E8*]

	£	s	d		£	s	d
William Powell	10	10	0	John Watkin & Howell John	3	0	0
Will: John Watkin	8	0	0	David Preece	1	0	0
Will: David Harry	1	10	0	Howell Powell	10	0	0
James Guilbert	6	10	0	Jo[n] Aleworth gen	15	0	0
Edward Griffith	1	0	0	John Phillipp	4	0	0
Anne Jenkin wid	5	0	0	Tho: Phillipp	5	0	0
Hugh Pritchard	3	0	0	Edward William Powell	1	6	8
Tho: Powell	5	0	0	Griffith John David	10	0	0
Mary Prichard wid	10	0	0	Eliz: John David	2	0	0
Tho: Lewis	11	10	0	Phillip Will: Watkin	2	0	0
John Harry	1	10	0	Tho: Watkin	3	10	0
Charles Phillipps	10	0	0	Will'm Phillipp	2	10	0
John Price	8	0	0	Will: Nicholas	5	0	0
Margaret Price wid	8	0	0	David Phillipp & Griff:			
David Gundy	4	10	0	Phillipp	5	0	0
Will: George	4	15	0	Phillip Will: Powell	2	0	0
Lewis Morgan & Johan				Tho: ap John	2	0	0
Thomas wid	8	0	0	Jane David wid	2	0	0
Walter Hugh	10	0	0	John Thomas	4	0	0
		(25r)		Will: Preece	1	5	0
Walter Cicilt	1	0	0				
Rich: William	1	0	0	Men charged towards the Horse			
Will: Gunter & Roger				John Delehay gen[20]	40	0	0
Gunter	5	0	0	The same for the Lands of			
Jo[n] Harry	4	0	0	the E of Salisbury[21]	24	0	0

---

18. The largest HT charges in 1664 were on John Miles (3), Thomas Jennings of
Newhouse (3) and William James with Katherine Waters (3).
19. Probably included Bwlch and Fwthwg (Foothog).   20. HT 1664 (8).
21. William Cecil, 2nd earl of Salisbury, 1591–1668; *Complete Peerage*, ed. Cokayne,
xi, p. 406.

Ewias Lacy: Waterston continued

	£	s	d
David John William for the late lands of the Lord Hopton	3	0	0
James Christopher for the same	2	10	0
Miles Powell for the same	2	0	0
Johan Gunter wid for the same	4	0	0
Mich: Thomas gen	10	0	0
			(25v)
Henry Prichard for ye same lands	8	0	0
Anne Pugh wid	6	0	0

	£	s	d
John Pritchard	2	0	0
Will: Jo^n Watkin for ye same lands	3	0	0
Nicholas Arnold Esq for ye tieth	30	0	0
Charge	315	0	0
	[*342*	*16*	*8*]

William Powell, Walter Hugh, Charles Phillipps. Raters.

The proportion is to be doubled

Graytree Hundred[1]

	Value Returned by the Raters £		The Value Horse Being Taken Out	Value according to ye contribution £ s d			The whole contribution at 2s per pound per annum for each particular parish in the Hundred £ s d		
1.	388	Aston Ingham		372	13	4	37	5	4
2.	474	Brampton Abbots		491	13	4	49	3	4
3.	300	Eaton Treagos		486	0	0	48	12	0
4.	792	Fownehope & Faley		1036	13	4	103	13	4
5.	255	Hope Mansell		273	3	4	27	6	4
6.	328	How Capell		366	0	0	36	12	0
7.	586	Linton & Lea		859	0	0	85	18	0
8.	525	Mordiford & Dormington		854	6	8	85	8	8
9.	1148	Much Marcle & Yatton		1702	6	8	170	4	8

1. The proportions of the hundred total charged here on the respective parishes were exactly the same as those in the 1677 assessment.

Hearth Tax return, Lady Day, 1664

Greytree Hundred	Total Charged Hearths	Total Houses	More than 10 hearths*	10	9	8	7	6	5	4	3	2	1	Total Exempt Houses
Aston Ingham	63	61								2	2	8	33	16
Brampton Abbotts	38	29								1	2	9	10	7
Eaton Tregoes	42	23						3			3	7	1	9
Fownhope	113	104					1			3	2	15	56	27
Hope Mansell	17	23									1	3	8	11
How Caple	28	20		1						2	1	2	3	11
Linton	69	82						1		2	5	9	21	44
Lea	23	14	11)									1	10	2
Mordiford, Frome & Dormington	100	91							3	3	3	12	40	30
Much Marcle	199	139	2 (14 & 14)			2	1	1	3	3	3	9	18	52	48
Putley	20	22										3	14	5
Ross Borough	396	226	1 (11)			1		5	4	2	17	26	53	55	62
Ross Foreign	101	84	1 (11)						3	1	9	11	22	37
Sollers Hope	32	23								2	2	3	12	4
Upton Bishop	69	70							1	3	2	6	27	30
Walford	114	69	1 (15)				1	1	1	1	8	8	33	15
Weston under Penyard	67	52							1	7	3	6	13	22
Woolhope	117	131					1		2	3	4	13	46	62
Total	1,608	1,263	6	1	3	3	9	11	14	49	82	187	456	442

* Actual charge in brackets.

57

Graytree Hundred continued

	Value Returned by the Raters		The Value Horse Being Taken Out	Value according to ye contribution		The whole contribution at 2s per pound per annum for each particular parish in the Hundred		
	£		£	s	d	£	s	d
10.	143	Putley	201	16	8	20	9	8
11.	919	Ross & Ross Forren	1523	13	4	152	3	4
12.	234	Sollers Hope	366	0	0	36	12	0
13.	815	Upton Bpp	859	0	0	85	18	0
14.	961	Walford	859	0	0	85	18	0
15.	459	West: under Peniard	859	0	0	85	18	0
16.	444	Woolhope & Brockhampton	1081	0	0	108	2	0

[Total £1219 4s 8d]

---

1. Aston Ingham   (27r)   [GeI]

	£	s	d		£	s	d
John Vaughan Esq for the demeasnes[2]	30	0	0	John Colwall	6	0	0
Charles Stock cler[3]	40	0	0	Tho: Cole	5	0	0
Will: Pitt Esq	20	0	0	John Brook his brother & sisters	6	0	0
James Collier[4]	20	0	0	John Giles & his Mother	10	0	0
John Rudge	20	0	0	Marlin Hurscock	4	0	0
Tho: Graile gen	18	0	0	Widow Trippett	3	0	0
William Philpotts	18	0	0	Jon Rudge & his mother for			
Will: Rudge	14	0	0	the Naylett	5	0	0
John Howell	14	0	0	The widow Reinolds	1	0	0
Tho: Hanbury	18	0	0	Will: Morse	4	0	0
Tho: Perkins	14	0	0	Will: Phillipps	4	0	0
Will: Perkins	12	0	0	Tho: Gibbes	1	10	0
John Nelme cler for ye				William Perry	2	0	0
Gammage	10	0	0	Tho: Read	2	0	0
William Reynolds	10	0	0	Anthony Rudge	3	0	0
Tho: Little	12	0	0			(27v)	
Will: Gardner	12	0	0	Rich: Cole	5	0	0
Tho: Wilse & Waltr Wilse				Christopher Walton		10	0
[Wilkes]	10	0	0	Gilbert Nurse & Waltr Nurse	4	0	0
Abraham Buckley	11	0	0	Rich: Burley	1	10	0
John Beale	6	0	0	James Sergeant	1	10	0
Will: Godsall	3	0	0	John Wingod	1	10	0

---

2. His real estate in the county in 1646 was valued at £400; Loan 29/15, pf. 2.
3. HT 1664 (4), the rectory.   4. HT 1664 (4).

Graytree: Aston Ingham continued

	£	s	d
Rich: Stallard	3	0	0
Tho: Nurse	2	10	0

Tho: Little, Will: Pirkins. Raters.

Charge	388	0	0
	[389	0	0]

The proportion is direct

2. Brampton Abbotts   [*Ge2*]

	£	s	d		£	s	d
John Vaughan gen or his				John Horton or ten't	6	0	0
ten't	1	0	0	Tho: Mayo	3	0	0
Sr John Scudamore for the				Tho: Read	1	10	0
Rector	60	0	0	Tho: Baynham	4	0	0
Tho: Apperley gen	6	0	0	Joseph Smart	15	0	0
John Newton Doctor	15	0	0	Rich: Careles	18	0	0
Tho: Addis	70	0	0	Mich: Millington	15	0	0
Tho: Hyett sen[r]	55	0	0			(28r)	
John Preece	35	0	0	Phillip Addis[6]	20	0	0
Rich: Gwatkin[5]	15	0	0				
Anne Pritchard wid	15	0	0	Charge	474	0	0
Tho: Hyett iun	20	0	0		[468	0	0]
Tho: Collins	50	0	0				
Tho: Dewe	15	0	0	Tho: Addis, Tho: Hiett. Raters.			
John Tailor	16	0	0				
John Hardwicke	5	0	0	**Proportion is direct**			
Rich: Powell	5	0	0				
John Streete	2	10	0				

3. Eaton Treagos   [*Ge3*]

	£	s	d		£	s	d
John Lord Scudamore	7	0	0	Walter Powell	10	0	0
John Abrahall Esq[7]	50	0	0	John Prosser	7	0	0
Tho: Apperlye gen[8]	28	0	0	Rich: Hannis	7	0	0
George Abrahall	33	0	0	Rich: Cooke	4	10	0
John Furney[9]	28	0	0				
James Collins iun[10]	50	0	0	Charge	300	0	0
Tennants att rack und[r] Ja:					[268	10	0]
Scudamore Esq							
Tho: Apperly gent	6	10	0	Tho: Apperlye, James Collins sen.			
James Collins sen	20	0	0	Raters.			
Charles Prosser	13	0	0				
Richard Meeke	4	10	0	**A third parte is to be added**			

5. HT 1664 (4).
6. Chief constable of Greytree, 1663; Loan 29/49, pf. 4, no. 69/15.
7. HT 1664 (6).   8. HT 1664 (6).   9. HT 1664 (6).
10. In 1663 a James Collins was chief constable for Greytree; Loan 29/49, pf. 4,
no. 69/15.

4. Fownehope & Faley [*Fawley*] (28v)   [*Ge4*]

	£	s	d		£	s	d
The Lady Marchioness of Hertford[11]	83	6	8	James Ravenhill	6	13	4
Sr John Kyrle Barronett	65	6	8	John Paine gent	6	0	0
Roger Letchmore Esq[12]	163	13	4	Thomas Gwatkin	11	6	8
Tho: Willis Dr of Physick	66	13	4	Rich: Meekes farmer	8	0	0
James Heref: Esq et mater	40	0	0	Henry Smith clerke	5	13	4
William Gregory Esq	33	6	8	Tho: Halls farme	8	0	0
Fitz William Coningsby Esq	13	13	4	Tho: Wood	6	13	4
Mr Oswell for Much Faley	53	6	8	Tho: Phillipps	8	0	0
Rich: Cope gen	40	0	0	Walter Knight	6	13	4
John Kidley gen	46	6	8	Edward Jones cler	8	6	8
Dr Shirborne for the Vicaridge	26	13	4				
John Havard	20	0	0	Charge	792	0	0
Mrs Traunter	14	6	8	[*768*	*7*	*4*]	
William Browne gent	9	6	8				
Roger Shiere	11	13	4	Rich: Cope, John Kidley. Raters.			
Mary Brandish	5	6	8	**A fifth parte to be added to the valuation**			

5. Hope Maunsell   (29r)   [*Ge5*]

	£	s	d		£	s	d
John Nurse Esq	15	0	0	John Keyse iun[13]	30	0	0
John Vaughan Esq & his tenn'ts	12	0	0	John Keyse sen	4	0	0
Tho: Tier Rector ibidem	40	0	0	Miles Sutton gen	20	0	0
Geo: Taylor & his sonne	30	0	0	James Palmer	6	0	0
John Nash	10	0	0	Roger Bonner	6	0	0
Charles Morgan	4	0	0	Henry Mills	16	0	0
Hester Grendon *Grindon*] wid	10	0	0				
Giles Tower	6	0	0	Charge	255	0	0
John Stritt [*Streete*]	13	0	0	George Taylor sen, John Keyse iun. Raters.			
John How	20	0	0				
Rich: Blast	13	0	0	**The proportion direct.**			

6. How Capell   [*Ge6*]

	£	s	d		£	s	d
Edw: Capell Esq[14]	200	0	0	John Knight	16	0	0
John Mayo cler[15]	50	0	0	James Churchyard	4	0	0
John Sergeant	21	0	0			(29v)	
Rich: Wineat [*Wynnyatt*]	55	0	0	Rich: Tyler	4	0	0

11. The manor had belonged to the marquis of Hertford (Harl. 6726), who became duke of Somerset in 1660 and died shortly afterwards (see Lyonshall, note 23).
12. FP 1661 (£3 unpaid); HT 1664 (9); will proved 1665 (PCC).
13. HT 1664 (3).   14. HT 1664 (10).   15. Rector, FP 1661 (£3 paid).

Graytree: How Capell continued

	£	s	d		£	s	d
Pearcy Mead'm [*Meadman*]	1	10	0	John Mutlow		10	0
William Gainsford	6	0	0	John Ketherow		10	0
Rich: Mutlow	3	0	0	Rich: Wineatt for his free			
Rich: Williams	5	0	0	land	3	0	0
Johan Taylor	1	10	0				
Will: Barrey	2	0	0	Charge	328	0	0
John Apperley	1	10	0	[*388*	*0*	*0*]	
Antho: Apperley	5	0	0				
Fran: Kerry gen		10	0	John Sergeant, John Knight. Raters.			
Rich: Cope gen	4	0	0				
For Osel's land	3	0	0				
John Abrahall	1	0	0	**The valuation direct.**			

7. Linton & Lea[16]   [*Ge7a*]

	£	s	d		£	s	d
The Countesse of Kent				Rich: Wintle	6	10	0
peere	82	0	0	John Cother	3	0	0
John Kyrle Barronett	30	0	0	Nich: Warre	3	10	0
The Vicaridge of Linton[17]	80	0	0	Tho: Packer	5	0	0
John Nourse gen	13	0	0	Guilbert Nourse	3	0	0
Mrs Rudhall	50	0	0	James Sergt &c	3	0	0
These are charged with Horse				Walter Nourse	3	10	0
Tho: Bonner	7	0	0	Will: Phelpotts	1	0	0
Robt Nourse	8	0	0	John Packer & his tenn't	2	0	0
John Hill	15	0	0	Tho: Turner	1	0	0
Tho: Phelps	14	0	0	William Nourse	2	0	0
		(30r)		William Taylor for his free			
John Sergeant	17	10	0	land	4	10	0
Rich: Barroll	11	0	0	John Bennet & his ten't	1	10	0
Will: Abrahall	17	0	0	Tho: Taylor & his ten't	1	0	0
John Ashman	11	0	0				
John Teagy	2	0	0	Charge	453	0	0
Will: Hall & his ten't	5	0	0				
John Davies & his ten't	1	10	0	John Hill, Guilbert Nourse, Raters.			
Wm How of the Crosse	5	10	0				
Wm Abrahall gen	6	0	0	**A third parte is to be added to the**			
Wm Taylor for Heygrove	10	0	0	**valuation**			
Rich: Phelps	6	0	0				
Robt Ayway [*Ayleway*] gen	4	0	0			(30v)	
John Keyse	4	0	0	**Lea**[18]		[*Ge7b*]	
Richard Stallard	1	0	0	Christopher Walton &c	4	0	0
Walter How	4	5	0	John Phillipps	23	0	0
Will: How &c	8	10	0	Rich: Stallard free land	19	0	0

16. The largest HT charge in 1664 was on John Barnes gent. (7).
17. John Elmhurst, vicar, paid £6 13s 4d to the FP 1661.
18. The largest HT charge in Lea in 1664 was on Thomas Pitt, gent. (11).

Graytree: Linton & Lea continued

	£	s	d
Rich: Stallard &c	11	10	0
Tho: Nourse	3	15	0
Christopher Walton free land		10	0
Will: Bower	11	0	0
Will: Dikes	1	10	0
John Dikes	2	0	0
Tho: Kidden	4	0	0
John Croose	2	0	0
John Rudge	2	0	0
Will'm Phelpotts	2	0	0
Rich: Edwards	6	0	0
Rich: Burley	4	0	0
Will'm Phelpotts iun	3	0	0
James Collyer	2	0	0
Rich: Wintle	2	0	0
Guilbert Nourse	1	10	0
Tho: Merrick	2	0	0

	£	s	d
John Teguy	1	0	0
John Ashman	1	15	0
William Phillipps sen	11	0	0
Tho: Stone	2	0	0
Hen: Davies	2	0	0
Mary Rudge wid	3	0	0
Will'm Hull	1	10	0
Walter James	3	0	0
James Voyce	1	0	0
Charge	133	0	0

William Bower. Rater.

Quere concerning the landlords of estates.

(31r)

8. Mordiford &c   [*Ge8a*]

	£	s	d
Fitz William Coningsby Esq	7	0	0
Tho: Price Esq	7	0	0
James Hereford gent & Fr: Hereford wid[19]	120	0	0
Tho: Smith &c	12	0	0
Will: Hodges iun	5	0	0
Anne Parsons wid	8	0	0

Lorpott   [*Ge8b*]

	£	s	d
Eliz: Cave wid[20]	25	0	0
Mary Bulckley wid	18	0	0
John Doberlow [*Dowberly*]	14	0	0
John Garston	5	0	0
John Hill & Tho: Morris	8	0	0
Tho: Seymore	4	0	0

Froome Priors   [*Ge8c*]

	£	s	d
William Garston of Eldersfield	18	0	0
Tho: Garston &c	16	0	0
Edw: Homes	9	0	0
Rich: Williams gen	7	0	0
Tho: Rock	5	0	0
Jo: Rock	5	0	0
Tho: Lovell	7	0	0

	£	s	d
Rich: Davies	4	0	0

Checkley   [*Ge8d*]

	£	s	d
John Turbill	7	0	0
John Archer	7	0	0
Rich: Turner of Dormington &c	4	0	0
John Baddam	4	0	0

Mordiford   [*Ge8e*]

	£	s	d
Walter Rogers Clre	25	0	0
Jo: Hide gen	4	0	0
Charge	355	0	0

Jo: Hereford, Edw: Holmes. Raters.

Noe valuation sett downe

(31v)

Dormington   [*Ge8f*]

	£	s	d
Sr John Kyrle Barronnett &c	4	0	0
Rich: Walwyn gen for Dormingtons wood	16	0	0
John Bridges gen[21]	42	0	0

---

19. FP 1661 (£2); HT 1664 (5).   20. HT 1664 (5).   21. HT 1664 (5).

Graytree: Mordiford &c.: Dormington continued

	£	s	d		£	s	d
Tho: Bowen	40	0	0	Edw: Rogers farme	16	10	0
Tho: Nuton	5	0	0	James Hodges	3	15	0
John Corbett	5	0	0	Tho: Davies for his owne	3	10	0
John Freeman	2	10	0	Tho: Davies for Mr Sands			
George Penrice	1	0	0	farme	7	0	0
Rowl: Crumpe		10	0	Anne Hide wid	4	10	0
Margery Poytheras	2	0	0	The widow Hodges for &c	16	10	0
Rich: Turner	6	0	0	John Dubberley	1	10	0
William Bickett	6	10	0	John Ward	1	10	0
John Cooke	6	10	0	Roul: Crump	2	15	0
Henry Baddam	1	0	0	Rich: Exon [*Exton*]	1	0	0
John Collins	8	0	0	James Felton	1	0	0
Roger Godsoll	7	10	0	Jam: Cooke		19	0
Roger Hill for &c	8	0	0	The wid Hodges for &c	2	10	0
Roger Hill for his owne	3	0	0			(32r)	
John Rawlins for ye Fleet	5	0	0	Roses plock	0		8
Tho: Pryse Esq for his tieth	18	0	0				

Charge 64 5 2
[*73 9 8*]

Charge 170 10 0
[*187 10 0*]

Tho: Newton, Edw: Rogers. Raters.

Bartestry [*Ge8g*]
Mr Reade for Mr Brincets
[*Bints*] land   10 10 0

**A third parte is to be added to the
Valuation**

---

9. Much Marcle [*and Yatton*]   [*Ge9*]

	£	s	d		£	s	d
Sr John Kyrle Baronett[22]	300	0	0	Humphrey Wood	3	0	0
Mrs Margarett Walwyne[23]	120	0	0	Elinor Edwards	6	0	0
Francis Lill Esq	100	0	0	Jam: Mayo	6	0	0
John Wallwyne Esq	35	0	0	Rich: Powell	6	0	0
Doctor Fell[24]	100	0	0	Rich: Meeke gen	10	0	0
John Vaughan	100	0	0	John Skynner for &c	8	0	0
Stephen Boughton	4	0	0	Edw: Sands gen	12	0	0
John Nelme sen	7	0	0	Jam: Gamond	8	0	0
Rich: Mayle	6	0	0	Anne Skelton	8	0	0
Will: Mayo	6	0	0	Rich: Whoopper	35	0	0
Rich: Castledine	6	0	0	Will: Smith	8	0	0
Rich: Drew	6	0	0	Tho: Shayle & his sonne	2	0	0
Rich: Winiatt	5	0	0			(32v)	
John Greeneaway	3	0	0	Rich: Powell	1	0	0

---

22. Succeeded 1650, died 1680 (*Baronetage*, ii, p. 18); JP q 1660; DL 1660; MP for the county 1661; HT 1664 (14).
23. HT 1664 (14).
24. In 1646 Dr Fell's personal estate in the county was valued at £100; Loan 29/15, pf. 2.

Graytree: Much Marcle [and Yatton] continued

	£	s	d		£	s	d
Mr Westfalling for the tieth	35	0	0	John Milward [*Millard*]	6	0	0
Thomas Wallwyn gen	44	0	0	Rich: Phillipps	5	0	0
Peter Nash for &c	8	0	0	Isaack Ayleway cler[25]	7	0	0
John Woodward	18	0	0	Joseph Skinner gen	4	0	0
John Apperley & Jo[n] Baker	35	0	0	John Hope	5	0	0
Francis Ayleway gen	44	0	0				
Edw: Sandes gen	1	0	0	Charge	1148	0	0
Rich: Burdestone	19	0	0	[*1165*	*0*	*0*]	
Will: Whopper	2	0	0				
Will: Mayo de la Porch	10	0	0	John Apperley, John Skynner. Raters.			
John Morris for Tantyes	10	0	0				
Rich: Mayo for &c	1	0	0	**A third part is to be added to the valuation**			

10. Putley   [*Ge10*]

	£	s	d		£	s	d
Thornton Jones gen	20	0	0	Rich: Hodges for &c	3	0	0
Rich: Wheeler Rector	20	0	0				
Eliz: Unett wid	40	0	0	Charge	143	0	0
Rich: Unett gen for &c	20	0	0				
Henry Gwillym for &c	15	0	0	Will: Gwillym, John Harris. Raters.			
Will'm Gwillym	8	0	0				
Will'm Hill	6	0	0	**A third part & a halfe is to be added to**			
John Harris	6	0	0	**the Valuation**			
Rich: Boucatt [*Boulcott*]	5	0	0				

		(33r)

11. Rosse Burrough[26]   [*Ge11a*]

	£	s	d		£	s	d
Anthony Alder	1	10	0	Phill: Addis	6	13	4
Rich: Tombes	2	0	0	Walter Merrick	3	0	0
Tho: Rudge	1	0	0	Tho: Taylor	8	5	0
Tho: Browne	3	0	0	Marga: Chapman wid	5	0	0
John Lovell	2	10	0	Tho: Addis	1	10	0
James Gulliford [*Gullafer*]	3	0	0	John Skinner iun	4	10	0
John Sargeant	3	0	0	Will'm Prichard	2	0	0
Francis Harris	2	10	0	Will: Whopper	5	7	6
Blanch Baker wid	8	13	4	Will: Baker	8	14	2
Aidonhigh [*Adoniah*] Maddock	7	16	8	Geo: Dubberley[27]	3	0	0
William Painter	2	10	0	John Cowles	2	0	0

25. Rector of Evesbatch, FP 1661 (20s).
26. The largest HT charge in Ross borough in 1664 was on the widow Bodenham (11).
27. He was the son of Christopher Dubberley and was referred to in the latter's will (proved 12 Feb. 1662 (PCC)).

Graytree: Rosse Burrough continued

	£	s	d		£	s	d
Tobie Stecknam [Fecknam]	4	0	0	John Mason	1	0	0
Guy Lane	1	10	0	Geo: Man	1	10	0
Will: Bellamy	22	6	8	Rich: Burropp	3	18	4
Guy Abrahall	4	10	0	Edw: Maddock	4	0	0
James Dubberley	3	0	0	Rich: Harris	20	0	0
Jane Merrick wid & her sonne	9	0	0	Nicho: Nelmes	4	0	0
Rich: Furney	4	10	0	James Merrick	3	0	0
Edw: Stanley [Staneley]	2	10	0	Tho: Preece	1	0	0
Anth: Dew	4	0	0	John Jones		10	0
Tho: Lovell	7	0	0			(34r)	
Walter Pearce	6	0	0	Rich: Prosser		15	0
Tho: Rodd	4	0	0	John Davis	1	0	0
Tho: Sparrie	4	0	0	Johan Weale	1	0	0
Christopher Mutlow	2	0	0	John Mutlow	2	0	0
Jo[n] Harbert	2	0	0	Phil: Prichard	1	10	0
Henry Perkes	1	10	0	Rich: Careless	1	5	0
		(33v)		Phil: Osburne[28]	3	8	0
John Bueman	2	0	0	Rich: Harris	2	13	4
Edw: Griffithes	3	0	0	Robt Merrick	2	13	4
Jam: Cowles	2	10	0	Will: Ball	2	0	0
Walter Maddocks	2	0	0	Roger Colla	1	0	0
John Hill	5	0	0	Johan Merrick	2	8	4
Gabriell Hill	5	0	0	Will: Man	5	0	0
Mrs Alice Kyrle	8	0	0	The widow Rudge	2	10	0
Martha Durley wid	4	0	0	Guy Bellamy	2	10	0
John Carter	3	10	0	Will: Langford	2	10	0
John Taylor	3	16	8	John Wheeler		18	0
Will'm Wensley [Winslow]	2	10	0	Joseph Taylor for &c	1	0	0
James Fisher	2	10	0	Edw: Man		10	0
Thomas Arundell	2	0	0	Stephen Baily		10	0
John Tuder	1	10	0	Guy Abrahall	2	10	0
Walter Jones	1	0	0				
Stephen Eudall	1	0	0	Charge	334	10	0
Will'm Pichard	1	0	0		[331	11	0]
John Grindon	3	0	0				
Mathew Phillipps	1	0	0	Will: Baker, Will: Bellamy. Raters.			
Antho: Taylor	2	10	0				
Mary Laviman	5	0	0	**Rosse Forren** [Gellb]			
John Sheares	5	18	4	Dr Newton[29]	14	13	4
Mary Cowrne wid	1	0	0	John Baldwyn [Baldinge]	22	0	0
Edw: Bower	1	10	0	John Vaughan gen[30]	18	0	0
Charles Stocke cler	5	0	0	John Markye gen	22	0	0
Arthur Davies	1	6	8	Daniell Kerry	30	0	0
John Paine	2	0	0	Rich: Clarke	31	10	0
Tho: Nicholls	1	10	0			(34v)	
Phill: Peterstow	3	13	4	Joseph Smart	20	0	0

28. Tanner; will proved 1667 (PCC).
29. Dr John Newton, vicar, paid £6 to the FP 1661.   30. HT 1664 (11).

Graytree: Rosse Forren continued

	£	s	d		£	s	d
Will: Merrick	10	0	0	John Young	15	0	0
John Mason	7	0	0	Guy Bellamy	6	0	0
John Bennett	14	10	0	John Lovell	10	0	0
Walter Cubberley	8	13	4	John Bennet	1	0	0
Rich: Hill	8	13	4	John Cowles of Rosse	4	0	0
John Jowline [*Joldinge*]	9	6	8	Will: Baker for &c	1	8	0
Will: Fisher	2	6	8	Margarett Chapman		10	0
Alice Chinne	16	0	0	Tho: Chinn	4	10	0
Will: Beale	9	6	8	Edw: Maddocke	1	10	0
Robt Mutlow	2	6	8			(35r)	
The wid Gorway [*Garway*]	5	0	0	Mrs Alice Kyrle	1	0	0
Tho: White	4	13	4	John Higgs		12	0
Will: Smith	4	13	4	John Cater	1	0	0
Christopher Mutlow	2	0	0	Tho: Browne	2	3	8
John Griffithes	36	0	0	John Mutlow	2	0	0
Will: Monn [*Mann*]	20	0	0	Phil: Osburne		10	0
Rich: Chinn	2	0	0	John Taylor	1	13	4
John Cowles	1	0	0	James Merrick	1	3	8
John Gorway	5	0	0	The wid Cowarne &c	15	0	0
Arth: Davis	1	0	0	John Jones		15	0
Tho: Jowlin	5	6	8	John Cowles of Alton	4	0	0
Countess of Kent for Cop-				John Baldwyn	1	10	0
pice wood in Penni'd				The widow Cowarne for &c	6	0	0
peere	30	0	0				
Gabriell Hill	5	0	0	Charge	585	5	0
Rich: Gwatkin	5	0	0		[596	0	8]
The widow Cowarne	9	0	0				
Sir John Scudamore for tieths	123	15	0	Joseph Smart, John Bennett. Raters.			
Rich: Meeke for &c	9	0	0	**Almost halfe added to the valuation**			

12. Sollers Hope[31] [*Ge12*]

	£	s	d		£	s	d
Sr John Kyrle per annum	5	0	0	Adam Perry	5	0	0
Mrs Mary Bodenham	20	0	0	The widow Jeffries	2	0	0
Edw: Capell Esq	4	10	0	Rich: Williams	3	0	0
Phillipp Addice gen	24	0	0	Anth: Apperlo	8	10	5
Henry Manscield [*Manfield*]				Rich: Winneatt	3	0	0
cler	40	0	0				
John Powell gen	50	0	0	Charge	234	0	0
Tho: Winneatt	40	0	0		[235	0	5]
Rich: Gammon [*Gamond*]	6	0	0				
Jam: Gamman	6	0	0	Tho: Winneatt, Rich: Gamman. Raters.			
Henry Gamman	1	10	0				
Will: Nurden [*Nurthen*]	2	0	0	**A third part is to be added to the**			
John Nelmes	13	10	0	**Valuation**			
Fra: Wall	1	0	0				

31. The largest HT charges in 1664 were on David Powell and Roger Mathews (4 each).

13. Upton Bishopp   (35v)   [Ge13]

	£	s	d
John Lo: Viscount Scuda-			
more	21	0	0
Ja: Scudamore Esq	50	0	0
Sr Jo: Kyrle Barronett	2	0	0
Sr Tho: How Kt[32]	3	0	0
Tho: Wigmore gen[33]	100	0	0
Mrs Mary Rudhall spinster	150	0	0
Jo: Keayse gen	39	0	0
Jo: Taylor cler	39	0	0
Jo: Vaughan gen	60	0	0
Jo: Bridge of Pomores			
[Palmers]	10	0	0
Elinor Fisher wid	38	0	0
Jo: Tomes	14	0	0
Edw: Fisher	3	10	0
Will: Nurthen	3	10	0
Gregory Hardwick	25		
Rich: Fisher of the Marsh	3	10	0
John Winniatt	10	0	0
John Beele	8	0	0
William Scudamore	18	0	0
John Sergent	1	10	0
Nathaniell Stephens	40	0	0
Henry Crumpe	6	10	0
Thomas Packer	6	10	0
John Phelps	2	10	0
Thomas Legeat	20	0	0
James Hardwick	4	10	0

	£	s	d
Thomas Phelps	2	0	0
Johan Nurthen wid	11	0	0
Tho: Clissold	25	0	0
Will: Treaven [Frewen]	8	0	0
Tho: Pingrie	12	0	0
Edw: Hichman	13	0	0
Katherine Smith	8	0	0
Will: Hartland	5	0	0
Will: Mathewes	5	0	0
James Tomes	6	0	0
Will: Sargent	8	0	0
		(36r)	
Will: Parlor	3	0	0
John Bridges of &c	2	10	0
Walter Gwatkin	4	0	0
Robt Nourse	8	0	0
John Davies	1	10	0
John Hardwicke	2	0	0
John Packer	2	0	0
Will: Bridge	10	0	0
Rich: Sargent	1	0	0

Charge 815 0 0
[816 0 0]

John Tomes, Will: Nurthen. Raters.

The proportion is direct.

14. Walford   [Ge14]

	£	s	d
The Dutchess of Som'sett	80	0	0
The Countess of Kent	15	0	0
The Lo: Scudamore	60	0	0
Robt Kyrle Esq[34]	200	0	0
John Markey Esq	75	0	0
Robt Stratford gen	40	0	0
Tho: Yeame [Yem] gen	50	0	0
Rich: Clarke gen	50	0	0
John Lee gen	45	0	0
Edm: Bond gen	90	0	0

	£	s	d
Dan: Kerry gen	20	0	0
Thomazine Dew wid	15	0	0
Henry Smith clarke	10	0	0
Will: Adams cler	10	0	0
Walter Pearce	12	0	0
Edmund Harris	20	0	0
Tho: Chinn	17	0	0
Jam: Smith	7	10	0
Anne Smith wid	7	10	0
Rich: Chinn	14	0	0

32. Probably Sir Thomas Grubham Howe of Kempley, Gloucs, who was knighted 15 Dec. 1660; Shaw, p. 232.
33. Captain of a militia company in the mid-1660s (Loan 29/49, pf. 4, no. 69/15); HT 1664 (7).   34. HT 1664 (15); will proved 1670 (PCC).

F

Graytree: Walford continued

	£	s	d		£	s	d
John Sybrance [*Sibrans or*				Mary Cowarne wid	3	0	0
Ciprians] sen	9	0	0	Anne Hardwick wid	1	0	0
Rich: Croose	2	0	0				
John Seymore	6	0	0	Charge	961	0	0
		(36v)					
Fortune Stratford wid	7	0	0				
Will: Bellamy	4	0	0	Robt Stratford, Rich: Clarke. Raters.			
Tho: Keare	3	10	0				
Alice Chinne wid	3	0	0	**Quere de peeres land peers land is £95**			
Alice Kyrle wid	5	0	0				
Stephen Phillipps for the							
tieth &c	80	0	0	**The proportion is direct.**			

---

15. Weston under Peniard[35] [Ge15]

	£	s	d		£	s	d
The Countess of Kent	10	0	0			(37r)	
Sr Jo: Scudamore in Tieth	40	0	0	John Rudge de Meadow	12	0	0
Mrs Rudhall &c	14	0	0	Will: Rudge	3	0	0
Doctor Newton in Tyth	20	0	0	Tho: Bonner	18	0	0
Mr Nourse[36]	32	0	0	Mrs Westerdell	12	0	0
Tho: Loyd	14	0	0	John Kayse de Hope	13	0	0
Tho: Sergeant	8	0	0	Rich: Stallard	4	0	0
Will: Roberts	10	0	0	Mr Prichard &c	4	10	0
Jam: Palmer	25	0	0	Francis Wynn	3	10	0
Mr Wynniatt	12	0	0	Do^r Phillipps &c	9	0	0
Kath: Rudge	10	0	0	Tho: Bridge for &c	8	0	0
John Merrick gen	25	0	0	Tho: Stone for &c	8	10	0
Walter Merrick	20	0	0	Robt Merrick	8	10	0
Tho: Swayne	8	0	0	Roger Bonner	1	0	0
Tho: Merrick	4	0	0	James Sergeant	1	0	0
Christian Hart	22	0	0	Tho: Rudge of Riford	1	0	0
Jo: Hardwick	20	0	0				
Jo: Nokes	3	10	0	Charge	459	0	0
Henry Rudge	14	0	0				
John Rudge de Wacton	2	0	0	John Rudge. Rater.			
Walter Lloyd	15	0	0				
Widow Smith	10	0	0	**Almost halfe is to be added to the**			
John Rudge de Marsh	14	0	0	**Valuation**			

---

35. The largest HT charge in 1664 was on John Bonner (5).
36. John Nourse Esq.

16. Woolhope & Brockhampton [*Ge16*]

	£	s	d		£	s	d
Mrs Mary Bodenham wid	60	0	0	Mr Hamden	———		
Mrs Bosworth wid	35	10	0	John Bradwell	———		
Edw: Bosworth gen	12	15	0	Will: Jones	———		
Will: Gregory Esq[37]	22	15	0	Henry Gwillime	———		
Edm: Ravenhill	9	0	0	Antho: Jones cler	———		
Tho: Stallard	6	3	0	Tho: Ravenhill	———		
John Winter	8	0	0	Jane Mayoe	———		
Anth: Brukley [*Buckley*]				Oswald Widderington	———		
cler[38]	18	15	0	Rich: Hill & John Hope	———		
Will: Watts cler	15	0	0	Tho: Whillar	———		
Rich: Wheeler cler[39]	14	0	0	Edw: Caple gen	———		
Henry Manfield cler	30	0	0	John Sergeant	———		
Tho: Howells	6	0	0	Tho: Church iun	———		
Anth: Apperley gen	9	10	0	Tho: Church sen[r]	———		
Tho: Apperley gen	27	0	0	Tho: Hodges & his sonne	———		
Jo: Wheelar	5	0	0	John Kethero	———		
Sparryes Landes	3	0	0	Will: Barry	———		
		(37v)		Tho: Willim	———		
Will: Bridges Esq	———			Hardins Lands	———		
John Ravenhill minor	———					(38r)	
Anne Chambers wid	———			John Davis		15	0
Roger Wood	———			Rich: Weaver	1	5	0
Stonehouse	———			Will: Bedow	1	0	0
Will: Winter	———			John Abrall	10	5	0
Garstons lands	———			Will: Kethero		15	0
John Ravenhill & his mother	———			John Mutlow	1	15	0
William Whooper	———			Will: Apperley gen	9	0	0
Tho: Tanty	———			Antho: Apperley	9	0	0
The widow Phillipps	———						
Wm Smith & his sonne	———			Charge	444	0	0
Thomas Wheelar	———			[*316*	*3*	*0*]	
John Lane	———						
John Davies	———			Tho: Wheeler, John Ravenhill. Raters.			
Rich: Smith	———						
Hatsfords farme	———			**The valuation is to be doubled.**			
Henry Gwillym	———						
Tho: Wallwyn gen	———						
Edw: Wheelar [*Whillar*]	———						

37. JP 1660; HT 1664 (9).
38. FP 1661 (£3 paid).
39. Will proved 8 Aug. 1663 (PCC).

Grimsworth Hundred[1] (39r)

	Value returned by the Raters		The Value Horse Being Taken Out — Value according to the contribution			The whole years contribution at 2s per pownd per annum for each particular parish in this Hundred		
	£		£	s	d	£	s	d
1	219	Bishopston	232	18	8	23	5	8
2	298	Byford	349	10	0	34	19	8
3	177	Brainton	275	3	4	27	10	4
4	203	Bridgsollers	367	16	8	36	15	8
5	333	Brinsopp	369	6	8	36	18	8

1. The proportions of the hundred charge allocated to the respective parishes are close to, but not the same as, those in 1677.

Hearth Tax return, Lady Day, 1664:

Grimsworth Hundred	Total Charged Hearths	Total Houses	Numbers of Charges of Each Magnitude											Total Exempt Houses
			More than 10 hearths *	10	9	8	7	6	5	4	3	2	1	
Bishopstone	36	33				1				1	2	1	16	12
Byford	38	37					1		1	1	3	2	9	20
Breinton	31	30				1					2	6	5	16
Bridge Sollers	26	15		1								5	6	3
Brinsop	30	19	1 (13)								2	2	7	7
Brobury	15	22									2		9	11
Burghill	95	72			1	1	1		2	2	5	6	26	28
Canon Pyon	97	80			2	1		2		2	2	8	29	34
Credenhill	27	21		1						2		1	7	10
Hampton Bishop & Tupsley	83	67						1	3	3	7	7	15	31
Holmer & Shelwick	89	61						4	2	2	1	8	28	16
Kenchester	35	18	1 (11)			1				1	1	3	3	8
Mansell Lacy	59	56							2	2	1	7	24	20
Mansell Gamage	39	34			2					1	1	4	7	19
Monnington	37	20	1 (20)								1	1	7	9
Moreton	40	25		1			1				3	2	4	13
Norton Canon	55	70						2	2	2	1	2	18	43
Pipe & Lyde	32	27					1				3	5	5	13
Staunton & Over Letton	62	111						2	2	2	1	3	23	78
Stretton Sugwas	22	14	1 (13)						1		1	1	2	9
Wellington	111	64	2 (14 & 11)					2	1	4	6	11	13	25
Wormsley	20	14					1				2		6	5
Yazor	44	45			1					1	2	5	15	21
Total	**1,123**	**895**	**6**	**3**	**6**	**8**	**4**	**11**	**17**	**25**	**50**	**90**	**284**	**391**

* Actual charge in brackets.

70

Grimsworth Hundred continued

	Value Returned by the Raters		The Value Horse Being Taken Out	Value according to the contribution		The whole years contribution at 2s per pound per annum for each particular parish in this Hundred		
	£			£	s	d	£	s	d
6	109	Brobury		146	10	0	14	13	0
7	816	Burghill als Burfield		940	0	0	94	0	0
8	890	Canon Pion		940	0	0	94	0	0
9	181	Credenhill		303	6	8	30	6	8
10	510	Hampton		963	3	4	96	6	4
11	655	Holmer		774	16	8	77	9	8
12	267	Kenchester		268	6	8	26	16	8
13	558	Mansell Lacy		630	6	8	61	4	4
14	261	Mansell Gamadge		383	16	8	38	7	8
15	380	Monington		349	10	0	34	19	8
16	235	Moreton upon Lugg		286	10	0	28	13	0
17	339	Norton Canon		699	0	0	69	18	0
18	260	Pipe & Lide		338	16	8	33	15	8
19	587	Stanton		699	0	0	69	18	0
20	336	Stretton		245	10	0	24	11	0
21	660	Wellington		929	0	0	92	18	0
22	148	Wormesley		184	0	0	18	8	0
23	426	Yazor		603	0	0	61	4	0

[*Total £1126 19s 8d*]

1. Bishopston (40r) [*Gm1*]

	£	s	d		£	s	d
Mr Berrington &c[2]	80	0	0	George Poule &c	4	0	0
John Courtler [*Curtler*] cler[3]	36	0	0	John Williams	1	0	0
John Adams &c	2	0	0	David Meredith &c		15	0
John Parlor	3	0	0	Franc' Basseter &c		10	0
Bartholomew Pillinger &c		13	4	Rich: Savaker &c	2	0	0
Rich: Colly &c	6	0	0	Geo: Painter	1	0	0
John Probert &c	2	15	0	Tho: Greene gent	1	0	0
John Poule &c	2	0	0	Geo: Eckley &c	24	0	0
The widow Berington	2	0	0	Rich: Foote &c	24	0	0
The wid Farmer	2	15	0	John Scandret [*Scaundrett*]	3	0	0
Will: Mathewes	7	0	0	Walter Eckley	6	0	0

2. Humphrey Berington's real estate in the county was valued in 1646 at £198 a year (Loan 29/15, pf. 2); he was fined $\frac{1}{6}$ of his estate, valued at £632; *CCC*, iii, p. 2000. The largest HT charge in 1664 was on Thomas Berington (8).
3. Rector, FP 1661 (20s paid).

Grimsworth: Bishopston continued

	£	s	d	
Phillip Gwillim	3	0	0	
The wid Hallings	2	0	0	
Tho: Welch &c	1	0	0	Walter Eckley, Phillip Gwillim. Raters.
Walter Arnell [*Ornell*] &c	1	0	0	
				The valuation direct.
Charge	219	0	0	

---

2. Byford[4]   [*Gm2*]

	£	s	d		£	s	d
Sr Tho: Tomkyns Knt	1	10	0	John Chambers &c	3	0	0
John Gomond gen[5]	60	0	0	Symon Mericke &c	5	0	0
Fra: Geeres gen	15	0	0	Walter Shepard	2	0	0
Awbrey Smith gen[6]	48	0	0	John Parlor	2	0	0
James Read for the Rectory[7]	40	0	0	John Maund	2	0	0
Rich: Bethell	10	0	0	Mrs Syllies	2	0	0
		(40v)		Will: Hodges	1	6	8
James Bethell for &c	20	0	0	John Geers gen	5	0	0
John Maund for &c	10	0	0				
John Palor [*Parlor*]	10	0	0	Charge	298	0	0
Tho: Probert &c	30	0	0				
Tho: Bell & Tho: Peirce	18	0	0	Rich: Bethell. Rater.			
James Prees	5	0	0				
Tho: Turner for &c	6	0	0	**Almost a third parte is to bee added to**			
Geo: Goodman &c	3	0	0	**the valuation**			

---

3. Brainton   [*Gm3*]

	£	s	d		£	s	d
Ja: Rodd gent	4	0	0	Bodenham Broadford			
Mary Deynall wid	40	0	0	[*Bradford*] gen[9]	12	0	0
Elinor Price wid	16	0	0				
Mary Elmhurst wid	10	0	0	Charge	177	0	0
Anthony Bullock	5	0	0		[*165*	*0*	*0*]
Wm Badham	24	0	0				
Capt John Booth[8]	24	0	0	Edw: Ravenhill, Antho: Bullock, Will:			
Alice Symmons wid	12	0	0	Snead. Raters.			
Tho: Davies & Wm Snead	6	0	0				
Edw: Ravenhill	12	0	0	**The valuation is to be almost doubled**			

---

4. The manor had belonged to the marquis of Hertford; Harl. 6726.
5. HT 1664 (7).
6. Chief constable of Grimsworth, 1663; Loan 29/49, pf. 4, no. 69/15.
7. Rector, 1660–1683.
8. Captain of a militia company in the mid-1660s; Loan 29/49, pf. 4, no. 69/15. HT 1664 (8).
9. He paid to the Exchequer a rent of £10 for his lands in Breinton in 1660; PRO, Various Accounts, E.101/630/30.

4. Bridge Sollers   (41r)   [Gm4]

	per ann'	£	s	d	
Tho: Geers gen[10]		120	0	0	
John Shepard		16	0	0	
Will: Geers gen		16	0	0	Roger Preese. Rater.
Mrs Monington for &c		28	0	0	
Will: Mathewes & others &c		8	0	0	**A 3rd parte & halfe a 3rd part is to bee**
Will: Istance [*Eustance*]		3	0	0	**added to the valuation**
The Vicaridge		12	0	0	
Charge		203	0	0	

5. Brinsop   [Gm5]

	£	s	d	
Will: Dansey Esq[11]	250	0	0	
Mr Bannaster[12]	25	0	0	
Will'm Taylor	30	0	0	Henry Walter, John Jones. Raters.
Mrs Coningsby	18	0	0	
Henry Walter	10	0	0	**valuation direct**
Charge	333	0	0	

6. Brobury   [Gm6]

	£	s	d	
John Stilling clarke[13]	25	0	0	
James Scudamore Esq	28	0	0	
Dr Evans[14]	25	0	0	James Kirwood, Edw: Lanford.
Anne Carwardine wid	18	0	0	Raters.[15]
Will: Davies	5	0	0	
Tho: Pirkes	2	10	0	**Almost a third part is to be added to the**
James Chambers	2	0	0	**valuation.**
John Chambers	3	10	0	
Charge	109	0	0	

10. HT 1664 (10).
11. The annual income from all sources of Roger Dansey of Brinsop Court was put at £800 in 1645; Harl. 911. The estimate was made by a visitor to the county and should be taken only as an indication of Dansey's relative standing. In 1646 William Dansey's real estate in the county was more reliably put at £160 a year and his personal estate at £102; Loan 29/15, pf. 2. Sheriff 1670. HT 1664 (13).
12. George Bannaster, vicar, FP 1661 (20s paid).
13. Instituted 27 Oct. 1664 (A. T. Bannister, *Diocese of Hereford Institutions, 1539–1900* (Hereford, 1923), p. 35), but he described himself as rector when certifying the transcripts of his register for 1661 and later years (Hereford CRO, Diocesan Archives), and was similarly described in the return of the FP 1661, to which he gave 40s.
14. Dr William Evans, prebendary of Hereford, and John Scudamore owned the two moieties of the manor; H. F. B. Compston, 'A Brobury Rent Roll', *TWC*, xxiv (1922), p. 120. Silas Taylor, however, states that the manor belonged to Evans and to Lord Scudamore; Harl. 6726.
15. HT 1664 (3 each).

7. Burghill (als Burfield) &c[16] (41v)   [Gm7]

	£	s	d		£	s	d
John Aubrey Esq	50	0	0	Nich: Taylor	4	10	0
Symon Paine	6	0	0	Rich: Bithell	12	0	0
Peter Jones of Heref	6	0	0	Tho: Hill	4	10	0
Hen: Caldicott of &c	3	0	0	Phill: Knapp	2	5	0
Dan: Holder of &c	9	0	0	Will: Herring	12	0	0
Jeremy Addis of &c	3	15	0	Mr Herring of Holmer &			
Dennis Smith	3	10	0	Licence Thomas of Heref	40	0	0
John Towne	6	15	0			(42r)	
John Howells	2	0	0	Roger Walter	4	10	0
John Mathewes	4	10	0	Will: Chambers	2	12	6
Hen: Caldicott of Heref	10	10	0	Tho: Bythell	16	10	0
Tho: Tomlins	4	10	0	Will: Hill	3	0	0
Tho: Gwillim gen	31	10	0	Rich: Hords	4	10	0
Anne Bennett	3	15	0	John Gwillim gen	13	0	0
Rich: Stephens	1	2	6	Hen: Rogers	2	5	0
James Exton	25	10	0	Tho: Jenkins sen	2	5	0
Anth: Stephens	25	10	0	Tho: Jenkins iun	2	14	0
Will: Gregory Esq	20			The Lady Lingen	20	0	0
Walter Taylor	1	17	0	The widow Gibbornes	4	10	0
Herbert Masters gen	60			James Exton	1	2	6
Tho: Farrington	3	15	0	Will: Cooke	1	2	6
Roger Williams	6	0	0	Dr Newton	1	0	0
Sam: Thomas &c	3	15	0	Nicho: Philpotts Esq	2	5	0
Franc' Dingley	27	0	0	Will: Yeomons	3	0	0
Mr Landon	17	10	0	Will: Dansey Esq	10	0	0
Tho: Herring	5	10	0	Morgan Price	1	2	6
Rich: Cox Esq for Gleab &				Sam: Smith cler	10	10	0
tieth	80	5	0				
Mr Middlebrooke for &c	5	5	0	Charge	816	0	0
John Aubrey Esq	18	0	0	[780	3	6]	
Wm Smith	24	0	0				
Anth: Baynham gen	45	0	0	Tho: Gwillim, Jo: Smith. Raters.			
Jo: Rogers	45	0	0				
Eliz: Herring	37	15	0	**The proportion direct**			

8. Cannon Pion   [Gm8]

	£	s	d		£	s	d
John Barnaby Esq for &c[17]	30	0	0	John Kinersley for &c	28	0	0
And for the tieth	40	0	0	Oliver Garnor for &c	6	6	8
George Sawyer Esq for &c[18]	30	0	0	Alice Pike wid for &c	5	10	0
And for the tieth	40	0	0	Tho: Griffiths vicar	26	6	8
John Barnaby Esq for &c	30	0	0	George Knapp	20	0	0

16. The largest HT charge in 1664 was on Thomas Carpenter, gent. (9).
17. His income was put at £300 a year in (?) *circa* 1677; Loan 29/182, fo. 313.
HT 1664 (9).   18. HT 1664 (9).

Grimsworth: Cannon Pion continued

	£	s	d		£	s	d
George Knapp for &c	3	0	0	Walter Nash	2	0	0
Rich: Syly for &c	6	0	0	Walter Nash for &c	2	10	0
Joⁿ Jones for &c	8	0	0	Walter Nash	3	0	0
Geo: Knapp for &c	25	0	0	Jo: Mason	4	10	0
		(42v)		Rich: Hodges	2	0	0
Richard Beynham	13	0	0	Rich: Baynham for &c	6	0	0
Tho: Stephens	11	0	0	Geo: Scarlett	2	6	8
Rich: Gayley	12	0	0	James Hodges	2	10	0
John Gwillim gen	8	0	0	Edw: Seaborne for &c	3	10	0
Mr Karvar	3	13	4	Tho: Jones	3	0	0
Joⁿ Munn	25	0	0	Griffith Jones	1	0	0
Rich: Burcher for &c	40	0	0	Will: Booll [*Bull*]	2	0	0
Rich: Burcher for &c	5	0	0			(43r)	
Tho: Berrington for &c[19]	50	0	0	John Burropp	2	0	0
Geo: Heynes for &c	66	6	8	Henry Knapp	2	0	0
Michaell Moore Esq	43	13	4	Will: Gittoes	4	0	0
Francis Kinersley	20	0	0	Will: Gittoes for &c	6	0	0
Tho: Jay	10	0	0	Arth: Thylor [*Taylor*] for &c	1	6	0
Kath: Jay	10	0	0	Dr Bridstock Harford	2	15	0
Roul' Garner [*Gardner*]	22	0	0	Tho: Bythell	2	0	0
Oliver Garner	10	0	0	Will Plene	1	0	0
Edw: Monnington	10	0	0	Phill: Syly	2	0	0
Mary Blayney	10	6	8	Hugh Syly	1	10	0
Ralph Darnell Esq	56	6	8	The chiefe rent to the Canons	24	4	0
Rich: Howard for &c	5	0	0				
Eliz: Knapp wid	19	0	0	Charge	890	0	0
Rich: Morgon [*Morvan*] for					[*923*	*11*	*8*]
&c	39	0	0				
Phil: Yeomans for &c	20	0	0	Edw: Monington, Rich: Baynham, Tho:			
Phil: Yeomans	12	0	0	Syly. Raters.			
Tho: Syly	13	0	0				
Will: Gayley & his sonne [?]	8	0	0	**The valuation direct**			

9. Credenhill

[*Gm9*]

	£	s	d		£	s	d
Mrs Anne Cholmely wid for				John Eckley for &c	2	0	0
&c[20]	70	0	0	and for Walter Meiricks			
Tho: Treherne cler for &c[21]	25	0	0	land	4	0	0
Mr Barker of Stretton for his				Rich: Probert for &c	8	0	0
&c	12	0	0				
Mr Silvanus Landon for &c	20	0	0	Charge	181	0	0
Will: Payne	12	0	0				
Mr Silvanus Smith cler	6	0	0	Will: Paine, Tho: Hill. Raters.			
Will: Browne & his mother	8	0	0				
James Meirick	8	0	0	**The valuation is to be doubled.**			
Phill: Eckley	6	0	0				

19. Of Little Pyon; will proved 1668 (PCC).   20. HT 1664 (10).
21. Rector, FP 1661 (40s paid).

(43v)

10. Hampton[22]   [Gm10]

[*There follows one blank page*]

(44r)

11. Holmer[23]   [*Gm11a*]

	£	s	d
Dr Edward Aldern	60	0	0
Humphrey Howorth gen[24]	30	0	0
Mrs Herring wid[25]	40	0	0
John Walsh gen	40	0	0
Jonathan Edwin gen[26]	30	0	0
Tho: Norman	20	0	0
Mrs Anne Church wid[27]	14	0	0
Anthony Stephens	10	0	0
Rich: Ravenhill gen	20	0	0
Jo: Edwine	12	0	0
Will: Gailey & the wid Wall	12	0	0
Tho: Sheppard	1	10	0
John Maiors [*Mayoes*] for			
&c	5	0	0
Will: Morris	1	0	0
Will: Winney	1	0	0
John Price	4	0	0
Phill: Wallis	1	0	0
Sr Jo: Scudamoʳ for &c	50	0	0
Mr Parry for &c[28]	40	0	0
Jo: Fox gen Q if not for h	50	0	0
Humph: Wilton	20	0	0
Jo: Hinton	5	0	0
Roger Leech	4	0	0
Rich: Knight	3	0	0
Nicho: Skyrme	1	0	0
Rich: Smith	1	10	0
Will: Heyward	1	10	0
Elinor Pountney wid	1	0	0
Nath: Brasier	1	0	0
Rich: Suter [*Shooter*]	1	0	0
Sr Jo: Scudamoʳ for &c	50	0	0
John Tully	3	0	0
Tho: Fletcher	1	0	0
Tho: Weaver	2	0	0
Rich: Tayler	7	0	0
The wid Long	1	0	0
Rich: Walker	1	0	0

	£	s	d
Phill: Symons	2	0	0
	(44v)		
John Jenkins	7	0	0
Rich: Philpotts gen	3	0	0
Rich: Benny gen	5	0	0
Geo: Exton	7	0	0
John Pye Esq[29]	40	0	0
Mrs Price wid	20	0	0
Edmund Weaver Esq	4	0	0
Hugh Rodd gen	2	0	0
Mr Phillipps	2	0	0
Wm Mailard gen	2	0	0
Mr Paynard	2	0	0
Dr Bridstock Harford	1	0	0

Charge   655   10   0

[*642   10   0*]

£94 upon Huntington to be added

A fifth part is to be added to the Valuation

Huntington in the parish of Holmer   [*Gm11b*]

	£	s	d
Mr Phillipps	40	0	0
Herbert Broughton cler	20	0	0
Stephen Skynner gen	18	0	0
Mrs Anne Herring wid	2	0	0
John Howells	5	10	0
John Walsh gen for &c	5	0	0
Mrs Price wid	1	0	0
Rowland Rees	2	10	0

Charge   94   0   0

Tho: Norman, Jo: Hinton, Jo: Howells. Raters.

22. Included Tupsley. The largest HT charge in 1664 was on Thomas Birch, clerk (6).
23. Included Shelwick.   24. JP q 1660.   25. Anne Herring, HT 1664 (6).
26. Chief constable of Grimsworth, 1663; Loan 29/49, pf. 4, no. 69/15. HT 1664 (6).
27. HT 1664 (6).   28. Richard Parry, gent., HT 1664 (6).
29. In 1646 his estate in the county was put at £80 a year; Loan 29/15, pf. 2.

12. Kenchester (45r) [Gm12]

	£	s	d
Mrs Vaughan[30]	120	0	0
James Lawrence Esq	80	0	0
Will: Tully	50	0	0
Will: Langford cler[31]	30	0	0
Will: Conyngsby gen	3	0	0
The widdow Hallings			
[Hawlins]	6	0	0
Will: Powell	3	0	0
Walter Pitt	2	0	0
Charge	267	0	0
	[294	0	0]

Will: Vaughan, James Lawrence, Wm Tully.

The valuation direct.

13. Mauncell Lacy [Gm13]

	£	s	d		£	s	d
James Rodd Esq[32]	62	10	0	The wid Jones	3	0	0
Francis Traunter gen	85	0	0	Jo: Ferra[r]	1	10	0
John Taylor gen	50	0	0	Wm Botchet [Bodgett]	7	0	0
Tho: Mason gen	60	0	0	Tho: Browne	2	0	0
Awbrey Smith gen	26	0	0	James Eckley	2	0	0
Edm: Thomas gen[33]	60	0	0			(45v)	
James Eckley	35	0	0	Rich: Bithell	1	10	0
Peter Eckley	24	0	0	Gregory More	2	10	0
Gervas Smith cler	26	0	0	Anne Haines	2	0	0
Abraham Mason[34]	6	0	0	John Harper & others	2	0	0
Edw: Davies	27	0	0	Margarett Eckley		10	0
Geo: Eckley	17	10	0	The wid Hallings		10	0
Arthur Hill	12	0	0	Jo: Probert		3	0
Tho: Hoskins [Hopkins]	7	0	0	Hodges Lands	7	0	0
Jo: Ireland	11	0	0	The Line Acres	1	10	0
Jo: Colly		14	0				
Wm Browne	4	15	0	Charge	558	12	0
Hen: Pantoll	5	0	0		[569	12	0]
Edw: Ireland	5	0	0				
Jo: Browne	7	10	0	Tho: Hopkins, John Ireland. Raters.			
Walter Hargest	1	10	0				
Hugh Dier	1	10	0	**The proportion.**			
Matth: James	1	10	0				

30. Elizabeth Vaughan together with John Prosser, HT 1664 (11).
31. Rector, FP 1661 (20s).
32. In 1646 the Herefordshire real estate of Thomas Rodd of Foxley was valued at £42 a year and his personal estate at £29; Loan 29/15, pf. 2.
33. HT 1664 (5).
34. HT 1664 (5).

14. Mauncell Gamage

[Gm14]

	£	s	d		£	s	d
Herbert Westfalling Esq[35]	100	0	0	Mr Berrington	7	10	0
Francis Geeres gen[36]	40	0	0	The wid Hodges	5	0	0
Mr Read vicar	10	0	0	Will: Mathewes	1	0	0
Dr Evans	35	0	0				
Tho: Bithell	15	0	0	Charge	261	0	0
Jo: Woodhouse	15	0	0				
Jo: Garrall	6	5	0	John Garrall, Tho: Bethell. Raters.			
Will: Jenkins	5	0	0				
Jo: Lurcott & his mother	7	10	0	**A third part is to be added to the**			
Joseph Bulcott [*Boucott*]	2	10	0	**valuation**			
Mr Rodd	11	5	0				

15. Monington

[Gm15]

	£	s	d	
Sr Tho: Tomkins Kt[37]	300	0	0	
Tho: Denis cler	40	0	0	**Valuation direct.**
Will: Hodges	40	0	0	
Charge	380	0	0	

16. Morton [*upon Lugg*] &c   (46r)

[Gm16]

	£	s	d		£	s	d
Sr Harbert Perrott Kt	20	0	0	tenance of a foote soldier			
John Price Esq	40	0	0	hath never as yet pd any-			
Garnons Daunser cler[38]	100	0	0	thing but hath refused &			
Rich: Walker cler	20	0	0	doth refuse.[39]	5	0	0
Charles Waston	20	0	0				
Tho: Jenkins	10	0	0	Charge	235	0	0
Hen: Lloid	10	0	0				
Jo: Heare & Will: Jenkins	5	0	0	Tho: Jenkins sen, Tho: Jenkins iun.			
Jo: Dyer	5	0	0	Raters.			
Wm Dunn for five pownds per annum which being ordered to pay propor- tionable tow'ds ye main-				**A third parte is to bee added to the valuation**			

35. JP q 1660; MP for Hereford 1660 and 1661, but the latter election was declared void. FP 1661 (£20 paid in Hereford); HT 1664 (9). His income was put at £200 a year in (?) *circa* 1677; Loan 29/182, fo. 313.   36. HT 1:664 (9).
37. JP 1660; DL 1660; MP for Weobley 1660 and 1661; knighted 2 Jan. 1661/2: Shaw, p. 236. In 1645 the annual income of Mr Tompkins of Monnington was estimated to be £1,200 (Harl. 911); in 1649 he compounded at $\frac{1}{3}$ on a value of £2,110; *CCC*, ii, p. 1035; HT 1664 (20).   38. HT 1664 (10).
39. The 1663 Militia Act imposed a penalty of £5 for not providing a foot-soldier when so charged; it seems that, although the previous Act implied that the smaller estates were liable to charge, there was no penalty for refusal.

17. Norton Canon   [Gm17]

	£	s	d		£	s	d
Mr Hyetts lands	64	0	0	Humph: Baker	12	0	0
Fr: Keery [Kerry]	30	0	0	Bellamies farme	20	0	0
Geo: Whitney	24	0	0	Mr Berrington	6	0	0
Tho: Carpenter	12	0	0	Ro: Rodd	3	0	0
Jo: Turner	11	0	0	Guilb: Cornewall gentl'[40]	40	0	0
Jo: Chabnor	16	0	0	Ja: Kirwood	8	0	0
The Demeanes of Norton	50	0	0				
Jo: Clarke vicar	12	0	0	Charge	339	0	0
Geo: Smith	9	0	0				
Rich: Greene	10	0	0	Rich: Chabnor, Geo: Whitney. Raters.			
Mr Scudamores landes							
quare h	8	0	0	**The proportion is to bee doubled**			
Ja: Clee	4	0	0				

18. Pipe [& Lide] &c   (46v)   [Gm18]

	£	s	d		£	s	d
Herbert Masters gen	45	0	0	Nicho: White & Edw:			
Edw: Wright gen	10	0	0	Badham	12	10	0
Jerom: Addis gen	4	0	0	Christopher Meeke	6	5	0
Jo: Addis gen[41]	39	0	0	Hugh Lewis	6	0	0
Rich: Walker cler[42]	18	0	0	Rich: Walker	1	14	0
Will: Westfalling gen for				Sr Herbert Parrott Kt	8	0	0
the glebe	5	0	0	Garnons Daunser cler	1	0	0
Jonathan Edwin gen	7	0	0				
Anne Herring wid	6	5	0	Charge	261	0	0
Mrs Powell wid	3	15	0		[251	14	0]
Wm Low cler	6	0	0				
Tho: Price Esq	16	5	0	Tho: Ravenhill, John Barrow, Rich:			
Nicho: Philpotts gen[43]	45	0	0	Chance. Raters.			
Jo: Chance	8	0	0				
Jo: Havard	3	0	0	**A third part is to be added to the valuation**			

(47r)

19. Sutton [Stanton][44]   [Gm19]

[There follow one and a third blank pages]

40. HT 1664 (6). Thomas Prosser was also charged on 6 hearths.
41. John Addis was punished for his Catholicism in 1684; Add. 36452, fo. 190; HT 1664 (4); he was also charged for 4 hearths at the Court of Lide.
42. Vicar.
43. Clerk of the Peace 1649–52 and 1660–70; Sir E. Stephens, *The Clerks of the Counties, 1360–1960* (1961), p. 99. He was also treasurer of the militia funds during the mid-1660s; Loan 29/49, pf. 4, no. 69. FP 1661 (£5 paid in Hereford).
44. Probably included Over Letton township. The manor had belonged to the Tomkins family; Harl. 6726. The largest HT charges in 1664 were on William Carpenter and James Rees (7 each).

20. Stretton &c (47v) [Gm20]

	£	s	d		£	s	d
Edw: Barker Esq[45]	200	0	0	The widow Hallings	2	0	0
Eliz: Kyrle wid	20	0	0	Will: Howells	1	10	0
Ann Herring wid	20	0	0	Will: Vaughan	1	10	0
Do^r Jo: Newton Rector	45	0	0				
Roger Cadwallader[46]	20	0	0	Charge	336	0	0
Tho: Gwillim gen	5	0	0				
Rich: Brinton gen	10	0	0	Roger Cadwallader, Morris Middle-			
Jo: Curier	5	0	0	brookes. Raters.			
Edw: Meirick	4	0	0				
Jo: Hincke [Linke]	2	0	0	**The valuation direct**			

21. Wellington[47, 48] [Gm21]

	£	s	d		£	s	d
Sr Herbert Parrott Kt[49]	120	0	0	Jo: Mathewes	2	0	0
The Lady Alice Lingen	4	0	0	Jo: Burchard	4	0	0
The Lady Weston	44	0	0	Giles Burchard	4	0	0
The parsonage Glebe &				Jo: Howles	2	0	0
Tieth	62	0	0	Walter Davies	2	0	0
Jo: Gwillim gen	64	0	0	Mills Lands	2	0	0
Tho: Mayo gen	58	0	0	Edw: Crumpe	1	10	0
Mr Hall	62	0	0	Lawfords Lands	1	0	0
Tho: Bridges gen	30	0	0	Rich: Hords	2	0	0
Hen: Rogers gen	15	0	0	Arth: Price [Prees]	2	0	0
Tho: Symmons gen	15	0	0	Phill: Gladwyn	2	0	0
Jo: Towne	18	0	0	Will: Allen	1	0	0
Rich: Burchard	12	0	0	Rich: Hords	1	0	0
Tho: Jenkins	15	10	0	John Hords	1	0	0
Mr Drake	13	0	0				
Mr Chapman cler	10	0	0	Charge	660	0	0
Jo: Hearing [Herring]	8	0	0		[617	0	0]
Rich: Walton	15	0	0				
Hugh Hords	8	0	0	Ezek: Davies, Will: Towne, Jo: Hards.			
		(48r)		Raters.			
Will: Burchard [Bircher]	4	10	0				
Mary Morvan & Jo: her				**A this [third] part is to be added to the**			
sonne	8	0	0	**valuation**			
Felice Price [Preece] wid							
for &c	5	0	0				

45. HT 1664 (13).
46. A Catholic, imprisoned 1682/4; Add. 36452, fo. 190.
47. Included Dinmore.
48. The largest HT charge in 1664 was on the widow Wolrich (14).
49. Knighted 14 Aug. 1660: Shaw, p. 231. JP q 1660; DL 1660; MP for Weobley 1660; sheriff 1661. He owned the Haroldston estate in Pembrokeshire, inherited from Sir James Perrot of that county; H. S. Grazebrook, *Heraldry of Worcestershire*, ii (1873), p. 426.

22. Wormesley [Gm22]

	£	s	d		£	s	d
Fra: Hall Esq[50]	70	0	0	Tho: Vaughan	1	0	0
Will: Browne	15	0	0	Saises farme	1	0	0
Marg: Eckley wid	15	0	0				
Jo: Colly	15	0	0	Charge	148	0	0
Jo: Exton	11	5	0				
Rich: Eckley	11	5	0	Jo: Colley, Geo: Haycox. Raters.			
Geo: Haycox [Hickox]	7	10	0				
Arth: Hill	2	0	0	**The valuation direct**			

23. Yazor (48v) [Gm23]

	£	s	d		£	s	d
Ja: Rodd Esq[51]	80	0	0	Roul' Watkins & his sonne	30	0	0
Ro: Rodd gen[52]	60	0	0	Jo: Hints	23	0	0
Herb: Westfaling Esq	8	0	0	Will: Watkins	1	10	0
Tho: Berrington gen	6	0	0	Jo: Taylor		10	0
Jane King wid	50	0	0	Tho: Hopkins	2	10	0
Rich: Immings vicar[53]	20	0	0	The wid Jones	12	0	0
Jane Hodges wid	8	0	0	Jo: Ireland		10	0
Rich: Moithen	3	0	0	Arth: Hill		10	0
Jo: Powell	2	0	0	Ja: Eckley for &c	1	0	0
Jo: Carpenter gen	30	0	0	The wid Eckley	3	0	0
Rich: Hodges	14	0	0	Ja: King for &c	5	0	0
Jo: Hodges	8	0	0	Mr Rodd for &c	5	0	0
Jo: Smith	4	0	0	Jam: Eckley		10	0
Grego: Pember	18	0	0	Hopless meadow	1	0	0
Jo: Bayley	10	0	0	Gills Lands		5	0
Edw: Bayley	6	0	0				
Phill: Romsall	1	10	0	Charge	426	0	0
The wid Prichard	1	10	0	[486	0	0]	
Ja: Hues	1	10	0				
Humph: Davis	15	0	0	Rowland Watkins, Tho: Like. Raters.			
Rich: Greene	4	0	0				
Will: Largoe	2	10	0	**A third parte is to be added to the**			
Rich: Moithen	1	10	0	**valuation**			
Tho: Like	23	0	0				
Tho: Winney	14	0	0				
Tho: Watkins	4	0	0				

(49r & v [blank])

50. HT 1664 (8); a farm called The Grange; will of Francis Hall of Ledbury, p. 97 *infra*.
51. The elder, will proved 1666 (PCC).
52. HT 1664 (9).
53. FP 1661 (20s paid).

	Value Return'd by the Raters (£)		The Value Horse Being Taken Out (£ s d)			Value according to the contribution			The whole years contribution at 2s per pound per annum for each particular parish in this Hundred (£ s d)		
1.	740	Bach Middlewood & Fominde	1080	0	0				108	0	0
2.	711	Brilley	911	6	8				91	2	8
3.	663	Clifford & Hardwick	1074	0	0				107	8	0
4.	1063	Eardesley	1353	0	0				135	6	0
5.	304	Huntington	353	0	0				35	6	0
6.	1384	Kington	1501	3	4				150	2	4
7.	221	Whittney	432	0	0				43	4	0
8.	463	Winforton	617	10	0				61	15	0

[Total £732 4s 0d]

1. The parish shares of the hundred total are similar to those of 1677 in proportion to the respective totals.

Hearth Tax return, Lady Day, 1664:

Huntington Hundred	Total Charged Hearths	Total Houses	More than 10 hearths*	10	8	7	6	5	4	3	2	1	Total Exempt Houses
Old Kington	24	22							1		6	8	7
New Kington: Lower	109	54			1	1	1	3	5	2	15	17	9
New Kington: Upper	87	50						1	4	7	15	15	8
Hergest	34	23		1						1	3	15	3
Bradnor & Rushock	35	31							1	1	2	24	3
Chickward	34	24					1		1	2	3	11	6
Total Kington	323	204		1	1	2	1	4	12	13	44	90	36
Bach, Middlewood &c	62	66					1		2		10	28	25
Brilley	85	95					2	1	1	6	10	26	49
Clifford & Hardwick	70	58					3		3		9	25	18
Eardisley	111	101				1		1	1	7	20	32	39
Huntington	38	29							1	5	4	11	8
Whitney	53	35	1 (15)					2	1	1	1	19	10
Winforton	57	52	1 (11)				1	1		1	6	20	22
Total	799	640	2	1	2	2	9	8	18	36	104	251	207

* Actual charge in brackets.

82

1. Bach [*Middlewood & Fominde*] (51r)   [*H1*]

	£	s	d		£	s	d
Robert Duppa	25	0	0	David Watkin David	9	0	0
Dame Elinor Williams	91	0	0	Will: Madey [*Maddy*] sen[2]	14	0	0
Philo Higgins	20	0	0	Posthume [*Posthumus*] Madey	9	0	0
Rich: Jones	20	0	0	Tho: Lewis	5	0	0
Rich: Jones	7	0	0	Will: Madey iun	18	0	0
Jo: Hall	18	0	0	Jo: Rouland	7	0	0
Tho: Nicholas	5	0	0	Jo: Watkins	8	0	0
Walter Hill	5	0	0			(51v)	
The widow Grove	4	0	0	Will: & Jo: Lewis	9	0	0
Wm Hughes	11	0	0	Sam: Tracy gen	12	0	0
Eliz: Wellington	6	0	0	Tho: Higgins gen[3]	66	0	0
Jesus Colledge Land	18	0	0	Phill: Holman Esq	14	0	0
Magdalen Scudamore	49	0	0	Tho: Bullocke	10	0	0
Rich: Bevan gen	22	0	0	Hen: Wellington	18	0	0
James Miles	3	0	0	Charles Pember	3	0	0
The wid Jenkins	8	0	0	Roger Vaughan Esq	8	0	0
Tho: Jenkins	16	0	0	Mr Parker Bodcott	12	0	0
James Jenkins	8	0	0	James Whiting cler	6	0	0
Tho: Smith	4	0	0	Jo: Rawlins cler	7	0	0
Isaack Morgan	22	0	0	The prediall tiethes of Bach			
Eliz: Smith spinster	20	0	0	Middlewood Broadmeadow			
Mrs Gravell	14	0	0	Vomynd & Bodcott	46	0	0
Tho: Penoyre gen	3	0	0				
Evan Harry	6	0	0	Charge	740	0	0
Will: Hill	6	0	0		[742	0	0]
James Watkins gen	4	0	0				
Evan Brace	10	0	0	Tho: Higgins, Will: Madey,[4]			
Tho: Prichard	9	0	0	Jo: Rowland. Raters.			
Watkin Madey	15	0	0				
Tho: Goodes	12	0	0	**A 4th part is to be added to the Valuation**			

2. Brilley[5]   [*H2*]

		£	s	d		£	s	d
Mr Pember of Newport for					The lands of Kinsley	40	0	0
the Tieth		40	0	0	Fra: Parry	30	0	0
The Cort Lands &c	**ho:**	105	0	0	Patrick Powell	30	0	0
Ph: Holman Esq[6]	**ho:**	57	0	0	Jo: Stead	21	0	0
The Lands of the Welsh-					The lands of Phillip Harper			
hood &c	**ho:**	20	0	0	dec'	18	0	0
Foot-soldiers					Tho: Duppa Esq	6	0	0
Abigall Warbarton wid		50	0	0	Hugh Lewis & Alice Lewis			
Marg: Prosser wid		36	0	0	wid	18	0	0
Griffith Hatley cler		30	0	0	Ja: Savaker	18	0	0

2. A William Maddy was a chief constable for Huntington in 1663; Loan 29/49, pf. 4, no. 69/15.   3. HT 1664 (6); will proved 1666 (PCC).   4. Of Voimind.
5. The largest HT charges in 1664 were on John Goode and William Williams (6 each).   6. He owned the manor; Harl. 6726.

G

Huntington: Brilley continued

	£	s	d		£	s	d
			(52r)	Bromth lands neere the pound			
Anne Bromth [*Bromich*] wid				and the Crump meadow	5	10	0
& Wa: Winston	12	0	0	Alexander Savaker	2	10	0
Walter Griffithes	12	0	0	Jo: Lewis	3	0	0
Rees Lewis	11	0	0	Jo: Harper	3	0	0
Bridge Cort landes	10	0	0	Marg: Morgan	3	0	0
Tho: Williams	10	0	0	Tho: Jones	3	0	0
Tho: Gibbon iun	9	0	0	Walter Powell	3	0	0
Tho: Higgins	10	0	0	Kath: Powell wid	2	0	0
Howell Bowen	9	0	0	Tho: Meredith	1	0	0
Johan Winston wid	8	0	0	Rich: Higgins	1	0	0
Rich: Lewis	8	0	0	Tho: Vaughan	1	10	0
Hugh Jones	6	0	0	Tho: Prosser	1	0	0
Johan Chambers wid	6	0	0	David Prichard	1	0	0
Wa: Prosser Ja: Prosser &				Rich: Preece	1	0	0
Ma: Pross[r] wid	6	0	0	Jo: Griffith	1	0	0
Balee [*Bulee*] Lands	6	0	0	Tho: Powell	1	0	0
Rees Jenkins	5	10	0				
Alice Lewis	5	0	0	Charge	711	5	0
Jo: Pembridge	5	0	0		[703	5	0]
Tho: Jenkins	4	5	0				
The other parte of Prosser's lands	4	0	0	Ja: Savaker, Tho: Gibbons. Raters.			
Eckleys lands	4	0	0	**A 5th part added to the Valuation**			

[3.] Clifford [*and Hardwick*] **&c**   (52v)   [*H3*]

	£	s	d		£	s	d
The Lady Whitney[7]	240	0	0	Tho: Harry Procer [*Prosser*]	2	0	0
The Lower Court of Clifford	50	0	0	Hugh Games Esq	4	0	0
Jam: Whitney gen	100	0	0	Roger Vaughan Esq	5	0	0
Hen: Williams Esq[8]	15	0	0	The Windhill Parke	2	0	0
Tho: Lewis	1	0	0	The wid: Poole	2	0	0
Hen: Wellington gen	1	10	0	The Chantry Lands of Clifford	3	0	0
Sam: Tracy gen	60	0	0	Will: Miles	4	0	0
Tho: Penoyre gen & Jam:				The wid: Davies	1	10	0
Penoyre gen	60	0	0	Walter Tho: Powell	2	0	0
Symon Brace	6	0	0	Philo: Higgins gen	10	0	0
Will: Hues [*Hughes*] gen	8	0	0	Jo: Ralins [*Rawlins*] cler[9]	10	0	0
David Smith gen	4	0	0	The Tiethes of Clifford	30	0	0
John Lewis	4	0	0	Will: Phillipps gen for ye			
Richard Aston	4	0	0	tiethes of Hardwick	12	0	0
Roger Boulcott gen	4	0	0	Fr: Lewis	1	0	0
Rich: Probert &c	4	0	0				
Jam: Bevan & Henry Rogers	6	0	0	Charge	663	0	0
Hen: Gwillim & his sonne	5	0	0	Jam: Penoyre, Sym: Brace, Jam: Rosse.			
Jam: Rosser	1	0	0	Raters			
Evan Harry	1	0	0	**Almost a 3rd part added to the valuation**			

7. HT 1664 (6) charged on Margaret Whitney.
8. HT 1664 (6). Albon Willis was also charged on 6 hearths.
9. Vicar, FP 1661 (20s).

[4.] Eardesley (53r) [H4]

	£	s	d		£	s	d
Tho: Baskervile Esq[10]	109	10	0	Tho: Harper for &c	8	5	0
Mr Mauncell	174	15	0	Will: Badham	13	2	0
Sir Samuell Tryan's lands[11]	69	15	0	Verny Higgins & his sonne	16	10	0
The parsonage	45	0	0	Tho: Harper of Spoone	12	0	0
The vicarage	37	10	0	Tho: Huett	14	2	0
The parocks	9	0	0	Eliz: Pember wid	9	0	0
Roger Havard gen	12	15	0	Walter Bengough	3	0	0
Hugh Lewis	12	15	0	Jo: George	2	10	0
Jo: Wellington	12	15	0	Jo: Hampton	2	10	0
Tho: Duppa gen[12]	77	10	0	Ja: Powell	2	10	0
Roger Crumpe & his sonne	19	0	0	Ro: Stephens	2	0	0
Will: Taylor	4	17	0	Henry Badham & Ro: Bad-			
Jam: Footes lands	30	0	0	ham	3	0	0
Katherin Rowden wid	26	5	0	Tho: Hughes & his mother	2	10	0
Jo: Rowlands	29	0	0	Humph: Bryan	2	0	0
Hen: Kerry	5	5	0				
Nicho: Baker	22	10	0	Charge 1071	0	0	
Humph: Baskervile	10	10	0	[992	8	6]	
Charles Jones	3	15	0				
Mrs Jane Cooke wid[13]	73	15	0	Will: Badham, Jo: Rowlands, Roger			
Henry Harper gen	41	5	0	Crumpe. Raters			
James Kedward	15	2	6				
Walter Badham	4	17	6	**a 5th parte is to be added to the**			
Tho: Harper for &c[14]	41	5	0	**Valuation**			
Tho: Harper for &c	10	17	6				

[5.] Huntington (53v) [H5]

	£	s	d		£	s	d
Phillipp Holman Esq	124	0	0	John Lewis	8	5	0
Dr Edwards	15	0	0	Griffith Price	6	0	0
Roger Mannering & the				Will: Johns [Jones]	6	0	0
occupiers of Penlan[15]	15	0	0	John Goode or &c	6	0	0
Tho: Gough gen & his sonne	18	0	0	Walter Burgwin	8	0	0
Hen: Cooke	9	0	0	Tho: Vaughan	3	10	0
James Poole	9	0	0	Wm Goode	3	0	0
Tho: Souch gen	13	0	0				
John Hall	3	0	0	Charge 304	0	0	
John Whitney	9	0	0	[264	15	0]	
John Probert	4	10	0				
Rich: Gittoes	4	10	0	Jo: Rogers, Jo: Probert. Raters.			

10. Sir Humphrey Baskervile of Eardisley was said in 1645 to have suffered a reduction in income from £3,000 to £300 a year; Harl. 911.
11. Sir Samuel Tryan, baronet, of Halstead, Essex, succeeded 1627 (*Baronetage*, i, p. 140); will proved 1665 (PCC). 12. HT 1664 (8).
13. Jane Coke of Quistmore left lands in Cambridgeshire; will proved 13 Dec. 1664 (PCC). 14. Of Bollinghill. 15. HT 1664 (4).

6. Kington

	£	s	d
Phil: Holman Esq[16]	120	0	0
Jo: Vaughan Esq[17]	153	0	0
Sam: Davies et Jo: Scaun-			
drett	33	0	0
Rich: Voare	8	0	0
Walter Scaundrett	12	0	0
Edw: Grenouse	12	0	0
Edw: King	18	0	0
Will: Knight[18]	5	13	0
Kath: Waythen &c	8	0	0
Tho: Greenway &c	6	13	0
Rich: Sergent	6	0	0
Mrs Serch &c	12	6	8
Rich: ap John	3	6	0
James Sergent	9	10	0
Humph: Baskervile &c	6	10	0
		(54r)	
Mr Hanley	12	0	0
Tho: Sayer	6	3	0
Tamberlaine Davies	4	0	0
Rich: Merroll & Tho: Morris	9	10	0
James Davies	3	0	0
Oliver Scaundrett &c	10	10	0
James Loyd gen	13	0	0
James Price gen	4	0	0
Tho: Traunter	6	10	0
Edmond Thomas	6	10	0
Walter Vaughan gen &c	24	0	0
Will: Day	6	13	0
Rich: Powell gen	3	0	0
Jo: Gough &c	7	13	4
Will: Addis	6	10	0
Stephen Scaundrett cler &c[19]	4	0	0
Mr Lewellin	64	0	0
Marchant Baugh	46	13	0
Dr Edwards[20]	40	0	0

	£	s	d
Wm Scaundrett	27	0	0
Rich: Scaundrett	25	0	0
Hugh Gwinn	3	10	0
Will: Sabin	6	10	0
Walter Knowles	6	0	0
Wm Greenely	7	0	0
Welstons Lands	4	0	0
Mrs Lewis &c	3	0	0
Will: Edwards gen	13	13	0
Tho: Price	33	0	0
Wm Scaundrett	12	0	0
Wm Wolfe &c	4	10	0
Geo: Dekins	11	0	0
Edw: Scaundrett	11	9	0
Rich: Scaundrett[21]	25	13	0
Rob*t*: Shipman	3	6	8
Tho: Johns	3	6	8
Will: Geeres gen	20	0	0
Jo: Traunter	3	0	0
		(54v)	
Simon Eastopp	4	0	0
Geo: Richards & Will:			
Meirick	4	0	0
Tho: Suter [*Shooter*] gen[22]	40	0	0
Walter Moore	11	10	0
Tho: Morris	10	0	0
David Williams	12	0	0
Alex: Davies	8	0	0
The heires of Walter Rogers	23	0	0
John Taylor & James Powell	3	0	0
The heires of Walter Pember	26	0	0
Jo: Pember & Tuthill &			
Empton[23]	33	0	0
Jo: Howles & James Price	20	0	0
Will: Mahallum	10	10	0
Tho: Harper & Jo: Philpotts	9	0	0

16. Holman acquired both moieties of the manor. He later enriched himself enough to enable his son to become a baronet in 1663 (Robinson, p. 161); he died in July 1669; *Baronetage*, iii, p. 277.
17. John Vaughan of Hergest Court; FP 1661 (£10 unpaid); HT 1664 (10); will proved 1670 (PCC); he also owned land in Kent.
18. HT 1664 (5) in Upper Ward of New Kington.
19. Vicar of Lyonshall; FP 1661 (20s paid).
20. In 1646 Thomas Edwards's estate in the county was valued at £10 real and £64 personal (Loan 29/15, pf. 2); HT 1664 (4) in Old Kington.
21. Chief constable of Huntington, 1663; Loan 29/49, pf. 4, no. 69/15.
22. Of Mahollam; uncle of John Vaughan of Hergest; will proved 1670 (PCC).
23. HT 1664 (7) in Chickward.

Huntington: Kington continued

	£	s	d		£	s	d
Walter Bengoe	11	0	0	Walter Serg't	2	10	0
Tho: Harper &c	11	0	0	Jo: Sayer	2	10	0
Gabriell Bassett	4	10	0	Jo: James	2	10	0
Varney Higgins & filius	4	13	0			(55r)	
Howel Stephens & filius	6	13	0	Tho: Webb	2	13	0
Wm Diron	3	0	0	Wm Garnons	2	0	0
Wm Badham	3	10	0	Wm Goare	2	10	0
Tho: Griffithes	3	10	0	Robert Probert	2	13	0
James Rodd	8	10	0	Rich: Garnons [*Garner*]	2	0	0
Charles Sayer	4	0	0	Joⁿ Taylor	2	13	0
Mich: Braughton [*Broughton*]				Rowdon Lands	2	0	0
gen	44	0	0	David Thomas	2	0	0
Do^r Josua Crosse	50	0	0	Phillip Richards	2	13	0
Edw: Bishopp	2	13	4	Joⁿ Rogers	1	0	0
Jo: Grimes &c	7	10	0				
The heires of Rich: Davies	6	0	0	Charg[24]	1384	0	0
Math: Price	10	10	0				
Wm Shepard	40	0	0				
Wm Taylor	2	10	0	Tho: Traunter, Will: Addis. Raters.			
Jo: Hall	1	0	0				
Jo: Hering	2	0	0	**The proportion direct.**			

[7.] Whitney [*H7*]

	£	s	d		£	s	d
Tho: Whitney Esq[25]	153	0	0	The occupiers of Tho: Bulls			
Dan: Wicherley clre	20	0	0	lands	2	6	8
Robt Duppa gen	7	0	0	Anth: Hussey	1	5	0
The occupiers of Fra: Boy-				Tho: Williams	1	5	0
cotts lands	7	11	3	Rich: Williams	1	4	0
Mary Bartluitt [*Bartlett*]				John Edmonds	1	5	0
wid	2	10	0				
Charles West	5	10	0	Charge	221	0	0
Rich: Hancorne	4	10	0				
Sam: Acton gen	4	12	0	Rich: Hunt, Phillip Renda. Raters.			
Phillip Renda	4	16	0				
Sam: Hancorne	2	6	0				
Phillip Wellington wid	2	6	8	**The Valuation is to be doubled**			

---

24. The largest HT charge in 1664 in Bradnor & Rushock was on Robert Mason (4) and in Lower Ward of New Kington on William Goods (8).
25. JP q 1660; listed as DL in 1660, but may not have been chosen; commissioner for the 18 months assessment 1662/3. In 1645 the income of Sir Robert Whitney was put at £4,000 a year; Harl. 911. Dame Anne Whitney, widow of Robert and mother of Thomas, was charged on 15 hearths in 1664.

[8.] Winforton[26]   (55v)   [H8]

	£	s	d		£	s	d
Thomas Whitney Esq	3	0	0	Sam: Woodcock	5	0	0
The lands of Phillip Holman				Walter Lewis	3	0	0
Esq in possession of Will:				Will: Woodcock	1	10	0
Andrews gen[27]	211	0	0	Edw: Vaughan	1	0	0
Tho: Higgins gen	26	0	0	Will: Andrews more	6	0	0
Tho: Dowsing [Dowdinge]				Walter Chambers	1	10	0
clre[28]	45	0	0	Will: Howles	1	10	0
John Larawnce	8	0	0	Barthol' Parrock	2	0	0
David Preece	8	0	0	Edm' Greene of Weere			
Tho: Boulter	8	0	0	Lesey	100	0	0
Robt Vaughan	7	0	0				
William Higgins	3	0	0	Charge	463	0	0
Robt Woolham	2	0	0				
Tho: Hunt	13	0	0	Tho: Higgins, Tho: Boulter, David			
Ja: Jenkins	2	0	0	Price. Raters			
Katherine Williams wid	4	0	0				
Tho: Chambers	2	0	0	**Something added to the Valuation.**			

26. For tax purposes Winforton usually included Willersley, but occasionally the latter was included with Eardisley, which may have occurred here.
27. William Andrews and others bought the manor of Winforton in 1653; it had previously belonged to Lord Craven; *CCC*, ii, p. 1625. Andrews was charged on 11 hearths in 1664.
28. Rector, FP 1661 (30s).

Radlow Hundred[1]

	Value Returned by the Raters		The Value Horse Being Taken Out	Value according to the contribution			The whole yeares contribution at 2s per pound per annum for each particular parish in this Hundred		
	£			£	s	d	£	s	d
1.	410	Ashperton		580	0	0	58	0	0
2.	162	Aylton		354	6	8	35	8	8
3.	580	Bish: froome		579	0	0	34	14	0
							[57	*18*	*0]*
4.	459	Bosbury		1502	0	0	154	4	0
							[150	*4*	*0]*
5.	438	Castle Froome		480	0	0	48	0	0
6.	431	Cannon Froome							
				[360	*0*	*0]*	*[36*	*0*	*0]*
7.	244	Coddington		288	0	0	28	16	0
8.	915	Collwall		1048	0	0	104	16	0
9.	1224	Cradley		1482	0	0	148	4	0
10.	211	Donington		252	0	0	25	4	0
11.	505	Eastnor		705	0	0	70	10	0
12.	114	Egleton		277	6	8	23	6	0
				[233	*0*	*0]*			
13.	349	Evesbach		377	6	8	34	14	8
							[37	*14*	*8]*
14.	——	Haymonds Frome		441	13	4	44	3	4
15.	663	Ledbury Burrough		649	6	8	64	18	8
16.	1167	Ledbury Forren		3631	7	6	363	2	9
17.	527	Ledon & Hatfield in Ledburies parish	531	11	8	53	3	2
18.	190	Little Marcle		484	3	4	84	8	4
							[48	*8*	*4]*
19.	416	Lugwardine		792	13	4	79	5	4
20.	224	Morton Gefferies		238	0	0	25	16	0
				[258	*0*	*0]*			

1. Most of the parish charges bear the same or similar ratios to each other as do those of 1677. The inserted figures have largely been derived by using the 1677 proportions. Others do not permit this kind of interpolation. The Bishops Frome charge seems to have been deliberately understated; were it not so, the total charge for Egleton, Bishops Frome and Haymonds Frome would bear exactly the same relation to the total as does the charge for the whole parish in 1677. There is, however, no agreement in the charges on the various parts of Ledbury parish. The charge for 'Ledbury Forren' is puzzling because the Foreign is already wholly covered by the charges on Wallhills etc., Wellington, Muchell and Leadon and Haffield. As the other hundred charges under the 1661 and 1672 quotas and in this document show very similar proportions to the county charge, there must be a presumption that the Radlow charge should be about 12·7% of the county (without Hereford) charge. This requires the deduction of the 'Ledbury Forren' charge of £363, leaving the final hundred total of £1,732 13s 4d. [*Footnote continued on page 91.*

Radlow Hundred continued

	Value Returned by the Raters		The Value Horse Being Taken Out			Value according to the contribution			The whole yeares contribution at 2s per pound per annum for each particular parish in this Hundred		
21.	478	Munsley	361	0	0				32	2	0
									[32	2	0]
22.	222	Pixley	320	6	8				22	16	8
			[328	6	8]				[32	16	8]
23.	337	Stoke Ideith	611	0	0				61	2	0
24.	521	Stretton Grandsome									
			[521	0	0]				[52	2	0]
25.	766	Taddington									
			[766	0	0]				[76	12	0]
26.	635	Upleadons side	635	0	0						
									[63	10	0]
27.	463	Wallhills Fairetree & Plaistow	531	8	4				53	2	10
28.	410	Wellington & Michell	531	9	2				53	2	11
29.	487	Westhide	456	0	0				45	12	0
30.	207	Weston	427	6	8				42	14	8
31.	448	Yarkhill	760	0	0				66	0	0
									[76	0	0]

[*Total* £2095 16s 0d]

---

1. Ashperton[2]   (57r)   [R1]

	£	s	d		£	s	d
The Lady Lingen	8	0	0	Rich: Hide for &c	15	0	0
Walter Hopton Esq	3	10	0	And for tuessen[4]	3	10	0
Ben: Mason Esq	4	0	0	Rich: Hooper de Sindrs	6	0	0
Will: Bridges Esq	4	0	0	Roger Hodges	8	0	0
Thorneton Jones Esq	65	0	0	Rich: Hooper de Villa	6	0	0
Rich: Dowdswell Esq	60	0	0	Eliz: Tomkins	8	0	0
Tho: Sextell gen	20	0	0	Jam: Chamberlaine	3	10	0
Joseph Skinner gen	7	0	0	Jo[n] Heath	5	0	0
Will: Hopkins	3	0	0	Jo: Ellis	1	10	0
Alexander Drew	20	0	0	Jo: Godsell	1	0	0
Tho: Taylor	25	0	0				
Anne Tomkins wid	28	0	0	Charge	410	0	0
Jo[n] Naske [*Nash*]	22	0	0				
James Baggard[3]	51	0	0	Jam: Baggard, Jo: Naske. Raters.			
Marg: Godsell	22	10	0				
Jo[n] Baggard	8	10	0	**A 5th parte is to be added to the**			
Wm Baggard	1	0	0	**Valuation**			

2. The largest HT charge in 1664 was on William George (4).
3. Chief constable of Radlow, 1663; Loan 29/49, pf. 4, no. 69/15.
4. Probably Tuston.

2. Aylton

	£	s	d		£	s	d
The parsonage[5]	20	0	0	Jam: Carwardine	5	0	0
Mr Bosworth	26	0	0	Mr Unett	4	0	0
Wm Webley	21	0	0	Wm Browne gen	3	0	0
Wm Hamond	21	0	0	Freemans field	4	0	0
Jo: Hawkins	15	0	0				
Fra: Caple[6]	22	0	0	Charge	162	0	0
Edw: Hall	4	0	0				
Jo: Heath	3	0	0	Fra: Caple, Wm Hamond. Raters.			
Mr Skinner	10	0	0				
Mr Wall	4	0	0	**The Valuation is to be doubled**			

Footnote continued from page 89]

Hearth Tax return, Lady Day, 1664:

Radlow Hundred	Total Charged Hearths	Total Houses	More than 10 hearths *	10	9	8	7	6	5	4	3	2	1	Total Exempt Houses
Ashperton	30	43								1	2	2	16	22
Aylton	20	16							1	1		3	5	6
Bishops Frome	52	43						1	4	2	2	3	6	25
Bosbury (1665 return)	66	27			1		1		2	2	2	7	12	0
Castle Frome	48	25	1 (12)						1	1	2	5	11	4
Canon Frome	26	18	1 (11)								2	2	5	8
Coddington	40	40								3	3	2	15	17
Colwall	130	84			1	1	1			4	7	15	39	16
Cradley	180	121					1	2	1	6	10	25	52	24
Donnington	24	16							1	2		2	7	4
Eastnor (1665 return)	85	45	1 (12)						2	2	3	9	28	0
Egleton	26	28									1	6	11	10
Evesbatch	55	30			1		1		2	3	1	3	8	11
Halmonds Frome	43	28		1			1		1	1	1	3	8	12
Ledbury Borough	291	227			3	1	2	5	7	15	17	21	24	132
Leadon & Haffield	53	47		1					1	2	3	3	15	22
Little Marcle	24	23								2	1	3	7	10
Lugwardine	83	49			1	1	1	1		1	2	9	25	8
Moreton Jeffreys	15	13						1				1	7	4
Munsley	22	23							1		3	1	6	12
Pixley	36	12			1			2			1	4	4	0
Stoke Edith	58	50	1 (17)					1	1	1		6	14	26
Stretton Grandison	49	25	1 (13)			1			1	2	1	3	6	10
Tarrington	54	71								1	4	3	32	31
Upleadon	73	56						1	1	5	2	9	18	20
Wallhills	58	31	1 (16				2				5		13	10
Wellington	73	45					1	1	5	3	1	2	16	16
Mitchel	38	24						2		1	1	5	9	6
Westhide	38	38							1	3		2	17	15
Weston Beggard	28	21							1		1	3	14	2
Yarkhill	56	61							2	1	2	6	24	26
Total	1,874	1,380	6	2	8	4	11	17	36	65	80	168	474	509

* Actual charge in brackets.

5. John Barston paid 14s to the FP 1661.   6. HT 1664 (5).

3. Bish'ps Froome [R3]

	£	s	d		£	s	d
Rich: Hopton Esq	45	0	0	Bellingham his sonne for			
Edw: Witherston clre[7]	36	0	0	Mr Jo: Huttons Estate[11]	160	0	0
Jo: Freeman gen[8]	13	0	0	John Arundell	4	0	0
Jo: Browne gen[9]	32	0	0	Ri: Homes	13	0	0
Fra: Freeman[10]	35	0	0	Ri: Arundell	8	10	0
Fra: Badham	18	0	0	Ri: Mayfield	7	0	0
Launcel' Skinner	32	0	0	Wm Badham	6	0	0
Humph: Joiner	25	0	0	Jo: Hawfield	4	0	0
Epiphian [*Epiphan*] Badham	12	0	0	Silvanus Baylis	6	0	0
Rich: Browne	24	0	0				
George Wright [*Right*]	10	0	0	Charge	580	0	0
Geo: Bennett	8	0	0				
Edw: Tomkins	8	0	0	Jo: Broome, Launcelott Skinner.			
The widow Holder	20	0	0			Raters.	
		(58r)					
Math: Cliffe gen	54	0	0	**The Valuation direct.**			
Edw: Slaughter gen & Mr							

4. Bosbury [R4]

	£	s	d		£	s	d
Tho: Dannett gen[12]	100	0	0	Edm: Powell	8	0	0
Jo: Bridges gen	40	0	0	Barthol' Brotin & his mother	5	0	0
Tho: Bridges gen	47	0	0	Tho: Bentley & his mother	5	0	0
Henry Broy	37	0	0	Jo: Watkins	5	0	0
Jo: Allen	22	0	0			(58v)	
Tho: Hanbury gen[13]	40	0	0	Guilb: Jones	5	0	0
Giles Powell	8	0	0	Jo: Bullock	5	0	0
Phil: Winston gen	23	0	0				
Will: Powell	22	0	0	Charge	459	0	0
Jo: Nash	15	0	0				
Paul Rumney	20	0	0	Tho: Dannett, Tho: Bridges, Jo: Allen,			
Ri: Marriott	10	0	0	He: Bray. Raters.			
Martha Pharley wid	15	0	0				
Johan Powell wid	27	0	0	**Twoe parts added to the Valuation**			

7. Vicar, FP 1661 (£4 paid); HT 1664 (5).
8. Chief constable of Radlow (Loan 29/49, pf. 4, no. 69/15); HT 1664 (5).
9. HT 1664 (5).
10. HT 1664 (5).
11. In 1646 the estate of Edward Slaughter of Cheyney's Court was valued at £134; Loan 29/15, pf. 2.
12. HT 1665 (9).
13. Probably Sir Thomas Hanbury, knighted *circa* 1665; A. Audrey Locke, *The Hanbury Family* (London, 1916), i, p. 103.

5. Castle Froome [R5]

	£	s	d		£	s	d
Fra: Unett Esq[14]	300	0	0	Wm Sawyer	20	0	0
Ro: Dobins gen	16	0	0	Rose Barkeley wid	8	0	0
Geo: Linager [Lenacre] cler[15]	50	0	0	Jane Godsall wid	8	0	0
Jo: Freeman	20	0	0				
Fra: Freeman	16	0	0	Charge	438	0	0

6. Cannon Froome [R6]

	£	s	d	
The Lady Hopton[16]	300	0	0	
Michaell Brampton [Brompton]	25	0	0	All this the Lady Hoptons estate paid per ten'ts
Tho: Taylor	20	0	0	
Tho: Drew	20	0	0	
Wm Tiler	15	0	0	Will: Tyler, Tho: Alderne. Raters.
Antho: Drew	16	0	0	
Fra: Badam [Badham]	15	0	0	**A 4th parte added to the Valuation**
Tho: Alderne	10	0	0	
Sibble Woorde [Woore]	10	0	0	
Charge	431	0	0	

7. Coddington (59r) [R7]

	£	s	d		£	s	d
Edm: Russell gen	38	0	0	Robt Powell	7	0	0
Farly Osborne[17]	20	0	0	The Parson	8	0	0
Fra: Brooke[18]	20	0	0	The names of those charged with Horse			
Wm Guilding	12	0	0				
Jo: Turner	5	0	0	Robt Bright gen[19]	43	0	0
Geo: Harbert	15	0	0	Tho: Bridges gen	11	0	0
Wm Ricketts	7	0	0	Tho: Baston	6	0	0
Hen: Bray	4	0	0				
Fra: Winn	12	0	0	Charge	244	0	0
Robt Holder	16	0	0				
Peter Holder	12	0	0	Fra: Brooke, Ro: Holder. Raters.			
Tho: Holder	8	0	0	**Something added to the Valuation**			

14. JP 1660; sheriff 1664; FP 1661 (£10 unpaid); HT 1664 (12).
15. Curate of Castle Frome, FP 1661 (30s).
16. Dame Elizabeth Hopton, FP 1661 (£3 unpaid); HT 1664 (11). Sir Edward Hopton, who appears nowhere in these valuations, was JP q 1660 and DL 1660. He was elected MP for Hereford in 1661, but the election was declared void. He commanded a militia company in the mid-1660s; Loan 29/49, pf. 4, no. 69/15.
17. HT 1664 (4).   18. HT 1664 (4).   19. FP 1661 (£3 paid).

8. Collwall[20] [R8]

	£	s	d		£	s	d
Bridstock Harford Do^r of				The wid Burford	8	0	0
Phisick	93	13	0	Jo: Hope gen	2	0	0
Robt Bright gen	78	6	0	Jo: Kings	16	0	0
Maurice Berkeley gen	70	0	0	The wid Thomas	5	6	0
The Parsonage new &c	75	18	0	Tho: Orkeley [*Oakeley*]			
The [*Tho:*] Hoards	33	19	0	weaver	4	0	0
Will: Gilding	16	6	0	Tho: Pitt	12	13	0
Jo: Bareston	17	6	0	Anth: Vobe	34	13	0
The wid Warner	6	0	0	Oakeridge	2	13	0
Roul' Pitt & Will' Hor'iblowe	33	6	0	Rich: Pitt glover	2	13	0
Jo: Pitt of Broadley	18	6	0	Rich: Cannock	4	0	0
Jo: Pillinger	14	13	0			(60r)	
		(59v)		Robt Turner	16	0	0
The Brooke house	12	13	0	John Nelmes	5	6	0
Edm: Dangerfield & Tho:				Edmond Tomlins	2	13	0
Dangerfield	32	0	0	Jo: Barston gen	3	6	0
Nich: Brooke	27	6	0	Fra: Pyfinche	2	13	0
Edm: Dangerfield iun	18	6	0	Jo: Pytt taylor	1	13	0
Jo: Drewe	26	13	0	Jo: Eales	3	6	0
The wid Pitt of Coddington	1	6	0	Wm Pritchard	2	13	0
Jo: Gilding	23	6	0	Ri: Turner	2	13	0
Ri: Hope	18	6	0	Gabr: Pitt	2	13	0
The widow Hartland iun	7	6	0	Geo: Pitt	2	0	0
Ri: Mason	1	6	0	Ro: Pitt	7	6	0
The widow Hartland sen	4	0	0	William Lissiman [*Lissman*]	2	0	0
Tho: Ockeleley [*Oakeley*] iun	5	6	0	Tho: Houlder	5	6	0
The wid Hatton	8	0	0	Demeasne	2	0	0
Will: Hill	5	16	0	Jo: Dangerfield	3	6	0
Jo: Holdr	8	0	0	Jo: Pitt of the old Castle	16	0	0
Ri: Cox	14	9	0	Ri: Ockley	3	6	0
Jo: Hope	8	13	0				
Jo: Pitt Tanner	9	6	0	Charge	915	0	0
Jo: James	10	13	0		[*916*	*1*	*0*]
Edw: Soley	13	6	0				
The wid Brooke	12	0	0	Jo: Barston, Jo: Guilding. Ratrs.			
Will: Hall	14	13	0	**A 10th part added to the Valuation**			

9. Cradley [R9]

	£	s	d		£	s	d
Leycest^r Viscount Hereff per				Edm: Skinner his temporall			
ann' p:[21]	50	0	0	estate	82	10	0
Mr Gowers Land	67	10	0	Rich: Hill gen	56	5	0
Edm: Skinner clre his				Anne Faulke wid	3	15	0
parsonage[22]	75	0	0	Adam Hough gen	45	0	0

20. The largest HT charge in 1664 was on Henry Wright (9).
21. Leicester Devereux, 6th viscount Hereford, succeeded between 1649 and 1658; *Complete Peerage*, ed. Cokayne, vi, p. 480.   22. Rector, FP 1661 (£10 paid).

Radlow: Cradley continued

	£	s	d		£	s	d
Leonard Hill	31	17	6	Tho: Hall	1	0	0
		(60v)		Edm: Thomas	1	10	0
Jo: Colles [*Coles*] gen	30	15	0	Jo: Collins		12	0
Roul' Harries	21	0	0	James Turnor[24]	14	0	0
Wm Hall	15	0	0	Anne Turnor wid[25]	13	2	6
Wm Turnor	26	5	0	Mr Johnsons	55	0	0
Jo: Long	13	10	0	Roul' Barkley gen	37	17	6
Rich: Long	26	5	0	Katherine Bullock wid	10	0	0
Tho: Stoakes	5	15	0	Wm Powell	13	2	6
Rich: Berwick	12	0	0	Edw: Powell	3	0	0
Jo: Rackster Dr of the				Susan Turner wid	13	2	6
Civill Law	15	10	0	Jo: Barrett	7	10	0
Wm Blackwell	6	0	0	Hugh Bullock	9	7	6
Wm Dunne	12	10	0	Tho: Collins	9	7	6
Edm: Clother	7	10	0	Eliz: Barrett wid	4	0	0
Mary Weaver wid	15	0	0	Wm Fyfield[26]	30	0	0
Tho: Eython	3	15	0	Rich: Harvey	3	15	0
Rich: Childe	7	10	0	Jo: Bullock	2	5	0
Johan Young wid	1	0	0	Ro: Parker	4	0	0
Rich: James &c	4	0	0	Wm Prichard	1	10	0
Rich: Stoakes	3	15	0	Rich: Duppa [*Dipper*]	4	0	0
Rich: Fawlke[23]	22	10	0	Jo: Smith	30	0	0
Anne Stockton wid	2	5	0	Roul' Hales	22	10	0
Jo: Powell	3	15	0	Jo: Woodiatt	35	0	0
Math: Noxon	7	10	0	Will: Comby	4	0	0
Wm Adcox	3	15	0	Mrs Pritchard	19	10	0
Wm Barrett	3	15	0	Rich: Wood	3	15	0
Tho: Hay	3	10	0			(61v)	
Tho: Shakle	1	5	0	Roger Hide	2	0	0
Rich: James	6	0	0	Rich: Shewster	5	15	0
Jo: Hill	1	10	0	Edm: Pennell	6	0	0
Jo: Williams	1	0	0	Tho: Wood	22	10	0
Fra: Pengriefe [*Penthriffe*]	1	10	0	The wid Hales	7	10	0
Jo: Stroud	1	0	0	Rich: Stokes	13	2	6
Robt Crumpe	7	10	0	Edw: Higgins	11	5	0
Jo: Cager [*Chager*]	9	0	0	Will: Hoggon [*Loggan*]	11	5	0
Robt Dreyton	1	10	0	Ralph Barton	2	5	0
		(61r)		Will: Harbert[27]	7	10	0
Geo: Warner	1	10	0	Jo: Turner	19	15	0
Rich: Wilmore	5	15	0	Eliz: Bullock wid	13	2	6
Geo: Woodiatt	2	5	0	Fra: Dymock	1	10	0
Rich: Leighton	1	10	0	Eliz: Farmer wid	2	0	0
Roger Millward [*Millard*]	3	0	0	Edgar Powell	3	0	0

23. Yeoman, will proved 4 July 1663 (PCC).
24. Gent., will proved 1668 (PCC).
25. HT 1664 (7); will proved 1670 (PCC).
26. Yeoman, will proved 1670 (PCC).
27. Yeoman, will proved 31 March 1664 (PCC).

Radlow: Cradley continued

	£	s	d
Geo: Cotton	1	10	0
Jo: Collins	2	0	0
Jo: Barrett collyer	1	10	0
Rich: Barrett	5	15	0
The wid Weaver	2	0	0
Will: Rainford [*Rainsford*]	1	0	0

Leo: Hill, Jo: Smith, Rich: Long.

Raters.

Almost a 4th parte added to the Valuation

	£	s	d
Charge	1224	0	0
	[*1225	4	6*]

---

10. Donington[28]   [*R10*]

	£	s	d		£	s	d
Emanuell Macon gen	33	0	0	The Parsonage[29]	23	0	0
Will: Skinner gen	27	0	0	Jo: Hill	12	0	0
John Warren gen	32	0	0				
Jon Cam	17	0	0	Charge	211	0	0
	(62r)						
Rich: Hankins	15	0	0	Edw: Hankins, Rich: Philpotts. Raters.			
Edw: Hankins	27	0	0				
Wm Grove	10	0	0	**Something added to the Valuation**			
Jo: Beale	15	0	0				

---

11. Eastnor   [*R11*]

	£	s	d		£	s	d
Tho: Cocks Esq[30]	140	0	0	Tho: Godfree	7	0	0
Rich: Read Esq	50	0	0	Tho: Tomkins	7	0	0
Jo: Skipp Esq	5	0	0	Edw: Buckenhill [*Bucknell*]	5	0	0
Rich: Cooke rector	30	0	0		(62v)		
Robt Higgins	20	0	0	Jo: Collins	12	0	0
Emanuell Machen gen	6	0	0	Will: Alderne	5	0	0
Humph Morton	40	0	0	Sam: Aston	5	0	0
Jo: Dugmore	30	0	0	Rich: Carles	7	0	0
Jo: Baldwyn	15	0	0	Rich: Sumbers	4	0	0
Anth: Lawrence	17	0	0	Jo: South	6	0	0
Edm: Knotsford	12	0	0	Ro: Sanford	4	0	0
Tho: Danford	17	0	0	Hester Baldwin wid	3	10	0
Guil: James	12	0	0	Edw: Tomlins	2	10	0
Jo: Elton gen	5	0	0				
Jo: Webley sen	10	0	0	Charge	505	0	0
Margery Pewtries wid	6	0	0				
James Baylies	13	0	0	Humph: Morton, Anth: Laurence.			
Jo: Cox gen	4	0	0			Raters.	
Anth: Bach	5	0	0				

---

28. The largest HT charge in 1664 was on John Perks (4).
29. William Lawrence paid 14s to the FP 1661.
30. JP 1660; sheriff 1663; FP 1661 (£10 paid); HT 1664 (12).

12. Eggleton [R12]

	£	s	d		£	s	d
Tho: Cooke Esq	20	0	0	The wid Taylor	5	0	0
Tho: Lingen Esq	7	0	0	John Serrell	4	0	0
Walter Hopton Esq	4	0	0	Isaac Knott	7	0	0
Jo: Mason	20	0	0	Tho: Sowth	5	0	0
Jo: Watts	10	0	0				
Geo: Mayfield	14	0	0	Charge	114	0	0
Rich: Norton[31]	10	0	0				
The wid Garner [Garners]	8	0	0	Tho: South. Rater.			

13. Evesbach (63r) [R13]

	£	s	d		£	s	d
Robt Dobins gen for &c } [32]	130	0	0	Tho: Berkley	12	0	0
Robt Dobins gen for &c				Edm: Peskell [Pennell]	5	0	0
Roul' Berkeley gen	10	0	0	Wm Bond	5	0	0
Tho: Wood	26	10	0	Wm Boswood	5	0	0
Jo: Beachamp	7	0	0	Roger White &c	5	0	0
Nath: Tomkins cler	50	0	0				
Jo: Powles	20	0	0	Charge	349	0	0
Will: Hay	20	0	0				
Jo: Hope gen	34	0	0	John Beacham, Jo: Asborn [Osborne].			
Jo: Nash	10	0	0	Raters.			
Jo: Baston	10	0	0				

14. Hamonds Froome.[33] [R14]

[There follow one and a quarter blank pages]

15. Ledbury Borrough (64r) [R15a]

	£	s	d		£	s	d
High Streete				Humph: Morton	14	0	0
Fra: Hall sen gen[34]	23	0	0	Humph: Morton or Ten'ts	—	—	—
Robt Stone[35]	3	10	0	Will: Baldwin	8	0	0
Sam: Willson Stocke	50	0	0	Mrs Rastell	14	0	0
Eliz: Hill wid	3	0	0	Rich: Moore &c	5	0	0
Edw: Buckenhill [Bucken-				Rich: Robinson	3	0	0
field]	6	0	0	John Stillings	1	0	0
Eliz: Berrow	6	0	0	Fra: Cale	4	0	0
Will: Mathewes	6	0	0	Tho: Baldwin	1	0	0

31. HT 1664 (3).   32. HT 1664 (9).
33. The largest HT charge in 1664 was on Bellingham Slaughter (10).
34. JP q 1655; FP 1661 (£5). clothier; will proved 1668 (PCC). He held land at Wormsley and Ledbury and left over £1,300 in bequests.   35. HT 1664 (9).

98   HEREFORD MILITIA ASSESSMENTS

Radlow: Ledbury Borrough: High Streete continued

		£	s	d
Anth: Branch		8	0	0
D[or] Benson		5	0	0
James Walcroft		2	0	0
Wm Meeke		5	10	0
Jo: Jones		7	0	0
Jo: Stone		2	10	0
Ja: Broome[36]		2	10	0
Randolph Randle	Stocke	100	0	0
James Bayliffes		13	0	0
Rich: Maddockes		3	0	0
Jo: Hall mercer		50	0	0
Jo: Berrow mercer	Stocke	50	0	0
		(64v)		
James Walcroft more		3	0	0
Southend	[R15b]			
Wm Skinner gen[37]		22	0	0
Edw: Skinner gen[38]		15	0	0
Ja: Gardiner		7	10	0
Tho: Hall		1	0	0
Tho: Page		3	10	0
Jo: Bridges gen &c		4	16	0
Will: Leadonton &c		1	10	0
Jo: Barnesley dyer		1	0	0
Mr Skinner for Capt' Elton		4	0	0
Ja: Gardiner for &c		6	0	0
Church Lane	[R15c]			
Henry Page vicar[39]		40	0	0
Charles Hoskins gen		7	10	0
Mr Phillipps &c		16	0	0
Tho: Wilde gen	Stock	50	0	0
Tho: Stone		5	0	0
Jo: Wilde gen[40]		6	0	0
Bystreete	[R15d]			
Mich: Skynner[41]		6	0	0
Rich: Hall		2	0	0
Edw: Adams		2	0	0
Hugh Jones		1	0	0
Tho: Gwinn		1	0	0
		(65r)		
Rich: Phelpotts		3	0	0

		£	s	d
Tho: Hill		2	0	0
Jo: Meeke			2	0
Newstreete	[R15e]			
Rich: Cocks [Coxe] gen[42]		13	0	0
Jo: Hall gen		2	10	0
Jo: Fishpoole		7	0	0
Jo: Elton		10	0	0
Homend	[R15f]			
Rich: Hankins		3	10	0
Capt' Millard &c		4	0	0
Jo: Mooreley		3	0	0
The wid Cooke		6	0	0
Jo: Gwillim for all		6	0	0
Anne Bibbs wid		1	0	0
Tho: Jones		1	10	0
Wm Nash		1	10	0
Tho: Browne &c		3	0	0
Jo: Meeke		1	0	0
Jo: Mutlow		1	10	0
Sam: Tinker &c		4	0	0
The Tenn'ts of Howtens		1	0	0
Jo: Hall tanner		8	0	0
Edw: Went &c		2	0	0
Jo: Taylor		2	0	0
Will: Hill		1	10	0
Fra: Hall jun gen		13	0	0
Will: Browne		6	0	0
Will: Hodges		3	0	0
Will: Mutlow		3	0	0
The wid Jenkins	Stock	40	0	0
Mich: Poole		3	0	0
Jo: Andrews		3	0	0
Fra: Smith		2	0	0
Rich: Dalley		1	0	0

Charge 663 0 0

[*763 18 0*]

Rich: Hankins. Raters.

Something to be added to the Valuation

---

36. Glover, will proved 1664 (PCC).
37. HT 1664 (9).
38. HT 1664 (9).
39. Vicar, FP 1661 (£4).
40. Clothier, will proved 1668 (PCC).
41. Clothier, will proved 1667 (PCC).
42. Clothier, will proved 1670 (PCC).

16. Ledbury Forren

[*There is no gap between this and the next title below*]

17. Leadon & Hatfield [*in Ledburies parish*]

	£	s	d		£	s	d
Ambrose Elton Esq[43]	200			Rich: Hankins for &c	4	10	
Jo: Beale gen for Woodfields				Will: Skinner gen for &c	52		
& Hatfield	25			Rich: Brook for &c	3		
Steph: Phillipps cler for				Tho: Gwillim	1		
Orlam	30			Jo: Skipp Esq for tieth &			
Peter Gwillim	6			Gleabe	17		
Steph: Skinner the elder	12			Jo: Elton gen for tieth &			
Will: Cam gen	15			Gleebe	15		
Jo; Williams for &c	3	10		Jo: Wilde for tieth &			
Joseph Bracy for &c Tho:				demeasne	2	6	8
Ranford	15			D[or] Benson for lands Tenth			
Tho: Cam	10			&c	25		
The wid White	14			Martin Morse	1	13	4
James Bradford [*Brodford*]	10			William Skinner for &c	2		
Will: Wall gen	30						
Robt Higgins gen	5			Charge	527	0	0
Edw: Hankins	1				[*529*	*10*	*0*]
Jo: Nethway for &c	8			John Hall. Rater.			
Eliz: Hill wid	1	10					
John Hall gen	20			**Valuation direct.**			

18. Little Marcle   (66r)

		£	s	d		£	s	d
Capt Jo: Hanbury[44]	h:	60	0	0	Being charged to maint: of			
Robt Holford gen	h:	60	0	0	foote soldiers &c			
Jo: Bridges gen	h:	26	0	0				
Being charged to maint' of					Charge	190	0	0
horse						[*191*	*0*	*0*]
Anne Carwardine wid[45]		15	0	0	Tho: Hill. Rater.			
Wm Ropier [*Roper*][46]		10	0	0				
Tho: Hill		10	0	0	**The Valuation to be doubled and**			
Ja: Greene		10	0	0	**halfe doubled**			

43. Of the Hasell; FP 1661 (£10 paid); HT 1664 (10).
44. (1594–1676); father of Sir Thomas Hanbury; he lost heavily in the service of Charles I; A. Audrey Locke, *The Hanbury Family* (London, 1916), i. p. 99 *et seq.*
45. Widow of Anthony Carwardine, yeoman, whose will was proved 16 May 1663 (PCC).
46. Yeoman, brother-in-law of Anthony Carwardine (see previous note); HT 1664 (4).

H

19. Lugwardine [R19]

		£	s	d			£	s	d
Rich: Reed Esq[47]	h:	71	0	0	Rich: Skirme		3	16	0
Nichol' Walwyn gen	h:	110	0	0	Will: Gregory gen	h:	6	6	0
Steph: Phillips cler[48]	h:	51	0	0	Roger Powell		3	0	0
Edw: Crump gen					Jo: Bevan		2	10	0
(Kings Servant)		30	0	0	Will: Tully		3	0	0
Anne Hide wid		6	0	0				(66v)	
Roul' Dubbey [*Dubberley*]		10	15	0					
Ja: Wellington	h:	30	0	0	Jo: Deeme of Thinghill		2	0	0
Tho: Hill		24	0	0	Jo: Deeme of Withington		2	0	0
Eliz: Skirme wid		13	17	0					
Jo: Skirme		9	0	0	Charge	416	0	0
Tho: Treherne	[?]	9	16	0		[*419*	*6*	*1*]
Jo: Williams sen		11	16	0					
Ja: Rogers	[?]	11	12	0	James Wellington, Tho: Hill. Raters.				
Jo: Trehearne	[?]	3	1	1					
Edw: Rawlings	[?]	4	17	0	**The Valuation to be almost doubled**				

20. Morton Jefferies [R20]

	£	s	d		£	s	d
Ja: Rodd Esq for &c[49]	90	0	0	The wid Powell	2	0	0
Ja: Rodd Esq for &c	26	0	0				
Tho: Davies	25	0	0	Charge	224	0	0
The wid Bauch	25	0	0				
Will: Mayfield	18	0	0	Tho: Rodd, Tho: Davies. Raters.			
Anth: Lawrence	13	0	0				
Jo: Hill	20	0	0	**The Valuation almost direct.**			
Tho: Bootfield [*Botfield*]	5	0	0				

21. Munsley [R21]

	£	s	d		£	s	d
Sʳ Robt Pye Kt	22	0	0	Will: Hopkins	160	0	0
Rich: Reede Esq	6	0	0	Will: Seycill[51]	70	0	0
Will: Dobbins cler[50]	45	0	0	Jo: Elton gen	40	0	0
Jo: Wilde gen ⎫				Edw: Went iunʳ	20	0	0
Fr: Hall gen ⎭	4	0	0	Edw: Went sen	10	0	0

47. JP q 1660; FP 1661 (£10 unpaid); HT 1664 (9).
48. Will proved 1667 (PCC). He came from a Ledbury family and was related to many merchant families of that town. He owned property in Little Dewchurch, Ballingham, Ledbury, Leadon, Wallhills and Tupsley, and held leases in Hereford-shire and Gloucestershire. He left legacies of about £950.
49. Will proved 1666 (PCC). His son Thomas Rodd was charged on 6 hearths in 1664.
50. Rector, FP 1661 (50s).
51. The largest HT charge in 1664 was on Thomas Seycell gent. (5).

Radlow: Munsley continued

	£	s	d		£	s	d
Jo: Freeman	8	0	0	Fr: Atherton	16	0	0
Rich: Freeman	24	0	0	Mrs Kyrle of Rosse	35	0	0
		(67r)		Will: Bridges Esq	10	0	0
Fra: Capell gen	4	0	0				
Jo: Hankins	18	0	0				
Jo: Ravenhill	4	0	0	Charge	478	0	0
Oswald Witherington	5	0	0		[538	0	0]
Wm Went	32	0	0	John Elton, Wm Hopkins. Raters.			
Thorneton Jones gen	5	0	0	The Valuation direct.			

22. Pixley   [R22]

	£	s	d		£	s	d
Ben: Mason Esq[52]	42	0	0	**Parke[53]**			
Thorneton Jones Esq	14	0	0	Jo: Bridges Esq	42	0	0
Joseph Skinner	24	0	0	Thorneton Jones Esq	8	0	0
Jo: Nash gen	23	0	0	Robt Bright Esq	11	0	0
The Tieth	14	0	0	Jo: Cooke	11	0	0
Jam: Cope	4	10	0	Rich: Hooper	4	10	0
Jo: Morgan	6	10	0	Hen: Gwillim gen	3	0	0
Jo: Hodges	3	0	0				
Hen: Gwillim gen	3	0	0	Charge	222	0	0
Tho: Gwillim	2	0	0	Joseph Skinner, Rich: Hooper. Raters.			
Edw: Godshall	2	0	0	A 3rd part is to be added to the			
Fra: Caple gen	5	0	0	Valuation			

23. Stoake Edith   (67v)   [R23]

	£	s	d		£	s	d
The Lady Lingen[54]	98	0	0	Jo: Stodart	6	0	0
Mr Scudamore[55]	60	0	0	Jo: Minton	4	0	0
Mr Cooke	60	0	0				
Mr Nash	48	0	0	Charge	339	0	0
Mr Frere [*Fryer*][56]	12	0	0		[337	0	0]
Rich: Hide	18	0	0				
Humph: Brooke	6	0	0	Tho: Smith, Wm Careles. Raters.			
Will: Carles	6	0	0				
Jo: Hodges	11	0	0	The Valuation almost doubled.			
Rich: Hodges	8	0	0				

52. JP q 1660; HT 1664 (9); will proved 1665 (PCC). He owned the manors of Pixley, Catley and Munsley and lands in Essex and Somerset.   53. Otherwise Parkhold.
54. Dame Alice Lingen was the widow of Sir Henry Lingen, who was buried at Stoke Edith on 22 Jan. 1661/2. He had been the most important royalist commander in the county during the Civil War. In 1646 his Herefordshire estates had been valued at £937 a year; Loan 29/15, pf. 2. HT 1664 (17). The Lingen estates later became the foundation of the Foley interests in the county; Robinson, p. 257.
55. Robert Scudamore, rector, paid £10 to the FP 1661; instituted 22 Jan. 1662/3; A. T. Bannister, *Diocese of Hereford Institutions, 1539–1900* (Hereford, 1923), p. 33.   56. Anthony Frere.

24. Stretton Grandsome [57]   [R24]

[There follow one and a half blank pages]

---

25. Taddington   (68v)   [R25]

	£	s	d		£	s	d
The Lady Lingen	60	0	0	Rich: Reece	10	0	0
Wm Cookes Esq	70	0	0	Fra: Caple gen	11	0	0
Jo: Ferers Esq	150	0	0	Anne Gallett wid[59]	10	0	0
Rich: Hopton Esq	35	0	0	Antho: Drew	10	0	0
Rich: Carwardine gen	92	0	0	Hen: Poole	8	0	0
Jo: Neale minister	50	0	0	Peter Nash gen	10	0	0
Tho: Vickeres gen	100	0	0	Alice Vines wid	5	0	0
Tho: Careles gen[58]	80	0	0	Rich: Poole & Rich: Cooke	5	0	0
Wm Gallett	15	0	0				
Oswall Widderington	7	0	0	Charge	766	0	0
Katherine Turner	10	0	0		[768	0	0]
Jo: Tomkins	20	0	0				
Robt Nurdbury	10	0	0	**The valuation direct**			

---

26. Upleadons Side   [R26]

	£	s	d		£	s	d
Sr Robt Pye Kt	100	0	0	Mr Cooke cler	15	0	0
Wm Bridges Esq[60]	100	0	0	Wm Stone	15	0	0
Tho: Bridges gen	40	0	0	Antho: Huck	12	0	0
Tho: Morton	33	0	0	Jo: Wood	12	0	0
Edw: Woodyatt	16	0	0	Mrs Bosworth	30	0	0
Tho: Symmonds	16	0	0	Ben: Mason Esq	20	0	0
Rich: Backer	12	0	0	Jo: Aston	7	0	0
Adon [*Adoniah*] Mutlow	33	0	0	Jo: Raxter Dr of Law	12	0	0
Hen: Millard	5	0	0	Jo: Dannett gen	4	0	0
		(69r)		Nich: Ellice	4	0	0
Jo: Alcott	21	0	0	Tho: Sycill	4	0	0
Wm Symmonds	8	0	0				
Tho: Treyherne	8	0	0	Charge	635	0	0
Ralph Bacon	30	0	0				
Rich: Gullen	7	0	0	Aydon Mutlow, Tho: Wooding. Raters.			
Will: Tyler	12	0	0				
Mr Games	4	0	0				
Jo: Powell	35	0	0	**Something is to be added to the**			
Tho: Wooding	20	0	0	**Valuation.**			

---

57. The free tenants had bought the manor; Harl. 6726. The largest HT charge in 1664 was on Walter Hopton Esq. (13).
58. HT 1664 (4).   59. Will proved 23 Feb. 1664 (Hereford).
60. Of Tyberton; his son Marshall Bridges was charged on 6 hearths in 1664.

27. Wallhills &c [*Faretree & Plaistow*] in Ledbury Parish[61]   [*R27*]

	£	s	d		£	s	d
Jo: Skipp Esq[62]	100	0	0	Will: Went	12	0	0
Ambrose Elton Esq	15	0	0	Will: Vobe	26	0	0
Mrs Mary Skinner wid	72	0	0	Rich: Watts	16	0	0
Jo: Elton gen	16	0	0	Eliz: Bennett wid	25	0	0
Jo: Wilde gen	3	0	0	Jo: Lewis	2	10	0
		(69v)		Ri: Jenkins	3	10	0
Anne Noeman [*Norman*] wid	20	0	0	Will: Ayleway	6	10	0
Stephen Skinner	10	0	0	Edw: Webb for &c	3	0	0
Stephen Skinner for &c	10	0	0	Will: Skinner gen	4	0	0
Sʳ Tho: Rich for &c[63]	4	10	0	Jo: Hall	4	0	0
Ro: Ayleway gen	13	10	0	The Ten'ts of Step: Skinner			
Ro: Stone	7	0	0	of Stone house	3	0	0
Mich: Skinner	8	0	0	Steph: Skinner for &c	5	0	0
Sarah Perrock wid	9	0	0				
Tho: Meeke	27	0	0	Charge	463	0	0
Guy Wood	16	0	0				
Rich: Taylor	19	0	0	Will: Vobe. Rater.			
For Mr Stephen Phillipps							
lands	2	10	0	**Something to be added to the Valuation.**			

28. Wellington &c in Ledbury Parish[64]

[*R28a*]

	£	s	d		£	s	d
Edm: Skinner cler	36	0	0	Will: Lilly	13	0	0
Jo: Skipp Esq	25	10	0	Edw: Cope	6	0	0
		(70r)		Leon: Smith & his sonne	5	0	0
Tho: Coale gen	25	0	0	Will: Hopkins for &c	52	0	0
Nicho: Ellis	13	0	0	Fra: Hall gen	6	0	0
Edw: Baldwyn	26	0	0	Ch: Hoskins gen	3	0	0
The wid Woodward	12	0	0	Rich: Ledington	4	0	0
Jo: Bray gen	24	0	0	Jo: Wilde gen	3	0	0
Fra: Skinner	24	0	0				
Will: Vobe	16	0	0	Charge	410	0	0
Anthony Vobe[65]	24	0	0		[*376*	*0*	*0*]
Mr Phillipps	2	10	0	Nich: Ellis. Rater.			
Tho: Hooper	40	0	0				
Jo: Elton gen	16	0	0	**The charge upon Muchill appeareth/**			

61. The largest HT charge in 1664 was on Edward Withers (16).
62. JP q 1660; captain of a militia company in the mid-1660s; Loan 29/49, pf. 4, no. 69/15. His real estate in the county was valued at £110 a year in 1646; Loan 29/15, pf. 2.
63. Probably Sir Thomas Rich of Sunning, Berks; baronet 20 March 1660/1: *Baronetage*, iii, p. 180.
64. The largest HT charge in 1664 was on Edward Coucher (7).
65. Yeoman, will proved 1669 (PCC); he owned land in Wellington and Collwall and left legacies of £900.

Radlow: Wellington &c in Ledbury Parish continued

	£	s	d
Muchell &c in Ledbury		[*R28b*]	
parish[66]			
Rich: Earle of Dorsett[67]	80	0	0
Tho: Cocks Esq	60	0	0
Fra: Hall iun	5	0	0
Humph: Morton	3	0	0
Edm: Tomblyns	25	0	0
Jo: Wheeler	6	0	0
Tho: Tomblyns [*Tomkins*]	8	0	0
		(71r)	
John Greene	5	0	0
The widow Brooke	4	0	0
John Bishopp	1	5	0
Henry Page clerke	2	10	0

	£	s	d
John Andrewes	3	10	0
John Skipp Esq	8	0	0
John Elton gen	6	0	0
Robt Stone		10	0
Margery Pewtres wid		15	0
Rich: Turner of Collwall	1	0	0
John Gwillym	3	0	0
Charge	223	0	0

Robt Hall. Rater.

Twoe partes are to be added to the
Valuation

29. Westhide[68]

	£	s	d
Humph: Baskervile Esq	146	0	0
Fitz Will' Coningsby Esq	10	0	0
Walter Hopton gen & Ro^t			
Berington g^t	10	0	0
Robt Scudamore cler	60	0	0
Anthon: Jauncie gen	46	0	0
Edward Chamberlaine gen	50	0	0
Fr: Smith	46	0	0
Edw: Smith	13	0	0
James Wellington	12	10	0
Rich: Parsons	13	0	0
John Holland	40	0	0
John Hanley	7	10	0
Wid' Bagnell	3	0	0

	£	s	d
Edward Rawlins	3	0	0
James Chamberlaine	14	0	0
Mrs Lee wid	9	0	0
John Chamberlaine	4	0	0
Tho: Binkes gen	13	0	0
Humph: Smith	7	0	0
Charge	487	0	0
	[*507*	*0*	*0*]

Fra: Smith, Rich: Parsons. Raters.

The Valuation direct.

66. The largest HT charges in Mitchel in 1664 were on Robert Dugmore and William Lewis (6 each).
67. Richard Sackville, 5th earl of Dorset; born 1622, succeeded 1652, died 1677 (*DNB*). The Herefordshire estates of the 4th earl were valued at £92 a year in 1646; Loan 29/15, pf. 2.
68. The largest HT charge in 1664 was on Edward Porter (5).

30. Weston (72r) [R30]

	£	s	d		£	s	d
Robt Scudamore cler	30	0	0	Mr Bakers Lands	5	0	0
John Mayo cler	30	0	0	Antho: Wood	8	0	0
Humph: Tailor gen[69]	46	0	0	The wid Alford	5	0	0
The wid Andrewes[70]	30	0	0				
Tho: Lane gen	14	0	0	Charge	207	0	0
John Berington Esq	5	0	0				
Tho: Binkes	6	0	0	Humph: Tailor, Rich: Alford. Raters.			
Tho: Hill gen	14	0	0				
Rich: Reede Esq for &c	5	0	0	**The Valuation is to be something**			
Henry Badham	9	0	0	**more then doubled**			

31. Yarkhill [R31]

	£	s	d		£	s	d
Mr Stedman cler[71]	20	0	0	Roul' Tailor for &c	12	0	0
Mrs Bodeham wid	200	0	0	Roul' Watkins	15	0	0
Mrs Whittington	40	0	0	Humph: Brook	6	0	0
Mrs Beale	20	0	0	Jo: Badham	6	0	0
The Church of Gloucester	20	0	0	Anth: Cole[73]	6	0	0
John Abrahall	30	0	0				
John Henley	15	0	0	Charge	448	0	0
Antho: Wood	8	0	0		[450	0	0]
Fr: Tomkins	20	0	0				
Anth: Hawlins [Hallings]	8	0	0	Jo: Whittington, Jo: Abrahall, Anth:			
Rich: Cook	7	0	0	Wood, Jo: Henley. Raters.			
Jo: Bridges Esq	7	0	0				
Tho: Abrahall[72]	10	0	0	**The Valuation is to almost doubled**			

69. HT 1664 (5).
70. Ursula Andrewes.
71. Francis Stedman senior, vicar of Yarkhill, paid 20s to the FP 1661.
72. HT 1664 (5).
73. Yeoman and blacksmith, will proved 20 September 1665 (Hereford); buried 14 Aug. 1665; his father, also Anthony Cole, died in 1659.

Stretford Hundred[1] (73r)

No.	Value returned by the Raters (£)	Parish	The Value Horse being taken out / Value according to the contribution (£)	s	d	The whole yeares contribution at 2s per pound for each particular parish in the Hundred (£)	s	d
1.	363	Amiley	1139	0	0	113	18	2
2.	173	Berley	247	0	0	24	14	3
3.	561	Dilwin	1118	0	0	111	16	0
4.	591	Eardesland	1110	0	0	111	1	7
5.	487	Kinnersley & Letton	960	0	0	96	10	0
6.	933	Kingsland	1744	0	0	174	8	0
7.	353	Kings Pyon	835	0	0	83	10	0
8.	536	Leonshall	1159	0	0	115	18	2
9.	236	Munkland	563	0	0	56	6	0
10.	794	Pembridge	1688	0	0	168	16	5

1. Both the order of magnitude and the parish proportions differ from those in 1677.

Hearth Tax return, Lady Day, 1664:

Stretford Hundred	Total Charged Hearths	Total Houses	More than 10 hearths *	10	9	8	7	6	5	4	3	2	1	Total Exempt Houses
Pembridge Borough	78	92		1	1				1		2	2	5	29	51
Bury & Weston	22	19							1	1	1	1	8		7
Moorcot	23	17					1			1	1	3	3		8
Marston	20	19							1	1		4	3		10
Broxwood	25	24										11	3		10
Noke	46	32					1	2	1	2			14		12
Total Pembridge	214	203		1	1		2	3	3	7	4	24	60		98
Almeley	89	62	1 (18)				2		2	4	1	4	20		28
Birley	22	25								1	2	2	9		12
Dilwyn	71	70						1	2	2	6	11	7		41
Eardisland	91	107					1	1		3	5	10	31		56
Kinnersley	60	49			1				1	4	2	3	18		20
Lower Letton	17	25								1		3	7		14
Kingsland	118	140				1			1	2	6	13	53		64
Kings Pyon	41	61						1	1		2	2	14		39
Lyonshall	90	86						1	1			22	35		27
Monkland	42	43						1	2	2		4	10		23
Shobdon	75	76		1						1	3	13	26		32
Staunton & Stocklow	21	38									1	2	14		21
Stretford	17	16								1	2	1	5		7
Weobley	142	126		1		1		1	1	7	7	20	24		64
Total	1,110	1,127	1	3	2	2	5	9	13	36	43	134	333		546

* Actual charge in brackets.

106

Stretford Hundred continued

Value Returned by the Raters			The Value Horse Being Taken Out	Value according to the contribution	The whole yeares contribution at 2s per pound for each particular parish in the Hundred
11.	541	Shobdon	1060 10 0		106 1 3
12.	145	Staunton & Stocklow	165 0 0		16 10 4
13.	97	Stretford	167 0 0		16 14 8
14.	680	Weobley	652 0 0		65 4 6

[*Total £1261 8s 4d*]

1. Amiley [*Almeley*]   (74r)   [*S1*]

	£	s	d		£	s	d
Mrs Moningtons Lands	60	0	0	Wm Driver of Wonton	35	0	0
Fr: Pember Esq[2]	70	0	0	John Smith	20	0	0
Fr: Price	3	10	0	Tim: Wood cler	3	10	0
Wm Knight	3	0	0	Sibbill Morris	3	10	0
Walter Ball	4	0	0	Mr Crumps lands	10	0	0
Walter Woodhill	20	0	0	Parker & Smiths lands	3	10	0
Walter Rochley [*Rushley*]	16	0	0	The parsonage	27	0	0
Will: Webb	8	0	0	The vicarage[4]	10	0	0
Will: Price	10	0	0	Tho: Woodhill	3	0	0
Perry Grasier	3	0	0				
Will: Driver of Hanley	7	0	0	Charge	363	0	0
James Mason	12	0	0		[*413*	*0*	*0*]
John Hawkins	12	0	0				
Tho: Harper[3]	12	0	0	Walter Woodhill, John Smith, Tho:			
Mr Carpenters Lands	50	0	0	Harper. Raters.			
John Foote	7	0	0	**Almost 2 partes added to the Valuation**			

2. Berley[5]   (75r)   [*S2*]

	£	s	d		£	s	d
Mr Darnell for the court	80	0	0	Simon Tomkins	2	0	0
John Sherriff iun	14	0	0	John Amies	2	5	0
Wm Trumper for the				John Crosse	2	0	0
Parsonage	15	0	0	Mr Middleton	2	10	0
Miles Adams	9	0	0	Edw: Shawe cler[6]	12	0	0
Tho: Munne for the Greene	7	10	0				
James Sheward	13	5	0	Charge	173	0	0
Anne Tomkin wid	9	0	0				
Edw: Lawrence	2	10	0	John Sherriff jun Rater			
Anne Saise wid	2	5	0	**The Valuation is to be doubled**			

2. Francis Pember together with Ann Pember bore the largest charge to the HT 1664 (18).   3. Of Upcott; buried 18 Nov. 1663.   4. Samuel Mathews, vicar.
5. The largest HT charge in 1664 was on Richard Walton (6).
6. Rector, FP 1661 (5s paid).

3. Dilwyn[7] [S3]

	£	s	d		£	s	d
That part of the parsonage						(76r)	
in Stretford Hundred[8]	60	0	0	Chadnor court	80	0	0
Richard Tuflin for &c	20	0	0	James Eckley sen	20	0	0
Mrs Elinor Carpenter for				Tho: Munne	15	0	0
her sonne[9]	36	0	0	Rich: Munne	5	0	0
Will: & Geo: Bradford	24	0	0	John Munne of Alton	24	0	0
Tho: Carpenter gen for &c[10]	20	0	0	Johan Munne wid	24	0	0
Arth: Carpenter gen	20	0	0	James Barnes	18	0	0
Wm Morris for &c	24	0	0	John Pearkes &c	20	0	0
Tho: Friser[11]	20	0	0	Rich: Tuflin for &c	20	0	0
Tho: & John Bennett	25	0	0	Tho: Tailor	5	0	0
Tho: Rosse	20	0	0				
Anne Tuflin [*Tuffly*] wid	15	0	0	Charge	561	0	0
Tho: Phelpotts	12	0	0				
Simon Herring	14	0	0	Tho: Bennett, Will: Bradford. Raters.			
Mrs Eliz: Monningtons							
farme at Hurst	20	0	0	**The Valuation is to be doubled**			

4. Eardesley [*Eardisland*][12] [S4]

	£	s	d		£	s	d
Rich: Dolphin Esq	40	0	0	John Croft gen	18	0	0
Will: Kinnersley	13	0	0	Wm Nicholls	3	0	0
Alexander Froysall	20	2	0	Mr Barbers Land	9	0	0
Tho: Trumper	14	0	0	Tho: Bridges gen	9	10	0
Henry Davies	5	10	0	Geo: Garnors	6	0	0
Kents Land	4	0	0	Jo: Trumper	5	0	0
Capt Booth	40	0	0	Robt Paine	4	0	0
Nicholas Dayos	25	0	0	Jo: Jackson & the wid:			
John Stallard	13	0	0	Carpenter	12	0	0
Nich: Kirwood gen	20	0	0	Jo: Griffitts	10	0	0
Robt Cutler gen	22	0	0				
Henry Hyett Esq	140	0	0	Charge	591	0	0
Edw: Lenthall	16	0	0		[*520*	*12*	*0*]
Wm Trumper	14	0	0				
Wm Colcombe	10	0	0	Alexander Froysell, Tho: Leynthall, Jo:			
Tho: Leyntholl	7	10	0	Trumper. Raters			
		(77r)					
Will: Lambe gen	40	0	0	**Valuation is to be doubled almost**			

7. Probably excluded Luntley, Little Dilwyn, Sollers Dilwyn and Homme, but included Alton, Hurst, Chadnor and Dilwyn.

8. Martin Johnson, vicar, paid 20s to the FP 1661.

9. HT 1664 (7).

10. For Fawley.

11. Chief constable for Stretford, 1664; Loan 29/49, pf. 4, no. 69/15.

12. The largest HT charge in 1664 was on John Brewster, gent. (7).

5. Kinnersley [& *Letton*]   [*S5a*]

	£	s	d		£	s	d
James Pitts Esq[13]	150	0	0			(78r)	
Jo: Viner cler	30	0	0	John Wellington	14	0	0
Hen: Mathewes	36	0	0	Wm Hughes	17	10	0
James Haynes for &c	35	0	0	Walter Hill	6	10	0
Tho: Edwyns	6	0	0	Edw: Baker	9	0	0
James Allen	4	0	0	Tho: Kirwood	14	0	0
Rich: Santt	4	0	0	Edw: Langford	6	10	0
Rich: Higgins	4	0	0	James Kirwood	7	0	0
The Little Farme	15	0	0	Tho: Wellington	5	0	0
Walter Hill	4	0	0				
Phil: Lawrence	4	0	0	Charge	487	0	0
Johan Hall	4	0	0		[540	10	0]
Wm Mathewes	3	10	0				

Hen: Mathewes, James Allen, Walter Hughes. Raters.

Letton	[*S5b*]		
John Booth Esq[14]	150	0	0
Wm Fabian cler[15]	11	10	0

The valuation is to be doubled almost

6. Kingsland[16]   [*S6*]

	£	s	d		£	s	d
Herbt Lord Bp of Hereff[17]	6	0	0	Nich: Daios	3	10	0
Sr Robt Harley[18]	200	0	0	Will: Bedford cler	8	0	0
Tho: Harley Esq	100	0	0	Tho: Walton		13	4
Ro: Cutler gen	80	0	0	Jo: Perry [*Pirry*]	3	0	0
Tim: Woodroff Rector[19]	200	0	0	Mr Evans cler	4	0	0
Rich: Whittall gen	20	0	0	Will: Bubb	18	0	0
John Colman	28	0	0			(79r)	
Rich: Newlar sen & Ro:				Jane Freeman wid	28	6	8
Chelmich	12	10	0	Joseph Woodhouse	7	0	0
Rich: Newlar [*Nular*] iun	5	10	0	Wm Jenkes	7	16	0
Jane Freeman wid	28	18	8	Tho: & Walter Higgins	7	16	0
Jo: Bartra' gen	38	0	0	Will: Higgins	7	16	0
Peter Harvey gen	11	0	0	Will: Luggar	6	16	0
John Chelmich	3	3	4	Marg: Powle wid	2	16	8
Walter Bach	1	16	8	Tho: Coleman	18	0	1

13. The manor of Kinnersley was bought for James Pitts in 1652; *CCC*, iii, p. 1714. HT 1664 (9).
14. He bought the manor of Letton in 1652; *CCC*, iii, p. 1714.
15. Rector of Letton, FP 1661 (50s paid).
16. The largest HT charge in 1664 was on Penelope Hereford widow with Richard Kinnersley (8).
17. Herbert Croft, consecrated bishop of Hereford 9 Feb. 1661/2.
18. (1626–1673), brother of Sir Edward and son of Sir Robert (1579–1656); his knighthood is not listed by Shaw, but is referred to in A. Collins, *The Peerage of England*, ed. Sir Egerton Brydges (London, 1812), iv, p. 55.
19. Rector, FP 1661 (£10 paid).

Stretford: Kingsland continued

	£	s	d		£	s	d
Johan Powell wid	7	0	0	Mr Masters & his tenants	4	19	6
Henry Gilley	3	13	4	Jo: Jauncy	8	0	0
John Coleman	1	0	0	Tho: Whitefoote	2	10	0
John Bubb & Tho: Hall				Tho: Rawlings	1	0	0
gen	4	6	8	Fr: Morgan	1	16	0
Wm Mathewes	3	3	4	Rich: Peirce	1	10	0
Bartholomew Wall gen	2	10	8	Rich: Barrar	4	13	0
Jo: Addis	6	10	0	Tho: Woodhouse	7	13	4
Henry Freeman	2	10	0	Nich: Daios	5	0	0
Will: Sugar senr	20	0	0	Tho: Harries	1	10	0
Hugh Dale	4	0	0	Jo: Nicholls	1	16	8
John Carter	6	6	8	Edm: Mitton & Tho:			
John Eales		10	0	Gates	1	10	0
Jane Toldervey wid	4	10	0	Wm Grismond sen[20]	23	0	0
John Addis iun		16	8	Wm Grismond iun	23	0	0
Tho: [sic]				Hen: Grismond	17	16	8
John Meiricke	1	6	8	Wm Grismond iun	17	10	0
James Elvell	1	6	0	Tho: Kington	14	10	0
Wm Butt	5	10	0	Tho: Barrar	8	0	0
Henry Wall gen	50	0	0	Tho: Kington & Henr:			
Mrs Moores Farme	13	13	0	Jenkes	2	0	0
Wm Tailor	5	10	0	Bartholom' Wall gen	4	6	9
Tho: Coleman	4	10	0	Henr' Baldwyn	7	0	0
James Davies	6	0	0	James Meirick		13	0
Henry Barrar	6	10	0	Johan Deswall wid	3	10	0
Wm Lugger	2	6	0	Wm Jenkes	6	16	8
Anne Burrop & John Price	2	16	0	Wm Baldwyn	1	10	0
James Caldwall	3	0	0	Jo: Kington		16	0
		(80r)		Anne Burrop wid	1	16	0
Jo: Maund	2	0	0				
Will: Powell	1	0	0	Charge	933	0	0
Geo: Pugh	1	0	0	[1213	10	4]	
Johan Bayes wid	1	0	0				
Tho: Vaughan		13	4	Wm Grismond, Tho: Kington, Wm			
Hen: Higgins	1	13	0	Bubb. Raters			
Tho: Gates	2	13	0				
Jo: Lewis	1	13	4	**Something above a third part to be added**			
				to the Valuation			

---

7. Kings Pyon[21]

(81r)   [S7]

	£	s	d		£	s	d
Mrs Eliz: Karver wid	70	0	0	Jam: Aylewood	20	0	0
Chr: Handley [Hanley] cler	10	0	0	Richard King gen	24	0	0
Jo: Karver gen	14	0	0	Tho: Suatt [Shuat]	29	0	0
Jo: Carpenter	20	0	0	Rich: Mason	5	0	0

---

20. Chief constable of Stretford, 1664; Loan 29/49, pf. 4, no. 69/15.
21. The largest HT charge in 1664 was on George Karver (6).

Stretford: Kings Pyon continued

	£	s	d
Tho: & Jo: Croose [Cross] gen	17	0	0
Roger Jenkins	18	0	0
Will: Oven [Owen]	17	0	0
Alex: Meredith	22	0	0
Tho: Tailor & for the tieth of Wotton	21	0	0
Jo: Staunton	14	0	0
Miles Tomkins	8	10	0
Will: Hall	2	0	0
John Spencer	2	0	0
John White iun	3	0	0
John White sen Anne White & Geo: White	3	0	0

	£	s	d
Wm Lem'e	1	10	0
James Barnes	2	10	0
Tho: Munne	2	0	0
Rich: Phillipps & Rich: Parrett	2	10	0
Rich: Bradford	1	0	0
Charge	353	0	0
	[329	0	0]

Tho: Croose, Jo: Carpenter. Raters

The Valuation is to be doubled

8. Lionshall [S8]

		£	s	d
Fra: Pember Esq[22]		90	0	0
John Loid gen		30	0	0
Stonybridge meadow		3	0	0
The Demesne belonging to the Dutches of Somersett[23]	h: p:	50	0	0
Dan Lisons gen for &c	gl: qr: h:	56	0	0
		(82r)		
Tho: Greene Esq & Mr Crosse	h:	35	10	0
Tho: Traunter gen	h:	20	0	0
Wm Wall gen		26	10	0
Rich: Hall	h:	6	0	0
Tho: Smith		1	10	0
Jam: Wathan		3	0	0
Edm: Thomas gen		15	10	0
Howell James		4	10	0
Jo: Davies		2	0	0
Rich: Hall & filius		8	10	0
Tho: Traunter		4	0	0
John Traunter		4	0	0
Jo: Watkins		1	10	0
Anne Knight		5	10	0

	£	s	d
Rich: Knight	3	0	0
Tho: Rogers	3	10	0
Jo: Rowell	6	0	0
Wm Addis	4	10	0
Rich: Widcocks [Willcox]	9	10	0
Jo: Knight gen	6	0	0
Evan Phillipps	2	0	0
Anne Vaughan & filius	2	0	0
Ralph Hopwood	3	10	0
Eliz: Bowyer wid	2	6	8
Jo: Sheere for &c	5	10	0
Edw: Hall	2	10	0
James Knight	1	10	0
Jo: Deykins	1	10	0
Kath: Deykins wid	1	10	0
Charles Knight	1	0	0
Tho: Nicholls	6	0	0
Walter Vaughan gen	4	0	0
Tho: Weaver	11	0	0
Wm Kent	9	13	4
Wm Bowyer	9	10	0
	(83r)		
Walter Wrotchley gen	5	0	0
Will: Adams gen	9	10	0

22. HT 1664 (6).
23. Frances Devereux, coheir of the 3rd earl of Essex, was widow of William Seymour, marquis of Hertford and 2nd duke of Somerset, who died in 1660; she died in 1674; *Complete Peerage*, ed. Cokayne, xii, part i, p. 73.

Stretford: Lionshall continued

	£	s	d		£	s	d
Hen: Mathewes for &c	1	0	0	Masons Lands	1	0	0
Edw: Scandrett gen	7	10	0	Jo: Rowell	1	0	0
Robt Dorson [*Dorston*]	1	10	0	Jo: Moore	1	0	0
Tho: Driver	4	0	0	Jo: Dayos gen	1	0	0
Tho: Wall	7	10	0	Geo: Rogers	1	0	0
Anne Driver wid	2	10	0	Sym: Traunter	1	0	0
Will Jones for &c	6	0	0	Wm Webb & Wm Evans	1	10	0
James Cooke gen	6	0	0				
Wm Shepard gen	4	0	0				
Wm Knight & his Mother	8	0	0	**The peeresland taken out £100**			
Rich: Harper	3	0	0	Personall estate			
Barnaby Traunter	3	0	0	Jo: Rogers	60	0	0
Hester Stephens wid & Eliz:				& Phil: Jones	20	0	0
Stephens wid	4	0	0				
Wm Moore	1	0	0	Charge[24]	536	0	0
Wm Wancklen	1	10	0		[636	10	0]
Jo: Traunter	2	0	0				
Jo: Deykins	2	0	0	Wm Kent, Barnaby Traunter,			
Philip Harris	2	10	0	Jo: Rowell. Raters.			
Jam: George	1	10	0				
Hugh Moore	2	10	0	**The Valuation is to be doubled**			

24. The valuation may be compared with the distribution of the charges for various rated taxes between 1636 and 1673. The charges for these were upon occupiers rather than owners as such. A comparison shows that the ownership of land was considerably more concentrated than was the occupation of land and that there was apparently a large number of small tenanted holdings.

Numbers of Charges of each Magnitude payable by Individuals
(expressed as proportions of the total Parish Charge and compared
with the 1663 Militia Valuations)

Proportions	1636 Shipmoney	1646 Assessment	1656 Assessment	1663 Valuation	1673 Assessment
Over 7½%	2	1	1	4	—
5–7½%	—	2	1	1	2
2½–5%	6	4	6	4	10
1–2½%	22	21	16	10	17
⅛–1%	51	63	62	52	67
⅛% or less	22	30	32	—	23
Total charges	103	121	118	71	119
Parish charge = 100%	£25 12s	£20 6s 8d	£49 1s 6d	£636	£52 0s 4d

(Hereford CRO, Diocesan Archives, Court Papers, I. and O.P., Box 5, bundle 27, Churchwardens of Lyonshall *v.* Powell.)

9. Munkland[25]   (84r)   [S9]

	£	s	d		£	s	d
Will: Bedford cler[26]	25	0	0	Waltr Beinham	2	15	0
Rich: Bedoes Esq	15	0	0	Jo: Gower	3	0	0
Jo: Walton	15	0	0	Jo: Viccares	3	10	0
Rich: Walton [*Walter*]	14	10	0	Tho: Morgan	1	5	0
Anne Bedford wid	23	0	0	Fr: Smalman	1	10	0
Alice Beacham wid	15	0	0	Tho: Walton	2	10	0
Eliz: Davies wid	14	0	0	Hen: Luggar	5	0	0
Rich: Gower	5	0	0	Meredith Thomas	1	0	0
Tho: Gower	15	0	0	David Preece	1	0	0
Jo: Stallard	45	0	0	Jo: Smith	2	0	0
Joice Smith wid	6	0	0				
Isaack Smith	6	0	0	Charge	236	0	0
Waltr Sheward	5	0	0				
Jo: Hill	1	5	0	John Stallard, Rich: Walton. Raters.			
Tho: Randle	3	0	0				
Arth: Dickins	2	0	0	**Valuation almost 3 partes added**			
Tho: Dickins	2	15	0				

10. Pembridge   (85r)   [S10]

	£	s	d		£	s	d
Tho: Hopwood gen[27]	76	0	0	Walt: Bithell gen & his			
Walter Mason gen	44	0	0	ten't	9	0	0
Miles Lochard [*Latchett*]				Jo: East	18	0	0
gen[28]	34	0	0	Tho: Smith	34	0	0
Tho: Wildish gen	5	0	0	Phil: Weale	7	0	0
Wm Wall gen[29]	12	0	0	Tho: Deswall	5	0	0
Mary Long wid & her ten'ts	10	0	0	Griffith Evans	5	0	0
Henry Taylor	6	0	0	Eliz: Stephens wid	5	0	0
Walter Knight	3	0	0	Jo: Jones	7	0	0
Jo: Godwyn	2	0	0	Geo: Crumpe	4	0	0
Mr Carre & his ten'ts	7	0	0	Tho: Tomkins[30]	5	0	0
Mrs Monington & her				Jo: Acton gen	15	0	0
ten'ts	h: 26	0	0	Jo: Croone	12	0	0
Jo: Stead	6	0	0	Dame Alice Lingen & her			
Anne Vaughan & fil & the				ten'ts	h: 23	0	0
wid Weaver	8	0	0	Walter Nash	12	0	0
Jo: Copnar & fil	6	0	0	Walter Weale & his ten't	14	0	0
Eliz: Bowyer wid	5	0	0	Wm Bayton	14	0	0
Rich: Bithell	5	0	0	Jo: Browne	3	0	0

25. The largest HT charges in 1664 were on James Barnes and Richard Wadeley att le Wallend (5 each).
26. Vicar, FP 1661 (40s paid).   27. Buried 4 Aug. 1664.
28. Of The Byletts; his real estate in the county was valued at £180 a year in 1646; Loan 29/15, pf. 2.   29. HT 1664 (7) in Noke.
30. He was executor of the will of his father Richard Tomkins, proved 16 April 1663 (Hereford); the latter was buried 22 Aug. 1662.

Stretford: Pembridge continued

		£	s	d
Wm and Tho: Wall		3	0	0
Jo: Warrall [*Warrold*]		3	6	8
Jo: Scaundrett		2	10	0
Will: Griffithes		3	0	0
		(86r)		
Waltr Vaughan gen & Mr				
James &c[31]		56	0	0
Mr Gould [*Bould*] & his				
ten'ts		10	0	0
Appolin: Llewellin wid & fil		4	0	0
Anne Poughnell wid & fil		10	10	0
Wm Adams		10	0	0
The Byletts Mr Barnabyes				
Land	**h:**	48	0	0
The Demesne of the Lady				
of the Mannor of P:	**p:**	52	0	0
Jo: Hall & his ten'ts		10	0	0
Edw: Smith		7	10	0
Wm Sharbourne Dr of				
Divinity		100	0	0

	£	s	d
Arth: Price gen	2	10	0
Tho: Daios	3	0	0
Rich: Griffithes	1	0	0
Ro: Evans	1	0	0
James Bengoe the elder	2	10	0
Essex Sherbourne gen[32]	5	0	0
Ja: Bengoe iun	1	0	0
Rich: Smith	1	0	0
Rich: Compton	1	0	0
Anne Parlor wid	2	0	0
Wm Higgins	2	10	0
Charge[33]	794	0	0
peeresland	84	0	0
[*789*	*6*	*8*]	

Arth[r] White, Walter Nash. Raters.

Almost doubled according to the valuation

---

11. Shobdon   [*S11a*]

		£	s	d
Jo: Handford Esq[34]	**h:**	200	0	0
Fr: Minton cler[35]		20	0	0
Tho: Woodhouse	**h:**	20	0	0
Joseph Woodhouse		9	0	0
Jo: Duppa		6	0	0
Jo: Woodhouse iun		16	0	0
Waltr Hoskins		11	0	0
Jo: Perry [*Pirry*]		14	0	0
		(87r)		
Jo: Dee		4	10	0
Jo: Bull		11	0	0

	£	s	d
Jo: Browne & Tho: Browne	40	0	0
Hen: Taylor	4	10	0
Wm Shepard the eldr	5	10	0
Anne Woodhouse wid	34	0	0
Jo: Woodhouse sen	6	10	0
Da: Woodhouse	9	0	0
Fr: Pyrry	9	10	0
Silvanus Gough	7	0	0
Morgan Price [*Press*]	6	10	0
Johan Tailor	5	0	0
Tobias Woodhouse	8	0	0

---

31. Walter Vaughan bore the largest HT charge in Morecott in 1664 (7). He and John James of Trippleton were trustees of the estate of Thomas Stead of Morecott, being respectively the latter's widow's second husband and son-in-law: C.6/19/127; C.6/234/64; C.6/9/147; C.6/18/173. The statement in Robinson (p. 226), that the Morecott estate had been held by John Stead by right of his wife a member of the Vaughan family, is incorrect; the Steads had been at Morecott in the 1570s.
32. Son of Dr William Sherborne; will proved 1695 (PCC).
33. The largest HT charges in 1664 in each township were: Pembridge Borough—John Rogers (10), Bury and Weston—Stead East (5), and Marston—John Crumpe (5).
34. Of Mitcham, Surrey; bought the manor of Shobdon from Lord Herbert: *CCC*, iii, p. 1713. Sheriff 1662; HT 1664 (10).
35. Vicar, FP 1661 (£3 paid).

Stretford: Shobdon continued

	£	s	d
Wm Bayly iun	5	10	0
Rich: Tailer	4	10	0
Will: Shepard iun	10	0	0
Ja: Woodhouse iun	16	0	0
Tho: Jones & Tho: Phipson	16	0	0
Jo: Dalley	5	10	0
Rogr Gallett & Jo: Gallett	11	0	0
Margery [*Margarett*] Gough wid	11	0	0
Jo: Bubb	5	0	0
Ja: Caldwall	3	0	0
Jo: Eules [*Eales*]	3	10	0

Joseph Woodhouse, Jo: Gallett.
Raters

	£	s	d
Land within the Townshipp of Lye [*S11b*]			
Fr: Caswall [*Caysall*] wid[36]	20	0	0
Wm Botterell	12	0	0
Rich: Hoskins	5	0	0
Wm Downes	3	10	0
Ro: Downes	1	10	0
Tho: Howells	1	10	0
Charge	541	10	0
	[*581*	*10*	*0*]

Rich: Hoskins. Rater.

The proportion is to be almost doubled

---

12. Staunton [*and Stocklow*] (88r) [*S12*]

	£	s	d
Will: Menheare gen for &c[37]	h: 67	0	0
Phil: Greenely for tyth[38]	16	0	0
Rich: Bebb cler[39]	9	0	0
Jo: Badland[40]	2	0	0
Peter Wykes	15	0	0
Tho: Hoskins & Mich: Hoskins	10	0	0
Rich: Badland[40]	4	10	0
Roger Withy & Walter Saice[41]	10	0	0
Alice Fletcher[42]	1	10	0

	£	s	d
James Fletcher[43]	4	10	0
Mary Stead	2	0	0
Edw: Ashley	2	0	0
Eliz: Lawrence wid	3	0	0
Charge	145	0	0
	[*146*	*10*	*0*]

James Fletcher, Mich: Hoskins. Raters.

Proportion to be doubled.

---

36. HT 1664 (4).
37. Will proved 1685 (PCC). He held the manor of Nether or Church Staunton and was believed to have been of Dutch or Flemish origin. His property there descended by marriage to the Sherbornes: Robinson, pp. 226, 228, 254.
38. The tithes of Church Staunton came into Crown hands when Wigmore Abbey was dissolved; they were sold in 1601 to a group of London speculators who re-sold them five months later to Philip Greenly, a member of a local family. His collectors were forcibly opposed by Richard Wigmore and John Badland (grandfather of John and Richard Badland assessed here); Sta. Cha. 8/154/8.
39. Vicar of Staunton, died 1668.
40. John Badland (died 1689) and Richard Badland of Hatfield (died 1710) were two of the sons of William Badland of Staunton, yeoman. John was father-in-law of Peter Wyke.
41. HT 1664 (3).
42. Widow of Roger Fletcher whose will was proved 1661 (Hereford).
43. Yeoman, will proved 1667 (Hereford).

I

13. Stretford   [S13]

		£	s	d
Rich: Immings [*Imans*] cler[44]		16	0	0
Mrs Norbon for the Court	h:	50	0	0
Edw: Hide		3	0	0
Fr: Wilkes		5	0	0
Wm Bedford[45]		16	0	0
Hen: Nash		1	0	0
Rich: Morris		1	0	0

	£	s	d
Hen: Powle	3	0	0
Walter Kinnersley	1	0	0
Jo: Gough	1	0	0

Charge 97 0 0

Roger Herring. Rater.

The proportion is to be doubled.

14. Weobley   (89r)   [S14]

		£	s	d
Mrs Eliz: Monington	h:	8	0	0
Jo: Birch Esq[46]	h:	300	0	0
Tho: Carpenter gen	p:	40	0	0
Nich: Philpott Esq	h:	30	0	0
Humph: Davies for Mr Berington	h:	20	0	0
Tho: Bridges gen	h:	60	0	0
Andr: Greenley gen	h:	5	0	0
Jo: Saise	p:	11	0	0
Jo: Welford	p:	5	0	0
Jo: Nurse		4	0	0
Tho: Tomkins		15	0	0
Da: Warnall	h:	4	0	0
Tho: & Roger Deyos for &c	h:	9	0	0
Wm Dansey Esq	h:	25	0	0
Howell Bevan		6	0	0
Henry Leatherborow		3	0	0
Wm Bayton		6	10	0
Jo: Carpenter gen for &c		6	10	0
Ja: Synnock		4	0	0
Wm Powell		3	0	0
Symon Gough		4	0	0
Howell Bevan & Rich: King	p:	12	0	0
Wm Bayton for &c[47]		5	0	0

		£	s	d
Howell Bevan & Mrs Cox		5	0	0
Tho: White for &c	h:	10	0	0
Edw: Synnock		4	0	0
John Alford		4	0	0
Jo: Price		6	10	0
Fr: Suett [*Shuett*]		10	0	0
Wm Saise	p:	6	10	0
Geo: Bowle		2	10	0
Ja: Hill sen		2	10	0
Anne Morgan wid		2	10	0
Rich: Davies		3	0	0
Simon Herring		4	0	0
Rich: Tuffling		4	0	0
Jo: Barnes		15	0	0
Anne Price wid		5	0	0
Roger Davies gen	p:	25	0	0
The widow Paschall		3	10	0

Charge 680 0 0
[*699 0 0*]

Rich: Davies, Will: Saise, Tho: White. Raters.

The valuation is to be almost doubled

44. Rector, FP 1661 (20s paid).
45. HT 1664 (4).
46. The former parliamentary commander bought Garnston from Roger Vaughan in 1661; J. G. Hillaby, 'The Parliamentary Borough of Weobley, 1628–1708', *TWC*, xxxix (1967), p. 104. JP q 1660; MP for Leominster 1660; FP 1661 (£100); HT 1664 (10).
47. For the Unicorn, HT 1664 (6).

Value Returned by Raters		The Value Horse being taken out	Value according to the contribution			The whole years contribution at 2s per pound per annum for each particular parish in this Hundred		
£			£	s	d	£	s	d
1.	164 Allensmoore		538	13	4	53	14	4
2.	154 Backton		202	0	0	20	4	0
3.	134 Blackmere		231	10	0	23	3	0

1. The proportions of the parish charges are not the same as those under the 1677 assessment.

Hearth Tax return, Lady Day, 1664:

Webtree Hundred	Total Charged Hearths	Total Houses	More than 9 Hearths *	9	8	7	6	5	4	3	2	1	Total Exempt Houses
Allensmore	70	65					2		2	2	8	28	23
Bacton	20	24			1							12	11
Blakemere	35	22		1		1		1			2	10	7
Bredwardine	50	61	1 (14)							2	7	16	35
Callow	22	21								2	3	10	6
Clehonger	43	41	1 (13)			1			1	1	1	14	22
Didley	29	23							3		6	5	9
Grafton	13	9						1		1		5	2
Dinedor	48	48	1 (14)					1		2	4	15	25
Dore	94	95		1	1	1		3	1	6	4	25	53
Dorston	57	66					1			2	7	31	25
Dulas	17	14			1						2	5	6
Eaton Bishop	48	51							3	3	6	15	24
Ewyas Harold	43	65					1		1	1	2	26	34
Holme Lacy	101	51	1 (48)					2	2	4	1	21	20
Kenderchurch	25	17				1				3	2	5	6
Kenchurch	64	52	1 (12)		1			1		1	8	20	20
Kingstone	39	49				1				3	4	15	26
Lower Bullingham	28	29						1	1	1	3	10	13
Madley	154	149	1 (11)		1		2	2	2	5	19	52	65
Moccas	37	41				1					4	22	14
Peterchurch	88	102			1		1	1	2	3	9	34	51
Preston on Wye	56	50					2	2	2	1	5	13	25
Thruxton	17	17				1				1	1	5	9
Tyberton	28	18		1					1		4	7	5
Turnastone	9	9						1			1	2	5
Vowchurch	58	49		1			1	2	1		9	11	24
Upper Bullingham	26	20			1				1	2	1	6	9
Wormbridge	21	23	1 (15)								1	4	17
Total	1,340	1,281	7	4	7	7	10	18	23	46	124	444	591

* Actual charge in brackets.

Webtree Hundred continued

	Value Returned by Raters		The Value Horse being taken Out	Value according to the contribution			The whole years contribution at 2s per pound per annum for each particular parish in this Hundred		
4.	540	Bredwardine		564	0	0	56	8	0
5.	50	Callow & Twyford		116	6	8	11	12	8
6.	170	Clehonger		340	0	0	34	0	0
7.	322	Didley & Grafton		309	10	0	30	19	0
8.	500	Dinder & Rotherwas		574	10	0	57	9	0
9.	615	Doore		867	10	0	86	15	0
10.	516	Dorson		372	0	0	37	4	0
11.	150	Dulas		154	0	0	15	8	0
12.	278	Eaton Bishopp		308	13	4	30	17	4
13.	296	Ewyas Harrold		318	0	0	31	16	0
14.	560	Homlacy		750	6	8	75	0	0
15.	157	Kenderchurch		267	13	4	26	15	4
16.	297	Kentchurch		402	6	8	40	4	8
17.	230	Kingston		436	0	0	43	12	0
18.	170	Lower Bullingham		235	13	4	23	11	4
19.	1146	Madley		1215	13	4	121	11	4
20.	134	Mockas		231	10	0	23	3	0
21.	156	Peterchurch		806	0	0	80	12	0
	[757]								
22.	443	Preston		385	0	0	38	10	0
23.	69	Thruxton		126	0	0	12	12	0
24.	159	Tiberton		231	10	0	23	3	0
25.	53	Turnaston		114	0	0	11	8	0
26.	446	Vowchurch		621	0	0	62	2	0
27.	114	Upper Bullingham		180	0	0	18	0	0
28.	117	Wormebridge		179	13	4	17	19	4

[Total £1107 15s 0d]

---

1. Allensmore   (91r)   [Wb1]

	£	s	d			£	s	d
James Siddall gen[2]	h: 24	0	0	Rich: Phelpotts		2	0	0
Tho: Symons gen	5	0	0	Wm Gethin [Geathing]		1	10	0
Wm Hill for &c	h: 4	0	0	Morgan Powell		1	10	0
Ri: Davies	3	10	0	Jo: Morgan gen	h:	10	10	0
Geo: Foote	8	0	0	Hugh Thomas		3	10	0
Tho: Price	2	0	0	Hugh Thomas for &c		3	10	0
Joseph Beall	2	0	0	Will: Bants [Banks]		3	10	0
Rich: Haines	2	0	0	Geo: Price		4	0	0

2. HT 1664 (6). Elenor Greene widow was also charged on 6 hearths.

Webtree: Allensmore continued

	£	s	d		£	s	d
Mrs Greene	12	0	0	Henry Barroll			
Rich: Williams for &c	12	0	0	Quer' de Tythes	4	0	0
Wm Barnett for &c	9	0	0	Jam: Low	1	5	0
Geo: Haines for &c	12	0	0	Wm Prosser	4	0	0
Jam: Wathen for &c	4	10	0	Jo: Lawrence	1	10	0
Jam: Wathen for &c	2	10	0				
The wid Walter	1	10	0	Charge	164	0	0
Ri: Barroll	1	10	0		[165	5	0]
Ri: Barroll for &c	3	0	0				
Hugh Russell gen	1	10	0	Jo: Morgan, Tho: Warrock, Wm Bur-			
Theophilus Dykes	1	0	0	nett. Raters			
Rich: Hunt	7	10	0				
The wid Sampson	2	0	0	**Two partes are to be added to the**			
Wm Marsh	2	10	0	**Valuation**			
Bodnam Gunter	1	10	0				

2. Backton (92r) [Wb2]

	£	s	d		£	s	d
Mrs Rachell Thomas	120	0	0	Jo: Lewis	3	0	0
Phil' Vaughan	8	0	0	Wm Pyton [*Peyton*] cler	9	0	0
Jam: Pritchard	6	0	0				
Rowl' Tailor	6	0	0	Charge	154	0	0
Will: Garson [*Garston*]³	6	10	0		[172	10	0]
Lewis Phillips	4	0	0				
Jam: Good	4	0	0	James Good, Lewis Phillipps. Raters			
Wm Pritchard	3	0	0				
Walter Phillipps	3	0	0	**The valuation is to be almost doubled**			

3. Blackmere [Wb3]

		£	s	d		£	s	d
Ja: Winston gen⁴	h:	40	0	0	Will: Hosier cler	10	0	0
Jo: Carwardine gen & Mr								
Holmes of Hereff		20	0	0	Charge	134	0	0
Mich: Witham		10	0	0		[124	0	0]
Tho: Fletcher		15	0	0				
Geo: Meate		8	0	0	Ja: Winston, Jo: Carwardine, Geo:			
Rowl' Vaughan		5	0	0	Meate. Raters.			
Wm Fletcher		2	0	0				
John Colcombe		4	0	0	**The proportion is to be doubled**			
Jo: Carwardine gen for								
Tieth		10	0	0				

3. The largest HT charge in 1664 was on William Garston (? Barston) (8).
4. HT 1664 (9).

4. Bredwardine

		£	s	d		£	s	d
The Lo: Scudamore	h:	8	0	0	Rich [*Higgins* DELETED]			
Roger Vaughan Esq[5]	h:	298	0	0	Williams	6	0	0
Tho: Lingen gen	h:	100	0	0	Arnold Harries	3	0	0
			(93r)		Edw: Williams	4	0	0
The Lady Alice Lingen	h:	36	0	0	Bethlin Parrie	3	0	0
Hen: Mellin gen		26	0	0				
Tho: Goods gen	h:	35	0	0	Charge	540	0	0
Herbt Walwyn gen		40	0	0		[654	0	0]
Jo: Stilling gen		30	0	0				
The Lo: Craven	p:	7	0	0	Waltr Hill, Wm Jenkings. Raters.			
Walter Hill		30	0	0				
Phillip Simonds		8	0	0	**Of peeresland**	7	0	0
Blanch Mills spinster		6	0	0				
Wm Higgins		8	0	0	**The proportion compleat**			
Anne George wid		6	0	0				

5. Callow [& *Twyford*][6]

	£	s	d			£	s	d
Will: Dobbins[7]	12	0	0	Tho: Hodges	charge with horse of these £26–10s	1	10	0
Fr: Davies	4	0	0					
Wm Lane	1	10	0	Ri: Baxter		3	0	0
Rich: Pothookes				[*Backster*][8]				
[*Pottlogge*]	2	0	0					
Geo: Mabberley	1	10	0	Charge		50	0	0
Tho: Blakeway	5	0	0			[47	10	0]
Tho: Wm Cocke	12	0	0					
Alice Demungott				Tho: Wilcox, Fr: Davies. Raters.				
[*Demounser*]	3	0	0	**Proportion is to be someth: above**				
Rich: Mathewes	2	0	0	**double**				

6. Clehunger

(94r)

		£	s	d		£	s	d
Herbt Awbrey Esq[9]	h:	50	0	0	Mrs Elinor Greene wid	9	0	0
Jam: Rodd Esq	h:	7	0	0	The Chauntrie house	10	0	0
Edw: Aldern Dr of the					The Well House	9	0	0
Civill Law[10]	h:	24	0	0	Mrs Elinor Badham wid	8	0	0
Jo: Booth gen		9	0	0	Sibill Overton wid	7	0	0

5. JP 1660; in 1660 he was considered as a deputy lieutenant but marked as being under age (S.P. 29/11, fo. 162); MP for Hereford 1662; captain of a militia troop in the mid-1660s; Loan 29/49, pf. 4, no. 69/15. He married Ann daughter of Sir Thomas Tomkins.

6. Included Twyford.   7. HT 1664 (3).   8. HT 1664 (3).

9. In 1646 his estate in the county was valued at £266 a year (Loan 29/15, pf. 2); FP 1661 (£10); HT 1664 (13).

10. His estate in the county in 1646 was valued at £53 a year; FP 1661 (£10); JP q 1660.

Webtree: Clehunger continued

	£	s	d		£	s	d
Johan Phipotts & Eustance				Tho: Hunt	1	10	0
Jones	4	0	0	The Tiethes att **Quaere de:**	15	0	0
Wm Goodman	3	10	0				
Mr Beales landes	3	0	0	Charge 170	0	0	
Geo: Haines	5	0	0				
Anne Bradford	2	0	0	Edm: Ballard, Eustance Jones. Raters.			
Ro: Morris	1	0	0				
The lands of Geo: Foote gen	2	0	0	**The proportion is to be doubled**			

7. Didley [& *Grafton*] &c[11]   [*Wb7*]

		£	s	d			£	s	d
Geo: Jones cler[12]		47	0	0				(95r)	
Tho: Goode gen	h:	25	0	0	Tho: Quarrell		7	0	0
Wm Powell for &c		13	6	8	The wid Smith		7	0	0
Mr Pye's lands	h:	13	6	8	Roger Garnons gen				
Jo: Hoskins		36	0	0	for &c	h:	15	6	8
Mrs Gravell		17	0	0	The said Roger Garnons				
Ri: Greene		12	0	0	for &c	h:	11	6	8
Bennett Hoskins Esq									
for &c	h:	22	0	0	Charge	322	0	0	
The sd Ben[tt] Hoskins						[*270*	*6*	*8*]	
for &c	h:	12	0	0					
Jo: Meendes for &c		12	0	0	John Hoskins, Tho: Goode. Raters.				
Tho: Smith &c ⎫									
Jo: Edwards &c ⎬		20	0	0	**The proportion direct**				
& Geo: Meiricke &c ⎭									

8. Dinder [& *Rotherwas*]   [*Wb8*]

		£	s	d		£	s	d
Mr Bodenham for					Rich: Churchyard	20	0	0
Rotheras[13]	h:	300	0	0	Tho: Torre & his sonne	20	0	0
Dinder Cort belonging to					Hen: Lane	15	0	0
Mr Porter	h:	90	0	0	Tho: Baggott [*Baggard*]	5	0	0
The demesne lands of					Ch: Lane	5	0	0
Mrs Bodenham	h:	10	0	0	Mr Carelesse land	5	0	0
Ro: Neham gen		20	0	0	Hen: Banes	2	10	0

11. The parish of St Devereux. The largest HT charge in 1664 was on William Westfaling (5).
12. Rector of St Devereux, FP 1661 (£3 paid).
13. Roger Bodenham's estates in Rotheras, Little Marcle, Weston Beggard, Holmer and Pipe were valued at £177 a year in 1646; Add. 19678. The same year his entire real estate in the county was put at £264 a year and his personal estate at £98; Loan 29/15, pf. 2. His whole fortune before the Civil War was estimated in 1684 at near £3,000 a year, but it was said that he had spent his estate on the king and so had to live obscurely; Add. 36452, fo. 190. HT 1664 (14).

Webtree: Dinder continued

	£	s	d
Eysams lands	2	10	0
Humph: Gullifer	2	0	0
Ri: Wild	2	0	0
The wid Greg	1	0	0
The wid Howells	1	0	0
Theodosia Turner wid	1	10	0
Tho: Butler	1	0	0

	£	s	d
Jo: Shepards land		10	0

Charge 514 0 0
[*504   0   0*]

Tho: Torre, Hen: Lane. Raters.

Something added to the Valuation.

---

9. Doore[14]   [*Wb9*]

		£	s	d
Jam: Scudamore Esq in revenue per annum[15]		200	0	0
Bennett Hoskins Esq[16]	**h:**	200	0	0
		(96r)		
Giles Bridges gen		60	0	0
Charles Morgan gen	**h:**	55	0	0
Jam: Bernard cler[17]		20	0	0
Peter Smith gen		20	0	0
Rich: Wild		20	0	0

		£	s	d
Rich: Parry gen		10	0	0
Jo: Morgan gen		10	0	0
Jo: Parry of Dulas Esq ['*gen*' DELETED]	**h:**	15	0	0
Edw: Baskervile gen		5	0	0

Charge 615 0 0

Peter Smith. Rater.

---

10. Dorson   [*Wb10*]

		£	s	d
Roger Vaughan Esq	**h:**	50	0	0
Herbert Awbrey Esq	**h:**	140	0	0
Jam: Whiting cler[18]		60	0	0
Jesus Colledge Lands		17	0	0
Hen: Wellington[19]	**h:**	24	0	0
Watkin Madley [*Maddy*]		20	0	0
Tho: Ravenhill		20	0	0
Jo: & Roger Smith		12	0	0
Edw: Bullock		16	0	0
Josias Price [*Prees*]		14	0	0
Jo: Partridge		10	0	0
Jo: Lewis		10	0	0
Anne Rickards [*Richards* wid		10	0	0
Tho: Goode	**h:**	18	0	0
Tho: Goode for &c	**h:**	8	0	0
David Smith		5	0	0
Jam: Woodhouse		3	0	0
Gabriell Pritchard & Tho: Watters		8	0	0
Tho: Powell		4	0	0
Jo: Probertt		5	0	0

	£	s	d
Wm Rowland	6	0	0
Tho: Parsons	7	0	0
Tho: Jenkins	8	0	0
Phil: Gilbert	8	0	0
Tho: Bullocke	6	0	0
Jo: Partridge for &c	3	0	0
	(97r)		
Jo: Bramptons lands	3	0	0
Wm Jenkins	3	0	0
Charles Pember	4	0	0
Wm Morris	3	0	0
Wm Prosser	3	0	0
Anne Goods landes	3	0	0
Ja: Fletcher	5	0	0

Charge 516 0 0

Henry Wellington, Watkin Madley. Raters.

The proportion direct.

---

14. The largest HT charge in 1664 was on Thomas Jenings (9).
15. JP q 1660; MP for the county 1661; DL 1663 (S.P. 29/87); died 1668.
16. JP 1655; JP q 1660.   17. Rector, FP 1661 (40s).
18. Vicar, FP 1661 (20s paid).   19. Gent., HT 1664 (6).

11. Dulas[20]   [Wb11]

Belongeth most parte to John Parry Esq
And is all charged with horse.   **The proportion direct.**

	£	s	d
Charge	150	0	0

---

12. Eaton Bishopp   (98r)   [Wb12]

	£	s	d		£	s	d
Mrs Eliz: Vaughan	2	10	0	The widow Read of Canon			
Jo: Davies gen[21]	15	0	0	bridge	1	10	0
Geo: Clerke cler[22]	35	0	0	Pembers landes	1	0	0
The wid Read & her				Griffith Reighnolds	1	0	0
daughter	15	0	0	Tho: Read of Single Bridge	1	0	0
John Badam	11	10	0	Jo: Simonds[24]	15	0	0
Rich: Bullock	12	0	0	Rich: Price	1	0	0
Tho: Teague	9	0	0	Ri: Probert	1	5	0
Walter Harwell	2	10	0	Anne Carwardine wid	1	0	0
Hosea Beast	2	0	0	Abell Price	1	0	0
Wm Husbands	11	10	0	Ja: Griffithes	1	0	0
Jo: Younger	19	0	0	Nich: Philpotts gen **h:**	2	10	0
Wm Barroll	17	0	0	Will: Price	18	0	0
Jo: Smith gen	10	10	0	Wm Vaughan gen	11	10	0
Wm Exton	10	10	0	Jo: Parry gen	11	0	0
Wm Clarke J[23]	11	0	0	Herbt Awbrey Esq	2	0	0
Jo: Squire	4	0	0				
Jam: Cook	8	10	0	Charge	278	0	0
Geo: Harris	2	0	0				
Ri: Gullifer	2	0	0	Jo: Yonger, Will: Price, Wm Barroll.			
Tho: Walker	2	0	0	Raters.			
Johan Carwardine	1	10	0				
Wm Carwardine	1	15	0	**A third part is to be added to the**			
Wm Cook	1	10	0	**Valuation**			
Jo: Cook	1	10	0				

---

13. Ewyas Harrald   (99r)   [Wb13]

		£	s	d		£	s	d
Humph: Baskervile Esq	**h:**	140	0	0	Valen' Parry gen	7	0	0
Bennett [Benjamin] Mason					Eliz: Parry wid	17	0	0
Esq	**h:** [25]	60	0	0	Tho: Gwillim	14	0	0
Jo: Parry Esq	**h:**	14	0	0	Wm Parry	6	0	0

---

20. The largest HT charge in 1664 was on David Grundy (8).
21. HT 1664 (4).   22. HT 1664 (4).
23. Chief constable of Webtree, 1663; Loan 29/49, pf. 4, no. 69/15.
24. HT 1664 (4).   25. HT 1664 (6).

Webtree: Ewyas Harrald continued

	£	s	d		£	s	d
Wm Watkins	5	0	0	Nich: Phillipps	4	0	0
Tho: Preece	5	0	0				
Roger Edmonds	5	0	0	Charge	296	0	0
John Parry	5	0	0				
Wm Pritchard	5	0	0	Tho: Preece, Roger Edmonds. Raters.			
Wm Trehearne	5	0	0				
Tho: Watkins	4	0	0	**Something to be added to the Valuation**			

14. Homlacey   [*Wb14*]

		£	s	d	
Jo: Lo: Viscount Scuda-					
more	h: [26]	500	0	0	John Crump, Henry Sampson. Raters.
He: Smith cler[27]		54	0	0	
He: Sampson gen		6	13	4	**Something is to be added to ye**
					Valuation
	Charge	560	0	0	

15. Kenderchurch &c   [*Wb15*]

		£	s	d		£	s	d
John Scudamore iunʳ arʼ[28]	h:	46	13	4	Alice Powell wid	2	0	0
Jo: Sayse		6	0	0	Jo: Watkins		15	0
Geo: Clive gen	h:	27	0	0	Mr Thorne	1	13	4
Allen [*Ellen*] Morgan wid		8	0	0	Wm Pytt for the Lo:			
Wm Pytt		9	5	0	Hollys[29] Tyth & for &c	10	0	0
Jo: Morgan		15	0	0				
Tho: Pytt		8	5	0	Charge	157	0	0
Wa: Phillipps		6	0	0				
Tho: Gwillim for &c		5	10	0	Tho: Pytt, Wm Pytt. Walt: Phillipps.			
			(100r)		Raters.			
Magarett Pitt		2	10	0				
Tho: Husbands for &c		5	0	0	**The proportion direct**			
Wm Baily for &c		3	10	0				

26. John Scudamore, Baron Dromore and Viscount Sligo (1601–1671); his income in 1645 was thought to be about £4,000 a year: Harl. 911. More exact evidence suggests that his receipts from his Herefordshire estates in 1641/2 were no more than £3,233; H. Reade, 'Account Books of the First Lord Scudamore', *TWC*, xxv (1925), p. 119. JP, *custos rotulorum*, 1660. FP 1661 (£100 paid); HT 1664 (48, the largest charge in the county, equalled only by the charge on the college of vicars choral).
27. Vicar, FP 1661 (£5).
28. Considered for appointment as a deputy lieutenant in 1660, but may not have been appointed; S.P. 29/11, fo. 162. HT 1664 (7).
29. Probably Denzil Holles, 1599–1680, created Baron Holles, of Ifield, Sussex, 20 April 1661; *Complete Peerage*, ed. Cokayne, vi, p. 545.

16. Kenchurch [Wb16]

		£	s	d			£	s	d
Jo: Scudamore Esq[30]	h:	30	0	0	Tho: Watkins iun		4	10	0
Humph: Baskervile Esq[31]	h:	30	0	0	Jo: Phillipps	h:	2	10	0
The same Baskervile for					Lewis Harris	h:	2	10	0
his forge &c[32]	h:	30	0	0	Wm Powell	h:	3	0	0
Jo: Tyler cler[33]		25	0	0	Nich: Wathame [Wathen]		4	10	0
Rich: Heath cler		10	0	0	Rich: Tailor	h:	4	0	0
Tho: Watkins sen		18	0	0	Jo: Weabe	h:	1	0	0
Mary Williams		5	0	0				(101r)	
Acon Greenlease &					Jo: Lambert		3	0	0
Anne Barnsley		6	0	0	Bumbur Lands		1	10	0
Walter Weabe		12	0	0	Johan Phillipps widow		15	0	0
Jo: Jenkins	h:	5	0	0	Jo: Rawlings		9	0	0
Rich: Lewis		3	10	0	Ri: Heath		5	10	0
Jo: Scudamore iun Esq	h:	3	10	0					
Marke Rawlings	h:	3	0	0					
Tho: Lewis	h:	3	0	0	Charge	297	0	0	
Char: Morgan		9	0	0		[285	0	0]	
Wm Jones		9	0	0					
Wm Lewis sen	h:	6	0	0	Tho: Watkins, Acon Greenelease. Raters				
Roger Bevan		5	10	0					
Mary Prosser vid		9	0	0	**A 4th part is to be added to the**				
Morgan Jones		6	10	0	**Valuation**				

---

17. Kingston [Wb17]

		£	s	d		£	s	d
John Parry gen[34]	h:	40	6	8	Edw: Jones	1	0	0
Bennett Hoskins Esq	h:	12	0	2	Ch: Morgan gen	20	0	0
Wm Vinall [Winall]		13	6	0	Edw: Baskervile gen	5	0	0
Anne Clarke wid		21	3	0	Ro: Mason gen[35]	5	1	6
Waltr Pye Esq		4	0	1	Hugh Russell gen	2	3	4
Wm Powell		4	13	4	Bodenham Gunter	1	13	4
Jo: Lane gen		6	2	0	Ja: Brace	1	5	4
Wm Marsh		9	0	0	Jo: Smith gen		13	0
Tho: Arundell Esq	h:	10	13	4	Edw: Collins gen		13	4
Mrs Eliz: Lucy		21	0	0	The: Cannons Tieth	8	0	0
Hugh Marsh		1	13	4				
Jo: Preece		1	13	4	Charge 230	0	0	
Wm Dansey Esq	h:	9	13	4	[238	4	3]	
Geo: Hill		20	0	0				
Edw: Jones		3	0	0	Wm Marsh, Hugh Marsh. Raters.			
Jam: Pritchard gen		10	13	4				
Tho: Mathews		1	3	4	**The Valuation is to be almost**			
Jo: Bennett		4	13	4	**doubled**			

---

30. HT 1664 (12); will proved 1670 (PCC).
31. JP 1660: sheriff 1669. HT 1664 (8).   32. Pontrilas Forge.
33. Rector, FP 1661 (40s).   34. HT 1664 (7).   35. Probably vicar of Kingston.

18. Lower Bullingham   (102r)

		£	s	d
Geo: Sayer Esq[36]	h:	120	0	0
Ri: Probin		16	0	0
Tho: Meirick		5	0	0
Mr Allen		4	0	0
The Tieth Corne		20	0	0
Charge		170	0	0
		[165	0	0]

Quere the tieth corne to whom it belonges
& whether chargeable for horse.

Tho: Rogers, John Davies, Tho:
Merrick. Raters.[37]

**A 3rd part is to be added to the
Valuation**

19. Madley[38]

	£	s	d			£	s	d
Mr Broughton [*Boughton*]					Jo: Williams for &c	4	0	0
for the Vicaridge[39]	40	0	0		Phillip Symonds gen	9	0	0
Jo: Carwardine	30	0	0		Mrs Moore[40]	80	0	0
Tho: Seaborne gen	30	0	0		Tho: Morgan gen	60	0	0
Tho: Carwardine	5	0	0		Tho: Carpenter gen	80	0	0
Geo: Rawlins lands	6	0	0		Wm Lawrence	8	0	0
Wm Greene for &c	5	0	0		Wm Foote	3	0	0
Mr Long	17	0	0		The widow Carwardine	35	0	0
Jam: Carwardine for &c	6	0	0				(103r)	
Mr Rogers lands	15	0	0		Jo: Walwyn	45		
Waltr Caunt for &c	14	0	0		Edw: Collins	28		
For Madley	14	0	0		Jo: Harper gen	12		
Jam: Carwardine for &c	6	0	0		wid Smith for &c	h: 26		
The Castle farme	10	0	0		The wid Tomkins	15		
Jo: Williams of Cublington	14	0	0		Jo: Cooke	15		
Jo: Lawrence	5	0	0		Walter Maddox	32		
Elinor Moggrid [*Mogridge*]					Rich: Merricke [*Meirick*]	8		
wid	5	0	0		Jo Moggridge	5		
Wm Rees	4	0	0		Ri: Symonds	30		
Jo: Lord:	7	0	0		Edw: Fode [*Foote*] sen &			
Pantolls Lands	5	0	0		iun	16		
Hugh Addams	16	0	0		Ri: Davies	14		
Jo: Paine	5	0	0		Ja: Maddox	11		

36. George Sawyer, will proved 31 Oct. 1665 (PCC). He also owned land in Berkshire.
37. The largest HT charge in 1664 was on Thomas Rogers, gent. (5).
38. An analysis of a survey of the parish made in 1813 (P. Morgan, 'An early 19th century survey of Madley', *TWC*, xxxiii (1950), p. 118), although based on acreage rather than value, suggests, when compared with this assessment, that between 1663 and 1813 there was a considerable increase in the interest of absentee landowners and a substantial diminution in the total and mean size of the interests of all classes of landowner and occupier except the largest.
39. Herbert Bowton, vicar, FP 1661 (£5 paid).
40. Mary Moore, HT 1664 (11).

Webtree: Madley continued

	£	s	d		£	s	d
Jo: Watkins	5			The Tythes of Madley	37		
Mr Jenkins	13			The Tythes of Cublington	27		
The Lands att Swynmore **h:**	28			The Tythes of Weston &			
Bridgett Greene	10			Brampton	25		
Tho: Laudington	10			The Tythes of Cannon			
Henry Eysam [*Eysham*] **h:**	65			Bridge	22		
Mr Sheldon And for Kts				The Tythes of Lullam	25		
farme **h:**	40						
Mr Green's lands in				Charge	131		
Tinberlim^e **Charged upon**	9			[*136*]			
Waltr Weale **Dr Alderne**	5						
Eliz: Lawrence	6			Tho: Morgan, Jo: Walwyn, Edw: Collins, Jo: Carwardine. Raters.			

Charge 1015
[*986*]

The Tiethes

Something is to be added to the Valuation

---

20. Mockas (104r) [*Wb20*]

	£	s	d		£	s	d
Edw: Cornewall Esq[41] **h:**	60	0	0	Jo: Kendrick	2	0	0
Ri: Bithell gen	7	0	0	Wm Brasier [*Bracer*]	1	10	0
Martha Williams wid	4	0	0	Ri: Smith	2	0	0
Wm Mathewes sen	4	0	0	Ri: Cox	1	0	0
Wm Mathewes iun	2	0	0	Hen: Vaughan	1	10	0
Jo: Tomkins	2	10	0	Wm Lurcott	1	10	0
Jo: Taylor gen	2	0	0	Ri: Hill	2	0	0
Ja: Winston gen **h:**	4	0	0	Wm Howells		15	0
Delabere Winston gen	3	0	0	Jo: Taylor cler	30	0	0
Tho: Heath	1	0	0				
Evan Williams	1	0	0	Charge	134	0	0
Walter Davies		15	0	[*136*	*6*	*0*]	
Jo: Harries	1	0	0				
Sibbill Mathewes		10	0	Jo: Taylor, Walter Davies. Raters.			
Jo: Gough		6	0				
Will: Preece [*Price*]		10	0	**The proportion is to be doubled**			
Rich: Shepard		10	0				

---

21. Peterchurch [*Wb21*]

	£	s	d		£	s	d
Tho: Delahay gen[42]	130	0	0	Esay Prosser[43]	5	0	0
Luke Lewis	5	0	0	Tho: Mason gen	25	0	0
Perin James wid	5	0	0	Ja: Vaughan gen	30	0	0
Lison Watkins	5	0	0	Ja: Penoyre gen	15	0	0

---

41. JP 1660: HT 1664 (7).　　42. FP 1661 (£2 15s paid); HT 1664 (8).
43. Tanner, will proved 1666 (PCC).

Webtree: Peterchurch continued

		£	s	d
Ja: Goode		5	0	0
		(105r)		
Jo: Smith Godway gen		30	0	0
Jo: Smith Willbrooke		40	0	0
Tho: Goode	h:	20	0	0
Wm Prosser	h:	60	0	0
Jo: Colcombe		15	0	0
Jo: Hunt		13	0	0
Anne Harris wid	h:	5	0	0
Jo: Parry		10	0	0
Wm Hall Snodell gen		20	0	0
Mr Hall for the Forge		20	0	0
Tho: Goode for &c	h:	80	0	0
Ri: Powell for &c		15	0	0
Jo: Price [*Prees*] for &c	h:	7	0	0
Elinor Shaw wid for &c		5	0	0

		£	s	d
Herbert Awbrey Esq	h:	20	0	0
Ja: Winston gen	h:	20	0	0
Esay Prosser & Jo: Smith				
for &c	h:	30	0	0
Roger Parry for &c	h:	10	0	0
Jo: Jenkins for &c		15	0	0

Charge 757 0 0
[*660 0 0*]

Ja: Vaughan, Tho: Mason, Jo: Smith, Jo: Parry. Raters.

A 6th part is to be added to the valuation

---

22. Preston

		£	s	d
The Court of Preston & the				
Tieth h:⎫ Deane and		126	0	0
Plowfield ⎬ Chapt^r				
Place &c h:⎭		30	0	0
Hunt Low				
&c	h:	32	0	0
Mr Halls				
Land	h:	24	0	0
Wm Bridges				
gen	h:	2	0	0
Mrs Carwardine wid		24	0	0
Wm Hosier cler		10	0	0
Ja: Meredith		28	0	0
Wa: Shepard		13	0	0
Ri: Bythell		10	0	0
Delabere Winston[44]		39	0	0
Jo: Haines		3	0	0
Ro: Delahay		11	0	0
Phil: Symonds[45]		24	0	0
Walter Lawrence		12	0	0
Jo: Greene		12	0	0

		£	s	d
				(106r)
Ri: Miles		2	0	0
Jo: Harris & Jo: Bainham		6	0	0
Wa: Hide & his Mother		6	0	0
Tho: Cood		6	0	0
The wid Jones		4	0	0
Rich: Cooke		3	0	0
The wid Lawrence		5	0	0
Landes belonging to				
Carwardine		4	0	0
Jo: Notts land		3	0	0
Jo: Colcombe		1	0	0
Ri: Harris		3	0	0
The Mill				
Deane & Chapter h:		6	0	0

Charge 443 0 0
[*449 0 0*]

Delab: Winston, Ja: Meredith. Raters.

Compleate without Alteration

---

44. Gent., HT 1664 (6). Walter Probert was also charged on 6 hearths.
45. Chief constable of Webtree, 1663; Loan 29/49, pf. 4, no. 69/15.

23. Thruxton [Wb23]

	£	s	d		£	s	d
Bodenham Gunter gen[46]	37	0	0	Marg: Pye	2	0	0
Hugh Russell gen	9	0	0	Mr Russell for &c	1	0	0
Ro: Mason cler for glebe	8	0	0				
Tho: Lampott [Lambert]	2	0	0	Charge	69	0	0
Wm Marsh	5	0	0				
Theophilus Dykes		16	0	Hugh Russell, Tho: Lambert. Raters.			
Johan Sansu' wid	1	0	0				
Alice Hunts land	2	0	0	**The valuation is to be almost**			
Jo: Mathewes	2	0	0	**doubled**			

24. Tiberton [Wb24]

	£	s	d	
Wm Bridges gen				
Mr Bridges £150[47]	100	0	0	Wm Bridges, Wm Greene. Raters.
Wm Greene gen	30	0	0	
Mr Walwyn & the wid Enoe	20	0	0	**A 3rd part to be added to the**
Jo: Greene	8	0	0	**Valuation**
Charge	158	0	0	

25. Turnaston (107r) [Wb25]

		£	s	d	
Humph: Howorth Esq	h:	15	0	0	
Nich: Philpott gen	h:	40	0	0	
Mrs Blanch Howorth		14	10	0	Tho: Price,[48] Evan Prosser. Raters.
Ja: Penoyre	h:	8	0	0	
Tho: Bowker cler		6	0	0	**The proportion is to be doubled.**
Charge		53	0	0	
		[83	0	0]	

46. Of Gwendor. He had been fined £50, at $\frac{2}{6}$, for his Herefordshire estates as a delinquent and papist: *CCC*, iv, p. 3002. HT 1664 (7).
47. Will proved 1668 (PCC). He held lands at Madley, Yazor, Weobley, Burton, Lyonshall, Mansell Lacy, Mansell Gamage, Bishops Frome, Preston on Wye, Bosbury, Munsley and Tyberton at the time of his death; HT 1664 (9).
48. HT 1664 (5).

26. Vowchurch   [Wb26]

		£	s	d			£	s	d
Sr Tho: Morgan Kt[49]	h:	120	0	0	Jo: Smith		5	0	0
Mrs Kemp wid[50]		15	0	0	Jo: Smith gen		11	0	0
James Cooksey		8	0	0	Mr Philpotts for &c	h:	71	0	0
Ch: Morgan gen	h:	8	0	0	The greate tiethes		15	0	0
Tho: Landon gen		20	0	0	Tho: Bowkers cler[51]		13	6	8
David Prosser		5	0	0					
Jo: Wilds for &c	h:	93	0	0	Charge		446	0	0
Humph: Howorth Esq							[443	6	8]
for &c	h:	10	0	0					
Esay Prossers farme		10	0	0	Ja: Cooksey, Humph: ——. Raters.				
Ja: Penoyre gen for &c		19	0	0					
The estate lately Mr Rogers		15	0	0	**A 3rd part is to be added to the**				
Ch: Jennings		5	0	0	**valuation**				

27. Upper Bullingham   [Wb27]

	£	s	d		£	s	d
Dr Rich: Bayly						(108r)	
Q if Mr Bayly be				Tho: Walker	3	10	0
chargeable for				Jo: Carpenter	3	10	0
Horse[52]	55	0	0	The Tyth Corne & graine	14	0	0
Ja: Davies	7	0	0				
Jo: Wilcox	7	0	0	Charge	114	0	0
—— Davies	7	0	0		[124	0	0]
Ed: Bullock	19	2	0				
Anne Codlicott wid	4	8	0	Jam: Davies, Jo: Wilcox, Walter Smith.			
Ro: Wade	3	10	0	Raters.			

28. Wormebridge   [Wb28]

		£	s	d	
Geo: Clive gen[53]	h:	40	0	0	
Mrs Mary Husbands	h:	50	0	0	
Bodenham Gunter gen		6	0	0	Tho: Husbands, Jo: Symonds. Raters.
Roger Garnons gen	h:	3	0	0	
Walt[r] Giles		12	0	0	**Something is to be added to ye Val:**
Roger Symonds		6	0	0	
Charge		117	0	0	

49. Created baronet 1 Feb. 1660/1. A former parliamentary commander, he was prominent in organising the militia after the Restoration; *DNB*. HT 1664 (9).
50. In 1646 the real estate in the county of Robert Kempe of Chenston was put at £20 a year and his personal estate at £72; Loan 29/15, pf. 2.
51. Vicar, FP 1661 (20s paid).
52. Doctor of Laws, HT 1664 (8).   53. HT 1664 (15).

Wigmore Hundred   (109r)

Value Returned by the Raters		Value Horse taken out	The valuation according to the contribution			The whole yeares contribution at 2s per pound per annum for each particular parish in the Hundred		
	£		£	s	d	£	s	d
1	292	Atforton Peytoe Stanway & Grange	423	0	0	42	6	0
2	55	Aston	90	0	0	9	2	1
						[9	0	0]
3	99	Aymestry & Shirley	241	0	0	24	2	0
4	223	Buckton & Coxhall	325	0	0	23	10	8
						[32	10	0]
5	169	Brompton Bryan	341	0	0	34	2	0
6	341	Burrington	338	0	0	33	16	0
7	150	Combe & Byton	514	0	0	51	8	0
8	60	Connopp	150	0	0	15	0	0
9	175	Downton	175	0	0	17	10	0
10	149	Elton	260	0	0	26	0	0
11	66	Kinton	192	0	0	19	4	3
						[19	4	0]
12	200	Knill & Harton	368	0	0	36	16	6
						[36	16	0]
13	194	Lenthall Earles	272	0	0	27	4	0
14	261	Lenthall Starkes	415	0	0	41	10	0
15	345	Leintwardine	345	0	0	34	10	4
						[34	10	0]
16	112	Letton & Newton	191	0	0	29	2	1
			[291	0	0]	[29	2	0]
17	175	Lingen & Limebrooke	440	0	0	44	0	0]
18	94	Litton & Cascobb	310	0	0	15	0	0
						[31	0	0]
19	——	Marlow & the Wood	——			——		
20	414	Mowley Waples Eves &c	514	0	0	51	8	6
						[51	8	0]
21	85	Netherly	152	0	0	15	1	4]
						[15	4	0
22	238	Rodd Nash & Brampton	549	0	0	54	18	0
23	302	Steppleton & Frog street	302	0	0	30	4	6]
						[30	4	0
24	138	Pedwardine & Boresford	341	0	0	34	2	5
						[34	2	0]
25	215	Tittley	614	0	0	61	8	0
26	250	Upper & Nether Kinsham	365	0	0	36	10	0
27	97	Walford	258	0	0	25	16	2
						[25	16	0]

K

Wigmore Hundred continued

	Value Returned by the Raters		Value Horse taken out	The valuation according to the contribution	The whole yeares contribution at 2s per pound per annum for each particular parish in the Hundred
28	105	Witton & Trippleton		214 0 0	21 8 0
29	260	Wigmore		346 0 0	34 12 6
					[34 12 0]
30	157	Willey		390 0 0	39 0 0
31	134	Yetton		276 0 0	27 12 0

[Total £981 2s 0d][1]

---

1. Hearth Tax return, Lady Day, 1664:

Wigmore Hundred	Total Charged Hearths	Total Houses	More than 10 hearths *	10	9	8	7	6	5	4	3	2	1	Total Exempt Houses
Adforton	32	27									1	3	23	0
Peyto &c	19	8			1							1	2	3	1
Aston	17	26							1			2	8	15
Aymestrey	60	41						1		3	4	7	16	10
Buckton & Coxhall	24	20				1						2	12	5
Brampton Bryan	36	13	1 (17)						1	1	1	1	5	3
Burrington	62	38				1				2	6	6	16	7
Covenhope	11	14						1				1	3	9
Downton	28	12		1							1	5	5	0
Elton	41	28					2			1	1	3	14	7
Kinton	23	21								1	1	5	6	8
Leinthall Earls	45	19	1 (11)							1	2	4	6	3
Leinthall Starkes	37	18					1		1		3	3	10	0
Leintwardine	82	70						1	1		6	14	25	23
Letton & Newton	25	25								1		4	13	7
Lingen &c	63	68							2	4		6	29	27
Marlow	13	11										1	10	0
Nether Lye	18	19								1	2	1	6	9
Pedwardine &c	31	33									3	1	20	9
Walford	22	16						1			2	3	4	6
Witton &c	23	14					1			1		2	8	2
Wigmore	98	83						1	2	2	6	11	33	28
Yetton	38	30					1			1	2	1	14	11
Total Wigmore Division	848	654	2	1	1	4	4	5	9	16	47	86	289	190
Lugharnes Division	416	266		1		2	3	4	12	9	24	37	103	71
Total	1,264	920	2	2	1	6	7	9	21	25	71	123	392	261

* Actual charge in brackets.

[1.] Atforton [*Peytoe Stanway & Grange*] **&c** (110r)
[*Wg1a*]

	£	s	d		£	s	d
Rich: Parramore²	10	0	0	Jo: Palfrey	2	5	0
Jo: Lane	6	0	0	Jo: Valiance [*Valients*]	1	0	0
Geo: Mitton		12	0	The Tieth of Atforton	17	0	0
Edw: Mitton	6	10	0				
Johan Langford wid	1	10	0	**Peyto Stanway & Grange** [*Wg1b*]			
Tho: Powell	3	0	0	Arth: Cockerham Esq³ h:	160	0	0
Edw: Bridgwater	4	15	0	Wm Smith	20	0	0
Tho: Taylor	4	15	0	Ja: Haddock	6	10	0
Wm Harris	10	5	0	Wm Bridgwater	2	0	0
Tho: Yates [*Gates*]	4	15	0	Rich Sont	2	0	0
Eliz: Garnor wid	2	0	0				
Fra: Edwards wid	3	0	0	Charge 292	0	0	
Jo: Devon [*Devins*]	5	10	0	[*288*	*2*	*0*]	
Ri: Bridgwater	2	10	0				
Wm Bridgwater	2	10	0	Wm Smith, Wm Harris. Raters			
Maudlin Whopper	1	10	0				
Edw: Bridgwater sen	8	5	0	**A 3rd part is to be added to the Valuation**			

---

2. HT 1664 (3).   3. JP 1655; Subs. 1663 (lands £2); HT 1664 (9).

Footnote continued from page 132

The royal aid charges eventually levied each quarter on each parish in this hundred were: Atforton, £10 6s 4d; Aston, £2 [*10s*] 7d; Aymestrey, £6 5s 7d; Buckton &c, £7 17s 4d; Brampton Bryan, £8 5s 7d; Burrington, £8 4s 1d; Combe &c, £12 12s 2d; Downton, £3 2s 10d; Elton, £6 6s; Kinton, £4 10s 10d; Knill &c, £8 19s [*9d*]; Leinthall Earls, £6 12s 1d; Leinthall Starkes, £10 2s 4d; Leintwardine, £8 4s 10d; Letton &c, £7 0s 7d; Lingen &c, £10 14s 10d; Litton &c, £7 [*1s*]; Marlow &c, £3 8s 10d; Mowley &c, £12 12s 2d; Nether Lye, £3 13s 11d; Rodd &c, £12 12s 2d; Stapleton, £9 10s 2d; Pedwardine &c, £7 14s 10d; Titley, £12 12s 2d; Kinsham, £9 10s 2d; Walford, £6 3s 10d; Witton &c, £5 2s 1d; Wigmore, £8 8s; Willey, £9 10s 2d; Yetton, £6 13s 9d; Loan 29/49, pf. 4, no, 69/14. These charges suggest that the figures in the right-hand column of the hundred schedule in Harl. 6766 for Buckton, Letton and Litton are incorrect. Connop was normally taxed with Shobdon in Stretford hundred. While the parish charges as proportions of the hundred charge were mostly the same for the royal aid as for the 1677 assessment, the proportions in Harl. 6766 are not quite the same. A partial explanation of this is the omission of a charge on Marlow, which, if it were the same as the final royal aid charge, would produce a greater similarity. The adjusted hundred total would therefore be about £970.

2. Aston [Wg2]

		£	s	d		£	s	d
Tho: Pooton for &c[4]		10	0	0	Jo: Hamand		13	4
Mr Salway	h:	10	0	0	Ja: Wood		13	4
The Parsonage		15	0	0	Meredith Wilcox		13	0
Tho: Colerick		5	10	0				
Jeffrie Beddoes		4	0	0	Charge	55	0	0
		(111r)						
Tho: Callowhill		2	10	0	Tho: Pooton, Tho: Colerick. Raters.			
Mich: Duson		2	10	0				
Tho: Richards		2	0	0	**The Valuation is to be doubled**			
Ro: Townsend		1	10	0				

3. Aymestrie [and Shirley] [Wg3]

		£	s	d		£	s	d
Roger Garnons gen[5]	h:	28	15	0	Jo: Hanley [Hinley]	7	0	0
Mrs Weaver	h:	17	15	0	Jo: Storr iun	8	0	0
The Tieth		6	0	0	Jo: Griffithes	4	0	0
Jo: Eales		1	0	0	Johan Storre	2	0	0
Edw: Elvell		4	0	0	Johan Woodhouse	2	0	0
Robt Emmett		1	6	8	Tho: Harper	2	0	0
Jo: Tomkins		5	5	0				
The wid Weaver		1	10	0	Charge	99	0	0
Wm Emmett		1	15	0	[104	14	2]	
Walter Nicholas		1	0	0				
Walter Nicholas for &c		4	5	0	Jo: Tomkins, Edw: Elvell, Jo: Storre			
Tho: Harris		1	2	6	jun. Raters.			
Edw: Peyto for &c		4	0	0				
Jo: Storr [Starr] sen		2	0	0	**The Valuation is to be doubled**			

4. Buckton [& Coxhall] [Wg4]

		£	s	d		£	s	d
Sr Edw: Harley Kt	h:	80	0	0	Tho: Stych	5	0	0
Priamus Davies[6]		60	0	0	Wm Palfrey	5	0	0
Benjamin Streater		10	0	0	Fr: Mathewes	2	10	0
		(112r)			Wm Davies	5	0	0
Tho: Barrear		15	0	0				
Ri: Powell		10	0	0	Charge	223	0	0
Tho: Valiance		10	0	0				
Wm Davies		6	0	0	Ri: Powell, Tho: Barwar. Raters.			
Jo: Mathewes		10	0	0				
He: Rudd		5	0	0	**The valuation to be doubled.**			

4. HT 1664 (5).
5. In 1646 the real estate in the county of Roger Garnons was put at £20 a year and his personal estate at £5; Loan 29/15, pf. 2. James Garnons was assessed on lands of £2 and as a recusant in the Subs. 1663; he was charged on 6 hearths in 1664.
6. A former parliamentary officer. HT 1664 (8).

5. Brompton Bryan [Wg5]

		£	s	d		£	s	d
Sr Edw: Harley Kt[7]	h:	140	0	0	Sam: Powell	3	0	0
Ralph Strettalls		11	0	0	Sam: Shilton gen	3	10	0
Tho: Stych for &c		11	0	0	Gleebe Land[8]	2	10	0
Edw: Nesse		11	0	0				
Jo: Lowke		6	0	0	Charge	169	0	0
Jo: Carter		3	10	0		[205	10	0]
Wm Child		3	10	0				
Meredith Evans		2	10	0	Edw: Nesse, Jo: Carter. Raters.			
Fr: Prosser		2	10	0				
Ri: Mellin [Melling]		3	10	0	**The Valuation is to be almost doubled**			
Ra: Jones		2	0	0				

6. Burrington[9] [Wg6]

	£	s	d		£	s	d
Ri: Wright gen	13	10	0	Edw: Collier	11	0	0
Will: Walker gen:				Nunnery grounds	4	0	0
his lands & ten'ts[10]	60	0	0	The wid Pooton	7	0	0
his Iron Workes[11]	30	0	0	Ri: Child	4	0	0
Edward Mathewes gen	26	6	0	Wm Smith	3	0	0
	(113r)			Tho: Colerick	2	0	0
Caleb Wright gen	12	0	0	Wm Lowke	2	0	0
Mrs Johan Gwilt	12	0	0	Burrington Pooles	16	0	0
Mrs Hodges	12	0	0				
The widow Duke	12	0	0	Charge	341	0	0
Roger Lowke	12	0	0		[320	12	0]
Burrington Mills	12	0	0				
Hay Mills	12	0	0	No personall estate except Mr Wakers			
Jo: Aston gen	8	0	0	Iron Mills rated in all Asseassmts at			
Ri: Collier	8	0	0	£30 per annum.			
Tho: Lewis	6	0	0				
Jo: Lowke	6	0	0	Tho: Colerick, Tho: Lowke. Raters.			
Ri: Coles [Cole]	17	16	0				
The wid Adams	6	0	0	**The valuation direct.**			
Jo: Poston	6	0	0				

7. In 1645 the income of Sir Robert Harley (1579–1656), father of Sir Edward, was estimated to be £1,500 a year; Harl. 911. Sir Edward Harley (1624–1700), K.B. 19 Nov. 1660, governor of Dunkirk, 14 July 1660 to 22 May 1661; *DNB*. JP q 1660; DL 1660; a man of keen antiquarian interests; the Harley Papers (Loan 29) show him to have been very active in the administration of the county militia. FP 1661 (£50 paid); Subs. 1663 (lands £20 assessed with Thomas Harley); HT 1664 (17).
8. Thomas Cole, rector, FP 1661 (30s).
9. The largest HT charge in 1664 was on Francis Walker (8).
10. Subs. 1663 (goods £5).
11. Bringewood Forge.

7. Combe & Byton[12]   [Wg7]

		£	s	d
Rich: Rodd Esq	h:	2	10	0
Ja: Price[13]	h:	20	10	0
Fr: Woodhouse & Wm				
Connopp		11	13	4
Jo: Sum'ers		6	0	0
Tho: Cam'ell		8	6	8
Fr: & Hugh Knoke		8	6	8
Jo: Blackpatch [Blackbatch]		3	3	4
Phil: Lewis cler		8	0	0
Owen Hawes cler[14]		10	0	0
Wm Menheire gen	h:	3	6	8
Ja: Woodhouse[15]	h:	25	0	0
Tho: Woodhouse[16]	h:	23	6	8
Tho: Hopwood	h:	5	4	2
Rich: Weaver[17]		16	13	4
		(114r)		
Wm Woodhouse		8	6	8

	£	s	d
Ja: Hoskins	5	4	2
Ri: Hoskins	2	14	2
Wm Hill	5	4	2
Ja: Woodhouse	2	10	0
Jo: Monn [Man]		14	2
Ri: & Wm Woodhouse	2	10	0
Ri: Browne	2	10	0
Ja: Godwyn	2	18	4
Jo: Woodhouse	2	0	0
Charge	150	0	0
	[186	12	6]

Tho: Camell, Ri: Weaver, Wm Woodhouse, Wm Hill. Raters.

3 parts are to be added to the Valuation

8. Connopp   [Wg8]

		£	s	d
Tho: Bridgwaters[18]		15	0	0
Wm Tyler		10	0	0
Tho: Smith		6	0	0
Ri: Cooke		6	0	0
The wid Whillard [Wheeler]		4	0	0
Margery Bull		1	10	0
Anne Woodhouse		2	10	0
The Lo: of the Mannors				
lands	h:	10	0	0

	£	s	d
The Impropriated Tiethes	5	0	0
Charge	60	0	0

Tho: Smith Rater.

2 parts to be added to the Val:

12. The hearth tax return for Lady Day, 1664, contains: (chargeable)—James Pirie (4), Thomas Sammell (2), Francis Knoke (2), Thomas Fletcher (3), Thomas Griffitts (1), Thomas Penny (2), Thomas Bent (1), John Blackbatch (1), Wm Harvy (1), Edward Sammell (1), Elenor Blackbatch (1), Owen Hawes clerke (2), Thomas Woodhouse (5), Richard Weaver (5), James Woodhouse (5), Wm Woodhouse (3), Wm Hill (1), James Woodhouse sen (2), Evan Davies (1), Wm Phillipps (1), Phillip Taylor (1), Wm Woodhouse glover (1), John Man (1), James Evans (1), Henry Willcox (1), Richard Browne (1), Wm Stannage (2); (not chargeable)—Richard Davis (1), Jonas Blayney (1), Richard Dymber (1), Thomas Preece (1), Elenor Phillipps (1), Thomas Morgan (1), David Williams (1), Richard Woodhouse (1), Thomas Griffitts (1), Richard Hinton (1), Thomas Fletcher sen (1); (chargeable hearths 52).
13. Gent., Subs. 1663 (lands £2).
14. Rector, FP 1661 (20s paid).
15. Chief constable of Wigmore, 1663; Loan 29/49, pf. 4, no. 69/15. Subs. 1663 (lands £2).   16. Gent., Subs. 1663 (lands £2).
17. Gent., Subs. 1663 (goods £3).   18. HT 1664 (6).

9. Downton [Wg9]

	£	s	d		£	s	d
Rich: Moore gen	80	0	0	Wm Morris	4	10	0
Will: Beale clarke	20	0	0	Jo: Davies	2	10	0
Sam: Hopkins	15	0	0				
Tho: Langford	15	0	0	Charge	175	0	0
Wm Duke [*Dukes*]	8	0	0				
Sim: Oliver	7	10	0	Sa: Hopkins, Wm Duke. Raters.			
Reece Morris	7	10	0				
Edm: Rusbach[19]	15	0	0	**The valuation direct.**			

10. Elton[20, 21] (115r) [Wg 10]

		£	s	d		£	s	d
Waties Corbett		20	0	0	Tho: Farmer	3	0	0
Sampson Weaver[22]	h:	20	0	0	Jo: Bridgwaters	4	0	0
Wm Williams[23]		25	0	0	Edw: Hopkins	5	0	0
Edw: Norgrove		7	0	0	Jo: Ingram	4	10	0
Jo: Hopkins		10	0	0	The wid Pitt	2	0	0
Jo: Hall		7	0	0	Jo: Knight	2	10	0
Jo: Harris		7	0	0				
Tho: Meredith		7	0	0	Charge	149	0	0
Ja: Haughton		10	0	0				
Jo: Brimell		5	0	0	Wm Williams, Tho: Colcombe. Raters.			
Wm Cooke		5	0	0				
The wid Flavell		5	0	0	**The Valuation is to be doubled**			

11. Kinton [Wg11]

	£	s	d		£	s	d
Tho: Froysell[24]	9	0	0	The wid: Meredith	1	10	0
Ri: Shepherd	7	10	0	Jonas [*Johan*] Watkins	1	10	0
Jo: Griffithes	7	10	0	John Davies	1	0	0
Jo: Powle	8	0	0				
Jo: Langford	7	0	0	Charge	66	0	0
Jo: Payto	7	0	0				
Brian Palphrey	5	0	0	Jo: Powle, Edw: Smallman. Raters.			
Edw: Smallman	5	0	0				
The widow Palfrey[25]	6	0	0	**The Valuation is to be doubled.**			

19. HT 1664 (10).
20. Probably included Patchfield.
21. The largest HT charge in 1664 was on John Mapp (7).
22. Gent., Subs. 1663 (lands £2).
23. Gent., Subs. 1663 (lands £2).
24. HT 1664 (4).
25. Margery Palfrey.

12. Knill [and Harton][26] &c   (116r)   [Wg12]

	£	s	d		£	s	d
Jo: Walsham Esq & Marg:				Jane Preece	1	0	0
Walsham[27] h:	66	6	8	Jo: Gough		10	0
Jo: Loyde & Roger Loyde				Hugh Paine	4	0	0
[Lyde][28]	20	0	0	Herb: Weston Esq	5	0	0
Rich: Knill	9	0	0	Griffith Paine	6	0	0
Tho: Davies	1	0	0	Rich: Knill	2	0	0
Roul' Stephens	6	10	0	Jo: Miles	3	10	0
Fr: Owen	1	10	0	Ri: Scaundrett	1	10	0
Ja: Rodd	2	13	4	Tho: Price	5	10	0
Tho: Scudmore	6	10	0	Hugh Gwin	3	10	0
Henr: Pyvinch	1	0	0				
Jo: Baugh Esq	3	10	0	Charge 200 0 0			
Jo: Lyde	4	0	0	[278 10 0]			
Tho: Woodcoke gen[29]	80	0	0				
Roger Lyde	10	0	0	Rowland Stephens, Tho: Powell Gough,			
Elinor Lyde	10	0	0	Jo: James. Raters.			
Barbara Walsham	10	0	0				
Anne Morris	9	0	0	**About a third parte is to be added to the**			
Jo: James	5	0	0	**valuation**			

13. Lenthall Earles[30]   (117r)   [Wg13]

	£	s	d			£	s	d
Herbert Lo: Bp of Hereff h:	20	0	0	Ro: Davies gen	h:	20	0	0
The La: Eure for &c[31] h:	60	0	0	Ja: Pitts wid		20	0	0

26. Included Lower Harpton; Upper Harpton was in Radnorshire. The hearth tax return for Lady Day, 1664, contains: Knill (chargeable)—John Walsham Esq (5), John Watkins (2), Roger Lide (3), Rowland Stephens (1), Richard Knill (1), Jenkin Knill (2), Francis Stephens (1), Edward Griffiths (1); (not chargeable)—John Thomas (1), Thomas Dayos (1), Roger Lewis (1), Wm Reece (1); (chargeable hearths 16). Herton (chargeable)—Thomas Woodcock (6), Mary Bull widow (3), Elenor Lyde widow (1), Ann Morrice vid (1), John James (1), Hugh Paine (1), James Prees (1), Richard Bull (1), John Pricherd (1); (not chargeable)—Thomas Powell Gough (1), Edward Powell Gough (1), Wm Jones (1), John Gough (1), Richard James (1), Herbert Jorden (1), Elizabeth Williams (1); (chargeable hearths 16).
27. Subs. 1663 (lands £3).
28. Roger Lyde, Subs. 1663 (lands £2).   29. Subs. 1663 (lands £4).
30. In 1646 Sir Sampson Eure's real estate was valued at £60 a year and his personal estate at £10; Loan 29/15, pf. 2. Lady Eure was charged on 11 hearths in 1664. A survey and assessment in 1666 for the additional aid gave these valuations: Lady Ewers £80, Tho. Oakeley £35 10s, James Land £8 15s, Rich. Browne and his tenants £35 10s, The Old Field £28 10s, Mr Rob. Davis £24 10s, Math. Langford for the Lo. Bishop's land £21 10s, Mr Rob. Tayler for the Mynd £2 10s, Mr John Davis and his sonne £21 10s, Clarkes tithes £17 10s, Tho. Croone £14, Mary Hopkins wid £12 5s, John Beddoes £4 5s, Sheappards lands £4 15s, Edw. Edwards £2 10s, John Elliotts £1 15s, Mr Whittle for tithes £5 5s; total £320; Hereford CRO, Gatley Park MSS. The 1677 assessment on half the 'new' quota appears at £13 7s 10d to follow the charge in Harl. 6766 rather than the 1666 revaluation: E.179/119/490.
31. Widow of Sir Sampson Eure, former attorney in Wales, who bought Gatley Park from the Crofts in circa 1634 and who died in 1659. Subs. 1663 (lands £3). She died in 1673; Robinson, p. 172.

Wigmore: Lenthall Earles continued

	£	s	d
Jo: Davies gen[32]	15	0	0
Jo: Beddoes	3	0	0
Tho: Croone senr	10	0	0
Tho: Clarke sen	15	0	0
Jo: Browne	15	0	0
Tho: Clarke	3	0	0
Ri: Griffith	2	0	0
Mary Hopkins & her sonne	10	0	0

Jo: Davies, Tho: Okeley.[33] Raters.

A 3rd part is to be added to ye Valuation

		£	s	d
Charge		194	0	0
		[*193	*0	*0*]

---

14. Leinthall Starkes   [*Wg14*]

	£	s	d			£	s	d
The Lo: Bp of Hereff	10	0	0		Hugh Dale	10	0	0
The Lady Eure	10	0	0		Rich: Bridgwater	26	0	0
Mr Goodier [*Goodyeare*][34]	60	0	0		Rich: Phlaven [*Flavell*]	10	0	0
Tho: Bridgwater	30	0	0		Edw: Allen	20	0	0
Mr Clogie cler	20	0	0		Sr Walter Long Kt[35]	6	0	0
Rich: Clarke for Tieth Hay	5	0	0					
Tho: Bridgwater	25	0	0		Charge	261	0	0
Wm Colerick	10	0	0					
Jo: Wright	2	10	0		Hugh Dale, Edw: Allen. Raters.			
Eliz: Dale [*Dalle*] wid	5	0	0					
Jo: Dale of Leintwardine	12	0	0		**Someth: is to be added to the Valuation**			

---

15. Leintwardine[36]   (118r)   [*Wg15*]

		£	s	d			£	s	d
The Lo: Cravens Estate there[37]	**p:**	84	0	0		Jo: James Esq his tenm'ts **h:**	6	0	0
Sr Edwd Harleys Tieth	**h:**	10	10	0		Jo: Dale	2	0	0
The Vicaridg Tieth		7	0	0		Ri: Dale	6	10	0
Ri: Bytheway & his sonne **h:**		50	0	0		The wid Bowyer	13	0	0
						Edw: Soly gen	7	10	0

---

32. Subs. 1663 (lands here and in Cowarne £2).   33. HT 1664 (6).
34. In 1646 his real estate in the county was put at £40 a year and personal estate at £19; Loan 29/15, pf. 2.
35. Probably Sir Walter Long of Whaddon, Wilts, created baronet 26 March 1661, died 1672; *Baronetage*, iii, p. 181.
36. In 1664 an assessment on Leintwardine parish for church repairs charged the constituent townships: Walford £6 9s; Adforton £6 2s 10d; Peyto £4 5s; Letton and Newton £7 15s 3d; Witton and Trippleton £5 18s 9d; Kinton £4 9s; Marlow and the Wood £3 8s 6½d; Leintwardine £9 6s 9d; Broxop and Brakes £2 5s 5d; Jay and Heath £3 17s 10d. Even if the last two townships are assumed to be included in the Leintwardine militia return, this church lewn was distributed differently from the militia valuations. Church assessments may well have been conventionally based on township allocations rather than rated equally across the parish; Hereford CRO, Diocesan Archives, Court Papers, I. and O.P., Box 485.
37. William, Earl Craven, 1606–1697 (*DNB*); his manor of Leintwardine had been bought by Robert Thorpe (*CCC*, ii, p. 1625), but he had apparently recovered it.

Wigmore: Leintwardine continued

	£	s	d		£	s	d
Wm Harley	1	1	0	Walter Woolaston	1	10	0
Geo: Lambe	8	10	0	Tho: Clarke	3	10	0
Tho: Heath	8	0	0	Ja: Duppa	2	13	4
Edw: Morris	6	13	4	Tho: Morris	3	10	0
Fr: Heath	2	0	0	Roger Bird	2	6	0
Brian Tailer	2	6	8	Tho: Hale	1	6	8
Tho: Bridgwaters	2	0	0	Tho: Clarke	1	6	8
The wid Hale [*Hall*]	6	0	0				
The wid Hooper	3	6	8	Charge[38]	345	0	0
The wid Davies	3	6	8		[*271*	*6*	*4*]
Tho: Durning	4	0	0				
Edw: Durning	2	6	0	peeres land belonging to the Lo: Craven			
Ro: Sayce	4	0	0	£84			
Ri: Mitton	2	6	8				
Ro: Owens	2	13	4	Ri: Bytheway, Geo: Lambe, Edw: Mor-			
Tho: Langford	2	13	4	ris. Raters.			
Julian Lawrence & Math:							
Clent	7	10	0	**The valuation direct**			

16. Letton [*and Newton*] &c   (119r)   [*Wg16*]

	£	s	d			£	s	d
Ri: Botfield gen[39]	30	0	0	Ro: Davies gen	**h:**	3	10	0
Jo: Pope	17	0	0	Ri: Langford		3	10	0
Edw: Blashfield	7	10	0	The tythe &c		5	0	0
Tho: Tayler	7	13	4	Tho: Taylor for &c		1	10	0
The wid Loyde	7	0	0					
Tho: Grenouse [*Green'ho:se*]				Charge		112	0	0
& Ja: Duppa	5	10	0			[*120*	*13*	*4*]
Tho: Tirpin	5	10	0					
Lewis Jones	3	10	0	Ri: Botfield, Edw: Wigmore. Raters.				
Edw: Wigmore gen	8	0	0					
Jo: Wharton	8	0	0	**The Valuation is to be doubled**				
Jo: Owens	7	10	0					

17. Lingen [*and Limebrooke*] &c[40]   [*Wg17*]

		£	s	d		£	s	d
Mary Wilkes wid		4	0	0	Phil: Brians	8	0	0
Tho: Davies gen	**h:**	12	0	0	Anne Powell wid	5	0	0
Johan Yapp wid		1	10	0	Ri: Carter	5	0	0
Jo: Cooke	**h:**	20	0	0	Tho: Brians	3	0	0
Tho: Tailer	**h:**	20	0	0	Addam Godwyn	1	10	0
Ch: Cooke		12	0	0	Tho: Williams & Da:			
Fr: Young		12	0	0	Meredith for Tith	14	0	0
Wm Davies[41]		12	0	0	Tho: Williams	1	0	0

38. The largest HT charge in 1664 was on the widow Harper (6).
39. Subs. 1663 (lands £2); HT 1664 (4).
40. The largest HT charges in 1664 were on William Rodd, gent., and John Cocke (4 each).   41. Will proved 19 June 1664 (PCC).

Wigmore: Lingen [and Limebrooke] &c continued

	£	s	d		£	s	d
David Meredith	1	0	0	Elner Dillow & Fr: Young	1	10	0
Abr: Mailard	4	0	0	Ri: Ward	1	10	0
Edm: Cooke	4	0	0	Jacob Greene	3	10	0
		(120r)		Edw: Legge for &c		10	0
Elinor Cooke	4	0	0	David Meredith for &c[42]	2	0	0
Katherine Clarke for &c **h:**	3	0	0				
Ja: Davies	3	0	0	Charge	175	0	0
Wm Clarke	3	0	0		[169	10	0]
Ro: Baker & Jo: Prothero	3	0	0				
Edw: Rider for &c	2	0	0	Wm Davies, Tho: Brians. Raters.			
Jo: Clarke	2	10	0	**The Valuation more then doubled**			

18. Litton *[and Cascobb]* **&c**[43]   [*Wg18*]

	£	s	d		£	s	d
Jo: Williams	9	0	0	Joh: Hold [*Howld*] wid &			
Rees Davies [*Davids*]	9	0	0	her sonne	7	0	0
Meredith Davies	9	0	0	Edw: Powell Gough	7	0	0
Hugh Pugh	4	10	0	Jo: Phillipps	8	0	0
Elinor Pugh wid	6	0	0	He: Holde	2	0	0
Elinor Morris wid	3	0	0	Hugh Stephens	2	0	0
Jo: Davies for &c	2	10	0				
Jo: Davies & Morg: Tho:				Charge	94	0	0
for tieth	3	10	0				
Marg: Grenous	4	0	0	Ja: Meredith, Hugh Pugh. Raters.			
Joh: Pugh wid	2	0	0				
Edw: Holde cler for his tieth	9	0	0	**Almost 2 partes are to be added to the Val:**			
Ja: Meredith	7	0	0				

19. Marlow *[and the Wood]* **&c** (121r)   [*Wg19*]

	£	s	d		£	s	d
Hen: Croone	7	0	0	Edw: Lawrence	2	10	0
Ri: Galliars	5	0	0				
Jo: Pierce[44]	7	0	0	Charge	43	0	0
The wid Wilding	4	0	0				
Edw: Morris	7	0	0	Ri: Galliers, He: Croone. Raters.			
Ri: Galliers	7	0	0				
The wid Bluck	3	10	0	**The Valuation is to be doubled**			

42. Subs. 1663 (goods £3).
43. The hearth tax return for Lady Day, 1664, contains: (chargeable)—John Williams (1), Reese Davis (2), John Davis (1), Elenor Pugh (3), Henry Hurston (1), Meredith Davis (1), Thomas Howld (4), Johan Howld (2), James Meredith (1), Edward Powell Gough (3), Edward Howld clerke (2), Elenor Morris widow (2), Hugh Pugh (2), Peter Pugh (1), Lewis Jones (1), Marga: Thomas (1), Evan Jenkin (1); (not chargeable)—Thomas Meredith (1), Phillip Morris (1), Howell Prees (1), Hugh ap Thomas (1), David Morgan (1), John Prichard (1), Thomas Sherman (1), Miles Evans (1); (chargeable hearths 29).   44. HT 1664 (3).

20. Mowley [*Waples Eves &c*] &c[45, 46]   [*Wg20*]

	£	s	d		£	s	d
Ri: Wigmore gen his tieth **h:**	14	10	0	Elinor Stead[49]	2	10	0
Andr: Greenely gen **h:**	19	0	0	Ro: Woodhouse	17	10	0
Walter Frizer	99	10	0			(122r)	
Jo: Greenely	99	10	0	Henry Taylor	1	6	8
Ja: Ashley [*Astley*] for &c[47]	19	13	4	Mary Stead	1	10	0
James Ashley	16	0	0	Wm Beavan	1	0	0
Phil: Greenely	10	0	0	Sim: Griffithes	1	0	0
Wil: Fletcher **h:**	10	0	0	Peter King	1	0	0
Jo: Fletcher	15	0	0	Jo: Phillipps	1	10	0
Da: Lochard	8	15	0	Rees Lewis	2	5	0
Jo: Badland & Peter Wikes[48]	16	15	0	Jane Godwin	1	0	0
Alice Godwyn	17	15	0	Jam: Fletcher		16	8
Wm Wall gen **h:**	6	13	4	Tho: Lewis		16	8
Wa: Knight	2	15	0	Wm Fletcher & Jo: Wood-			
Jo: Steenton	2	5	0	house	4	10	0
Tho: Lewis for &c	5	16	8				
Tho: & Mich: Hoskins	2	5	0	Charge	414	0	0
Ri: Bebb cler	5	0	0	[*416*	*1*	*8*]	
Eliz: Lawrence	1	3	4				
Ja: Thomas	1	0	0	Ja: Ashtley [*Ashley*], Walt^r Frizer.			
Miles Thomas for &c	1	0	0			Raters.	
Jo: Brians	2	10	0				
Wm Fletcher	2	10	0	**A 5th part is to be added to the Val:**			

---

21. Nether Lye   [*Wg21*]

	£	s	d		£	s	d
Will: Phillipps[50]	20	0	0	Wm Tyler	11	10	0
Jo: Tyler[51]	11	10	0	Tho: Browne	7	0	0
Sampson Grubb	11	10	0	Jo: Jones	7	0	0

---

45. The hearth tax return for Lady Day, 1664, contains: (chargeable)—Andrew Greenly (5), Phillip Greenly (5), John Fletcher (1), Edward Hudson (2), Francis Ricards (1), Symon Griffitts (1), James Astley (5), John Hunt (6), Phillipp Bleeke(1), Robert Woodhouse (4), Walter Frizer (3), John Greenly (1), Thomas Fletcher (1), Elenor Steade (1), Thomas Lewis (1), Wm Fletcher (1), Wm Frizer (2), Wm Bevan jun (1), David Lochard (1), John Badland (4), Henry Williams (4), Mary Stead (1), Beniamin Bryan (2), James Bevan (1), John Stinson (1), Peter Kinge (1), John Phillipps (1); (not chargeable)—James Thomas (1), Wm Bevan (1), Elizabeth Higgins (1), Thomas Greenly (1), Richard Powell (1), Wm Glover (1), Sibill Greenley (1), Thomas Davis (1), Edward Greenly (1), Thomas Godwyn (1), Richard Phillipps —, Wm Tuder (1), John Bevan (1), Robert Morris (1), Thomas Parker (1); (chargeable hearths 58).
46. Anne Hunt was assessed to the Subs. 1663 on lands of £3 (on 1 May).
47. Of Ashley and of Bircher; will proved 1671 (PCC).
48. This estate was the subject of a marriage settlement in 1656; Hereford City Lib., Local Collection. Subs. 1663 (lands £2).
49. Of Stansbach; will proved 1672 (Hereford).
50. Subs. 1663 (lands £2); HT 1664 (4).   51. Subs. 1663 (lands £2).

Wigmore: Nether Lye continued

	£	s	d
The Lady Lingen for &c **h:**	20	0	0

Wm Phillipps, Jo: Brunt. Raters.

Charge	85	0	0
	[*88*	*10*	*0*]

**A 3rd parte to be added to the
Valuation**

---

22. Rodd [*Nash & Brampton*] &c[52]

Rodd [*Wg22a*]	£	s	d
Ri: Rodd gen[53]	65	0	0
Edm: Gough gen	12	0	0
Wa: Evans & Ja: Lyde	12	0	0
Ja: Rodd for &c[54]	8	0	0
Ja: Rodd for &c[55]	2	0	0
Tho: Rodd for &c	5	0	0
	(123r)		
Nash [*Wg22b*]			
Jo: Gough for &c[56]	30	0	0
Will: Connopp for &c	8	0	0
Jo: Lyde[57]	13	0	0
Tamberlaine Passey & Da:			
Passey	8	0	0
Roger Badland[58]	4	0	0
Charge	63	0	0

Brompton [*Little Brampton*]	£	s	d
[*Wg22c*]			
Fra: Owen[59]	32	0	0
Jo: Browne & Wm Browne[60]	17	0	0
Hen: Pyvinch	8	10	0
Tamberlaine Passy for &c	6	10	0
Ri: Lyde	5	10	0
Tho: Skydmore [*Scudamore*]	1	0	0
Mr Phillip Lewis cler for			
Tieth[61]	10	10	0
Charge	238	0	0
	[*248*	*0*	*0*]

Francis Owen, Hen: Pyvinch. Raters.

The Valuation is to be doubled

---

52. The hearth tax return for Lady Day, 1664, contains: Rodd (chargeable)—
Richard Rodd Esq (10), James Rodd (3), Walter Evans (2), John Lyde (1); Nash,
(chargeable)—Henry Pyvinch (5), John Lyde (3), Wm Connopp (4), Roger Badland
(2), Richard Stead (1), Evan Watkins (2); Brampton, (chargeable)—Francis Owen
(5), John Browne (3), Henry Pyvinch (3), Richard Lyde (1), Tamberlaine Passey (1),
Thomas Scudamore (2), Peter Lewis (1), Mr Owens mill (1); Rodd, Nash & Brampton, (not chargeable)—Evan Powell (1), John Rees (1), Richard Lewis (1), Ann
Thomas (1), Elenor Powell (1), Sibill Powell (1), Margaret Meredith ap John (1),
Wm Thomas (1), Edward Woodhouse (1), Wm Trooper (1), Joan Ashley (1), John
Clerke (1), David Steephens (1); (chargeable hearths 49 struck through becoming
50).
53. His real estate in 1646 was valued at £80; Loan 29/15, pf. 2. Subs. 1663 (lands
£3).
54. For Heads land.
55. For Passey's estate.   56. Possibly Baugh.
57. Subs. 1663 (lands £2).
58. (1610–1694), brother of John Badland of Staunton.
59. Subs. 1663 (lands £2).
60. Subs. 1663 (for Massey's land £2).
61. Vicar of Presteigne from 1660. He gave £20 to the FP 1661 and is there described
as rector, although it is likely that he did not recover the rectory until 1664; Lord
Rennell of Rodd, *Valley on the March* (London, 1958), p. 246.

23. Steppleton [and Frog street]⁶² [Wg23]

		£	s	d		£	s	d
Tho: Cornewall Esq⁶³	h:	70	0	0	Jo: Price gen	15	0	0
Ro: Weaver gen	h:	60	0	0				
Giles Whittall gen⁶⁴		40	0	0	Charge	302	0	0
Wm Jones gen		30	0	0	[307	0	0]	
Ro: Young⁶⁵		15	0	0				
Edw: Hill⁶⁶ & Ri: Hill⁶⁷		14	0	0	Wm Jones, Jo: Price. Raters.			
The Tieth		20	0	0				
Mrs Bridgett & Eliz: Jones		25	0	0	The valuation direct			
Mrs Dorothy Rodd wid⁶⁸		18	0	0				

(124r)
24. Pedwardine [& Boresford] &c [Wg24]

	£	s	d		£	s	d
Tho: Child⁶⁹	20	0	0	Tho: Crumpe	5	0	0
Fr: Rudd	5	0	0	Jo: Powell	4	0	0
Wm Lowke	5	0	0	Jane Powell wid	3	0	0
Jo: Prince	6	0	0	The wid Carters Land	2	0	0
Tho: Rudd	5	0	0	Tho: Collins	3	0	0
Alice Bankes wid	5	0	0	The wid Crumps Land	5	0	0
Kath: Williams wid	5	0	0	Tho: Rogers for &c⁷⁰	10	0	0
Ri: Lucas	8	0	0				
Jonathan Smith	10	0	0	Charge	138	0	0
Ri: Gough	2	0	0	[147	10	0]	
Stannardine Rudd	7	0	0				
Ri: Millichapp	20	0	0	Ri: Lucas, Tho: Crumpe. Raters.			
Tho: Lingen	12	0	0				
Lewis Pritchard	4	0	0	The Valuation is to be above doubled			
Tho: Carter	1	10	0				

62. The hearth tax return for Lady Day, 1664, contains: (chargeable)—Thomas Cornewall Esq (8), Wm Jones gent (7), John Price gent (7), Thomas Wheeler (3), Richard Gronows (2), Robert Younge (3), Wm Ruston (1), John Hill (2), John Younge (1), Robert Clerke (2), Richard Rodd gent (1), James Ruffe (1), Thomas Younge (2), Wm Pyvynch (1), Edward Hill (2), Richard Hill (1), Thomas Vaughan (1), John Fox (1), Thomas Davis (1), Peter Younge (1); (not chargeable)—none; (chargeable hearths 48).
63. Baron of Burford, lord of the manor of Stapleton; JP q 1660. Subs. 1663 (lands £6). A manorial rentroll of 1681 shows that his rents from Stapleton and Frogstreet were lesst han £13 a year; Shrewsbury Borough Library Deeds 2603.
64. Subs. 1663 (lands £2).
65. Will proved 1669 (Hereford).
66. Yeoman, will proved 1682 (Hereford), inventory £118.
67. Yeoman, brother of Edward, will proved 1669 (Hereford).
68. Will proved 1666 (PCC).
69. HT 1664 (3).
70. HT 1664 (3).

25. Titley[71]   [Wg25]

		£	s	d		£	s	d
Tho: Traunter gen	h:	72	0	0	Walter Higgins	1	0	0
Andr: Greenely gen[72]	h:	26	13	4	Mary Bird	1	6	4
Jo: Knight gen[73]		26	18	4	Tho: Abraham	3	6	8
Wm Passey gen[74]		22	13	4	Walter Knight de Flinsham	1	6	4
Wm Scaundret gen		12	0	0	Jenkin Lewis	2	0	0
Edw: Greenowes		8	0	0	Tho: Foxall	4	10	0
Will: Wolfe[75]		10	0	0	Mary Godwin	1	0	0
		(125r)			James Ashley	11	0	0
Marg: Search wid		6	0	0	Sim: Griffithes	1	6	4
Edm: Thomas		6	0	0	Walter Knight	7	6	8
John Grimes [Greyms]		6	0	0	St Mary Colledg of			
Tho: Pace[76]		17	6	8	Winchester[78]	20	0	0
Jo: Traunter		4	13	4	The Lo: Farmer of the Priory	12	0	0
Jo: Davies		4	13	4				
Humph: Mills & Jo: Davies		10	13	4	Charge	215	0	0
Wm Greenely		10	0	0		[325	13	8
Phil: Greeneley of Mowley		6	10	0				
Rees [Rice] Evans		1	0	0	Jo: Knight, Wm Passey. Raters			
Anne Passy[77]		1	6	4				
Will: Rodd		6	13	4	**The Valuation is to be doubled**			

---

71. The hearth tax return for Lady Day, 1664, contains: (chargeable)—Thomas Traunter gent. (7), Andrew Greenley gent. (5), John Knight jun (6), Wm Passey (5), Wm Scandrett (4), John Greyms (3), Edward Greenous (3), Richard Hill (3), Wm Wolfe (1), John Watkins (3), Wm Rodd (2), Anne Passy (1), John Davis (2), Walter Higgins (1), Wm Griffitts (1), Mary Byrd (1), Mary Godwyn (1), Evan Powell (1), Symon Higgins (1), Phillipp Davies (1), John Deykes (1), Wm Greenly (2), John Williams (1), Thomas Foxall (1), George Llewellyn (2), Rice Evans (1), Jenkin Lewis (1), Richard Greenley (1), John Angell (1); (not chargeable)—none; (chargeable hearths 63).
72. Subs. 1663 (lands £2).
73. Subs. 1663 (lands £2).
74. Subs. 1663 (lands £2).
75. Buried 20 Aug. 1665.
76. Thomas Parris *alias* Pace, administration granted 19 Oct. 1665 (Hereford).
77. Buried 18 May 1665.
78. Titley manor extended over the eastern part of the parish; it had belonged to Winchester College since the early 15th century; Winchester College MSS.

26. Upper & Nether Kinsham[79]   [Wg26]

		£	s	d
Tho: Cornewall Esq[80]	h:	8	0	0
Ri: Rodd Esq for &c	h:	45	0	0
The said Ri: Rodd for &c	h:	10	0	0
The said Ri: Rodd for &c	h:	3	0	0
The said Ri: Rodd for &c	h:	2	0	0
The said Ri: Rodd for &c	h:	1	0	0
Tho: Blayney Esq[81]	h:	30	0	0
		(126r)		
Tho: Wheeler		8	0	0
Ja: Woodhouse		8	0	0
Tho: Tyler		8	0	0
Roger Dirrand [Derand or Dirrance]		5	0	0
Giles Whittall for &c		14	0	0
The said Giles for &c		5	0	0
Ro: Hibbins		4	0	0
Ri: Mason		4	0	0

	£	s	d
Jo: Hunt[82]	6	0	0
Mary Fortescue for &c[83]	15	0	0
Wm Symes [Sims]	5	0	0
Jo: Duppa	3	0	0
Jo: Smith	3	0	0
Ja: Price	3	0	0
Tho: Guilbert	1	0	0
Owen Hawes cler	5	0	0
Charge	250	0	0
[196	0	0]	

Ri: Grenowes,[84] Tho: Wheeler. Raters.

Almost a 3rd part is to be added to the Valuation

27. Walford   [Wg27]

	£	s	d
Sr Edward Harley Kt	30	0	0
Jo: Rusbach[85]	15	0	0
Jane Marsden[86]	20	0	0
Tho: Stych iun[87]	12	0	0
Tho: Stych sen	8	0	0
Tho: Mason	3	10	0
Jo: Prince	3	10	0
Anne Lane	3	0	0

	£	s	d
Jane Everall	2	0	0
Charge	27	0	0
[97	0	0]	

Tho: Stych sen, Tho: Stych jun. Raters.

The Valuation is to be doubled

79. The hearth tax return for Lady Day, 1664, contains: (chargeable)—Thomas Blayney Esq (8), Richard Greenhouse (6), Wm Price (1), James Woodhouse (3), Ralph Tippins (2), Roger Derand (1), — Hunt widow (1), Wm Davis (1), Phillipp Hew (1), Henry Brians (1), James Price (1), Anthony Harris jun (1), Bridget Tyler widow (1), John Smith (1), John Duppa (1), Wm Sims (1), Anthony Harris sen (1), James Starr (2), Anthony Tippins (1), Richard Mason (1), Robert Yabins (1), Luke Hanford (1), Thomas Wheeler (4), John Derand (2), Richard Derand (1); (not chargeable)—Johan Jenkins (1), Sibill Walton (1), Stephen Meredith (1), Elenor Edwards (1), Richard Price (1), Margaret Harris (1), John Phillipps (1), Joshuah Davis (1); (chargeable hearths 45).
80. Lord of Kinsham manor; in 1681 his rents therefrom totalled £1; Shrewsbury Borough Library Deeds 2603.
81. JP 1660; FP 1661 (£6 13s 4d paid); Subs. 1663 (lands £2). Buried 10 Jan. 1666/7.
82. Buried 6 Dec. 1663; will proved 11 Mar. 1663/4 (PCC); he owned land in Kinsham, Mowley and in Worcestershire and Warwickshire.
83. Subs. 1663 (goods £3).   84. Subs. 1663 (lands £2).
85. clerk.   86. Subs. 1663 (lands £2).   87. HT 1664 (6).

(127r)

28. Witton [*and Trippleton*] **&c**   [*Wg28*]

		£	s	d		£	s	d
Jo: James Esq[88]	h:	50	0	0	Ri: Okeley	4	0	0
Wm Smith		5	0	0	The Tieth	5	0	0
Ri: Edwards		2	0	0				
Tho: Bowen		12	0	0	Charge	105	0	0
Wm Collier		11	0	0				
Wm Holland		5	0	0	Tho: Bowen, Wm Holland. Raters.			
Walter Harris		5	0	0				
Tho: Colcombe		6	0	0	**The Valuation is to be doubled**			

---

29. Wigmore   [*Wg29*]

		£	s	d		£	s	d
Sr Edward Harley Kt of					Wm Winde	2	0	0
&c[89]	h:	150	0	0	The Lady Long	2	0	0
Tho: Davies gen[90]		27	0	0	Roger Low	3	0	0
Tho: Tirpin [*Turpin*]		5	0	0	Tho: Mason	2	10	0
Wm Rickards [*Richards*] gen		10	0	0	Ri: Hoskins	3	10	0
Mrs Johan Bond wid		8	0	0	Hugh Harris	3	10	0
Tho: Dewsall		3	10	0	Mr Alexander Clogie vicar	8	0	0
Tho: Bridgwaters		5	0	0				
Tho: Millichapp		10	0	0	Charge	260	0	0
Anne Lewis wid		4	0	0				
Fra: Abbotts wid		2	10	0	Tho: Millichapp, Tho: Bridgwaters.			
Wm Lewis		3	0	0	Raters.			
Arnold Gilley[91]		2	10	0				
Ri: Hopkins		2	10	0	**Something added to the Valuation**			
Ri: Clarke		2	10	0				

---

30. Willey[92]   (128r)   [*Wg30*]

	£	s	d		£	s	d
Mrs Bridgett & Eliz: Jones	4	0	0	Edm: & Tho: Legge	15	0	0
Jo: Vaughan & his mother[93]	15	0	0	Edm: Hackluit	20	0	0
Ri: Millichapp[94]	20	0	0	Jo: Powell	13	0	0

---

88. Sheriff 1649; *custos rotulorum* 1655; S.P. 18/95/72 (ii). FP 1661 (£10 unpaid); Subs. 1663 (lands £4); HT 1664 (8).   89. HT 1664 (7).   90. HT 1664 (7). 91. With Richard Hopkins he was charged to the Subs. 1663 on lands of £3. 92. The hearth tax return for Lady Day, 1664, contains: (chargeable)—Charles Vaughan (3), John Vaughan (4), Roger Prosser (3), Thomas Childe (3), Edward Legge (2), Richard Millichopp (5), Edmund Hacklett (3), John Powell (2), Wm Paine (1), Wm Gittins (2), Owen Powell (3), John Woodhouse (1), Peter Hill (3), Thomas Davis (2), Walter Powell (2); (not chargeable)—David Prees (1), Henry Kedward (1), Lucy Davies widow (1), Alice Griffiths (1), John Higgs (1); (chargeable hearths 39).   93. Elizabeth Vaughan of Stocking, Subs. 1663 (lands £1). 94. Subs. 1663 (lands £2).

Wigmore: Willey continued

	£	s	d		£	s	d
Edw: Legge iun	7	0	0	Jo: Price	2	0	0
Will: Paine[95]	7	0	0	Ri: Millichapp for &c	3	0	0
Will: Gittins for &c	7	0	0				
Ri: Strangwell	6	0	0				
Owen ap Howell [Powell]	6	0	0	Charge	157	0	0
Jo: Woodhouse	6	0	0		[142	0	0]
Walter Powell	7	0	0	Phillip Lewis, Edw: Legge. Raters.			
Flory Tyler	2	0	0				
Hugh Grenous	2	0	0	The Valuation is to be doubled			

31. Yetton   [Wg31]

		£	s	d	
Mrs Weavers estate[96]	h:	60	0	0	
Jo: Tyler gen		15	0	0	
Hen: Tyler iun		15	0	0	
Ro: Taylor[97]		15	0	0	Sampson Weaver, Tho: Croone. Raters.
Edw: Woodyatt		2	0	0	
Wm Phillipps		3	0	0	The Valuation is to be doubled
Tho: Budgett		4	0	0	
The Tyth	h:	15	0	0	
	Charge	134	0	0	
		[129	0	0]	

95. Subs. 1663 (goods £3).
96. Anne Weaver, Subs. 1663 (lands £3). Robert Weaver Esq bore the largest charge to the HT 1664 (8).
97. Chief constable of Wigmore, 1663; Loan 29/49, pf. 4, no. 69/15.

Wolphey Hundred[1]

	Value Returned by the Raters		Value Horse Being Taken out	The Value according to the contribution			The whole years contribution at 2s per pound per annum for each particular parish in this Hundred		
	£			£	s	d	£	s	d
1.	241	Brimfield		512	0	0	51	4	0
2.	—	Croft		196	3	0	19	13	4
3.	478	Eaton &c		567	0	0	56	14	0
4.	208	Edvin Ralph		371	10	0	37	3	0
5.	790	Eye parish		1474	10	0	147	9	0
6.	94	Farlow		132	10	0	13	5	4
7.	490	Hatfield & Docklow		941	8	0	94	2	8
8.	462	Hope Hampton Winsley		682	0	0	68	4	0
9.	207	Humber		427	10	0	42	15	0
10.	154	Hide Hill Wintercot		454	0	0	45	8	0
11.	717	Ivington Brierly &c		1044	0	0	104	8	0
12.	461	Kimbolton		928	10	0	92	17	0
13.	146	Laisters		248	6	0	24	16	8
14.	895	Leominster		999	12	0	99	12	0
15.	250	Little Dilwin &c		690	6	0	60	18	8
				[609	0	0]			
16.	543	Little Hereford		682	10	0	68	0	0
17.	228	Lucton & Eyton		560	0	0	56	0	4
18.	200	Ludford		160	10	0	16	1	0
19.	258	Midleton		618	13	0	61	17	4
20.	162	Newchurch &c		470	0	0	47	0	0
21.	301	Orleton		712	6	0	71	4	0
22.	315	Richards Castle		332	0	0	33	4	0
23.	150	Rochford		253	18	0	25	7	8
24.	170	Sarnsfeeld		419	0	0	41	8	4
25.	320	Stagbach & Cholst:		621	10	0	62	3	4
26.	270	Stoake Prior &c		709	6	0	70	18	8
27.	145	Upton		231	3	0	23	2	4
28.	429	Warton & Newton		704	10	0	70	9	0
29.	—	While		—			—		
30.	232	Yarpoole		196	3	0	19	13	4

[*Total £1625*]

---

1. The proportions of the hundred charge allotted to the individual parishes are not the same as those of 1677.

[*Footnote continued on page 150*

1. Brimfield[2]　　　　(130r)　　　　　　　　　　[Wp1]

	£	s	d			£	s	d
Tho: Marston	29	0	0	Johan Lingen		7	0	0
Hercules Underhill	22	0	0	Jo: Baker		12	10	0
Ri: Perkes	16	0	0	Tho: Hunt sen		15	0	0
Will: Connopp	12	0	0	Anth: Bird		4	0	0
Tho: Hemming	9	0	0	Tho: Hunt iun		8	0	0
Ri: Phillipps	5	10	0	Phil: Bird		7	0	0
Wm Hunt	3	10	0	Joice Turner		5	10	0

Footnote continued from page 149]

Hearth Tax return, Lady Day, 1664:

Wolphey Hundred	Total Charged Hearths	Total Houses	More than 10 hearths *	10	9	8	7	6	5	4	3	2	1	Total Exempt Houses
Brimfield	56	61						1			4	6	26	24
Croft	18	18											18	0
Eaton, Hennor & Stratford	51	34	1 (13)					1	2	1		4	10	15
Edvin Ralph	43	27								1	3	11	8	4
Eye, Ashton & Moreton	60	44				1	1	1	1		3	7	11	19
Luston	57	72			1		1			1	2	8	18	41
Farlow	24	27										5	14	8
Hatfield	41	24	1 (13)						2			3	12	5
Docklow	61	34						1	1	4	5	4	11	8
Hope, Hampton & Winsley	79	27	1 (35)	1				1	1	1		7	5	10
Humber	39	30					1		1	2	2	1	11	12
Hide, Hill & Wintercott	33	38								1	4	6	5	22
Ivington	80	46		1		1		1	1	3	4	5	7	21
Kimbolton	60	49						1		6	2	5	14	21
Laysters	39	23							1	1	1	7	13	0
Leominster	579	446	2 (13 & 14)		2	2	2	7	9	19	53	61	60	229
Little Dilwyn	74	49	1 (13)			1	2		1		3	5	15	20
Little Hereford	61	59							3	1	2	5	26	22
Lucton	32	21	1 (12)								3	2	7	8
Eyton	21	25								2	1	2	6	14
Ludford	37	13	1 (17)								1	6	5	0
Middleton	51	38						1		2	7	4	8	16
Newchurch &c	43	38					1			1	2	6	14	14
Orleton	67	93					1			3	1	6	33	49
Richards Castle	51	33		1					2			6	19	5
Rochford	34	38								1	1	6	15	15
Sarnesfield	27	23	1 (11)							1		4	4	13
Stagbach & Cholstrey	25	19									4	4	5	6
Stoke Prior	95	59				2		1	1	1	5	12	25	12
Wharton	71	37	1 (12)			1		2		2	4	4	4	19
Upton	26	27	1 (12)								2	1	6	17
While	26	16				1			1			1	5	7
Yarpole & Bircher	69	72							1	2	9	6	22	33
Total	**2,130**	**1,660**	**11**	**3**	**4**	**7**	**7**	**20**	**30**	**61**	**126**	**220**	**462**	**709**

* Actual charges in brackets.

2. The largest HT charge in 1664 was on John Holland gent. (8).

Wolphey: Brimfield continued

	£	s	d		£	s	d
Jo: Cecill	4	0	0	Roger Griffithes	2	0	0
Edw: Brians	4	0	0	Jo: Powell	2	0	0
Tho: Maund	4	0	0	Will: Penson	1	0	0
Geo: Galey	7	0	0	Alice Bytheway	1	0	0
Jo: Bytheway	4	10	0	Abraham Penson	1	0	0
Ri: Connopp	10	10	0				
Ri: Weare	9	10	0	Charge 241	0	0	
Tho: Hunt	6	0	0				
Rich: Hunt	7	0	0	Tho: Heming, Tho: Hunt. Raters.			
Tho: Gilley	3	0	0				
Ralph Winwood	15	10	0	**The Valuation is to be doubled**			
Tho: Besand	2	10	0				

2. Eaton &c[3, 4] (131r) [Wp2]

		£	s	d			£	s	d
Wallop Brabazon Esq[5]	h:	200	0	0	Geo: Trumper		11	6	8
Hen: Brabazon Esq	h:	100	0	0	Ri: Collins		8	6	8
Tho: Burgwin		15	0	0	Ri: Cleeveley [*Clively*]		10	0	0
Tho: Pateshall		18	6	8	Edw: Pitts		4	0	0
Jo: Hallard iun & Johan					Ri: Wanklin		2	4	0
Serrill		9	6	8	Johan Wind	h:	6	0	0
Eliz: Baylies		5	6	8	Ro: Wigmore Esq	h:	6	10	0
Jo: Badham		5	6	8	Roger Mcrris		2	13	4
Wm Paine		16	13	4					
Wm Leintoll		11	13	4	Charge 478		0	0	
Tho: Nicholas		21	6	8					
The Lo: Scudamore	h:	6	0	0	Tho: Pateshall, Wm Leintell, Rich:				
Wm Davies		2	13	4	Cleevely. Raters				
Jo: Pateshall		7	0	0					
Fitz: Wm Coningsby Esq	h:	9	0	0	**The valuation direct.**				

3. Edvin Ralph [Wp3]

		£	s	d			£	s	d
Phineas Jackson Minister[6]	h:	18	0	0	Roger Yeomans		12	0	0
Edw: Burwall[7]		18	0	0	Edw: Winwood		12	0	0
Edw: Wike	h:	18	0	0	Wm Turbervile		12	0	0
The Lords Meadowes		5	0	0	Will: Probarts		6	0	0
Tho: Evans		12	0	0			(132r)		
Ri: Perry		12	0	0	Hugh Bailies	h:	6	0	0

3. Included Hennor and Stratford.
4. The largest HT charge in 1664 was on Edmund Gittoes (13).
5. In 1645 his estates were valued at £1,000 a year (Harl. 911); a more reliable estimate in 1646 put his Herefordshire estate at £303 a year; Loan 29/15, pf. 2. JP q 1660. DL 1660 (listed): S.P. 29/11, fo. 162.
6. Rector, 1662-7; FP 1661 (£6).   7. HT 1664 (4).

Wolphey: Edvin Ralph continued

		£	s	d
Jo: Smith		10	0	0
Ri: Yeomans	h:	9	0	0
Geo: Bailies		9	0	0
Wm Bruton		9	0	0
John Smith delesar'		4	0	0
Buchers Land		4	0	0
Tho: Hall		4	0	0
Hen: Pyvinch		4	0	0
Jo: Holland		4	0	0
Tho: Oliver		3	0	0
Eliz: Barker [*Barber*]		3	0	0
The Court Close		1	0	0

		£	s	d
Will: Perry		1	10	0
Tho: Jay		1	0	0
Wm Bosswood			10	0

Charge 208 0 0

[*198 0 0*]

Edw: Burwall, Jo: Smith. Raters.

A 3rd part and a halfe 3rd part is to be added to the Valuation.

4. Eye Parish

		£	s	d
Eye Ashton & Morton [*Wp4a*]				
Humph: Cornewall Esq[8]	h:	200	0	0
Tho: Norris gen[9]	h:	200	0	0
Wa: Phillipps & his sister				
Mary		32	0	0
Tho: Crump		20	0	0
Tho: Tyler		8	0	0
Jo: Patis		3	0	0
Jo: Brimell		24	0	0
Ro: Whittall		32	0	0
Tho: Nott		5	0	0
Jo: Banaster		8	0	0
Jo: Gailey		3	0	0
Christopher Haines		5	0	0
Johan Pooton		3	0	0
			(133r)	
Fitz: Will: Coningsby for				
&c	h:	35	0	0
Merivale Farme	h:	35	0	0
Little Ashwood		10	0	0
Roger Maund		10	0	0
Jo: Garnons cler[10]		35	0	0
Ri: Blakeway [*Blackway*]	h:	23	0	0
Ri: Hayward		5	0	0
Jo: Bach		24	0	0

		£	s	d
Anth: Symes		4	0	0
Tho: Edwards		5	0	0
Jo: Caldwall [*Caldway*]		10	0	0
Roger Cocks [*Cox*]	h:	28	0	0
Sam: Powell gen		12	0	0
Miles Blount gen		1	0	0
Alex: Nelme		1	10	0
Jo: Stephens		1	10	0
Jo: Goode		1	0	0
Giles Whittall gen		1	0	0
Wm Powle		1	10	0
Jo: Coleman of Laughton		1	10	0
Ri: Wancklin		1	0	0
Ri: Vale		1	0	0

Charge[11] 790 0 0

Walter Phillips, Jo: Brimell. Raters.

A 3rd part is to be added to the valuation

Luston[12]	[*Wp4b*]			
Herb: Lo: Bp of Her' for				
&c	h:	53	0	0
Fra: Caldwall		6	0	0

---

8. JP 1660; DL 1660 *et seq.* In the mid-1660s he was a major in command of a company of the county militia; Loan 29/49, pf. 4, no. 69/15. MP for Leominster 1661. HT 1664 (7). His income was estimated to be £200 a year in ? *circa* 1677: Loan 29/182, fo. 313.

9. Will proved 1670 (PCC).   10. Vicar, FP 1661 (40s paid).

11. The largest HT charge in Moreton in 1664 was on John Walter (8).

12. The largest HT charge in Luston in 1664 was on Peter Young (8).

Wolphey: Eye Parish: Luston continued

	£	s	d
Simon Bailies gen	13	0	0
Jo: Wanklen & Wm Wancklen	8	0	0
Math: Collier	4	0	0
Jo: Winde	4	0	0
Hugh Freeman	5	0	0
Walter Hickmans	9	10	0
	(134r)		
Hen: Hayward	5	10	0
Ri: Morris	1	0	0
Ja: Kington	2	10	0
John Bithell	2	0	0
Walter Wind	8	0	0
Tho: Cotes	1	0	0
Ri: Price [Prees]	4	6	0
Tho: Wancklen	1	15	0
Wm Evans	18	0	0
Jo: Garnons	2	6	0
William Bithell	6	0	0
Anne Wynd wid	1	0	0
Roger Maund	1	16	0
The wid: Deakins	2	0	0
Wm Wancklen	1	0	0

		£	s	d
Sim: Wind		1	0	0
Wm Bailies		1	0	0
Roger Hill		1	0	0
Jo: Daniell		1	0	0
Tho: Burgin [Borgin]		1	0	0
Alice Bickett & her sister		2	13	4
Wm Burges			16	0
Hen: Garrett		1	0	0
Sim: Seward gen	h:	10	0	0
Fr: Powle gen	h:	9	0	0
The wid Wheeler		1	0	0
Budgett for &c		2	0	0
Hugh Butler		1	0	0
Ja: Peytoe		1	0	0
Jo: Stephens gen		1	5	0
Sr — Jervice for the Tieth	h:	23	0	0
Charge		219	0	0

Fr: Caldwall, Math: Collyar. Raters.

The valuation is to be doubled

5. Farlow   (135r)   [Wp5]

		£	s	d
Sr Wm Child & his underten'ts[13]	h:	50	0	0
Tho: Nicholls [Nicholas]		10	0	0
Tho: Low		10	0	0
Tho: Tart		6	0	0
Marg: Harper wid		4	0	0
Ri: Palmer		4	0	0
Tho: Hamons gen		4	0	0
Ben: Wilding cler for ye tieth		6	0	0

	£	s	d
Roger Harper	2	0	0
Charge	94	0	0
[96	0	0]

Roger Harper, Edw: Gennings. ¯ aters.

The valuation is to be doub .

6. Hatfield [& Docklow] &c[14]   [Wp6a]

		£	s	d
Tim: Colles Esq[15]	h:	100	0	0
Edm: Smith		15	0	0
Roul' Pitt		15	0	0
Jo: Woodyatt[16]		10	0	0

	£	s	d
Jo: Perry	9	0	0
Wm Dennes	7	0	0
Tho: Cox	7	5	0
Edm: Smith	6	12	0

13. Of Kinlet, a Master in Chancery, knighted 12 May 1661: Shaw, p. 234.
14. Probably included Brockmanton and Westwood.
15. JP q 1660. In 1646 his real estate in the county was valued at £72 a year; Loan 29/15, pf. 2. HT 1664 (13). Will proved 1670 (PCC).
16. Of Bilfield; will proved 1668 (Hereford).

Wolphey: Hatfield continued

	£	s	d			£	s	d
Jo: Harttree	6	12	0	Jo: Vaston & Wm Vaston	23	0	0
Jo: Luston	3	10	0	Jo: Broy [Bray]	16	0	0
Humph: Bailies[17]	5	0	0	Jo: Luston for &c	14	0	0
Wm Perkins	1	10	0	Nich: Grubb for &c	10	0	0
Jo: Bailies	1	10	0	Tho: Cook & Tho: Nicholls	12	0	0
Ri: Nicholls	3	10	0	Walter Hankocks	2	0	0
Ri: Badland[18]	3	0	0	Tho: Oliver & Tho: Vernall	12	0	0
Jo: King	2	10	0	Jo: Vernall	10	0	0
Luke Botwood	1	10	0	Jo: Hall & Alice Eaton wid	5	0	0
				Tho: Vernall	3	0	0
Charge	199	0	0	Jo: & Johan Wind	40	0	0
				Tho: Mason	12	0	0
Humph: Baylies. Rater.				Jo: Goode	16	0	0
				Wm Waties	1	10	0

The Valuation is to be almost doubled

Charge 292 0 0

Docklow[19]	[Wp6b]	(136r)

		£	s	d
Jo: Cornewall gen	h:	40	0	0
Edm: Smith for &c		30	0	0
Wm Morris[20]		23	0	0
Wm Broy		23	0	0

Jo: Vernall, Jo: Vaston, Tho: Mason.
    Raters.

The valuation is to be doubled.

---

7. Hope [Hampton Winsley   [Wp7]

		£	s	d			£	s	d
Mr Wise & his ten't					Will: Caswall		13	0	0
&c[21]	h:	200	0	0	Will: Davies		13	0	0
Jo: Berrington Esq[22]	h:	80	0	0	Tho: Higgins		15	0	0
The Bury of Hope	p:	40	0	0	Will Sucker		13	0	0
Wm Goodman		18	0	0	Jo: Maund	h:	6	0	0
Hen: Higgins		15	0	0	Jo: Bluck		5	10	0
Ri: Savaker for Perbin							(137r)		
[Pervin]	h:	15	0	0	Ri: Bruer		2	10	0

---

17. Yeoman, will proved 1669 (Hereford).
18. Yeoman, will proved 1710 (Hereford); he owned the St Mary House in Staunton on Arrow.
19. Included Hampton Wafer.
20. HT 1664 (6).
21. Sampson Wise of Clerkenwell, Middlesex; will proved 30 Oct. 1663 (PCC); in it he resigned his interests in the estates of his father-in-law, Fitzwilliam Coningsby, and of Humphrey Coningsby to them respectively; he also left a legacy to his servant for his years of service at Hampton Court.
22. Of Winsley; alleged to have suffered plunder during the Interregnum; Add. 36452, fo. 190. FP 1661 (£3).

Wolphey: Hope [Hampton Winsley] continued

		£	s	d	
Ri: Rogers	There is upon	2	0	0	
Wm Brewer	review taken upon ye 21 of	2	0	0	
Will: Paschall	March 1663	3	0	0	A 3rd part is to be added to the Val:
The Tieth	taken out for Horse a part	16	0	0	
Jo: Farrinton	being added 5[24]	3	0	0	
	Charge[23]	462	0	0	

8. Humber[25, 26] [Wp8]

	£	s	d			£	s	d
Geo: Cornewall gen &c	h: 50	0	0	He: Caswall		10	10	0
Rowland Pitt &c	h: 28	0	0	Jo: Caswall		24	0	0
Jo: Stansby				Ri: Bull[27]		12	10	0
[Stansbury] &c	h: 27	0	0	Ro: Hill &c	h:	8	10	0
Jo: Staple &c / Will: Stansby (The Lo: Scudam: upon Rack)	h: 5	10	0	Jo: Stansbye &c		6	10	0
&c	h: 7	0	0		Charge	207	0	0
	Charge 117	0	0	Ri: Bull, Jo. Caswall. Raters.				
Jo: Angell cler his parsonage	28	0	0	**The valuation is to be doubled**				

9. Hide [Hill Wintercot] &c[28] [Wp9]

	£	s	d		£	s	d
Jo: Jay	18	0	0	Roger Nash	4	0	0
Jo: Butler	8	10	0			(138r)	
Jo: Mun	8	10	0	Wm Morris	2	0	0
Ri: Mun	8	10	0	Tho: Davies	14	10	0
Tho: Pritchard	8	0	0	Humph: Hay	2	0	0
Tho: Walton	8	10	0	Jo: Mun	16	0	0

23. Fitzwilliam Coningsby and his sons compounded at ⅓ of their estates, valued in all at £4,243; these probably included property outside the county as his Herefordshire estates were put at £950 in 1650; *CCC*, iii, p. 2064. In 1645 his income was by repute £4,000 a year; Harl. 911. Another, more exact, valuation put his real estate in the county at £558 a year and his personal estate at £270 in 1646; Loan 29/15, pf. 2. According to Robinson (p. 146), he had been reduced to absolute want in the Civil War and its aftermath. In his will, proved in 1666 (PCC) he left lands in Bodenham and in Worcestershire, Leicestershire, Salop and Radnorshire. JP q 1660; DL 1660. In 1664 he was charged on 35 hearths in Hampton; probably his estate at Hampton Court is represented here by the charge on Sampson Wise.
24. In the MS this comment is an annotation in the margin opposite the names Rogers to Farrington.
25. The largest HT charge in 1664 was on John Carter (7).
26. Included Risbury and Prittleton.
27. Chief constable of Wolphey, 1663; Loan 29/49, pf. 4, no. 69/15.
28. The largest HT charge in 1664 was on Henry Browne (4).

Wolphey: Hide [Hill Wintercot] continued

	£	s	d		£	s	d
Hugh Powle	14	10	0	For the Lo: Bp	10	0	0
Marg: Powle	14	10	0				
Eliz: Powle	4	10	0	Charge	154	0	0
Ro: Davies	4	0	0				
Edw: Hide	4	10	0	Jo: Mun, Tho: Jay. Raters.			
Wm Pascoll	2	0	0				
Jo: Davies	2	0	0	**2 parts are to be added to the Valuation**			

10. Ivington [*Brierly &c*] &c   [*Wp10a*]

		£	s	d			£	s	d
Ja: Pitt Esq	**h:**	225	0	0	Hen: Bedford		30	0	0
Ri: Acton gen		27	5	0	Tho: Vye		18	15	0
Will: Browne		30	0	0	Edw: Apperley		18	15	0
Fr: Willkes	**h:**	40	0	0	Tho: Tomkins		7	10	0
Peter Southall		22	10	0	Jo: Tomkins gen		4	0	0
Tho: Goodith		7	10	0					
Oliver Hagley		7	10	0	**Brodward** [*Wp10c*]				
Will: Pascall		1	0	0	Wallop Brabazon Esq		6	0	0
Joice Towne wid		1	0	0	Will: Bailies Esq		11	5	0
Ri: Clarke		1	0	0	Will: Harris gen	**h:**	40	0	0
Eliz: Michaell		1	0	0	Johan Bond wid		15	0	0
Wa: Powell		3	15	0	Tho: Rawlings		7	10	0
Roger Nash		3	15	0	Ro: Wigmore Esq	**h:**	11	5	0
Jo: Harper		1	0	0	The occupiers of the Tieth				
Jo: Booth Esq	**h:**	4	10	0	&c		10	0	0
Fr: Lacon gen[29]		22	10	0	Edw: Williams for &c		2	10	0
Mary Norgrove wid		30	0	0					
Jo: Norgrove gen	**h:**	27	10	0	Charge		717	0	0
Tho: Walton		1	0	0			[*707*	*15*	*0*]

Brierley [*Wp10b*]		(139r)	Wm Browne, Peter Southall, Edw: Ap-	
Audrey Tomkins wid	22	10	0	perley, Tho: Rawlings. Raters.
Jo: Pearkes	22	10	0		
Anne Adams wid	22	10	0	**A 4th part is to be added to the valuation.**

11. Kimbolton[30]   [*Wp11*]

		£	s	d		£	s	d
The Duke of Buckingham					Wm Gittoes & Ch: Phillips	20	0	0
for &c	**h:**	100	0	0	Edm: Powell &c	6	0	0
For the Tieth Cap: Booth					Jo: Wancklen	5	0	0
	h:	60	0	0	Jo: Carpenter	8	0	0

29. HT 1664 (10).
30. The largest HT charge in 1664 was on Sibill Goode (6). The churchwardens of this parish who appear in this schedule were: 1662, William Bilwyn and Thomas Vernall; 1663, William Coleman, Humphrey Wall and Richard Browne; 1664, Walter Wancklen, Humphrey Smith and William Yeomans; 1665, John Bach; 1665/6, Alexander Jauncey; 1667, William Gittoes; 1668, Edmund Powell; 1669, John Wancklen; 1670, John Carpenter; 1671, John Coleman and Thomas Jay; 1673, William Yeomans and Ethelbert Jay.

Wolphey: Kimbolton continued

	£	s	d		£	s	d
Lewis Powell &c	10	0	0	Humph: Wall &c	25	0	0
Jo: Coleman	10	0	0	Jo: Wancklen &c	16	10	0
Will: Powle & Wm Yeomans	10	0	0	Tho: Jay	10	0	0
Will: Bilwyn	5	0	0	Ethelbert Jay	10	0	0
	(140r)			Ro: Vale	20	0	0
Jo: Bach &c	4	0	0	Ri: Browne	8	0	0
Wm Coleman	10	0	0	Humph: Smith	20	0	0
Wm Powle	10	0	0	Tho: Vernall	5	10	0
Alex: Jauncey	6	10	0	Jo: Caldwall	3	0	0
Jo: Goode	16	10	0				
Jo: Bennett	16	0	0	Charge	461	0	0
Giles Whittall	15	0	0				
Wa: Wancklen & his mother	15	0	0	Wm Yeomans, Rich: Browne. Raters.			
Wa: Wancklen &c	6	0	0				
Jo: Bach	10	0	0	**The proportion is to be doubled**			

12. Laysters[31]

[Wp12]

		£	s	d		£	s	d
Nich: Acton Esq		25	0	0		(141r)		
Jo: Barnaby Esq[32]	h:	30	0	0	Jo: Bennett	5	0	0
Susan Clarke wid	h:	6	0	0	Ri: Bennett	15	0	0
Mary Gough wid		8	0	0	Ethelbert Jay	4	0	0
Jo: Adams		9	0	0	Humph: Aldred	3	0	0
Jo: Barnaby gen		9	0	0	Hen: Browne	3	0	0
Edw: Jones		4	0	0	Ri: Holt	1	10	0
Jo: Hughes		2	5	0				
Will: Wilkes		8	0	0	Charge[33]	146	0	0
Ri: Hodges		12	0	0				
Jo: Gittoe [*Gittoes*]		2	0	0	He: Browne. Rater.			

The valuation is to be almost doubled.

31. Often taxed with While, although the implication here is that they were separate; Susana Clarke was charged to hearth tax in 1664 in While, but John Pateshall of Pudleston, also charged to hearth tax in While, does not appear in this schedule.
32. Of Brockmanton; his real estate in the county in 1646 was put at £58 a year and personal estate at £25; Loan 29/15, pf. 2. JP 1660.
33. The largest HT charge in 1664 was on John Cornewall (5).

13. Leominster Burrough[34]

The Nether Marsh Ward	£	s	d
[*Wp13a*]			
Herb: Bach & Fr: Giles	2	0	0
Margery Robbins wid &			
Wm Robins	3	0	0
Ri: Smith for &c	2	0	0
Alex: Nelme	8	0	0
Jo: Pateshall sen of Pudle-			
stone gen **h:**	6	0	0
Jo: Alcox	1	10	0
Tho: Wancklen of London	20	0	0
Joseph Pateshall	5	0	0
Phil: Nicholls	3	0	0
Eliz: Winton wid	4	0	0
Jo: Becy [*Beysey*]	5	0	0
Ri: Caswall	6	0	0
Hen: Seward	30	0	0
Tho: Taylor	8	0	0
Jo: Higgison for &c **h:**	2	0	0
Fra: Bishopp	4	0	0
Ri: Browne of Hamnash	3	0	0
Ri: Wigmore Esq & his			
ten't **h:**	3	0	0
Mary Crowther	4	0	0
Wm Broy of Docklow	4	0	0
Jo: Tombes iun	17	0	0
Jo: Streete gen	12	0	0
Charge	152	0	0

Ri: Bach, Ri: Nash, Alex: Nelme, Tho:
Hardick, Tho: Evans, Hugh Davies.
Raters.

The Middle Marsh Ward	(142r)		
[*Wp13b*]			
Ri: Dolphin gen for &c[35] **h:**	25	0	0
Johan Panck wid	4	0	0

	£	s	d
Kath: Williams wid &			
Jo Wms	12	0	0
Edw: Bangham [*Baughan*]	20	0	0
Sim: Seward	12	0	0
Mr — Hunt for &c	6	6	8
Jo: Booth Esq **h:**	30	0	0
Ri: Nash	1	10	0
Walter Phillipps	2	0	0
Jo: Pateshall of Leom'	3	0	0
Will: Hammons [*Hamonds*]	3	0	0
Ri: Stead of Eyton	3	0	0
Edm: Stephens	3	0	0
Wm Ditcher [*Dicher*]	2	0	0
Johan & Marg: Robbins			
spinst'	1	10	0
Ri: Bach labourer	1	10	0
Tho: Catstree	16	0	0
Jo: Jay	3	0	0
Evan Jones &c	1	10	0
Henr: Bryan	2	10	0
Wm Vernall	1	10	0
Charge	153	0	0
	[*154*	*6*	*8*]

Ri: Bach, Ri: Nash, Alex: Nelme, Tho:
Hardick, Tho: Evans, Hugh Davies.
Raters.

Something added to the valuation.

The Ward betweene the Crosse & Pinsley			
[*Wp13c*]			
Fr: Powle gen **h:**	70	0	0
Jane Bedford wid & Tho:			
Gittoes	3	0	0
Tho: Mannings	6	0	0
Ja: Caswall	3	0	0
Elinor Greene wid	3	0	0

34. The 1678 assessment (E.179/237/46) for which the half year's charge under the 'half' quota was £24 16s 11d, the same as the 1677 charge, suggests that the town's proportionate quota within the hundred was unchanged after 1664. In 1678 the charge respectively laid on the wards was very different from that in this schedule, High Street ward being much higher and Cross and Pinsley much lower in 1678. In the latter year the number of individuals charged was, at 302, almost double the number in 1663, 78 of them being charged 6½d or less, the equivalent of a £1 valuation.
35. HT 1664 (14).

Wolphey: Leominster: The Ward between the Crosse & Pinsley continued

		£	s	d
Edw: Hay [*Hayes*][36]		8	0	0
Tho: Burne		8	0	0
Rich: Crockett		1	10	0
Tho: Scarlett		9	0	0
		(143r)		
Jane Wellington wid &				
Roul' Stead		12	0	0
Jo: Norgrave gen for &c				
& teiths &c	h:	10	0	0
Ri: Hodges of Middleton		4	0	0
Tho: Jones for &c		4	0	0
Jo: Tomkins gen		9	0	0
Tho: Hardwick		4	0	0
Eliz: Bond wid		3	0	0
Ro: Wigmore Esq		20	0	0
Tho: Badnage		3	0	0
Ro: Butler of Chorlestree		2	0	0
Sam: Tailor		1	10	0
Waltr Powell		10	0	0
Ch: Barnett		2	0	0
Wm Caswall		3	0	0
Eliz: Toldervie wid		4	0	0
Sampson Wise Esq	h:	20	0	0
The Priory of Leominster	h:	20	0	0
	Charge	243	0	0

Ri: Bach, Ri: Nash, Alex: Nelme, Tho: Hardick, Tho: Evans, Hugh Davies. Raters.

The High Street Ward

[*Wp13d*]

	£	s	d
Kath: Perkes wid	2	10	0
Ri: Pitt	2	0	0
Tho: Foord	1	10	0
Tho: Tomkins	2	0	0
Edw: Russell cler	15	0	0
John Tomkins	2	0	0
Patience Marre [*May*]	1	10	0
Jo: Stephens	15	0	0
Fr: Peirce	12	0	0
Tho: Leeth	2	0	0
Jo: Chubb	1	10	0

	£	s	d
Jer: Clarke for &c	2	0	0
Jo: Stead[37]	5	0	0
Wm Toldervie	7	0	0
Edw: Williams	2	0	0
	(144r)		
Ri: Parry	2	0	0
Anne Woodhouse	2	0	0
Tho: Evans	2	0	0
Jo: Walton	2	10	0
Jacob Greene [*Grine*]	2	0	0
Wm Badnedge	3	0	0
Tho: Yeomans	1	10	0
Hen: Burt	2	0	0
Will: Cartwright			
[*Cartricke*]	2	0	0
Tho: Penson	2	0	0
John Noblett	5	0	0
Charge	99	0	0

Ri: Bach, Ri: Nash, Alex: Nelme, Tho: Hardick, Tho: Evans, Hugh Davies. Raters.

The South Streete Ward

[*Wp13e*]

	£	s	d
Marg: Powle wid	2	0	0
Jo: Bayly	4	0	0
Tho: Perkes	3	0	0
Jo: Rowbery [*Rubery*]	2	0	0
Fr: Moore & Edw:			
Rawlings	4	0	0
Marg: Wancklin wid	5	0	0
James Prece of Combe	2	0	0
Tho: Rawlings of Broad-			
ward	3	0	0
Hugh Davies	1	10	0
Tho: Whetstone	1	10	0
Wm Michaell [*Mikill*]	4	0	0
Tho: Caswall	2	0	0
Anne Skinner	3	0	0
Henry Bedford	10	0	0
Tho: Havard for &c	2	10	0
Dan: Shepard	3	10	0

36. Gent.; month's tax collector for Stretford, 1664; Loan 29/49, pf. 4, no. 69/16.
37. Bailiff 1663, town clerk 1660–88; G. F. Townsend, *The Town and Borough of Leominster* (Leominster, *circa* 1861), pp. 293, 295.

Wolphey: Leominster: The South Streete Ward continued

	£	s	d
Geo: Carver[38]	2	0	0
Rachell Carver	2	0	0
Miles Blount sen de Orleton	3	0	0
Jo: Gwatkins	2	0	0
	(145r)		
Roger Flecher	2	10	0
Tho: Rickards [*Richards*]	1	10	0
Rich: Bithell for &c	2	0	0
Ri: Scudamore	2	0	0
Charles Seward	4	0	0
Marg: Jones for &c	1	10	0
Walt^r Bedford for &c	1	10	0
Ro: Foord	4	0	0
Charge	81	0	0

Ri: Bach, Ri: Nash, Alex: Nelme, Tho:
Hardick, Tho: Evans, Hugh Davies.
Raters

Etnham streete Ward

[*Wp13f*]

	£	s	d
Ro: Powle	3	0	0
He: Caswall for &c	1	10	0
Tho: Smith	2	0	0
Alice Nicholls wid	2	0	0
Caleb Moore	2	0	0
Ri: Hemmings	2	0	0
Tho: Pateshall sen of Hennor	10	0	0
Ri: Bach sen	5	0	0
Will: Gittoes	3	0	0
Fr: Hay	4	0	0

		£	s	d
Marg: Caldwall [*Caldre*] spinster		2	10	0
Jo: Giles		1	10	0
Ja: Powle		1	10	0
Will: Bailies		16	0	0
Jo: Boise		2	10	0
Tho: Leech for &c		1	10	0
Will: Geeves [*Jeves*]		3	0	0
Ri: Rowbery		2	0	0
Tho: Mascoll		1	10	0
Anne Nicholson wid		2	10	0
Will: Vaston[39]		6	0	0
Humph: Becy [*Beysey*]		7	0	0
Edw: Rawlings		3	10	0
Ri: Caswall of Docklow		3	0	0
Johan Wind wid	h:	5	0	0
		(146r)		
Wallop Brabazon Esq[40]		50	0	0
Reece Jones		4	0	0
Jo: Leech		3	0	0
Ri: Lloyd		1	10	0
Will: Gyles		3	0	0
Mary Drew wid & Wm Taylor		2	0	0
Charge		157	0	0

Ri: Bach, Ri: Nash, Alex: Nelme, Tho:
Hardick, Tho: Evans, Hugh Davies.
Raters.

Something added to the valuation

14. Little Dilwin &c[41]

[*Wp14*]

		£	s	d		£	s	d
The Tieth	h:	40	0	0	Ri: Brodford [*Bradford*]	15	0	0
Will: Lambe gen[42]	h:	40	0	0	Ri: Wadley [*Wadeley*]	10	0	0
Ja: Mun		25	0	0	Jo: Mun	25	0	0
Ri: Morris		20	0	0	Wm Brodford	20	0	0
Walt^r Melling		13	0	0	Ja: Rosse & his sonne	5	0	0
Wm Parker		12	0	0	Tho: Carpenter gen	20	0	0

38. Collector of the month's tax for Wolphey, Wigmore and Stretford.
39. Month's tax collector for Wigmore, 1664.
40. HT 1664 (13).
41. See Dilwyn (p. 108) for constituent townships.
42. HT 1664 (13).

Wolphey: Little Dilwin &c continued

	£	s	d
Jo: Saice [*Sayse*] & his sonne	12	0	0
Mrs Bridges	5	0	0
Ja: Eckley	12	0	0
The wid Bowyer of Luntley	40	0	0
Jo: Bennett	13	0	0
Hen: Bowyer	6	0	0
Ri: Seward	12	0	0
Jo: Jackson	5	0	0

Ja: Mun, Wm Melling, Jo: Bennett.
Raters.

The valuation is to be doubled.

		£	s	d
Charge		250	0	0
		[*350*	*0*	*0*]

---

15. Little Hereford[43]   (147r)   [*Wp15*]

		£	s	d
Anne Dansey wid & Jo:				
Dansey Esq[44]	h:	93	10	0
Edw: Whitchcott Esq		4	0	0
Rowland Archer Esq[45]	h:	86	0	0
Alex: Grafton [*Garston*][46]		28	0	0
Edw: Starre		20	0	0
Roger Debitor [*Debitot*]		26	0	0
Ri: Perkes		20	0	0
Wm Maylard		12	0	0
Edm: Cheese		10	0	0
Jo: Seward		14	0	0
Andr: Seward		11	0	0
Hen: Rawlings		11	0	0
Ja: Shepard		3	10	0
Jo: Powell		3	10	0
Jo: Bowker		4	10	0
Wm Houton		7	10	0
Foulke Dillow		3	10	0
Tho: Cupper		10	0	0
Wm Andrewes sen		4	10	0
Tho: Martin		12	0	0
Jo: Penson		7	0	0

	£	s	d
Math: Whittall	7	0	0
The widow Dobles	7	0	0
Ri: Carter	5	0	0
Andr: Seward sen	8	0	0
Anne Lea wid	3	0	0
Wm Cheese	8	0	0
Jo: Hill	9	0	0
Jo: Dillow	18	10	0
Jeffery Debitor [*Debitot*] for			
Middletons tith	16	0	0
Mr Comby[47]	3	10	0
Mr Cooke for the tith of			
Easton	16	0	0
Will: Cuper [*Cooper*]	25	0	0

		£	s	d
Charge		543	0	0
		[*517*	*10*	*0*]

Alex: Grafton, Tho: Martin. Raters.

**A 5th part is to be added to
the valuation**

---

43. In 1659 the manor had belonged to Mr Dansey and Mr Archer; Harl. 6726.
44. HT 1664 (5).
45. HT 1664 (5).
46. HT 1664 (5).
47. John Comby, FP 1661 (clerical) (5s).

16. Luckton [and Eyton] &c.   (148r)
[Wp16a]

		£	s	d
Robt Wigmore Esq[48]	h:	60	0	0
Silvanus Taylor gen		16	0	0
Tho: Penny		9	0	0
Will: Barber		9	0	0
Peter Marsh		7	0	0
Ralph Perpoint for the tith				
	h:	10	0	0
Jo: Clee		5	0	0
Hen: Gilley		2	0	0
Ri: Davies		1	10	0

Charge 63 0 0
[119 10 0]

Will: Barber. Rater.

The Valuation is to be doubled

Eyton	[Wp16b]	£	s	d
The Lo: Bp of Hereff	h:	10	0	0
Sr Gervise Elves[49]	h:	10	0	0
Tho: Harley Esq	h:	20	0	0
Ri: Marston	h:	25	0	0
Tho: Marston	h:	40	0	0
Mr Weaver		15	0	0
Wm Cadd	h:	15	0	0
Ri: Stead		10	0	0
Mr Pritchard	h:	8	0	0
Mr Tombes		3	0	0
Hen: Seward		2	10	0
Tho: Jones		3	0	0
Hen: & Wm Baldwyn		3	0	0

Charge 164 0 0

Ri: Stead. Rater.

The valuation is to be doubled.

---

17. Ludford   [Wp17]

	£	s	d
Sr Job Charlton K[nt50]	200	0	0

Valuation direct.

Wm Davies, David Roberts. Raters.

---

18. Middleton   (149r)   [Wp18]

	£	s	d		£	s	d
The Lo: Duke of				Fr: Brace iun gen	10	0	0
Buckingham for &c	50	0	0	Tho: Yapp	12	0	0
Bennett Prior gen[51]	18	0	0	Jo: Phillips	24	0	0
Fr: Brace sen gen[52] & his				Ri: Maund	12	0	0
grandsonn	18	0	0	Jo: Maund	12	0	0

---

48. Lucton manor belonged to the Wigmores; Harl. 6726. In 1646 Wigmore's real estate in the county was put at £62 a year and his personal estate at £15; Loan 29/15, pf. 2. HT 1664 (12).
49. Of Stoke, Suffolk; created baronet 22 June 1660; died 1705; *Baronetage*, iii, p. 51.
50. JP q 1660. He owned the manor: Harl. 6726. FP 1661 (£50); HT 1664 (17). His income was put at £1,000 a year in ? *circa* 1677; Loan 29/182, fo. 313.
51. Major in command of a militia company in the mid-1660s; Loan 29/49, pf. 4, no. 69/15.
52. Buried 8 Mar. 1664.

Wolphey: Middleton continued

	£	s	d		£	s	d
Jo: Wind	12	0	0	Ri: Brock	3	0	0
Ri: Hodges[53]	10	0	0	Tho: Holt	2	0	0
He: Browne	12	0	0	Ethelbert Perkes	2	0	0
Wm Cock[54]	12	0	0	Eliz: Morris	2	0	0
Eliz: Smith wid[55]	12	0	0	Tho: Tyler	1	0	0
Ri: Poston[56]	10	0	0				
Jo: Seward	6	0	0	Charge	258	0	0
Fr: Farmer	6	0	0				
Will: Phillipps gen	3	0	0	Fr: Brace, Tho: Yapp. Raters.			
Tho: Pascall	3	0	0				
Jo: Cox	3	0	0	**The valuation to be doubled**			
Ja: Pembridge	3	0	0				

---

19. Newchurch &c.   [*Wp19a*]

		£	s	d		£	s	d
Walter Bythell[57]	h:	25	0	0	Phill: Lenthall. Rater.			
Tho: Morley		4	0	0				
Mr Mitton		4	0	0	**2 partes added to the Valuation**			
Ja: Price & Wm Webb	par:	3	10	0				
Lydons		3	0	0	Hoplesse Greene [*Wp19c*]			
part of the Parsonage of					Will: Collier	13	0	0
Kynnersley within the sd					Tim: Wood	8	10	0
Towneship		6	0	0	Tho: Church	5	10	0
					The Parsonage	5	10	0
					The Vicaridg	1	10	0
Charge		45	0	0				

Wa: Bythell. Rater.

	Logaston [*Wp19d*]			
	Anne Smith wid	15	0	0
2 partes added to the valuation	Geo: Stead	2	10	0
	Sibbill Hill & her sonne	1	10	0

Hursley	[*Wp19b*]	(150r)			Mr Bithells mead'	1	9	0
Mr Bosworth's Landes		26	0	0				
Mr Simonds Landes		10	0	0	Charge	54	9	0
Phil' Lenthall		10	0	0				
Jo: Harper		4	10	0	Roger Smith Rater.			
Jo: Chambers		4	0	0				
Parte of the parsonage of					**2 parts added to the valuation.**			
Letton within the sd								
Towneship vizt		8	0	0				
Charge		62	10	0				

---

53. HT 1664 (5).
54. Buried 14 Mar. 1667.
55. Buried 21 Sept. 1666.
56. Buried 7 Aug. 1669.   57. HT 1664 (7).

M

20. Orleton   [Wp20]

	£	s	d		£	s	d
Miles Blount gen[58]	30	0	0	Tho: Phillipps	8	0	0
Wm Dawes gen	50	0	0	Jo: Yapp	8	0	0
Jo: Cank	15	0	0	Tho: & Jo: Keyall [Keysall]	9	0	0
Geo: Bytheway	25	0	0	Jo: Hughes sen	3	0	0
Tho: Crump	20	0	0	Wm Glover	4	0	0
Wm Stepple	15	0	0	Tho: Comber	4	0	0
Ri: Seward	18	0	0	Ch: Boton	7	0	0
Marg: Howton wid	15	0	0	Mr Dobins for &c	7	0	0
Tho: Brompton [Bampton]	16	0	0	Jo: Cootes	3	0	0
Jo: Connopp	20	0	0	Edw: Wellings	4	0	0
	(151r)			Mr Coningsbyes Landes			
Fr: Hints	14	0	0	&c h:	50	0	0
Humph: Wall	12	0	0	Mr Cornewall	10	0	0
Will: Mason	10	0	0				
Anne Brymeld [Brimell]							
wid	9	0	0	Charge	301	0	0
Ri: Cheese	3	0	0		[412	0	0]
Wm Seward for &c	7	0	0				
Edw: Hall	8	0	0	Jo Cank, Ri: Seward. Raters.			
Jo: Phillipps	8	0	0	**The Valuation is to be doubled.**			

21. Richards Castle   [Wp21]

	£	s	d		£	s	d
Ri: Salloway [Sallway]				Will: Colerick	1	0	0
gen[59]	150	0	0	Tho: Farmer	1	10	0
Jo: Salloway cler	20	0	0	Tho: Tomkins	1	0	0
Jo: Davies	32	0	0	Marg: Hoggins	2	0	0
Ar: Bradshaw gen	3	0	0	Wm Gilley	1	0	0
Tho: Chambers	20	0	0	Wm Seward	3	0	0
Ri: Higgins	16	0	0	Edw: Hall	1	10	0
Ri: Gilley[60]	16	0	0	Wm James	1	10	0
Jo: Towne	6	10	0	Geo: Gilley	1	0	0
Sim: Higgins	6	10	0	Tho: Brooke	1	10	0
Nich: Gilley	6	10	0				
Ja: Tompkins	6	10	0	Charge	315	0	0
Ri: Camme	3	10	0				
Johan Besand wid	4	0	0	Ri: Higgins, Tho: Towne. Raters.			
	(152r)						
Ri: Penson	2	10	0	**Someth: added to the Valuation which**			
Edw: Gilley	2	10	0	**ought to be doubled, They not paying**			
Jo: Ingram	3	0	0	**much above is per annum in the pownd**			
Will: Cavoke	1	10	0	**Contribution**			

58. Died 27 Nov. 1663; Robinson, p. 223. Will proved 18 Aug. 1664 (PCC). He had
a 99-year lease, from 1640, of lands in Orleton, Yarpole, Bircher and Eye, and also
held land in Warwickshire. In 1660 he rented from the Exchequer his lands in
Orleton and Eye for £19; PRO, Various Accounts, E.101/630/30. In the HT 1664
his widow was charged for 7 hearths.
59. The Salways owned the manor; Harl. 6726. FP 1661 (£20 paid); HT 1664 (10).
60. Chief constable of Wolphey, 1663: Loan 29/49, pf. 4, no. 69/15.

of the faculty, the
officers, the Board
cerning changes in

g with and making
d other administra-
s, and student groups
e of the College.

ident of the College,
 department involved
 the faculty who are
ted member of the com-
s chairman. When the
for tenure, he will be
red member of his de-
 involves the depart-
cted member will be

22. Rochford [*Wp22*]

	£	s	d		£	s	d
Tho: Arundell Esq for &c	22	0	0	Jo: Holland	2	0	0
Mary Morris wid	16	0	0	Alice Wiatt	2	0	0
Hen: Gomery[61]	9	0	0			(153r)	
Tho: Morris	8	0	0	Tho: Frece & the wid Lane	5	0	0
Wm Downes	14	0	0				
Kath: Fidoe	8	0	0	Charge	132	0	0
Edm: Gomery	5	0	0				
Jo: Fidoe	3	0	0	Tho: Morris. Rater.			
Mr Jo: Cornewall &c[62]	6	0	0				
Jo: Grove cler for Glebe				Mr Nicholetts &c h:	8	0	0
& Tieth	10	0	0	one meadow more at h:	6	0	0
Fr: Gregg	3	0	0	Twoe parcells of Land			
Edm: Fidoe sen	3	0	0	more & a ten't h:	4	0	0
Edw: Griffin of Eastham	3	0	0				
Edm: Fermiston				Charge	18	0	0
[*Farrington*]	2	0	0				
Miles Clent	3	0	0	Tho: Morris. Rater.			
Phil: Morris Landes &c	4	0	0				
Jo: Smith	2	0	0	**The proportion is to be doubled**			
Roger Layland	2	0	0				

23. Sarnsfield [*Wp23*]

		£	s	d	
Eliz: Monington wid[63]	h:	100	0	0	
The Ley Court	h:	30	0	0	Wm Foule, Wm Jenkins. Raters.
Tho: Gomond gen	h:	15	0	0	
Rich: Hopley gen		5	0	0	**The Valuation is to be doubled**
The parsonage		20	0	0	
Charge		170	0	0	

24. Stagbach [& *Cholstree*] &c [64] [*Wp24*]

		£	s	d			£	s	d
The Lo: Scudamore for					Wallop Brabazon Esq	h:	5	0	0
the Tieth	h:	40	0	0	Wancklens farme[65]	h:	40	0	0
Ro: Wigmor of Lucton					Ri: Bach of Leom[r] gen		5	0	0
Esq	h:	40	0	0	Rebecca Seward of Leom[r] wid		6	0	0

61. HT 1664 (4).
62. The manor belonged *circa* 1659 to Sir Gilbert Cornewall and Mr Morris; Harl. 6726.
63. In 1646 her real estate was valued at £102 and her personal estate at £130: Loan 29/15, pf. 2. In 1660 ⅔ of her estate in Sarnsfield and Almeley was valued at £135; PRO, Various Accounts, E.101/630/30. HT 1664 (11).
64. The largest HT charge in 1664 was on John Ballard (3).
65. The duke of Buckingham's estates in Ivington and Stagbach were let in 1648 to John Wanklen, ironmonger, of Leominster, at a rent of £32 a year; Add. 19678.

Wolphey: Stagbach [& Cholstree] &c continued

	£	s	d		£	s	d
Fra: Powle of Leom[r] gen **h:**	12	0	0	Ro: Pascall	20	0	0
Hen: Powle[66] **h:**	23	0	0	Will: Knight	16	0	0
Hen: Birch	16	0	0		(154r)		
Ri: Acton[67]	9	0	0	Walter Powell	9	0	0
Fr: Pierce	9	0	0	Wm Woodhouse	9	0	0
Sibbill Viccarrs [*Viccaris*]							
wid	9	0	0	Charge 320	0	0	
Will: Peytoe [*Peto*]	10	0	0				
Ro: Butler[68]	12	0	0	Ri: Acton, Wm Peytoe. Raters.			
Tho: Bedford	12	0	0				
Jo: Carpenter gen	18	0	0	**Valuation is to be doubled.**			

25. Stoake Prior &c [69, 70]   [*Wp25a*]

	£	s	d			£	s	d
Dr Watson	**h:**	40	0	0	Wickton &c [*Wp25b*]			
The wid Wind	**h:**	20	0	0	Fitz: Wm Coningsby Esq **h:**	5	0	0
Ben: Coningsby gen	**h:**	25	0	0	Hen: Caswall[71]	20	0	0
Rich: Simpson	**h:**	15	0	0	Tho: Holt	20	0	0
Ri: Lane		7	0	0	Ri: Munke	8	0	0
Will: Nicholls		7	0	0	Ri: Kinge	20	0	0
Tho: Norris		10	0	0	The wid Stansbury	8	0	0
Wm Walton		7	0	0	Jo: Stansbury	3	10	0
Jo: Yapp		7	0	0				
Will: Kington		7	0	0	Charge 270	0	0	
Wm Caldwall		7	0	0				
Hen: Vaston		7	0	0	He: Caswall, Will: Caldwall, He: Vas-			
Ri: Bull gen		20	0	0	ton. Raters.			
Jo: Vaston		3	0	0				
The wid Clarke	**h:**	2	0	0	**A third part is to be added to the**			
Jo: Banke		2	0	0	**valuation.**			

(155r)

Wharton [*and Newton*] **&c** [*Wp25c*]

	£	s	d			£	s	d
Herbt Awbrey Esq	**h:**	110	0	0	Mr Wise	**h:**	10	0	0
Ri: Hopton Esq[72]	**h:**	70	0	0	Jo: Hallard	20	0	0
Tho: Price Esq[73]	**h:**	10	0	0	Tho: Nicholls & his Mother	17	0	0
Ri: Whittall gen[74]	**h:**	55	0	0	Miles Scull gen	8	0	0
Jo: Berrington gen	**h:**	15	0	0	Hugh Gittoes	15	0	0

66. HT 1664 (3).   67. Gent., HT 1664 (3).   68. HT 1664 (3).
69. Normally included Risbury.
70. The largest HT charges in 1664 in Stoke Prior were on John Higgason and Richard Pennell (8 each).
71. HT 1664 (6); gent.   72. Sheriff 1654; JP 1655; JP q 1660. HT 1664 (9).
73. JP q 1660; DL 1660; MP for the county 1661. His income was put at £400 a year in ? *circa* 1677; Loan 29/182, fo. 313.   74. HT 1664 (12).

Wolphey: Wharton [and Newton] &c continued

	£	s	d			£	s	d
Dan: Shepard	7	0	0	Tho: Higgins		17	0	0
Ri: Edwards	17	0	0	Hen: Philly cler[75]	h:	15	0	0
Hugh Wind & Tho: Brock	4	0	0	Jam: Grafton			15	0
Jo: Gittoes	7	0	0	Mr Pitt & Hen: Browne	h:	1	0	0
Edw: Apperley	3	0	0					
Jane Wellington wid		15	0					
Wm Nicholls		3	0	Charge	429	0	0
Mr Burne		14	0	Her: Walton, Jo: Gittoes. Raters.
Hugh Davies	1	0	0					
Herb: Walton	15	0	0	**A 3rd parte is to be added to the**
Geo: Hill	5	0	0	**Valuation**
Wm Goodman	5	0	0	

26. Upton   [*Wp26*]

	£	s	d			£	s	d
Jo: Carver [*Karver*] gen[76]	57	0	0	Roger Dillow		2	0	0
Ar: Winwood gen	21	0	0	Will: Hackluit		1	0	0
Ri: Collins gen	24	0	0	Will: Glace		1	0	0
Jo: Shepard gen	21	0	0					
Ri: Marston gen	6	0	0	Charge	145	0	0
Ri: Perkes gen	5	0	0					
Jo: Seward	3	0	0	Edw: Prodger, Rater.
	(156r)							
John Maund	2	0	0	**A 3rd part added to the val:**
Ri: Cradock	2	0	0	

28. While[77]   [*Wp28*]

[*There follows more than half a blank page*]

(157r)

29. Yarpooll [78]   [*Wp29*]

	£	s	d		£	s	d
Herbt Lo: Bp of Hereff:	5	0	0	Tho: Venmore iun	9	10	0
Hen: Philley Mr of Artes	23	0	0	Tho: Venmore sen	5	0	0
Miles Blount gen	9	10	0	Tho: Hardwick	1	10	0
Tho: Derry	14	0	0	He: Wall	5	0	0
Ja: Cook	14	10	0	Ri: Grove	1	6	0

75. Rector of Croft and treasurer of Hereford cathedral; will proved 1669 (PCC).
76. HT 1664 (12).
77. The symbol Wp28 has been allocated to While rather than Wp27 in order that the symbols shall parallel the original numbering of the schedules in the MS. It will be noted that the latter has at this point become a little disordered.
78. Included Bircher.

Wolphey: Yarpooll continued

	£	s	d
Anne Payne wid	4	6	0
Fra: Fowler wid	5	0	0
Tho: Higgins	10	0	0
Mr Low: cler	4	0	0
Jo: Wall & his father	2	0	0
Fra: Peakins [*Perkins*]	2	0	0
Tho: Wall	2	0	0
Ri: Deswall [*Dewswall*]	4	0	0
Jo: Venmore	1	0	0
Geo: Gold	1	0	0
Wm Kent	1	0	0
Jo: Wind	1	0	0
Tho: Gold	1	0	0
Wm Powle	1	0	0
Edm: Matts		15	0
Jo: Yapp	1	0	0
Wm Grismond	1	0	0
Wm Evans	1	0	0
Jo: Cheese		10	0
Jo: Phillipps	1	0	0
Tho: Nash[79]	19	0	0
Mr Habberley cler	11	0	0
Ro: Croft Esq[80]	1	0	0
John Browne	9	10	0
Jam: Rosse	12	0	0
Anne Collins wid	8	0	0
Tho: Bedford	5	0	0
Tho: Pitt	1	10	0

		£	s	d
			(158r)	
John Daniell		2	6	0
Eliz: Bythell wid		1	0	0
Jo: Hambleton		1	0	0
Ri: Wheeler			15	0
Wm Owens cler[81]		1	0	0
Geo: Phillipps		2	0	0
Will: Coston [*Cesson*]		1	10	0
Ri: Peakins [*Perkins*]		1	6	0
Fra: Weaver		1	0	0
Ro: Bedford			11	0
Fra: Phillpotts			6	0
Eliz: Alcocks		2	0	0
Ro: Deakins			13	4
Arnold Weaver		1	6	8
Edw: Weaver		1	6	8
Tho: Marsh		2	10	0
Henry Grismond			15	0
Alice Ridgley [*Rigley*]		1	0	0
Sr Jervis Elves Tyth	**h:**	17	0	0

Charge 232 0 0
[*239 2 8*]

Ri: Grove, Tho: Bedford. Raters.

**Two partes are to be added to
the valuation.**

(159r)
30. Croft[82]   [*Wp30*]

[*There follows a blank page*]

---

79. HT 1664 (4).
80. HT 1664 (4).
81. Curate of Yarpole, FP 1661 (2s 6d paid).
82. The chief property owner appears to have been Bishop Croft on whom the entire HT 1664 charge (18) fell.

Wormilow Hundred[1] (160r)

	Value Returned by the Raters £		Value Horse Being Taken out	Value according to the contribution £ s d	The whole yeares contribution at 2s per po'd per annum for each particular parish in this Hundred £ s d
1.	228	Ballingham &c		528 16 8	52 17 8
2.	329	Bridstow		903 16 8	90 7 8
3.	132	Dewsall		169 1 0	16 19 0

1. The charge on Much Dewchurch bears the same proportion to the hundred charge (assuming a £120 charge on Llangarren) as the charge in the 1677 assessment. It does not seem possible that the valuation has been miscopied. A deliberate doubling of the charge apparently due must therefore be assumed. The other charges are equal to or close to the proportions in the 1677 tax.

Hearth Tax return, Lady Day, 1664:

Wormilow Hundred	Total Charged Hearths	Total Houses	More than 10 hearths *	10	9	7	6	5	4	3	2	1	Total Exempt Houses
Ballingham	34	16	1 (14)							3	3	5	4
Bolstone	24	21			1					2	4	4	10
Bridstow	94	74					1	4		5	13	27	24
Dewsall	14	8					1			1	1	2	3
Garway	103	76			1			3	4	6	10	25	27
Goodrich	101	92				1		1	4	7	13	26	40
Hentland	146	94	3 (12, 14, 15)						2	9	13	42	25
Kings Caple	46	41						1	1	2	7	17	13
Kilpeck	49	38							4	1	5	20	8
Treville	26	36							3	1	2	7	23
Llanhithog	6	10										6	4
Llandinabo	13	9								1	4	2	2
Llangarren	187	86	2 (11, 11)		1	2	2	4	7	12	16	36	6
Llanrothall	49	14		1	1			1			2	4	3
Llanwarne	60	49					1	1	1	4	6	18	18
Little Birch	25	27			1						7	7	12
Aconbury	18	17				1				1	1	4	10
Little Dewchurch	23	20								2	5	7	6
Marstow	27	23						1		1	4	11	6
Much Birch	57	44							3	3	8	20	10
Much Dewchurch	111	74	1 (23)				1	2	1	2	14	32	21
Orcop	38	63								1	4	27	31
Pencoyd	31	24						1	2	1	4	7	9
Peterstow	67	62						1	2	5	10	19	25
St Weonards	100	83	1 (11)				1	1	2	7	13	22	36
Sellack & Foy	60	32				1		3	2	1	8	9	8
Tretire & Michaelchurch	35	21							4	1	3	10	3
Welsh Newton	67	45	1 (11)				1	1	3	2	5	17	15
Whitchurch & Ganarew	89	65				1			3	5	9	37	10
Total	1,700	1,264	9	1	5	6	8	25	48	86	194	470	412

* Actual charges in brackets.

169

Wormilow Hundred continued

	Value Returned by the Raters		Value Horse Being Taken out	Value according to the contribution			The whole yeares contribution at 2s per po'd per annum for each particular parish in this Hundred		
4.	318	Garway		650	10	0	65	1	0
5.	304	Gudridge		860	0	0	86	0	0
6.	—	Haywood		103	3	4	10	6	4
7.	279	Hentland		607	10	0	61	13	0
							[*60*	*15*	*0*]
8.	221	Kings Capell		743	10	0	74	7	4
9.	279	Killpeck &c.		638	6	8	63	16	8
10.	71	Landinabo &c		212	0	0	21	4	0
11.	1162	Langarran		1200	0	0		blank	
							[*120*	*0*	*0*]
12.	247	Lanrothall		200	3	4	20	0	4
13.	311	Lanwarne		556	3	4	55	12	4
14.	423	Little Birch &c		501	6	8	50	2	8
15.	215	Marstow		200	3	4	20	0	4
16.	98	Much Birch		267	16	0	26	15	8
17.	446	Much Dewchurch		505	13	4	101	5	4
18.	207	Orcopp		334	10	0	33	9	0
19.	162	Pencoyd		242	3	4	24	4	4
20.	348	Peterstow		333	6	8	33	6	8
21.	240	St Wennards		762	3	4	76	4	4
22.	710	Seliack & Foy		743	10	0	74	7	4
23.	170	Tretire & Mi: ch:		291	6	8	29	2	8
24.	262	Welch Nuton		229	13	4	22	19	4
25.	387	Whitech: & Gunardo		386	10	0	38	13	0

[*Total £1267 8s 0d*]

---

1. Ballingham &c

	£	s	d			£	s	d
Sr John Scudamore Baronett				Jo: Drew		5	0	0
& Kt of the Bath[2]	100	0	0	Wm Cole	h:	6	0	0
Jo: Daniell &c	20	0	0	Tho: Roberts		2	0	0
Wm Seycell	10	0	0	Ja: Roberts		1	10	0
Wm Roberts	10	0	0	Wm Caldicott		1	10	0
Rich: Williams **past**	5	0	0	Jo: Caldicott		1	10	0

---

2. Created baronet 1644; succeeded by his son Sir John; *Baronetage*, ii, p. 227. JP q 1660. Subs. 1663 (lands £10); HT 1664 (14).

Wormilow: Ballingham &c continued

	£	s	d
Howell Jones	1	0	0
Charge	163	10	0

Wm Seycell, Jo: Drew, Ri: Williams. Raters.

The Valuation is to be doubled

Bowston[3]   [*Wm1b*]
Jo: Lo: Viscount Scuda-
more &c   **h:** 36 0 0

		£	s	d
Mr Ri: Cox[4]	**h:**	16	0	0
Jo: Garrald[5]		2	0	0
Mr Henry Smith cler		6	10	0
Jo: Bennett		1	10	0
Wm Pyttman		1	10	0
Jo: Symonds		1	10	0
Charge		65	0	0

Tho: Manfield, Jo: Garrald. Raters.

2. Bridstow   [*Wm2*]

		£	s	d			£	s	d
Sr Ja: Bridges Kt &					Mrs Baker		23	0	0
Barronett[6]	**h:**	170	0	0	Ch: Eckley		3	0	0
Sr Wm Powell Kt &					Mary Fisher wid		23	0	0
Barronett[7]	**h:**	150	0	0	Tho: Mills		15	0	0
Mrs Mary Rudhall	**h:**	120	0	0	Roger Weeb [*Webb*]		3	0	0
Jo: Vaughan Esq	**h:**	15	0	0	Tho: Addis		11	0	0
Jo: Nurse Esq	**h:**	16	0	0	The heires of Tho: Holder		11	0	0
Jo: Abrahall gen		70	0	0	Jo: Bennett		7	0	0
Roger Rees[8]		24	0	0	Tho: Philpotts		7	0	0
Mrs Kyrle	**h:**	15	0	0	Mary Cowarne wid[10]		30	0	0
Ri: Smith		15	0	0	Jo: Bennett of Over Rosse		4	0	0
Phil: Rees		4	0	0	Ri: Addis		3	0	0
			(162r)		Phil: Addis		3	0	0
Ri: Minde		2	0	0	Alice Chine wid		15	0	0
Waltr Carrier		4	0	0	Jo: Lea gen		5	0	0
Symon Carrier		4	0	0	Jo: Tuder		3	0	0
Ri: Marratt gen		7	0	0	Jo: Markey gen		3	0	0
The wid Minde		4	0	0	Ch: Bridges Esq		8	0	0
Ga: [*Gabriel*] Hill[9]		11	0	0	Wm Bonner cler[11]		37	0	0
Mrs Darley		11	0	0	The wid Stanner		3	0	0
Tho: Wincell [*Wintle*]		4	0	0	Mrs Merrick		3	0	0

3. The largest HT charge in Bolstone in 1664 was on Philip Taylor (6).
4. Gent., Subs. 1663 (lands £1).
5. Subs. 1663 (lands £1).
6. Succeeded to baronetcy 1652; inherited barony of Chandos 1676; *Baronetage*, ii, p. 15. JP q 1660; DL 1660; sheriff 1667. FP 1661 (£30 paid).
7. Sir William Powell *alias* Hinson of Pengethley, created baronet 23 Jan. 1660/1, died 1680/1; *Baronetage*, ii, p. 1903. Sheriff 1657; JP q 1660; DL 1660. FP 1661 (£30 paid).
8. HT 1664 (6).   9. Subs. 1663 (lands £1).
10. Subs. 1663 (lands £1).   11. Vicar, FP 1661 (£2 paid).

Wormilow: Bridstow continued

	£	s	d		£	s	d
Anth: Collyer	4	0	0	Will: Philpotts	2	0	0
Jo: Hall	3	0	0	Jo: Jones	1	0	0
Wm Puckmore	2	0	0	Will: Parry	1	0	0
Tho: Browne	2	0	0	Ro: Mutlow	1	0	0
Alice Andrewes spinster	2	0	0	Will: Fisher	1	0	0
Ro: Prichard	2	0	0	Jo: Pritchard	1	0	0
David James	2	0	0				
Jo: Lane	2	0	0	Charge	329	2	0
Jo: Gwillett [*Gwilt*]	2	0	0		[*898*	*0*	*0*]
The wid Gwillim	2	0	0				
Will: Edwards	1	0	0	Ri: Smith, Jo: Tomy. Raters.			
	(163r)						
Roger Jones	1	0	0	**The valuation is to be doubled**			

3. Dewswall[12]   [*Wm3*]

		£	s	d		£	s	d
Sr Wm Powell Kt &					Mr Clark for ye tieth of			
Barronett	**h:**	100	0	0	Dewsall & Callow	20	0	0
Sr Jo: Scudamore Kt &								
Barr'tt	**h:**	6	0	0	Charge	132	0	0
Ri: Davies gen		6	0	0				

Wm Hitchman, Jo: Seabourne, Wm Williams. Raters.

4. Garway[13]   [*Wm4*]

		£	s	d		£	s	d
Tho: Pearle Esq	**h:**	89	0	0	Ri: Pierce	2	10	0
Hen: Milbourne Esq	**h:**	7	0	0	Da: Lewis	3	10	0
Hugh James gen		46	10	0	Jo: Willim	3	10	0
Johan Bevan wid[14]		27	0	0	Jo: Howman	1	10	0
Will: Baskervile gen[15]		22	0	0	Tho: Morgan	2	10	0
Ri: Scudamore gen		5	0	0		(164r)		
Will: Phillipps		14	0	0	John Phillipps	2	10	0
Jo: Edwards gen	**h:**	3	0	0	Charles Morgan	2	10	0
Geo: Jenkins		7	0	0	Ri: Hughes	1	10	0
Ri: Jones		6	10	0	Ja: Philpott	1	10	0
Will: Treherne		4	0	0	Wm Morgan	4	0	0
Geo: Loope		12	0	0	Mary Coules	4	10	0
Jo: Pierce		6	0	0	Jo: Coope [*Cope*]	3	0	0

12. The largest HT charge in 1664 was on Edward Hitchman, gent. (7).
13. The largest HT charge in 1664 was on Richard Barry, gent. (9).
14. Subs. 1663 (lands £1).
15. Of Cummadog (Cwm Madoc); it was alleged that he had been plundered and sequestered by parliament before 1660; Add. 36452, fo. 190. Subs. 1663 (lands £1).

Wormilow: Garway continued

	£	s	d		£	s	d
Tho: Williams	4	0	0	Fr: Allen	1	0	0
Anne Harris	2	0	0	Jo: Walker	1	0	0
Tho: Watkins	4	0	0	Tho: Phillipps	1	10	0
Phil: Roberts	2	0	0	David Jones	1	0	0
Edw: Gwillim gen[16]	8	0	0				
Jo: Hoskins	5	10	0	Charge	318	0	0
Wm Davies	2	0	0				
David Gwillim	2	10	0	Will: Baskervile, Will: Phillipps. Raters.			
Wm Crowther		10	0				
Wm Looke [*Leeke*]		10	0	**The Valuation is to be doubled**			
Wm Prichard	1	0	0				

5. Gudridge [*Wm5*]

	£	s	d		£	s	d
Wm Tringham vicar	17	11	3	Tho: Rea	4	3	6
More for the glebe land	5	12	6	Wm Neve		8	8
Ri: Tyler	4	11	10	Eliz: Swift & her sonne	6	3	9
The Castle demeasnes	34	15	8	Lettice Goodwyn wid[21]	17	18	5
Whites land[17]		2	0	Will: Bellamy	16	0	3
Jo: Savaker[18]	8	5	0	Tho: & Rich: Scudamore[22]	14	7	9
The parsonage Tieths	17	0	0	Tho: Daniell	11	15	10
Tho: Philpotts[19]	4	2	3	Edw: Fisher		13	1
Roger Howell & Wm Hall	10	0	0	Wm Charles or Jones		5	10
Anth: Grubb	22	4	4	Jo: Thomas		6	1
Tho: Weare[20]	13	4	4	Anth: Dower		6	1
	(165r)			Phil: Hannis		7	0
Lewis Weare	1	13	9	Robt Lambert		2	0
Wm Fisher	1	14	0	Tho: Edward		3	0
Wm Vaughan [*Boughan*]				Jo: White	17	6	9
of Bryans	4	12	7	Jo: Jones	1	15	0
Phil: Leech	3	15	0	Waltr Vaughan for &c	3	2	6
Ja: Lane	4	0	9	Tho: Nicholls	5	13	6
Wm Hannis	3	2	2	Tho: Morris		17	9
Ro: Hannis	1	0	0	Tho: Hannis	1	15	9
Marg: Catchmeyd	1	18	4	Tho: Hall		3	10
Jo: Fletcher		12	0	Jo: Nicholls	5	11	0
Ethelb: Gardinar		6	6	Jo: Powell	1	5	0
Tho: Howell	1	14	1	Wm Boughan of Ash	4	15	10

16. Subs. 1663 (lands £1).
17. John White, Subs. 1663 (lands £1).
18. Gent., Subs. 1663 (lands £1).
19. Gent., Subs. 1663 (lands £1).
20. Subs. 1663 (lands £1).
21. Subs. 1663 (with Elizabeth Swift, lands £1); HT 1664 (7).
22. Subs. 1663 (lands £1).

Wormilow: Gudridge continued

		£	s	d
Wm Puckmore		4	7	10
Charles Fisher		5	14	3
Wm Boughan		3	0	3
Rich: Hannis[23]		8	4	3
	(166r)			
Tho: Boughan		2	18	9
Ro: & Tho: Boughan		1	0	8
Tho: Mills		8	5	0
Idem for lease land		3	0	0
Phil: Harris			5	6
Phil: Jenkins		1	8	1
Tho: Havard iun			11	6
Outdwellers holding land				
in the parish:				
Rudhall Gwillim Esq	h:	1	4	6
Ri: Vaughan Esq	h:	3	0	0
Phil: Vaughan gen		1	10	0
Jo: Hoskins gen	h:	1	10	0
Wm Edwards		2	0	0
Wm Chynn		2	5	0

			£	s	d
Jo: Fisher	past [part] Horse		5	3	9
Wm Smith	& charged only			6	1
Roger Hall	for Horse 012				
or Tho:	the Remainders				
Vaughan	the Value doub		1	8	0
Anne Jones	led belongeth				
wid	to the Countess			9	4
Tho: Marrett	of Kent			10	10
Ro: Smith	Excepting Tho:			11	0
Tho: Philpott	Howells land wch				
of Brelston	is but small		2	16	3
Tho: Vaughan				10	9
Phil: Prichard				3	0
Giles Jowling				4	11
Tho: Hennond				7	6
	Charge		304	0	0
			[334	18	2]

Jo: Savaker, Tho: Weare. Raters.

(167r)

6. Haywood[24]   [Wm6]

[There follows a blank page]

7. Hentland   (168r)   [Wm7]

		£	s	d
Sr Wm Powell Barr'tt	h:	52	10	0
Jo: Smith[25]		12	0	0
Idem Jo: Smith			18	0
Ja: Smith		2	13	0
Jo: Bennett	h:	12	10	0
Ro: Smith		1	11	6
Ri: Chest	h:	6	0	0
Idem Chest		4	0	0
Jo: Seymore		8	13	0
Jam: Rodd	h:	3	7	0
Jo: Hannis		1	18	0
The wid Chyn			19	0

		£	s	d
Edw: Goodman			19	0
Phil: Symonds			18	0

[There follows a half page gap and the next entries start at the head of a page]

(169r)

		£	s	d
The wid Pelletory			10	0
Tho: Meredith			18	0
The wid Joulin			10	0
Tho: Meynde	h:	2	16	0
Tho: Weaver & Jo: Weaver			9	0
Phil: Pilstow [Pitstow]		1	14	0
Jo: Machin		3	5	0
Phil: Davies			19	0

23. Subs. 1663 (lands £1, with Roger Howells).
24. Normally taxed with Dewsall.   25. Gent., Subs. 1663 (lands £1).

Wormilow: Hentland continued

		£	s	d
Tho: Mynde for Abrell			16	0
Roger Jones		1	5	0
Jo: Hoskins gen	h:		18	0
Ri: Creese [Croose]			5	0
Tho: Vaughan			12	0
Tho: Rawlins Esq for				
&c	h:	12	10	0
Jo: Rickards			4	0
Jo: Glyn[26]		12	10	0
Will: Meynde [Minde]		24	14	0
Tho: Meynde			15	0
Wm Beale	q for h:	8	4	0
Tho: Machin		2	18	0
Will: Streete		5	10	0
Tho: Hopkin [Hopkins]		2	16	0
Jo: Roberts		2	13	0
Edw: Lewis		1	15	0
Tho: Roberts			15	0
Wm Gwatkin			11	0
Ro: Myles	h:		10	0
Ja: Scudamore Esq[27]	h:	10	0	0
Bennett Hoskins Esq	h:	5	0	0
Tho: Beale cler		4	0	0
Sands Hulmes cler	h:	7	14	0
Mrs Evans[28]		7	0	0
Ja: Roberts iun		4	10	0
Jo: Bennett		7	0	0
Will: Puckmore		1	7	0

		£	s	d
Will: Roberts of Cary	h:	3	11	0
Will: Roberts of Traissock		3	15	0
Jo: Hopkins		2	4	0
Humph: Wilcocks			11	0
			(170r)	
And: Brodle [Brodley]		1	0	0
Ch: Fisher			12	0
Oliver Glyn	h:		14	0
The wid Underwood			14	0
Jo: Kidley gen	h:	3	0	0
Guilb: Wilcocks		3	14	0
Fra: Gibons			19	0
Tho: Jones		1	11	0
Jo: Puckmore		1	0	0
Jo: Davis now Guilb:				
Wilcockes			4	0
Ri: Wilcockes	h:	1	0	0
Tho: Wilcockes for &c	h:	1	2	0
Tho: Bluck [Black]			9	0
Jo: Hopkins & And: Brodle			5	0
Wm Roberts of Cary &c			19	0

Charge 279 0 0

[273 13 6]

Wm Mynde, Jo: Bennett. Raters.

The valuation is to be doubled

---

8. Kings Caple
[Wm8]

		£	s	d
Sr Jo: Kyrle Barr[tt]	h:	40	0	0
Sr Jo: Scudamore Barr[tt]	h:	40	0	0
Jo: Vaughan Esq	h:	40	0	0
Tyrer Dr in divinity	h:	12	0	0
Wm Gwillim gen	h:	20	0	0
Tho: Marrett gen[29]	h:	40	0	0
Tho: Apperley gen	h:	5	0	0
Tho: Hyett		10	0	0
Jo: Bridges gen	h:	6	0	0

	£	s	d
Jo: Payne gen & his			
moth[r30]	35	0	0
Anth: Grubb & Tho:			
Gwillim gen	40	0	0
Jo: Paine sen[31]	18	0	0
Jo: Puckmore	13	0	0
Mrs Katherine Gwillim wid	15	0	0
Jo: Minde sen	18	0	0
Fra: Pricherd[32]	13	0	0

---

26. Yeoman, Subs. 1663 (lands £1). Will proved 18 Oct. 1664 (PCC).
27. HT 1664 (15).
28. Anne Eavons, widow, Subs. 1663 (with William Roberts, lands £1).
29. Subs. 1663 (lands £1). HT 1664 (5).   30. Subs. 1663 (lands £1).
31. Subs. 1663 (lands £1).   32. Gent., Subs. 1663 (lands £1).

Wormilow: King's Caple continued

	£	s	d
Ri: Mynd & Will: Beale	15	0	0
Wm Rogers	13	0	0
Fortune Holder[33]	10	0	0
	(171r)		
Will: Nurse[34]	10	0	0
Waltr Underwood	6	0	0
Tho: Griffitts	5	0	0
Jo: Hullutt	5	0	0
Roger Gwillim gen	5	0	0
Charge	221	0	0
	[434	0	0]

Jo: Payne, Anth: Grubb, Jo: Puckmore. Raters.

2 partes are to be added to the Valuation

---

9. Killpeck &c   [Wm9]

[There follows a blank half page]

(172r)

		£	s	d
Trevill				
The Lady Pye &c[35]	h:	20	0	0
Ro: Russell gen[36]	h:	12	13	4
Jo: Hoskins &c	h:	4	13	4
Old Mr Scudamore of				
Kench: &c	h:	14	13	4
Tho: Good gen	h:	1	15	0
Hugh Russell		1	15	0
Roger Garnons gen	h:	9	0	0
Ri: Dobbins gen[37]	h:	9	6	8
Walter Giles	h:	5	6	8
Jo: Pye & Marg: Pye		2	13	4
Tho: Jones & his sisters	h:	4	13	4
Deverox Quarrell &c		12	0	0
David Quarrell &c	h:	5	6	8
Ri: Hunt & his mother		2	13	4
Jo: Edwards		4	0	0
Tho: Wathen &c	h:	2	13	4
Jo: Edwards Geo: Meirick				
& Tho: Smith &c		8	0	0

		£	s	d
Jo: Seysell		1	6	8
Jo: Jones			13	4
Will: James			13	4
Phil: Harry &c	h:	1	6	8
Sim: Preece [Price] &c	h:		13	4
Ja: Gardiner & Wm				
Thomas &c	h:	4	13	4
Will: Price	h:	1	13	4
Charge		127	0	0
		[132	3	4]

Ri: Dobins, Jo: Pye, Jo: Edwards. Raters.

The valuation is to be doubled.

Llanhithock

[There follows a blank three-quarters of a page]

---

33. Spinster, Subs. 1663 (lands £1).
34. Gent., Subs. 1663 (lands £1).
35. Widow of Sir Walter Pye who died 1 Dec. 1659; Robinson, p. 88.
36. HT 1664 (4).
37. HT 1664 (4).

10. Landinabo &c[38]   (173r)   [Wm10]

		£	s	d		£	s	d
Ri: Carlis Minister		4	0	0	Jo: Meyrick		5	0
Bennett Hoskins Esq[39]	h:	1	0	0	Joh: Tomy wid	1	0	0
Rudhall Gwillim Esq	h:	12	0	0	Tho: Willim for &c	1	0	0
Jo: Nurse & Edw: Jones					Florish Griffitts	1	0	0
Esq	h:	1	0	0				
Jo: Kidley gen	h:	10	0	0	Charge	79	0	0
Wm Andrewes gen		15	0	0		[69	15	0]
Phil: Andrewes gen [40]		15	0	0				
Tho: Patershall gen		1	0	0	Jo: Ketherough, Ri: Woodward. Raters.			
Ri: Woodward		1	0	0				
Will: Morse		3	10	0	**2 partes are to be added to ye**			
Jo: Ketheroughe		3	0	0	**Valuation**			

[11.] Langaran   (174r)   [Wm11]

		£	s	d			£	s	d
He: Milbourne Esq	h:	90	0	0	Mr Halls for Trereers	h:	30	0	0
Rich: Ballard gen	h:	75	0	0	Mr Vaughan of				
Phil: Jones gen		30	0	0	Trebumfrey	h:	30	0	0
Oswald Hoskins gen		15	0	0	Jo: Gwillim		5	0	0
Jo: Kemble gen		15	0	0	Jo: Tombes & Jo: Bennett		15	0	0
Jo: Phillipps		15	0	0	Tho: Rawlins Esq[42]	h:	60	0	0
Ro: Edwards[41]		20	0	0	Tho: Grifitts[43] & Jo:				
Ja: Collins		20	0	0	Grifitts		70	0	0
Will: Howells iun		10	0	0	Ri: Rees		45	0	0
Tho: Edwards		15	0	0	Jo: Taylor		10	0	0
Ri: Jenkins		10	0	0	Mr Myno[rs] Land	h:	15	0	0
Jo: Philpotts of Trewen		5	0	0	Tho: Taylor & Roul:				
Jo: Philpotts of Trewaren		15	0	0	Smith		15	0	0
Will: Howells sen		5	0	0	Mary Daniell wid		10	0	0
Tho: Donne		30	0	0	Wm Lewis		5	0	0
Tho: Wathen for &c		10	0	0	Grace Hart wid		20	0	0
Ri: Drew		2	10	0	Wm Gwillim gen[44]	h:	120	0	0
Ralph Wathen		2	10	0	Sr Jo: Scudamores land	h:	35	0	0
Walter Lewis		2	10	0	Jo: Philpotts		10	0	0
Jo: Hoskins gen	h:	65	0	0	Joh: Penn wid		5	0	0
Wa: Hill gen	h:	65	0	0	Tho: Williams		5	0	0
Will: Browne gen		20	0	0	Tho: Hopkins		2	10	0

38. Probably included Harewood.
39. Subs. 1663 (lands £8).
40. Subs. 1663 (lands £2). Elinor Andrews was charged on 3 hearths in 1664.
41. Subs. 1663 (with his son Thomas and the widow Edwards of Lancran, lands £1).
42. FP 1661 (£13 6s 8d paid); Subs. 1663 (lands £3).
43. HT 1664 (9).
44. FP 1661 (£5).

Wormilow: Langaran continued

	£ s d			£ s d
	(175r)	Rich: Williams		2 0 0
James Scudamore gen	5 0 0			
Mr Halls[45] & Mr			Charge	1162 0 0
Ballards	h: 15 0 0			
Jo: Tovey gen	60 0 0	Phe: Jones, Ri: Reece, Tho: Griffitts.		
Grace Gwatkins	20 0 0	Raters.		
Ja: Wathen	10 0 0			
The wid Powells land	5 0 0	**The Valuation direct.**		

12. Lanrothall[46]   [Wml2]

[There follow two blank half pages]

(176r)
13. Lanwarne   [Wml3]

	£ s d		£ s d
Jam: Scudamore Esq	h: 30 0 0	Will: Adrewes [*Andrewes*]	
Sr Ja: Scudamore Barr^t	h: 8 0 0	gen	6 10 0
Sr Wm Powell Barr^t	h: 7 0 0	Roger Webb	4 0 0
Ben: Hoskins Esq	h: 60 0 0	Will: Geathing	4 0 0
Jo: Hoskins Esq	h: 41 0 0	Ja: Gunter	2 0 0
Jo: Nurse[47] & Edw:			(177r)
Jones Esqs	h: 102 0 0	Will: Webb	1 0 0
Jo: Kidley gen	h: 1 0 0	Will: Powell	1 10 0
Jo: Browne gen & Ces:		Jo: Coules	1 0 0
Hoskins	32 0 0	Howell Williams	3 0 0
Edw: Beatham cler	14 0 0	Tho: Morse	3 0 0
David Powell	32 0 0	Tho: Morse of Pencoyd	10 0
Ri: Willim	8 0 0		
Oliver Willim	8 0 0	Charge	311 0 0
Tho: Rouck [*Rocke*]	6 0 0		[*414 0 0*]
Tho: Willim	4 0 0		
Jo: Willim	8 0 0	Da: Powell, Wi: Morse. Raters.	
Wm Morse	8 0 0		
Tho: Woodward	3 0 0	**A 4th part is to be added to**	
Walt^r Underwood	3 10 0	**the Valuation**	
Jo: & Hen: Ketherough	12 0 0		

45. Walter Hall, FP 1661 (£3 paid).
46. The largest HT charges in 1664 were on Henry Milbourne Esq and William Morton (11 each).
47. JP q 1660. In 1646 his real estate in the county was put at £25 a year and his personal estate at £93: Loan 29/15, pf. 2. Subs. 1663 (lands £4); HT 1664 (9).

14. Little Birch &c [Wm14a]

		£	s	d
Jo: Lo: Viscount				
Scudamore	h:	10	0	0
Jo: Kidley gen[48]		10	0	0
Wm Guillim gen		8	0	0
Jo: Guillim gen		9	0	0
Wm Higgs cler		7	0	0
Mary Abrahall wid		7	0	0
Tho: Parsons		3	0	0
Jo: Gwatkin		4	0	0
Tho: Weaver		3	0	0
Tho: Binkes		4	0	0
Ri: Rogers		2	0	0
Tho: Banton		1	0	0
	Charge	68	0	0

Jo: Gwillim, Tho: Parsons. Raters.

Aconbury[49] [Wm14b]

		£	s	d
The Lo: Visc: Scudamore		10	0	0
Sr Ja: Bridges[50] & Sr Wm				
Powell		120	0	0
	Charge	—	—	—

Tho: Binckes, Rater.

Little Dewchurch [Wm14c]

		£	s	d
Rudhall Gwillim Esq	h:	2	10	0
Tho: Rawlins Esq	h:	18	0	0
Mr Gething[51]		37	0	0
Mr Helmes		3	0	0

		£	s	d
Mr Voile		6	0	0
Mr Barnes	q h:	6	0	0
Mr Edwins		4	0	0
Tho: Jones		4	0	0
			(178r)	
Rich: Jones		5	0	0
Jo: Hey		10	0	0
Phil: Witherstone		6	0	0
Phil: Lambert		5	0	0
Phil: Osburne		2	10	0
Ja: Billingsley		6	0	0
Tho: Wilcocks	h:	20	0	0
The wid Williams		4	0	0
Jo: Jones jun		5	0	0
Tho: Biggs		1	10	0
David Freyer		1	10	0
Walter Underwood		1	10	0
Jo: Bennett		6	15	0
Guilb: Wilcocks		1	10	0
Jo: Hopkin			5	0
Wm Roberts			2	6
Tho: Biggleston		2	0	0
Wm Pitman		1	0	0
Ri: Combe		1	10	0
Ja: Andrewes		3	0	0
Edw: Witherston		1	10	0
Ja: Linke		3	0	0
Charge		225	0	0
		[169	2	6]

Tho: Jones, Ja: Billingsley. Raters.

15. Marstow [Wm15]

	£	s	d
Tho: Philpotts[52]	30	0	0
Jo: Chest	24	0	0
Will: Chinn	11	0	0
Tho: Philpotts of			
Coroxstone [Ruxton]	4	0	0

	£	s	d
Tho: Philpotts for &c	4	10	0
Phil: Vaughan	14	10	0
Tho: Philpotts		10	0
Ro: Edwards	5	0	0
Tho: Edwards of Lancrall	9	0	0

48. Subs. 1663 (lands £1).
49. The largest HT charge in Aconbury in 1664 was on Giles Wilton (9).
50. In 1646 the personal estate in the county of Sir John Bridges of Aconbury was valued at £289; Loan 29/15, pf. 2.
51. Probably Richard Gething, gent., Subs. 1663 (lands £1).
52. Probably of Trebandy, Subs. 1663 (lands £2); HT 1664 (5).

N

Wormilow: Marstow continued

	£	s	d		£	s	d
Ro: Edwards for &c	1	0	0	Tho: Edwards of Pencreck			
Anne Hennond wid	7	0	0	and Nich: Hill	12	10	0
Tho: Philpotts of Brelston	8	0	0	Anne Jones wid	1	10	0
Mrs Swift	5	0	0	Jo: Philpotts of Brelston	1	10	0
		(179r)		Phil: Hennond	1	0	0
Will: Edwards of Whitfield	2	4	6	Marg: Nicholls		8	0
Tho: Edwards of the same	2	4	6	Ri: Thomas		10	0
Rog Hall	6	0	0	Tho: Tyrer	20	0	0
Tho: Hannis		15	0				
Tho: Marrett [*Marryott*]		2	0	Charge	215	0	0
Phil: Leech		8	0		[*175*	*7*	*0*]
Tho: Morris		3	0				
Rog Jones	1	14	0	Tho: Philpotts, Will: Chinn. Raters.			
Tho: Vaughan		18	0				

Nothing added to the valuation

---

16. Much Birch   [*Wm16*]

	£	s	d		£	s	d
Edw: Jones gen	3	0	0	Jo: Coope [*Cope*]	3	0	0
Jo: Kidley gen	11	0	0	Will: Roberts	3	0	0
Jo: Bennett[53]	6	0	0	Jo: Cowles[55]	3	10	0
Ro: Hiett & Ri: Chance	9	0	0	Wm Rogers & his Mother	6	0	0
Ri: Parsons[54]	5	0	0	Jo: Williams & his Mother	3	0	0
Ja: Lawrence [*Lanwarne*]				The Tieth	20	0	0
& his mother	9	0	0				
Tho: Foy [*Toy*]	6	0	0	Charge	98	10	0
Ri: Rogers	4	0	0				
Ri: Rogers of Beyliston	3	0	0	Jo: Bennett, Tho: Toy, Ri: Rogers, Ri:			
Tho: Parsons	4	0	0	Parsons. Raters.			

---

17. Much Dewchurch   (180r)   [*Wm17*]

		£	s	d			£	s	d
Sr Wm Powell Knt	h:	60	0	0	Jane Bodenham wid[57]	h:	60	0	0
Walter Pye Esq[56]	h:	80	0	0	Jo: Hopkins gen		10	0	0
Geo: Mason gen		10	0	0	Phil: Markie gen		10	0	0
Herb: Boughton cler		25	0	0	Ch: Rogers gen		20	0	0
Mrs Bodeham of Rosse	h:	60	0	0	Ri: Rogers gen		15	0	0

---

53. Gent., Subs. 1663 (lands £1).
54. Gent., Subs. 1663 (lands £1); HT 1664 (4).
55. HT 1664 (4). Morgan Thomas was also charged for 4 hearths.
56. HT 1664 (23).
57. In 1646 the real estate of Jane Bodenham of Bringwen, a papist, was valued at £60 a year; Loan 29/15, pf. 2. In 1660 her estate was rented from the Exchequer by herself for £25; PRO, Various Accounts, E.101/630/30. Subs. 1663 (lands £2).

Wormilow: Much Dewchurch continued

		£	s	d
Tho: Goode gen	h:	10	0	0
Eliz: Staine [*Stacie*]		10	0	0
Walter Gwatkin		10	0	0
Tho: Smith sen		10	0	0
Tho: Smith iun		12	0	0
Fr: Webb		10	0	0
Jo: Howells		4	0	0
Nich: Griffitts } h: Bp		10	0	0
Floris Griffitts		5	0	0
Ri: Ince		4	0	0
Jo: Gronnowe		3	10	0
Will: Gronnowe		3	10	0
Kath: Vaughan & her sister		3	10	0

	£	s	d
Jo: Rogers gen	5	0	0
Jo: Wackline [*Walkley*]	2	0	0
Jo: Williams	2	0	0
Lewis Harris	2	0	0
Charge	446	0	0
[*456*	*10*	*0*]

Wa: Gwatkin, Tho: Smith, Jo: Howells. Raters.

The valuation not much varying

---

18. Orcopp[58]   [*Wm18*]

		£	s	d
Waltr Pye Esq	h:	50	0	0
Jo: Scudamore Esq	h:	1	10	0
The heires of Geo: Jones Esq	h:	8	0	0
Phil: Cecill Esq	h:	12	0	0
Tho: Phillpotts gen	h:	6	10	0
			(181r)	
Sr Nich: Powell for the tieth	h:	15	0	0
Edw: Betham Ministr		1	6	8
Wm Webb		5	6	8
Ro: Baron gen		13	13	7
Jo: Morgan gen		3	16	8
Jo: Lambert sen		1	6	8
Hugh Gouff [*Gough*]		9	3	4
Mr Weale & Mr Rogers		14	13	4
Tho. Powell[59]		5	6	8
Will: Abrahall		3	6	8
Guil: Jones		5	6	8
Phil: Bevan		5	0	0
Will: Oliver		5	6	8

	£	s	d
Jo: Gunter	1	11	2
Jo: Price	2	13	4
Jo: Emme'tts	2	13	4
Jo: Lambert iun	3	10	8
Tho: Price	1	11	0
Roul: Jones	2	13	4
Tho: Lambert	2	17	6
Jo: Jones	1	1	4
Jo: Rogers	2	6	8
Walter Pridith	6	0	0
Rich: Powell	1	15	7
Charge	207	0	0
[*195*	*7*	*6*]

Jo: Clogan, Jo: Lambert, Wm Oliver. Raters.

A 3rd part is to be added to the Valuation

---

58. The largest HT charge in 1664 was on Thomas Bodenham, gent. (3).
59. Yeoman, will proved 14 Feb. 1665/6 (PCC).

19. Pencoyd

	£	s	d			£	s	d
Will: Gwatkins[60]	20	0	0	Jo: Nurse Esq	h:	13	10	0
Jo: Roberts[61]	16	0	0	Edw: Betham cler		1	10	0
Edw: Morse[62]	15	10	0	Tho: Tyrer cler		6	13	4
Anne Hopkins[63]	20	0	0	Roger Webb		2	13	4
Robt Tomy	3	6	8	Ja: Rodd for tieth		13	6	8
Ri: Gwatkins	5	6	8	Will: Morse			13	4
Jo: Brace	4	13	4	Tho: Yeareworth for				
Phil: Heane [Neave] for &c	3	15	0	&c	h:	12	0	0
Tho: Hopkins	2	13	0	Tho: Yeareworth for				
Jo: Roberts for Tieth	2	10	0	&c	h:	2	0	0
	(182r)			Tho: Yeareworth for				
Tho: Wathen & Jo: Cope				&c	h:	1	13	4
for &c	4	0	0					
Will: Tomy iun	1	0	0	Charge		162	0	0
Tho: Brace	3	6	8					
Will: & Ro: Tomy	3	6	8	Jo: Roberts, Edw: Morse. Raters.				

		£	s	d
Outdwellers				
Bennett Hoskins Esq	h:	1	10	0
Ro: Myno[rs] Esq	h:	1	10	0

**A 3rd parte is to be added to
the Valuation**

---

20. Peterstow

(183r)

		£	s	d			£	s	d
Ro: Braborne minister[64]		44	0	0	Ri: Chest		5	0	0
Sr Wm Powell Bar[tt]	h:	37	0	0	Will: Ruckell		25	0	0
Sr Ja: Bridges Bar[tt]	h:	43	0	0	Rogr Jones		13	10	0
Rich: Merrett [Marrett]					Will: Jones		6	10	0
gen[65]		10	0	0	Wa: Hill gen	h:	6	0	0
Will: Edwards[66]		19	0	0	Ri: Vaughan Esq	h:	7	0	0
Phil: Pitstow[67]		18	0	0	Jo: Prosser		11	0	0
Phil: Davies[68]		19	0	0	Jo: Hennis [Hannis]		1	10	0
Wm Phelpott[69]		6	0	0	Jo: Phelpott			10	0
Jo: Vaughan		6	0	0	The wid Bennett			10	0
Tho: Edwards		8	10	0	Jane Pye wid		3	0	0
Tho: Phelpott		6	10	0	Owen Mynde			10	0
Jo: Hoskins gen	h:	7	10	0	Blanch Leker wid, Jo: Hill,				
Will: Abrahall		6	10	0	Ri: Jones		6	10	0
Tho: Flenders [Flanders]		4	0	0	Tho: Miles		1	0	0
Ro: Vaughan		5	0	0	Tho: Philpotts gen	h:	19	0	0

---

60. Subs. 1663 (lands £1); HT 1664 (5).
61. Subs. 1663 (lands £1).
62. Subs. 1663 (lands £1).
63. Subs. 1663 (lands £1).
64. Rector, FP 1661 (£1).
65. Subs. 1663 (lands £1).
66. Gent., Subs. 1663 (lands £1).
67. Gent., Subs. 1663 (lands £1).
68. Subs. 1663 (with Roger Davies, lands £1).
69. Subs. 1663 (lands £1).

Wormilow: Peterstow continued

	£	s	d
Jo: Prichard		10	0
Ri: Stephens[70]	1	0	0
Charge	348	0	0

Wm Edwards, Phil: Pitstow, Rogr Jones. Raters.

The valuation direct.

21. St Waynards   [*Wm21*]

		£	s	d
Tho: Bedford cler		5	0	0
Ro: Minors Esq[71]	h:	80	0	0
Jo: Minors gen		8	0	0
Hen: Lawes gen		8	0	0
Will: Hall gen		11	0	0
Tho: Clifford for &c		16	0	0
Jo: Edwards for &c	h:	16	0	0
Ri: Kidley gen for &c	h:	6	0	0
Jo: Williams gen		6	0	0
Alice Mullins wid		3	0	0
Jo: Horseman[72]		6	0	0
Jo: Weare		2	0	0
Edw: Willim		6	0	0
Tho: Philpotts for &c	h:	6	0	0
Wa: Priddith		6	0	0
Jo: Jeyne		8	0	0
Will: Davies for &c		8	0	0
Jo: Kidley for &c	h:	10	0	0
Geo: Martin		3	0	0
Ri: Powell		2	0	0
Tho: Howells		4	0	0
Wm Parlor		2	10	0
Edw: Pridith		1	10	0
Tho: Pridith		1	0	0
Wm Cecill & Jo: Howman		2	0	0
Ri: Ware [*Weare*]		2	0	0
Tho: Horne for &c		1	0	0
Jam: Weare		1	0	0
Jo: Paine		2	0	0
		(184r)		
Jo: Walker		1	0	0
Jo: Willims			10	0
Tho: Gwillim		2	0	0
Jo: Reece [*Prees*] for &c			10	0

		£	s	d
Anne Phillipps wid		1	0	0
Watkin Cary		1	0	0
Tho: Church		1	0	0
Charge		240	0	0
Outdwellers				
Giles Rawlins gen		20	0	0
Rudhall Gwillim Esq	h:	2	0	0
Henry Milbourne Esq	h:	7	0	0
Wm Abrell gen		2	0	0
Tho: Griffitts		1	0	0
Ri: Reece		1	0	0
Marge: Philpotts wid		2	0	0
Joh: Bevan wid		5	0	0
Ri: Barry gen		2	10	0
Ri: Preece		1	0	0
Waltr Webb		1	0	0
Jo: Tovey gen			10	0
Jo: Machin		1	0	0
Edw: Morse		2	0	0
Tho: Yarrett for &c		3	0	0
Hugh Stephens for &c		2	0	0
Ri: Williams & Rich Neaves for &c		6	0	0
Jo: Davies		1	0	0
Jo: Woodward		1	0	0
Charge		61	0	0
		[*59*	*0*	*0*]

Jo: Edwards, Jo: Williams, Jo: Weare. Raters.

2 parts are to be added to the Valuation

---

70. HT 1664 (5).
71. Subs. 1663 (lands £2); HT 1664 (11).
72. Yeoman, Subs. 1663 (lands £1).

22. Sellack [& Foy] &c   (185r)   [Wm22]

		£	s	d		£	s	d
Jam: Scudamore Esq[73]	h:	150	0	0	Wil: Lucas	7	10	0
Sr Will: Powell Kt &					Jo: Hannis	5	0	0
Barr[74]	h:	140	0	0	Wm Grag	6	10	0
Ben: Hoskins Esq for					Ri: Phelpotts [Phelps]	3	15	0
&c[75]	h:	120	0	0	Jo: Phelpotts	3	15	0
Mr Tho: Tyrer cler[76]	h:	50	0	0	Jo: Glynn for &c	7	10	0
Mr Geo: Abrahall					The Tieth of Strangford	15	0	0
cler[77]	h:	25	0	0	Rich: Merrick	2	10	0
Peter Oswald gen[78]		45	0	0	Will: Merrett	3	0	0
And for Heyetts farme		7	0	0	Tho: Merrett	2	10	0
Mrs Eli: Cole wid		35	0	0	Walter Hinner [Binner]	2	0	0
Mrs Susan Burhill					The widow Bennett	2	0	0
[Burghill] wid		16	0	0				
Mrs Mary [Margery]					Charge	710	0	0
Burhill wid		26	0	0	[708	10	0]	
Ri: Weaver for &c		15	0	0				
Jo: Carrier now Jo: Hill		4	10	0	Ri: Phelps, Ro: Vaughan. Ratrs.			
Waltr Meeke for &c		6	10	0				
Tho: Grove		7	10	0	**The Valuation neere direct**			

---

23. Tretyre [& Mi: ch:]   (186r)   [Wm23]

		£	s	d			£	s	d
Dan: Manby cler[79]		20	0	0	Ben: Hoskins Esq	h:	7	0	0
Will: Abrahall gen[80]		30	0	0	Mr Hall	h:	3	10	0
Math: Sough [Shough][81]		15	0	0	Jo: Hopkins		4	10	0
Edw: Powell	h:	12	0	0	Tho: Cooke		1	0	0
Edw: Jones gen & Paul					Hen: Milbourne Esq	h:	1	0	0
Jones gen	h:	15	0	0	Mary Dun		1	0	0
Jo: Scudamore Kt &									
Barr[tt]	h:	20	0	0	Charge		170	0	0
Ri: Vaughan Esq	h:	6	0	0	[167	10	0]		
Ro: Mynors Esq	h:	2	0	0					
Jo: Machin[82]		10	0	0	Wm Abrahall, Math: Slough [Shough].				
Ri: Daniell		7	0	0	Raters.				
Jo: Philpotts		3	10	0					
Wm Gwillim gen	h:	4	0	0	**Valuation as it was given in**				
Jo: Tovey gen		1	10	0	**charged wth Horse £70**				
Edw: Morse		3	10	0					

---

73. FP 1661 (£100 paid); Subs. 1663 (lands £10); commissioner for this subsidy.
74. Subs. 1663 (lands £10); commissioner for the subsidy.   75. HT 1664 (9).
76. Vicar of Sellack, FP 1661 (£3).   77. Vicar of Foy, FP 1661 (£5).
78. Chief constable of Wormilow; Loan 29/49, pf. 4, no. 69/15.
79. Rector of Tretire, FP 1661 (£1 paid); HT 1664 (4).
80. Subs. 1663 (lands £1); HT 1664 (4).
81. Subs. 1663 (lands £1).   82. HT 1664 (4).

24. Welsh Newton [Wm24]

		£	s	d
Mrs Scudamore	h:	46	0	0
Fr: Allen gen[83]		38	0	0
Geo: Kemble gen[84]		10	0	0
Ch: Tudor[85]		17	0	0
Geo: Powell gen		6	0	0
Phil: Hopkin		16	0	0
Jo: Watkins		9	0	0
Phil: Donne[86]		24	0	0
Will: Daniell		3	0	0
Alice Donne		2	10	0
Nath: Dobbins		2	0	0
Eliz: Baker		6	0	0
Marg: Taylor		6	0	0
Will: Lewis gen		5	0	0
Jo: Philpott		3	0	0

		£	s	d
Tho: Pearle Esq	h:	48	0	0
Tho: Phillipps		10	10	0
Jo: Winston		2	0	0
Rogr Bayly		2	0	0
Jane Raynolds		2	0	0
Marga: Catchmay		1	0	0
Jo: Kemble gen		1	0	0
Ri: Tydor		2	0	0
Charge		262	0	0

Phil: Hopkin, Phil: Donn. Raters.

Valuation direct.

25. Whitchurch [& *Gunardo*] (187r) [Wm25

		£	s	d
Rudhall Gwillim Esq[87]	h:	30	0	0
Sr Tho: Dorrell[88]		40	0	0
The Countess of Kent	p:	30	0	0
Will: Gardiner gen		10	0	0
Phil: Vaughan gen		20	0	0
The Lands of Jo: Nurse				
gen	h:	12	0	0
Will: Howells[89]		20	0	0
Jo: Davies		20	0	0
Jo: Fisher		20	0	0
Jo: Jennings		20	0	0
Tho: Potter		10	0	0
Tho: Philpotts of Crebandy				
[*Trebandy*] gen	h:	5	0	0
Ro: Taylor		1	10	0
Ch: Mainston		4	0	0
Tho: Philpott of Ruxton		5	0	0

		£	s	d
Roger Morris		2	0	0
Phil: Jennings		4	0	0
Ja: Dew		3	0	0
Tho: Dew		10	0	0
The wid Cutta [*Cutt*]		3	0	0
Mrs Catchway		5	0	0
Kath: Philpotts		4	0	0
Will: Lucas		4	0	0
Jo: Vaughan		2	0	0
Ro: Tomy		2	0	0
Jo: Philpotts of Sellersbrook		3	0	0
The wid Gardiner		5	0	0
Ro: Davies cler		1	0	0
Will: Chyn		1	0	0
Roger Rickards		2	0	0
Lands belonging to the				
Count: of Kent	p:	6	0	0

83. Subs. 1663 (lands £1); HT 1664 (11).
84. In 1646 his real estate in the county was valued at £36 a year; Loan 29/15, pf. 2. Subs. 1663 (lands £1).
85. Subs. 1663 (lands £1).
86. Chief constable of Wormilow; 1663; Loan 29/49, pf. 4, no. 69/15. Gent., Subs. 1663 (lands £1).
87. JP q 1655 and 1660; captain of a militia company 1664; Loan 29/49, pf. 4, no. 69/15. FP 1661 (£10 unpaid); Subs. 1663 (lands £3); HT 1664 (7).
88. Probably Sir Thomas Darrell of Lillingstone Dayrell, Bucks; Shaw, p. 202.
89. Gent., Subs. 1663 (lands £1).

Wormilow: Whitchurch [& Gunardo] continued

	£	s	d			£	s	d
							(188r)	
Jo: Jones of the Gockett	1	0	0					
Will: Smith of the Laies	4	0	0	Rich: Jennings	2	0	0
Ri: Philpott of the same	2	0	0	Lands belonging to the			
Ja: Collins	4	0	0	Countess of Kent	1	0	0
Ro: Jennings	3	0	0	Jo: Taylor of Doward side	1	0	0
Tho: Phillipps for &c	6	0	0	Tho: Meeke	2	0	0
The widow Weaver	2	0	0	Mr Bonner	3	0	0
Jo: Dew	1	0	0	Edw: Betham parson of			
Ro; Edwards	2	0	0	Whitch: & Ganareu			
Jo: Jones	1	10	0	for the Gleb[90]	40	0	0
Ri: Gwillim	1	0	0				
Tho: Roberts	1	0	0	Charge	387	0	0
Ja: Probin	1	0	0		[385	0	0]
Lands belonging to the							
Count: of Kt	p: 1	0	0	Phill: Vaughan, Will: Howells. Ratrs.
Will: Bennett	1	0	0	

Nothing added to the Valuation.

---

90. Rector of Whitchurch, FP 1661 (50s).

Finis[1]

Broxash Hund:
1. Wigton

Grimsworth Hund:
2. Hampton
3. Staunton

Radlow Hund:
4. Hamonds Froome
5. Stretton Gransome

Wolphey Hund:
6. While
7. Crofte.

---

1. This is a list of parishes for which no nominal schedules are included in the MS, although totals are included for all but two. There are other nominal schedules apparently missing, but only those for Kilpeck and Llanhithog are unlikely to be represented under other parish schedules.

INDEX OF NAMES

Each name in the assessment schedules has been indexed in the following pages to the particular schedule in which it appears. This has been done by giving each parish or township list an alpha-numerical symbol. Where a parish or township schedule is further subdivided another alphabetical character has been added. The first alphabetical code indicates the hundred in which the parish is situated. The numerical suffixes are in series following consecutively the order of the parish schedules.

Alphabetical code	Hundred	
B	Broxash	pp. 29–47
E	Ewias Lacy	pp. 48–56
Ge	Greytree	pp. 57–69
Gm	Grimsworth	pp. 70–81
H	Huntington	pp. 82–88
R	Radlow	pp. 89–105
S	Stretford	pp. 106–116
Wb	Webtree	pp. 117–130
Wg	Wigmore	pp. 131–148
Wp	Wolphey	pp. 149–168
Wm	Wormilow	pp. 169–186

All common Christian names have been abbreviated. Where the text itself uses a shorter abbreviation this has been adopted in the index when there is any doubt as to what was intended. If there is more than one reference to a name in a schedule the number of references is added to the parish symbol against the name. Thus two references to William Baker in Ross Borough will be indexed: 'Will: Ge11a(2).'

Abrahall; Abrall; Abrell
Geo: Ge3; Wm22; Guy: Ge11a(2); John: Ge3; Ge6; Ge16; R31(2); Wm2; Mary: Wm14a; Thos: B24; R31; Will: Ge7a(2); Wm18; Wm20; Wm21; Wm23(2).

Abraham
Thos: Wg25.

Acton
Mrs: B19; Hum: B16; John: S10; Nich: Wp12; Ri: Wp10a; Wp24(2); Sam: H7; Will: B11; B14a; B20.

Adams; Addams
Mr: B2; B10d; wdw: Wg6; Anne: Wp10b; Edwd: R15d; Hugh: Wb19; John: Gm1; Wp12; Miles: S1; Will: B6; Ge14; S8; S10.

Adcock; Adcox
Joseph: B4; B6; Will: R9.

Addis; Addice
Jeremy: Gm7; Jerome: B19; Gm18; John: Gm18; S6(2); Phil: Ge2; Ge11a; Ge12; Wm2; Rich: Wm2; Thos: Ge2(2); Ge11a; Wm2; Will: H6(2); S8.

Alcott; Awkett
John: B6; R26.

Alcox; Alcocks
Eliz: Wp29; John: Wp13a.

Alder
Anth: Ge11a.

Aldern; Alderne; Aldren
Dr: Wb19; Dan: B27c; Edwd: Gm11a; Wb6; Thos: R6(2); Will: B6; R11.

Aldred
Hum: Wp12.

Aleworth
John: E8.

Alford
Wdw: R30; John: S14; Rich: R30.

Allen
Mr: Wb18; Edwd: Wg14(2); Fran: Wm4; Wm24; Jam: S5a(2); John: R4(2); Will: Gm21.

Amies
John: S1.

Andrews; Andrewes; Andrew; Adrewes
Wdw: R30; Alice: Wm2; Chris: B2; B7; Dan: B25; Jam: Wm14c; John: R15f; R28b; Lewis: E7; Phil: Wm10; Thos: B13(2); Will: B13; H8; Wp15; Wm10; Wm13.

Angell
John: Wp8.

Apperley; Apperlo
Anth: Ge6; Ge12; Ge16(2); Edwd: Wp10b(2); Wp25c; John: Ge6; Ge9(2); Thos: Ge2; Ge3(3); Ge16; Wm8; Will: Ge16.

Archer
John: Ge8d; Rowl: Wp15.

Arden
John: B11(2); B25.

Arnell
Walt: Gm1.

Arnold
Arnold's: E1; Nich: E8.

Arundell
John: R3; Rich: R3; Thos: Ge11a; Wb17; Wp22.

Asborn; see Osburne
John: R13.

Ashley; Ashtley; Astley
Edwd: S12; Jam: Wg20(3); Wg25.

Ashman
John: Ge7a; Ge7b.

Aston
John: R26; Wg6; Rich: H3; Sam: R11.

Atherton
Fran: R21.

Aubrey; Awbrey
Herb: Wb6; Wb10; Wb12; Wb21; Wp25c; John: Gm7(2); Ursula: B28.

Ayleway; Ayway
Fran: Ge9; Isaac: Ge9; Rob: Ge7a; R27; Will: R27.

Aylewood
Jam: S7.

Babe
Babe's: B6; Rich: B6; Will: B6.

Bach
Anth: R11; Herb: Wp13a; John: Wp4a; Wp11(2); Rich: Wp13a; Wp13b(2); Wp13c; Wp13d; Wp13e; Wp13f(2); Wp24; Walt: S6.

Bachley
Bachley's: B8.

Bacon:
Ralph: R26.

Badham; Baddam
Anne: B7; Edwd: Gm18; Elin: Wb6; Epiphian: R3; Fran: B6; R3; R6; Henr: Ge8f; H4; R30; Hum: H4; John: B7; Ge8d; R31; Wb12; Wp2; Joyce: B7; Mary B23; Rob: H4; Thos: B10g; Walt: H4; Will: Gm3; H4(2); H6; R3.

Badland
John: S12; Wg20; Rich: S12; Wp6a; Rog: Wg22b.

Badnage; Badnedge
Thos: Wp13c; Will: Wp13d.

Baggard; Baggott
Jam: R1(2); John: R1; Thos: Wb8; Will: R1.

Bagnall
Wdw: R29.

Bailies; Baylies; Baylis
Eliz: Wp2; Geo: B11; B22; Wp3; Hugh: Wp3; Hum: Wp6a(2); Jam: R11; John: Wp6a; Martha: B27c; Silvanus: R3; Sim: Wp4b; Will: B6; B22; Wp4b; Wp10c; Wp13f.

Baker; Backer
Mr: B19; R30; Mrs: Wm2; wdw: B2; Anne: B19; Blanch: Ge11a; Edwd: S5b; Eliz: Wm24; Hum: Gm17; John: B2; Ge9; Wp1; Nich: H4; Phil: B10a(2); Rich: B2; B19; R26; Rob: Wg17; Thos: B2(2); B6(2); B12; Will: Ge11a(2); Ge11b.

Baldwin; Baldwyn
Edwd: R28; Henr: S6; Wp16b; Hester: R11; John: Ge11b(2); R11; Thos: R15a; Will: R15a; S6; Wp16b.

Bale; or Bulee
Balee: H2.

Ball
An: B4; John: B1; B3; B4; B9; Walt: S1; Will: Ge11a.

Ballard
Mr: Wm11; wdw: B5b; Edm: Wb6; Geo: B5b; John: B15; Rich: Wm11.

Banes
Henr: Wb8.

Bangham
Edw: Wp13b.

Banks; Bankes
Alice: Wg24; John: Wp25a; Will: Wb1

Bannaster; Banaster
Mr: Gm5; John: Wp4a.

Banton
Thos: Wm14a.

Barber
Barber's: S4; Will: Wp16a(2).

Barker
Mr: Gm9; Edwd: Gm20; Eliz: Wp3.

Barnaby; Barneby; Barnabie
Mr: S10; John: B4; B9; B11; B24; B26; Gm8(2); Wp12(2).

Barnes
Mr: Wm14c; Jam: S3; S7; John: B20(2); S14; Rich: B18(2); B26; Rob: E5; Rowl: B14a(2); Will: B25.

Barnett
Ch: Wp13c; Johan: B6; Will: Wb1(2)

Barnsley; Barnesley
Anne: Wb16; John: R15b.

Baron
Ro: Wm18.

Barrar; Barwar; Barrear
Henr: S6; Rich: S6; Thos: S6; Wg4(2).

Barrell; Barroll
Henr: Wb1; Rich: Ge7a; Wb1(2); Will: Wb12(2).

Barrett; Burrett
Eliz: R9; Fran: B14a; John: R9; Joyce: B5a; Rich: R9; Will: R9.

Barrow
John: Gm18; Math: B5a.

Barry; Barrey
Rich: Wm21; Will: Ge6; Ge16.

Bartluitt
Mary: H7.

Barton
Henr: B2; B10d; Ralph: R9.

Bartram
John: S6.

Baskervile
Edwd: Wb9; Wb17; Hump: H4; H6; R29; Wb13; Wb16(2); Thos: B5a; H4; Will: Wm4(2).

Basseter
Fran: Gm1.

Bassett
Gabriell: H6.

Baston; Barston; Bareston
John: R8(3); R13; Thos: R7.

Batman
Jam: B20; John: B20.

Baugh; Bauch
Wdw: R20; John: Wg12; Marchaunt: H6.

Baughan; Boughan
Ro: Wm5; Thos: Wm5(2); Will: Wm5.

Baxter
Rich: Wb5.

Bayes
Johan: S6.

Bayliffe; Bayliffes
Wdw: B21; Jam: R15a.

Bayly; Baylie; Baily
Edwd: Gm23; Henr: B27a; Johan: B12; John: Gm23; Wp13e; Rich: B27b; Wb27(2); Rog: Wm24; Steph: Ge11a; Will: S11a; Wb15.

Bayton
Will: S10; S14(2).

Beacham; Beachamp
Alice: S9; John: R13(2).

Beale; Beele; Beall
Mr: Wb6; Mrs: R31; John: Ge1; Ge13; R10; R17; Joseph: Wb1; Thos: Wm7; Will: Ge11a; Wg9; Wm7; Wm8.

Beast
Hosea: Wb12.

Beatham; Betham
Edwd: Wm13; Wm18; Wm19; Wm25.

Beaver
Rich: R7.

Bebb
Rich: S12; Wg20.

Braine
Mr: E4.

Brampton; see Brompton
John: Wb10; Michael: R6.

Branch
Anth: R15a.

Brandish
Mary: Ge4.

Brasier; Brazier
Nath: Gm11a; Rog: B24(2).

Bray; Brey; see Broy
Henr: R4; R7; John: R28a; Rog: B5b(2); Thos: B11.

Brewer; Bruer
Rich: Wp7; Will: Wp7.

Bridges; Bridge
Mr: B2; B9; Mrs: Wp14; Ch: Wm2; Giles: Wb9; Jam: Wm2; Wm14b; Wm20; John: Ge8f; Ge13(2); R4; R15b; R18; R22; R31; Wm8; Thos: Ge15; Gm21; R26; R4(2); R7; S4; S14; Will: B19; Ge13; Ge16; R1; R21; R26; Wb22; Wb24(2).

Bridgewater; Bridgewaters
Edwd: Wg1a(2); John: Wg10; Rich: Wg1a; Wg14; Thos: Wg8; Wg14(2); Wg15; Wg29(2); Will: Wg1a; Wg1b.

Bright
Rob: R7; R8; R22.

Brimell; Brymeld
Anne: Wp20; John: Wg10; Wp4a(2).

Brincet
Mr: Ge8g.

Brinton
Rich: Gm20.

Brock
Rich: Wp18; Thos: Wp25c.

Brodle
And: Wm7(2).

Brompton; see Brampton
Jam: B6; Thos: Wp20.

Bromth; or Bromich
Bromth: H2; Anne: H2.

Brooke; Brook
Wdw: R8; R28b; Fran: R7(2); Hump: R23; R31; John: Ge1; Nich: R8; Rich: B17; R17; Thos: Wp21.

Broome
Jam: R15a; John: B1; B27c; B28(2); R3

Brotin
Barthol: R4.

Broughton; Braughton; see Boughton
Mr: Wb19; Herb: Gm11b; Michael: H6.

Browne; Brown
Wdw: B10a; Geo: B9; Giles: B17; Henr: Wp12(2); Wp18; Wp25c; John: B1(2); B4; B26; Gm13; S10; S11a; R3; Wg13; Wg22c; Wp29; Wm13; Rich: B9; R3; Wg7; Wp11; Wp13a; Thos: Ge11a; Ge11b; Gm13; S11a; R15f; Wg21; Wm2; Will: B27c; Ge4; Gm9; Gm13; Gm22; R2; R15f; Wg22c; Wp10a(2); Wm11.

Broy; see Bray
Henr: R4; John: B4; Wp6b; Will: Wp6b; Wp13a.

Brukley; see Buckley
Anth: Ge16.

Bruton
Will: Wp3.

Bryan; Brian; Brians
Edwd: Wpl; Henr: Wp13b; Hump: H4; John: Wg20; Phil: Wg17; Thos: Wg17(2).

Bubb
John: S6; Will: S6(2).

Buckenhill
Edwd: R11; R15a.

Buckingham
Duke: B2; Wp11; Wp18.

Buckley; see Brukley
Abraham: Ge1.

Budgett
Budgett: Wp4b; Thos: Wg31.

Bueman
John: Ge11a.

Bulckley
Mary: Ge8b.

Bulcott; Boulcott; Boucott; Boucatt
Joseph: Gm14; Rich: Ge10; Rog: H3.

Bull; see Booll
John: S11a; Margery: Wg8; Rich: Wp8(2); Wp25a; Thos: H7.

Bullock; Bullocke
Anth: Gm3(2); Edwd: B23; Wb10; Wb27; Eliz: R9; Hugh: R9; John: R4; R9; Kath: R9; Rich: Wb12; Thos: H1; Wb10.

Carwardine—*continued.*
R2; Wb19; Johan: Wb12; John: B19;
B27b; Wb3(3); Wb19(2); Rich: B27b(2);
B27c; R25; Thos: Wb19; Will: Wb12.

Cary
Watkin: Wm21.

Casson
Mrs: B19.

Castledine
Rich: Ge9.

Caswall
Fran: S11b; Henr: Wp8; Wp13f;
Wp25b(2); Jam: Wp13c; John: Wp8(2);
Rich: Wp13a; Wp13f; Thos: Wp13e;
Will: Wp7; Wp13c.

Catchmay; Catchmeyd; Catchway
Mrs: Wm25; Marg: Wm5; Wm24.

Cater; see Carter
John: Ge11b.

Catstree
Thos: Wp13b.

Caunt
Walt: Wb19.

Cave
Eliz: Ge8b.

Cavoke
Will: Wp21.

Cecill; see Seycill; Cicilt
John: Wp1; Phil: Wm18; Will: Wm21.

Chabnor
John: Gm17; Rich: Gm17.

**Chamberlain; Chamberlen; Chamber-
laine**
Edwd: B12; B27b; R29; Jam: R1; R29;
John: B12(2); B23; R29.

Chambers
Anne: Ge16; Jam: Gm6; Johan: H2;
John: Gm2; Gm6; Wp19b; Thos: H8;
Wp21; Walt: H8; Will: Gm7.

Chance
John: Gm18; Rich: Gm18; Wm16.

Chapman
Mr: Gm21; Marg: Ge11a; Ge11b.

Chappell
Rob: B25.

Charles
Hugh: E1(2); E4; Rich: E4; Will:
Wm5.

Charlett
Rob: B1(2).

Charlton
Job: Wp17.

Cheese
Edm: Wp15; John: Wp29; Rich: Wp20;
Thos: B2; Will: Wp15.

Chelmich; Chelmicke
John: S6; Ro: S6.

Cherry
John: B5b(2).

Chest
John: Wm15; Rich: Wm7(2); Wm20.

Cheston
Cheston's: E7.

Childe; Child
Rich: R9; Wg6; Thos: B14a; B28;
Wg24; Will: Wg5; Wp5.

Chinn; Chinne; Chine; Chyn; Chynn
Wdw: Wm7; Alice: Ge11b; Ge14;
Wm2; Rich: Ge11b; Ge14; Thos:
Ge11b; Ge14; Will: Wm5; Wm15(2);
Wm25.

Cholmely
Anne: Gm9.

Christopher
David: E3; Jam: E8.

Chubb
John: Wp13d.

Church
Mrs: B27b; Anne: Gm11a; Thos:
Ge16(2); Wp19c; Wm21.

Churchyard
Jam: Ge6; Rich: Wb8.

Chute
Mr: B10b.

Cicilt; see Cecill; Seycill
Walt: E8.

Clarke; Clark; Clerke
Wdw: Wp25a; Mr: Wm3; Anne: Wb17;
Arth: B4; Geo: Wb12; Jam: B24; Jer:
Wp13d; John: B4(2); B6; Gm17; Wg17;
Kath: Wg17; Rich: B24; Ge11b;
Ge14(2); Wg14; Wg29; Wp10a; Susan:
Wp12; Thos: B6; E5(2); Wg13(2);
Wg15(2); Will: Wb12; Wg17.

Clee
Jam: Gm17; John: Wp16a; Rich: B6(2);
Thos: B6(4).

Clements
John: B27c; Sarah: B11.

Clent
Math: Wg15; Miles: Wp22.

Cleveley; Cleeveley
Rich: Wp2(2).

Cliffe
Math: R3.

Clifford
Thos: Wm21.

Clissold
Thos: Ge13.

Clive
Geo: Wb15; Wb28.

Clogan
John: Wm18.

Clogie
Mr: Wg14; Alex: Wg29.

Clother
Edm: R9.

Cockerham
Arth: Wg1b.

Cocks; Cocke; see Cox
Rich: R15e; Rog: Wp4a; Thos: R11;
R28b; Thos Will: Wb5; Will: Wp18.

Colcombe
John: Wb3; Wb21; Wb22; Thos: Wg10;
Wg28; Will: S4.

Cole; Coale
Anth: R31; Elin: Wm22; Rich: Ge1;
Thos: Ge1; R28; Will: Wm1a.

Colerick
Thos: Wg2(2); Wg6(2); Will: Wg14;
Wp21.

Coles; see Cowles
John: R9; Rich: Wg6.

Colla
Rog: Ge11a.

Collas
Rich: B27a(2).

Colley; Colly
John: B25; Gm13; Gm22(2); Rich: B11;
B12; Gm1; Thos: B9; B25.

Collier; Collyer; Collyar
Anth: Wm2; Edwd: Wg6; Jam: Ge1;
Ge7b; Math: Wp4b(2); Rich: Wg6;
Will: Wg28; Wp19c.

Collins; Collyns
Mr: B27c; Anne: Wp29; Christopher:
B27c; Edwd: B22(2); Wb17; Wb19(2);
Greg: B4; Jam: Ge3(3); Wm11; Wm25;
John: Ge8f; R9(2); R11; Margery:
B25; Rich: B25; Wp2; Wp26; Sim:
B20; Thos: Ge2; R9; Wg24.

Colman; Coleman
John: S6(2); Wp4a; Wp11; Thos:
S6(2); Will: Wp11.

Colwall
John: Ge1.

Combe
Rich: Wm14c.

Comber
Thos: Wp20.

Comby; see Comley
Mr: Wp15; Will: B14a; B25; R9.

Comley; see Comby
Edm: B14a.

Compton
Rich: S10.

Coningsby; Coningesby; Conyngsby
Mr: B2; B19(2); Wp20; Mrs: Gm5;
Ben: Wp25a; FitzWill: Ge4; Ge8a;
R29; Wp2; Wp4a; Wp25b; Thos: B2;
Will: Gm12.

Conney; Cony; Cunney
Kath: B20; John: B1; B26.

Connop; Connopp
John: Wp20; Rich: Wp1; Will: Wg7;
Wg22b; Wp1.

Coode; Cood; see Goode
Thos: B5b; Wb22.

Cook; Cookes
Mr: R23; R26; Wp15; wdw: R15f;
Ch: Wg17; Edm: Wg17; Elin: Wg17;
Henr: H5; Jam: Ge8g; S8; Wb12;
Wp29; Jane: H4; John: B9; B10b;
B20; B25; Ge8f; R22; Wb12; Wb19;
Wg17; Rich: B2; B10c; Ge3; R25;
Wb22; Wg8; Thos: R12; Wp6b;
Wm23; Walt: B14a(3); Will: B9;
Gm7; R25; Wb12; Wg10.

Cooksey
Jam: Wb26(2).

Cootes; see Cotes
John: Wp20.

Cope; Coope
Edwd: R28; Jam: R22; John: Wm4;
Wm16; Wm19; Rich: Ge4(2); Ge6.

Copnar
John: S10.

Corbett
Anne: B1; John: Ge8f; Rich: B1(3); B3; Thos: B4; Waties: Wg10.

Cornwall; Cornewall
Mr: Wp20; Edwd: Wb20; Geo: Wp8; Guilb: Gm17; Hump: Wp4a; John: B13; Wp6b; Wp22; Thos: Wg23; Wg26.

Coston
Will: Wp29.

Cotes
Tho: Wp4b.

Cother
John: Ge7a.

Cotton
Geo: R9.

Courtler
John: Gm1.

Cowarne; Cowrne
Wdw: Ge11b(3); Mary: Ge11a; Ge14; Wm2.

Cowles; Colles; Coules; see **Coles**
Jam: Ge11a; John: Ge11a; Ge11b(3); R9; Wm13; Wm16; Mary: Wm4; Tim: Wp6a.

Cowper; Couper; Cupper; Cuper
Christ: B26; Thos: B3; Wp15; Will: Wp15.

Cox; see **Cocks**
Mrs: S14; John: R11; Wp18; Rich: Gm7; R8; Wb20; Wm1b; Thos: Wp6a.

Cradock
Rich: Wp26.

Craven
Lord: Wb4; Wg15(2).

Creese; see **Croose**
Rich: Wm7.

Crockett
Rich: Wp13c.

Croft; see **Hereford**
John: S4; Ro: Wp29.

Croone
Croone's: B2; Henr: Wg19(2); John: S10; Thos: Wg13; Wg31.

Croose; see **Creese**
John: Ge7b; Rich· Ge14; Tho: S7(2).

Crosse
Mr: S8; John: H6; S2.

Crowther; Chrowther
Mr: B2(2); Mary: Wp13a; Thos: B1; Will: Wm4.

Crump; Crumpe
Crump meadow: H2; Mr: S1; wdw: Wg24; Edwd: Gm21; R19; Geo: B10a; S10; Henr: Ge13; John: B14a; Wb14; Rob: R9; Rog: H4(2); Rowl: Ge8f; Ge8g; Thos: Wg24(2); Wp4a; Wp20.

Cubberley
Walt: Ge11b.

Curier
John: Gm20.

Cutler
Rob: S4; S6.

Cutta
Wdw: Wm25.

Dale
Elin: B27b; Eliz: Wg14; Hugh: S6; Wg14(2); John: Wg14; Wg15; Rich: Wg15.

Dalley
John: S11a; Rich: R15f.

Dancer; Daunser
Mr: B27c; Garnons: Gm16; Gm18.

Danford
Thos: R11.

Dangerfield
Edm: R8(2); Thos: R8.

Daniell
John: Wp4b; Wp29; Wm1a; Mary: Wm11; Rich: Wm23; Thos: Wm5; Will: B10; Wm24.

Dannett
John: R26; Thos: R4(2).

Dansey
Anne: Wp15; John: Wp15; Will: Gm5; Gm7; S14; Wb17.

Darley
Mrs: Wm2.

Darnell
Mr: S2; Ralph: Gm8.

Daunce
Henr: B26.

David
David: H1; Eliz: E8; Griffith: E7(2);

David—*continued.*
E8; Jane: E8; John: E1; E6; Lison: E5;
Lucas: E5; Mary: E6; Phillip: E5(2);
Thos: E6; Watkin: E1; E5; Will: E4;
E5; E6; E7.

Davies; Davis
Davies: B2; Wb27; Mr: B6; wdw: H3;
Wg15; Alex: H6; Arth: Ge11a; Ge11b;
Edwd: Gm13; Eliz: S9; Ezek: Gm21;
Fran: Wb5(2); Henr: Ge7b; S4; Hugh:
Wp13a; Wp13b; Wp13c; Wp13d;
Wp13e(2); Wp13f; Wp25c; Hump: B4;
B6; B18; B26; Gm23; S14; Jam: H6;
S6; Wb27(2); Wg17; John: B25; Ge7a;
Ge11a; Ge13; Ge16(2); S8; Wb12;
Wb18; Wg9; Wg11; Wg13(2); Wg18(2);
Wg25(2); Wp9; Wp21; Wm7; Wm21;
Wm25; Mary: B19; Meredith: Wg18;
Phil: Wm7; Wm20; Priamus: Wg4;
Rees: Wg18; Rich: E2; Ge8c; H6;
S14(2); Wb1; Wb19; Wp16a; Wm3;
Rob: Wg13; Wg16; Wp9; Wm25; Rog:
S14; Tamberlaine: H6; Thos: B23;
Ge8g(2); Gm3; R20(2); Wg12; Wg17;
Wg29; Wp9; Walt: B27b; Gm21;
Wb20(2); Will: B10e; Gm6; Wg4(2);
Wg17(2); Wp2; Wp7; Wp17; Wm4;
Wm21.

Dawes
Will: Wp20.

Dawkes
John: B19(2).

Day
Will: H6.

Dayos; Daios; Deyos
John: S8; Nich: S4; S6(2); Rog: S14;
Thos: S10; S14.

Deakins; Deikins; Dekins; Deykins
Wdw: Wp4b; Geo: H6; John: S8(2);
Kath: S8; Mary: B21; Ro: Wp29;
Thos: B21.

Debitor; see **Dubitott**
Jeff: Wp15; Rog: Wp15.

Dee
John: S11a.

Deeme
John: B12; B19; B27a; B27b; B27c(2);
R19(2); Marg: B19; Thos: B27a;
B27c.

Delahay; Delehay; De La Hay
Geo: E4; John: E5; E8; Ro: Wb22;
Thos: E5(2); E6; Wb21; Walt: E7.

Demungott; Demounser
Alice: Wb5.

Denis; Dennes
Thos: Gm15; Will: Wp6a.

Derry
Thos: Wp29.

Deswall
Johan: S6; Rich: Wp29; Thos: S10.

Devon; Devins
John: Wg1a.

Dewe; Dew
Anth: Ge11a; Jam: Wm25; John:
Wm25; Thos: Ge2; Wm25; Thomasine:
Ge14.

Dewsall
Thos: Wg29.

Deynall
Mary: Gm3.

Dickes
Mr: B19.

Dickins
Arth: S9; Thos: S9.

Dikes; Dike; Dykes; Dyke
John: Ge7b; Theophilus: Wb1; Wb23;
Will: Ge7b.

Dillow
Elin: Wg17; Foulke: Wp15; John:
Wp15; Rog: Wp26.

Dimocke; Dymock
Eliz: B15; Fran: R9; Rich: B15.

Dingley
Fran: Gm7.

Diron; Dirrand
Rog: Wg26; Will: H6.

Ditcher
Will: Wp13b.

Doberlow; see **Dubberley**
John: Ge8b.

Dobins; Dobbins
Mr: Wp20; Nath: Wm24; Rich:
Wm9(2); Ro: R5; R13(2); Will: R21;
Wb5.

Dobles
Wdw: Wp15.

Dolphin
Rich: S4; Wp13b.

Donne; see **Dunne**

Emmett; Ement
John: Wm18; Rob: Wg3; Will: B10f; Wg3.

Empton
Empton: H6.

Enoe
Wdw: Wb24.

Ensell; Ensoll
Rog: B23(2).

Eudall
Steph: Ge11a.

Eules; or Eales
John: S11a.

Eure
Lady: Wg13; Wg14.

Eustance; Istance
Henr: E7; John: E5.

Evans
Evans: B2; Dr: Gm6; Gm14; Mr: S6; Mrs: Wm7; Griffith: S10; John: B10c; Meredith: Wg5; Rees: Wg25; Rich: B10c; Ro: S10; Thos: Wp3; Wp13a; Wp13b; Wp13c; Wp13d(2); Wp13e; Wp13f; Walt: Wg22a; Will: S8; Wp4b; Wp29.

Everall
Jane: Wg27.

Evett
Elin: B19; Will: B19.

Evisham
Jam: B7(2); John: B7(2).

Exon; see Exton
Rich: Ge8g.

Exton; see Exon
Geo: Gm11a; Jam: Gm7(2); John: Gm22; Will: E6; Wb12.

Eysham; Eysam
Abel: B27c; Eysams: Wb8; Henr: Wb19.

Eython
Thos: R9.

Fabian
Will: S5b.

Farley; Pharley
John: B1(2); Martha: R4; Rich: B1; Will: B1.

Farmer
Wdw: Gm1; Eliz: B27d; R9; Fran: Wp18; Rich: B2; Thos: Wg10; Wp21.

Farrington; Farrinton
John: Wp7; Thos: Gm7.

Faulke; Fawlke
Anne: R9; Rich: R9.

Fecknam; see Stecknam

Fell
Dr: Ge9.

Felton
Jam: Ge8g.

Fermiston
Edm: Wp22.

Ferrar; Ferers
John: Gm13; R25.

Ferrington
Wdw: B2.

Fidoe
Edm: Wp22; John: Wp22; Kath: Wp22.

Fincher
Geo: B22.

Fisher
Charles: Wm5; Wm7; Edwd: Ge13; Wm5; Elin: Ge13; Jam: Ge11a; John: Wm5; Wm25; Mary: Wm2; Rich: Ge13; Will: Ge11b; Wm2; Wm5.

Fishpoole
John: R15e

Flavell
Wdw: Wg10.

Flenders; Flanders
Thos: Wm20.

Fletcher; Flecher
Alice: S12; Jam: S12(2); Wb10; Wg20; John: Wg20; Wm5; Rog: Wp13e; Thos: Gm11a; Wb3; Will: Wb3; Wg20(2).

Fode; see Foote
Edwd: Wb19(2).

Foord
Ro: Wp13e; Thos: Wp13d.

Foote; see Fode
Geo: Wb1; Wb6; Jam: H4; John: S1; Rich: Gm1; Will: Wb19.

Fortescue; Fastescue
Mrs: B10a(2); Mary: Wg26.

Foule
Will: Wp23.

Fowler
Fran: Wp29.

Fox
John: Gm11a.

Foxall
Thos: Wg25.

Foy; Toy
Thos: Wm16(2).

Francis
Rich: E4.

Franke
Anth: B27a; B27b.

Frece
Thos: Wp21.

Freeman
Freemans: R2; Edwd: B11; Fran: R3; R5; Henr: S6; Hugh: Wp4b; Jane: S6(2); John: Ge8f; R3; R5; R21; Rich: R21;

Freene
Thos: B6.

Frere
Mr: R23.

Frewen; see Treaven

Freyer
David: Wm14c.

Friberie
Friberies: E7.

Frizer; Friser
John: B14a; Thos: S3; Walt: Wg20(2).

Froysall; Froysell
Alex: S4(2); Thos: Wg11.

Furney
John: Ge3; Rich: Ge11a.

Fyfield
Will: R9.

Gabb
John: E3.

Gailey; Galey
Geo: Wp1; John: Wp4a.

Gainsford
Will: Ge6.

Gallett
Anne: R25; John: S11a(2); Rog: S11a; Will: R25.

Galliars
Rich: Wg19(3).

Games
Mr: R26; Hugh: H3.

Gamond; Gammon; Gamman; Gomond
Henr: Ge12; Jam: Ge9; Ge12; John: Gm2; Rich: Ge12(2); Thos: Wp23.

Gardner; Gardiner
Wdw: Wm25; Ethelbert: Wm5; Jam: R15b(2); Wm9; Nath: B6(2); B19; Thos: B25; Will: B25; Ge1; Wm25.

Garner; Garnors
Wdw: R12; Eliz: Wg1a; Geo: S4; Oliver: Gm8(2); Rowl: Gm8.

Garnons
John: Wp4a; Wp4b; Rich: H6; Rog: Wb7(2); Wb28; Wg3; Wm9; Will: H6.

Garrall; Garrald
John: Gm14(2); Wm1b(2).

Garrett
Henr: Wp4b.

Garston; Garson; Grafton
Garston's: Ge16; Alex: Wp15(2); John: Ge8b; Thos: Ge8c; Will: Ge8c; Wb2·

Gates
Thos: S6(2).

Gayly; see **Galey; Gailey**
Rich: Gm8; Will: Gm8; Gm11a.

Geeres; Geers; Geare
Fran: Gm2; Gm14; John: Gm2; Thos: Gm4; Will: Gm4; H6.

Geeves
Will: Wp13f.

Gennings
Edwd: Wp5.

George
Wdw: E4; Anne: Wb4; Hump: E5(2); Jam: S8; John: E5(2); H4; Will: E8.

Gethin; Geathing
Mr: Wm14c; Will: Wb1; Wm13.

Gibbins; Gibbons; Gibbornes; Gibbon; Gibons
Wdw: Gm7; Fran: Wm7; Henr: B19(2); Jane: B19; Thos: B19(2); H2(2); Will: B14a.

Gibbs; Gibbes
Thos: Ge1.

Gilding; Guilding
John: R8(2); Will: R7; R8.

Giles; Gyles
John: Ge1; Wp13f; Walt: Wb28 ;Wm9; Will: Wp13f.

Gille
Gille: Gm23.

Gilley
Arnold: Wg29; Edwd: Wp21; Geo: Wp21; Henr: S6; Wp16a; Nich: Wp21; Rich: Wp21; Tho: Wp1; Will: Wp21.

Gittins
Will: Wg30.

Gittoes
Edm: B13; Hugh: Wp25c; John: Wp12; Wp25c(2); Rich: H5; Thos: Wp13c; Will: Gm8(2); Wp11; Wp13f.

Glace
Will: Wp26.

Gladwyn
Phil: Gm21.

Glover
Will: Wp20.

Glyn; Glynn
John: Wm7; Wm22; Oliver: Wm7.

Goare
Will: H6.

Godfree
Thos: R11.

Godsall; Godsoll; Godsell; Godshall
Edwd: R22; Jane: R5; John: R1; Marg: R1; Rog: Ge8f; Will: Ge1.

Godwin; Godwyn; Goodwyn
Adam: Wg17; Alice: Wg20; Jam: Wg7; Jane: Wg20; John: S10; Lettice: Wm5; Mary: Wg25; Thos: B27c.

Gold; Gould
Geo: Wp29; Thos: Wp29, Mr: S10.

Gomery
Edm: Wp22; Henr: Wp22.

Goodduggan
David: E2.

Goode; Good; Goodes; Goods; see Coode
Good's: B6; Anne: Wb10; Hump: B22; Jam: E1; Wb2(2); Wb21; John: B4; B22; H5; Wp4a; Wp6b; Wp11; Thos: B22; H1; Wb4; Wb7(2); Wb10(2); Wb21(2); Wm9; Wm17; Will: H5.

Goodier
Mr: Wg14.

Goodith
Thos: Wp10a.

Goodman
Edwd: Wm7; Geo: Gm2; Will: Wb6; Wp7; Wp25c.

Gorway; Garway
Wdw: Ge11b; John: Ge11b.

Gough; Gouff
Edm: Wg22a; Edw: Wg18; Geo: B1; Hugh: Wm18; John: H6; Wb20; Wg12; Wg22b; Margery: S11a; Mary: Wp12; Rich: Wg24; Silvanus: S11a; Sim: S14; Thos: B11; H5; Wg12.

Gower
Mr: R9; John: S9; Rich: S9; Thos: S9.

Grafton; see Garston
Jam: Wp25c.

Grag
Will: Wm22.

Graile
Thos: Ge1.

Grasier
Perry: S1.

Gravell
Mrs: H1; Wb7.

Greeg; Greg
Wdw: Wb8; Fran: Wp22; Johan: E7; Sarah: E7.

Greene; Green
Mrs: Wb1; Wb19; Bridget: Wb19; Edm: H8; Elin: Wb6; Wp13c; Jacob: Wg17; Wp13d; Jam: R18; John: B13; R28b; Wb22; Wb24; Rich: Gm17; Gm23; Wb7; Thos: B22; Gm1; S8; Will: B10e; Wb19; Wb24.

Greeneaway
John: Ge9; Thos: H6.

Greenhouse; Grenowse; Grenous; Grenouse; Greenowes
Edwd: H6; Wg25; Hugh: Wg30; Marg: Wg18; Rich: Wg26; Thos: Wg16.

Greenlease
Acon: Wb16(2).

Greenly; Greenely; Greenley
Andr: S14; Wg20; Wg25; John: Wg20; Phil: S12; Wg20; Wg25; Will: H6; Wg25.

Gregory
Will: Ge4; Ge16; Gm7; R19.

Grendon; see Grindon
Hester: Ge5.

Gretton
Alex: B1.

Griffin
Edwd: Wp21.

Griffiths; Griffithes; Griffith; Griffitts
Mr: B17; Blanch: E1; Edwd: B25; E8;
Ge11a; Florish: Wm10; Wm17; Geo:
E4; Giles: E3; Henr: E1; E7; Jam:
Wb12; John: Ge11b; H2; S4; Wg3;
Wg11; Wm11; Nich: Wm17; Rog: Wp1;
Rich: S10; Wg13; Sim: Wg20; Wg25;
Thos: B28; E1; Gm8; H6; Wm8;
Wm11(2); Wm21; Walt: H2; Will:
S10.

Grimes
John: H6; Wg25.

Grindon; see Grendon
John: Ge11a.

Grismond
Henr: S6; Wp29; Will: S6(4); Wp29.

Gronnowe
John: Wm17; Will: Wm17.

Groome
Will: B25.

Grove
Wdw: H1; John: Wp22; Rich: Wp29(2);
Thos: Wm22; Will: R10.

Grubb
Anth: Wm5; Wm8(2); Nich: Wp6b;
Sampson: Wg21; Thos: B5b; Will: B11.

Guilbert; Gilbert
Wdw: E1; Eliz: E1; E5; Henr: E5; Jam:
E8; John: E4(2); Lewis: E3(2); E4;
Phil: Wb10; Thos: E4; Wg26; Will:
E1(2); Zakery: E1.

Guise
Thos: B19.

Gullen
Rich: R26.

Gulliford; Gullifer
Hump: Wb8; Jam: Ge11a; Rich: Wb12.

Gundy
David E8.

Gunter
Bodnam: Wb1; Wb17; Wb23; Wb28;
Jam: Wm13; Johan: E8; John: E2;
Wm18; Rog: E8; Will: E8.

Guy
Rich: B27c.

Gwatkin; Gwatkins
Grace: Wm11; John: Wp13e; Wm14a;
Rich: Ge2; Ge11b; Wm19; Thos: Ge4;
Walt: Ge13; Wm17(2); Will: Wm7;
Wm19.

Gwillim; Gwilliam; Gwillime; Gwillym
Mr: B7; wdw: Wm2; David: Wm4;
Edwd: Wm4; Henr: Ge10; Ge16(2);
H3; R22(2); John: B10a; E3; Gm7;
Gm8; Gm21; R15f; R28b; Wm11;
Wm14a(2); Kath: Wm8; Peter: R17;
Phil: Gm1(2); Rich: Wm25; Rog: Wm7;
Rudhall: Wm5; Wm10; Wm14c; Wm21;
Wm25; Thos: E3; E5; Gm7(2); Gm20;
R17; R22; Wb13; Wb15; Wm8; Wm21;
Will: E5; Ge10(2); Wm8; Wm11;
Wm14a; Wm23.

Gwilt; Gwillett
Johan: Wg6; John: Wm2.

Gwin; Gwinn
Hugh: H6; Wg12; Miles: B6(2); Thos:
R15d.

Habberley
Mr: Wp29.

Hackett
John: B1.

Hacklett; Hackluit
Edm: Wg30; Rich: B20; Will: Wp26.

Haddock
Jam: Wg1b.

Hadland
Henr: B19.

Hagley
Oliver: Wp10a.

Haines; Heynes; Haynes
Anne: Gm13; Christ: Wp4a; Geo:
Gm8; Wb1; Wb6; Jam: S5a; John:
B2; Wb22; Rich: Wb1.

Hale; Hales
Wdw: R9; Wg15; Rowl: R9; Thos:
Wg15.

Hall
Mr: B2(5); Gm21; Wb21; Wb22;
Wm11(2); Wm23; Anne: B10e; Bene-
dict: B19; Edwd: R2; S8; Wp20; Wp21;
Fran: Gm22; R15a; R15f; R21; R28a;
R28b; Johan: S5a; John: H1; H5; H6;
R15a; R15e; R15f; R17(2); R27; S10;
Wg10; Wp6b(2); Wm2; Math: B28(2);
Rich: R15d; S8(2); Rob: R28b; Rog:
Wm5; Wm15; Thos: B4; Ge4; R9(2);

Hall—*continued.*
R15b; S6; Wp3; Wm5; Will: E3; Ge7a;
R8; R9; S7; Wb21; Wm5; Wm21.

Hallard
Henr: B5; John: Wp2; Wp25c; Sarah:
B11.

Hallings; see **Hawlins; Hayling**
Wdw: Gm1; Gm12; Gm13; Gm20.

Hambleton
John: Wp29.

Hamden
Mr: Ge16.

Hamond; Hamand; Hamons; Hammons
John: Wg2; Thos: Wp5; Will: R2(2);
Wp13b.

Hampton
John: H4.

Hanbury
John: R18; Thos: Ge1; R4.

Hancorne
Rich: H7; Sam: H7.

Handcox; Hancock; Hancox; Hankocks
Alex: B15; Rich: B1(2); Walt: Wp6b.

Hanford
John: S11a.

Hankins
Edwd: R10(2); R17; John: R21; Rich:
R10; R15f(2); R17.

Hanley; Handley
Mr: H6; Chris: S7; John: R29; Wg3.

Hannis; Hennis
John: Wm7; Wm20; Wm22; Phil: Wm5;
Rich: Ge3; Wm5; Ro: Wm5; Thos:
Wm5; Wm15; Will: Wm5.

Hardin
Hardins: Ge16.

Hardwicke; Hardwick; Hardick
Anne: Ge14; Greg: Ge13; Jam: Ge13;
John: B26; Ge2; Ge13; Ge15; Thos:
Wp13a; Wp13b; Wp13c(2); Wp13d;
Wp13e; Wp13f; Wp29.

Hare
Rich: B2(2); Thos: B2.

Harford
Bridstock: Gm8; Gm11a; R8.

Harley
Edwd: Wg4; Wg5; Wg15; Wg27; Wg29;
Rob: S6; Thos: S6; Wp16b; Will:
Wg15.

Harper
Henr: H4; John: Gm13; H2; Wb19;
Wp10a; Wp19b; Marg: Wp5; Phil: H2;
Rich: S8; Rog: Wp5(2); Thos: H4(4);
H6(2); S1(2); Wg3.

Harris; Harries
Anne: Wb21; Wm4; Arnold: Wb4;
Edm: Ge14; Fran: Ge11a; Geo: Wb12;
Hugh: Wg29; John: Ge10(2); Wb20;
Wb22; Wg10; Lewis: Wb16; Wm17;
Phil: S8; Wm5; Rich: Ge11a(2); Wb22;
Rowl: R9; Thos: S6; Wg3; Walt: B19;
Wg28; Will: Wg1a(2); Wp10c.

Harry; Harrie
Eliz: E1; Evan: H1; H3; Harry: E7;
John: E4; E8(2); Lewis: E1; E4; Phil:
E1; E4; E7; Wm9: Rice: E1; Will:
E1(2); E5; E8.

Hart
Christian: Ge15; Grace: Wm11.

Hartland
Wdw: R8(2); Will: Ge13.

Hartree
John: Wp6a.

Harvey
Peter: B25; B26; S6; Rich: R9.

Harwell
Walt: Wb12.

Hatch
Rich: B2.

Hathway
Jam: B10a.

Hatley
Griffith: H2.

Hatsforde
Hatsfordes: Ge16.

Hatton
Wdw: R8.

Haughton
Jam: Wg10.

Havard
John: Ge4; Gm18; Rog: H4; Thos:
Wp13e; Wm5.

Hawes
Owen: Wg7; Wg26.

Hawfield
John: R3.

Hawkins; Haukins
John: R2; S1; Rich: B12.

Hawlins; Hallins; Hawlings; see **Hayling; Hallings**
Anth: R31; Rich: B18(2); Walt: B18; B23.

Haworth; Howorth
Blanch: Wb25; Hump: E7; Gm11a; Wb25; Wb26.

Hay; see **Hey**

Haycox
Geo: Gm22(2).

Hayling; Hallinges; see **Hawlins**
Thos: B6(3).

Hayward; Heyward
Henr: Wp4b; Rich: Wp4a; Thos: B13; Will: Gm11a.

Heane
Phil: Wm19.

Heare
John: Gm16; Thos: B2.

Heath
Fran: Wg15; John: R1; R2; Rich: Wb16(2); Thos: Wb20; Wg15.

Helline
Mr: B27d.

Helmes
Mr: Wm14c.

Hemming; Hemmings
Rich: Wp13f; Thos: W1(2).

Henley
John: R31(2).

Hennond
Anne: Wm15; Phil: Wm15; Thos: Wm5.

Herbert; Harbert
Geo: R7; John: Ge11a; Reece: E6; Will: R9.

Hereford
Bishop of (see Croft): S6; Wg13; Wg14; Wp4b; Wp9; Wp16b; Wp29; Fran: Ge8a; Leicester Viscount: B18; R9; Jam: Ge4; Ge8a; John: Ge8e.

Hergest; Hargest
Walt: Gm13.

Herring; Hearing; Hering
Mr: Gm7; Mrs: Gm11a; Anne: Gm11b; Gm18; Gm20; Eliz: Gm7; John: Gm21; H6; Rog: S13; Sim: S3; S14; Thos: Gm7; Will: Gm7.

Hertford
Marchioness of: Ge4.

Hey; Hay
Edwd: Wp13c; Fran: Wp13f; Hump: Wp9; John: Wm14c; Steph: B23; Thos: R9; Will: E2; R13.

Hibbins
Ro: Wg26.

Hichman; Hickmans; Hitchman
Edwd: Ge13; Walt: Wp4b; Will: Wm3.

Hide
Anne: Ge8g; R19; Edwd: S13; Wp9; John: Ge8e; Rich: R1; R23; Rog: R9; Walt: Wb22.

Higgins
Edwd: R9; Henr: B27c; S6; Wp7; Leon: E2(3); Philo: H1; H3; Rich: H2; S5a; Wp21(2); Rob: R11; R17; Sim: Wp21; Thos: B13; H1(2); H8(2); S6; Wp7; Wp25c; Wp29; Verny: H4; H6; Walt: E2; S6; Wg25; Will: E1; H8; S6; S10; Wb4.

Higgison
John: Wp13a.

Higgs
John: Ge11b; Phil: B19; Will: Wm14a.

Hill
Wdw: B2; Anne: B6; Arth: Gm13; Gm22; Gm23; Edm: B14a(2); Edwd: B18; Wg23; Eliz: R15a; R17; Gabriel: Ge11a; Ge11b; Wm2; Geo: Wb17; Wp25c; Jam: S14; Jane: B25; John: B2; B5a; B7; B14a; B20(2); B23(7); B27b; Ge7a(2); Ge8b; Ge11a; R9; R10; R20; S9; Wp15; Wm20; Wm22; Leon: R9(2); Nich: Wm15; Ralph: B9; Rich: B2(2); B20; Ge11b; Ge16; R9; Wb20; Wg23; Rob: B23; Wp8; Rog: Ge8f(2); Wp4b; Sam: B27d; Sibbill: Wp19d; Thos: B6; B13(2); B14a; B14b; B19; B23; Gm7; Gm9; R15d; R18(2); R19(2); R30; Walt: H1; S5a; S5b; Wb4(2); Wm11; Wm20; Will: B7; B11; B21; Ge10; Gm7; H1; R8; R15f; Wb1; Wg7(2).

Hinchman
Rich: B25.

Hincke; or **Lincke**
John: Gm20.

Hinner; or **Binner**
Walt: Wm22.

Hinton
John: Gm11a; Gm11b.

Hints
Fran: Wp20; John: Gm23; Rich: Wm17.

Hitchcocks
Hitchcocks: B17.

Hodges
Hodges: Gm13; Mrs: Wg6; wdw: Ge8g(2); Gm14; Edwd: B27d; Jam: Ge8g; Gm8; Jane: Gm23; John: B2; B21; Gm23; R22; R23; Rich: Ge10; Gm8; Gm23; R23; Wp12; Wp13c; Wp18; Rog: R1; Thos: B27d(2); Ge16; Wb5; Will: Ge8a; Gm2; Gm15; R15f.

Hodnet
Hump: B14a.

Hoggan; see **Loggan**

Hoggins
Marg: Wp21.

Holde
Edwd: Wg18; Henr: Wg18; Johan: Wg18.

Holder; Howlder; Houlder
Wdw: R3; Dan: Gm7; Eliz: B20; Fortune: Wm8; John: R8; Peter: R7; Rob: R7(2); Thos: R7; R8; Wm2; Will: B5a(2).

Holford
Rob: R18.

Holland
John: R29; Wp3; Wp22; Rich: B22; Will: Wg28(2).

Holloway
Edwd: B17(2); Thos: B5a; B17(2); Will: B14a.

Hollys
Lord: Wb15.

Holman
Phil: H1; H2; H5; H6; H8.

Holmes; Homes
Mr: Wb3; Edwd: Ge8c(2); Rich: R3.

Holt
Phil: B18; Rich: Wp12; Thos: B23; Wp18; Wp25b.

Hooper
Wdw: Wg15; Rich: R1(2); R22(2); Thos: R28.

Hope
John: B2; Ge9; Ge16; R8(2); R13; Rich: R8; Will: B2.

Hopkin; Hopkins
Anne: Wm19; Edwd: Wg10; John: Wg10;Wm7(2);Wm14c;Wm17;Wm23; Mary: Wg13; Phil: Wm24(2); Rich: Wg29; Sam: Wg9(2); Thos: Gm13; Gm23; Wm7; Wm11; Wm19; Will: B25(2); R1; R21(2); R28.

Hopley
Rich: Wp23; Thos: B19.

Hopton
Lady: R6(2); Lord: E4(2); E5; E6; E7; E8; Rich: B3; B4; B16; B26; R3; R25; Wp25c; Walt: B6; R1; R12; R29.

Hopwood
Ralph: S8; Thos: S10; Wg7.

Hords; Hards; Hoords; Hoards
Hugh: Gm21; John: Gm21(2); Rich: Gm7; Gm21(2); B10f; Thos: R8.

Horne
Thos: Wm21.

Horniblowe
Will: R8.

Horseman
John: Wm21.

Horton
John: Ge2.

Hosier
Will: Wb3; Wb22.

Hoskins
Bennet: Wb7(2); Wb9; Wb17; Wm7; Wm10; Wm13; Wm19; Wm22; Wm23; Ces: Wm13; Charles: R15c; R28; Jam: Wg7; John: Wb7(2); Wm4; Wm5; Wm7; Wm9; Wm11; Wm13; Wm20; Mich: S12(2); Wg20; Oswald: Wm11; Rich: S11b(2); Wg7; Wg29; Thos: Gm13; S12; Wg20; Walt: S11a.

Hough
Adam: R9.

How
John: Ge5; Thos: Ge13; Walt: Ge7a; Will: Ge7a(2).

Howard
Rich: Gm8.

Howells; Howell; Howles
Wdw: Wb8; Henr: E3; E5; John: Ge1; Gm7; Gm11b(2); Gm21; H6; Wm17(2);

Howells; Howell; Howles—*continued.*
Rees: E4; Rog: Wm5; Thos: B19; Ge16; S11b; Wm5(3); Wm21; Will: Gm20; H8; Wb20; Wm11(2); Wm25(2),

Ap Howell
Owen: Wg30.

Howman
John: Wm4; Wm21; Thos: B11.

Howton; Howten; Houton
Howtens: R15f; Marg: Wp20; Will: Wp15.

Huck; Hucke
Anth: R26; John: B25.

Huett
Thos: H4.

Hugh
Thos: E1; Walt: E8.

Hughes; Hues
Jam: Gm23; John: Wp12; Wp20; Rich: Wm4; Thos: H4; Walt: S5b; Will: H1; H3; S5b.

Hull
Will: Ge7b.

Hullutt
John: Wm8.

Hulmes
Sands: Wm7.

Hunt
Mr: Wp13b; wdw: E4; Alice: Wb23; John: Wb21; Wg26; Miles: E4; Rich: H7; Wb1; Wp1; Wm9; Thos: H8; Wb6; Wp1(4); Will: Wp1.

Hurscock
Marlin: Ge1.

Husbands
Mary: Wb28; Thos: Wb28; Will: Wb12.

Hussey
Anth: H7; Giles: B10a; Thos: B10e.

Hutton
John: R3.

Hyett; Hiett; Heyett
Mr: Gm17; Heyetts: Wm22; Henr: S4; Ro: Wm16; Thos: Ge2(3); Wm8.

Immings; Imans
Rich: S13; Gm23.

Ince; see Hints

Ingland
Thos: B20.

Ingram
John: Wg10; Wp21; Will: B14a.

Ireland
Edwd: Gm13; John: Gm13(2); Gm23.

Istance; see Eustance
Will: Gm4.

Jackson
John: S4; Wp14; Phineas: B4; B23(2); B26; Wp3.

James
Mr: S10; David: E7; Wm2; Gilb: R11; Howell: S8; Hugh: Wm4; John: B3(2); E1; H6; R8; Wg12(2); Wg15; Wg28; Launcelot: B6; Math: Gm13; Morgan: B22; Perin: Wb21; Phil: E6; Rees: E4; Rich: E2(2); E7; R9(2); Thos: E2; Walt: Ge7b; Will: Wp21; Wm9.

Jauncey; Jauncie; Jauncy
Anth: R29; Jam: B4; B9(2); John: B6(3); S6; Thos: B6.

Jaunsons; see Johnsons
Mr: B4.

Jay
Ethelbert: Wp11; Wp12; Geo: B5b; Henr: B2; John: B5b; Wp9; Wp13b; Kath: Gm8; Thos: Gm8; Wp3; Wp9; Wp11.

Jefferys
Mr: B19.

Jenkins; Jenkings; Jenkin
Mr: Wb19; wdw: H1; R15f; Anne: E5; E8; Geo: E1(2); E4; Wm4; Jam: H1; H8; John: B2; E1; E5; Gm11a; Wb16; Wb21; Phil: Wm5; Rich: R27; Wm11; Rees: H2; Rog: S7; Sibbill: E5; Thos: E5(2); Gm7(2); Gm16(3); Gm21; H1; H2; Wb10; Walt: E5(2); Watkin: E1; Will: Gm14; Gm16; Wb4; Wb10; Wp23.

Jenks; Jenkes
Henr: S6; Will: S6(2).

Jennings; Jenninges
Charles: E5; E7; Wb26; Johan: E7; John: B4; E5; Phil: Wm25; Rich: Wm25; Rob: Wm25; Rowl: E5(2); Sibble: E7; Thos: E7(3).

Jervice; see Elves
Sir: Wp4b.

Jewe
Margery: B25.

Knowles
Walt: H6.

Kyrle
Mrs: R21; Wm2; Alice: Ge11a; Ge11b; Ge14; Eliz: Gm20; John: Ge4; Ge7a; Ge8f; Ge9; Ge12; Ge13; Wm8; Rob: Ge14.

Lacon
Fran: Wp10a.

Lambe
Geo: Wg15(2); Will: S4; Wp14.

Lambert; Lampott
John: Wb16; Wm18(3); Phil: Wm14c; Rob: Wm5; Thos: Wb23(2); Wm18.

Landon
Mr: Gm7; Elin: E3(2); Silvanus: Gm9; Thos: Wb26.

Lane
Wdw: Wp22; Anne: Wp22; Ch: Wb8; Geo: B20; Guy: Ge11a; Henr: Wb8(2); Jam: Wm5; John: B21; Ge16; Wb17; Wg1a; Wm2; Rich: Wp25a; Thos: R30; Will: Wb5.

Lanford; Langford
Edwd: Gm6; S5b; Johan: Wg1a; John: Wg11; Rich: Wg16; Thos: Wg9; Wg15; Will: Gm12.

Langley
Dr: B15; John: B4; Will: Ge11a.

Largoe
Will: Gm23.

Laudington
Thos: Wb19.

Laviman
Mary: Ge11a.

Lawes
Henr: Wm21.

Lawford
Lawfords: Gm21; wdw: Wb22; Walt: Wb22.

Lawrence; Larawnce
Anth: B6; B18; R11(2); R20; Charles: B6; Edwd: S2; Wg19; Eliz: S12; Wb19; Wg20; Jam: B6(3); Gm12(2); Wm16; John: H8; Wb1; Wb19; Julian: Wg15; Phil: S5a; Will: Wb19.

Lawton
Henr: B2.

Layland
Rog: Wp22.

Lea; Lee
Mrs: R29; Anne: Wp15; Anth: B20; John: Ge14; Wm2.

Leadonton; Ledington
Rich: R28; Will: R15b.

Leatherborow
Henr: S14.

Lechmere; Lechmore
Rog: Ge4.

Leech
Alice: B19; John: B19; Wp13f; Phil: Wm5; Wm15; Rog: Gm11a; Thos: Wp13f.

Leeth; see Seeth
Tho: B2; Wp13d.

Legeat
Thos: Ge13.

Legge
Edm: Wg30; Edwd: Wg17; Wg30(2); Thos: Wg30.

Leighton
Rich: R9.

Leker
Blanch: Wm20.

Leme; Lemme
Will: S7.

Lenthall; Leyntholl; Leintoll
Edw: S4; Phil: Wp19b; Thos: S4(2); Will: Wp2(2).

Leonard
Susan: E2.

Lewellin; Llewellin
Mr: H6; Appolin: S10.

Lewis
Mrs: H6; wdw: E4; Alice: H2(2); Anne: B20; Wg29; David: E4; Wm4; Edwd: Wm7; Eytham: E2; Fran: H3; Hugh: Gm18; H2; H4; Jam: E2; Jenkin: Wg25; Johan: B2; John: E3; E4; H1; H2; H3; H5; R27; S6; Wb2; Wb10; Lewis: E2; Luke: Wb21; Marmaduke: E5(2); Morgan: E7; Phil: E1; Wg7; Wg22c; Wg30; Rees: H2; Wg20; Rich: B14a(2); E2; H2; Wb16; Thos: B13; B20; E1; E2; E8; H1; H3; Wb16; Wg6; Wg20(2); Walt: H8; Wm11; Will: H1; Wg29; Wm11; Wm24; Zachery: E5.

Like
Thos: Gm23(2).

Lill
Fran: Ge9.

Lilly
Will: R28.

Linager; Lenacre
Geo: R5.

Lingen
Lady (Dame) Alice: B10a(2); B10d; B10f(2); B19; Gm7; Gm21; R1; R23; R25; S10; Wb4; Wg21; Mr: B19; Johan: Wp1; Luke: B19; Rog: B19; Thos: B6; R12; Wb4; Wg24; Will: B19.

Linke; Lincke; see Hincke
Jam: Wm14c.

Lisons
Dan: S8.

Lissiman
Will: R8.

Little
Thos: Ge1(2).

Lloyd; Loyd; Lloid; Loid; Loyde
Wdw: Wg16; Arth: B10b; Eliz: E2; Henr: Gm16; Jam: H6; John: S8; Wg12; Rich: Wp13f; Rog: Wg12; Thos: Ge15; Walt: Ge15.

Lochard
David: Wg20; Miles: S10.

Loggan
Will: R9.

Long
Mr: Wb19; Lady: Wg29; wdw: Gm11a; John: R9; Mary: S10; Rich: R9(2); Walt: Wg14.

Looke; Leeke
Will: Wm4.

Loope
Geo: Wm4.

Lord
Hugh: E1; John: Wb19.

Love
John: B1; Thos: B23.

Lovell
John: Ge11a; Ge11b; Rich: B2; B10a; Thos: Ge8c; Ge11a.

Low
Mr: Wp29; Hunt: Wb22; Jam: Wb1; Rog: Wg29; Thos: Wp5; Will: Gm18.

P

Lowke
John: Wg5; Wg6; Rog: Wg6; Thos: Wg6; Will: Wg6; Wg24.

Lucas
Jam: E5(2); Lewis: E5; Rich: Wg24(2); Will: B1; Wm22; Wm25.

Lucy
Eliz: Wb17.

Luggar
Henr: S9; Will: S6(2).

Lurcott
John: Gm14; Will: Wb20.

Luston
John: Wp6a.

Lyde; see Lloyd
Elin: Wg12; Jam: Wg22a; John: Wg12 Wg22b; Rich: Wg22c; Rog: Wg12.

Lydons
Lydons: Wp19a.

Mabberley
Geo: Wb5.

Mace
Henr: B24(2).

Machin
Emanuell: R11; John: Wm7; Wm21; Wm23; Thos: Wm7.

Maddox; Madox; Madocks; Maddock Maddocks; Maddocke; Maddockes
Aidonhigh (Adoniah): Ge11a; Edwd: Ge11a; Ge11b; Jam: Wb19; John: E6; Oliver: E5; Rich: R15a; Thos: E3; E6; Walt: Ge11a; Wb19; Will: B7.

Madey
Posthume: H1; Watkin: H1; Will: H1(3).

Madley; see Madey
Watkin: Wb10(2).

Mahallum
Will: H6.

Mainston
Ch: Wm25.

Maiors; see Mayoes
John: Gm11a.

Man
Edwd: Ge11a; Geo: Ge11a; Will: Ge11a.

Manby
Dan: Wm23.

Oswell; Oswald
Mr: Ge4; Peter: Wm22.

Oven; Owen; Owens
Fran: Wg12; Wg22c(2); John: Wg16;
Ro: Wg15; Will: S7; Wp29.

Overton
Sibill: Wb6.

Pace
Thos: Wg25.

Packer
John: Ge7a; Ge13; Thos: Ge7a;
Ge13.

Page
Henr: R15c; R28b; Thos: R15b.

Paine; Payne
Anne: Wp29; Griffith: Wg12; Hugh:
Wg12; John: Ge4; Ge11a; Wb19;
Wm8(3); Wm21; Rob: S4; Sim: Gm7;
Will: Gm9(2); Wg30; Wp2.

Painter
Geo: Gm1; Will: Ge11a.

Palfrey; Palphrey
Wdw: Wg11; Brian: Wg11; John:
Wg1a; Will: Wg4.

Palmer
Jam: Ge5; Ge15; Rich: Wp5.

Panck
Johan: Wp13b.

Pantoll
Pantolls: Wb19; Henr: Gm13.

Parker
Parker's: S1; Mr: H1; Rob: B16; R9;
Solomon: B13; Will: Wp14;

Parlor; Palor
Anne: S10; Edm: B8; John: Gm1
Gm2(2); Will: Ge13; Wm21.

Parramore
Rich: Wg1a.

Parrock; Perrock
Barthol: H8; Sarah: R27.

Parry; Parrie
Mr: Gm11a; Ben: E4(2); Bethlin: Wb4;
Eliz: Wb13; Fran: H2; Geo: E4(3);
Jam: B20; E5; John: E3(2); E4; E5(11);
E6; Wb9; Wb11; Wb12; Wb13(2);
Wb17; Wb21(2); Mabell: E5; Rich:
Wb9; Wp13d; Rog: Wb21; Valen:
Wb13; Will: Wb13; Wm2.

Parsons
Anne: Ge8a; Hugh: B9(2); John: B27a;
Mary: B4; Rich: R29(2); Wm16(2);
Thos: Wb10; Wm14a(2); Wm16.

Partridge
John: Wb10(2); Thos: B4.

Pascall; Paschall
Wdw: S14; Ro: Wp24; Thos: Wp18;
Will: Wp7; Wp9; Wp10a.

Passey
Anne: Wg25; David: Wg22b; Tamberlaine: Wg22b; Wg22c; Will: Wg25(2).

Pateshall; Patershall
Mr: B8; John: Wp2; Wp13a; Wp13b;
Joseph: Wp13; Thos: Wp2(2); Wp13f;
Wm10.

Patis
John: Wp4a.

Paynard
Mr: Gm11a.

Payto; see Peyto

Pearce; Peirce; Pierce; see Pers
Fran: Wp13d; Wp24; John: Wg19;
Wm4; Rich: S6; Wm4; Thos: Gm2;
Walt: Ge11a; Ge14.

Pearle
Thos: Wm4; Wm24.

Pelletory
Wdw: Wm7.

Pember
Pember's: Wb12; Mr: B2; H2; Charles:
H1; Wb10; Eliz: H4; Fran: S1; S8;
Greg: Gm23; John: H6; Walt: H6.

Pembridge
Jam: Wp18; John: B1(2).

Pengriefe; Penthriffe
Fran: R9.

Penn
Johan: Wm11.

Pennell; Penell; see Peskell
Edm: R9; Henr: B26; John: B10d.

Penny
Thos: Wp16a.

Penoyre; Pennogre
Jam: H3(2); Wb21; Wb25; Wb26;
Thos: E2; H1; H3.

Penrice
Geo: Ge8f.

Penson
Abraham: Wp1; John: Wp15; Rich: Wp21; Thos: Wp13d; Will: Wp1.

Perkins; Pirkins
Edwd: B14a; John: B6; Kath: B5a; Rich: Wp29; Thos: Ge1; Will: Ge1(2); Wp6a.

Perks; Perkes; Pirkes; Pearkes
Ethelbert: Wp18; Henr: Ge11a; John: S3; Wp10b; Kath: Wp13d; Rich: Wp1; Wp15; Wp26; Thos: Gm6; Wp13e.

Perpoint
Ralph: Wp16a.

Perrins
Rich: B4.

Perrott; Parrott; Parrett
Herbert: Gm16; Gm18; Gm21; John: E1; Rich: S7.

Perry; Pirry; see Pyrry
John: B5a; S6; S11a; Wp6a; Rice: E1; Rich: B15; Wp3; Will: Ge1; Wp3.

Pers; see Pierce
John: B12.

Peskell; see Pennell
Edm: R13.

Peterstow
Phil: Ge11a.

Pewtries; Pewtres
Margery: R11; R28b.

Peyto; Peytoe
Edwd: Wg3; Jam: Wp4b; John: Wg11; Will: Wp24(2).

Pharley; see Farley

Phelps
John: Ge13; Rich: Ge7a; Wm22; Thos: Ge7a; Ge13.

Philips; Phillips; Phillipp; Phillipps
Dr: Ge15; Mr: B4; B27c; Gm11a; Gm11b; R15c; R28; wdw: Ge16; Anne: Wm21; Charles: E8(2); Wp11; David: E3; E8; Evan: S8; Geo: Wp29; Griffith: E8; Howell: E1; Johan: Wb16; John: E3; E8; Ge7b; Wb16; Wg18; Wg20; Wp18; Wp20; Wp29; Wm4; Wm11; Lewis: Wb2(2); Mary: Wp4a; Math: Ge11a; Nich: Wb13; Oliff: E5; Rich: Ge9; S7; Wp1; Sim: E4; Steph: Ge14; R17; R19; R27; Thos: E4; E8; Ge4; Wp20; Wm4; Wm24; Wm25; Walt: B10d; E2; E7; Wb2; Wb15(2);

Wp4a(2); Wp13b; Will: E8; Ge1; Ge7b; H3; Wg21(2); Wg31; Wp18; Wm4(2).

Philley
Henr: Wp25c; Wp29.

Philpotts; Phelpotts; Phelpots; Philpott
Mr: Wb26; Fran: Wp29; Hugh: B7; Jam: Wm4; Johan: Wb6; John: H6; Wm11(3); Wm15; Wm20; Wm22; Wm23; Wm24; Wm25; Kath: Wm25; Margery: Wm21; Nich: Gm7; Gm18; S14; Wb12; Wb25; Rich: Gm11a; R10; R15d; Wb1; Wm22; Wm25; Thos: B12(2); S3; Wm2; Wm5(2); Wm15(5); Wm18; Wm20(2); Wm21; Wm25(2); Will: Ge1; Ge7a; Ge7b(2); Wm2; Wm20.

Phipson
Thos: S11a.

Phlaven
Rich: Wg14.

Pichard
Will: Ge11a.

Pike
Alice: Gm8.

Pillinger
Barthol: Gm1; Eliz: B11; John: R8.

Pilstow; see Pitstow
Phil: Wm7.

Pingrie
Thos: Ge13.

Pitman; Pyttman
Will: Wm1b; Wm14c.

Pitstow; see Pilstow
Phil: Wm20(2).

Pitt; Pytt; Pitts
Mr: Wp25c; wdw: R8; Wg10; Anne: B7; B20; Edwd: B19(2); Wp2; Gabriel: R8; Geo: R8; Henr: B1; B9; Jam: B7(2); B19; E6; S5a; Jane: Wg13; Wp10a; John: B5b; B7; B14b; B21; R8(4); Marg: Wb15; Rich: R8; Wp13d; Rowl: R8; Wp6a; Wp8; Thos: B13; B25; R8(2); Wb15(2); Wp29; Walt: Gm12; Will: E5(2); Ge1; Wb15(3).

Plaine
John: B2.

Plene
Will: Gm8.

Poole
Wdw: H3; Henr: R25; Jam: H5; Mich: R15f; Rich: R25; Will: B5a.

Pooton
Wdw: Wg6; Johan: Wp4a; Thos: Wg2(2).

Pope
John: Wg16.

Porter
Mr: Wb8; Edwd: B1; B4.

Poston
John: Wg6; Rich: Wp18.

Pothookes; Pottlogge
Rich: Wb5.

Potter
Thos: Wm25.

Poughnell
Anne: S10.

Pountney
Elin: Gm11a.

Powell; Poule; Powle
Mr: B10e; Mrs; B27c; Gm18; wdw: R20; Wm11; Alice: Wb15; Anne: Wg17; Charles: E3; David: Wm13(2); Edwd: E8; R9; Wm23; Edgar: R9; Edm: R4; Wp11; Eliz: Wp9; Elizeor: B19; Fran: Wp4b; Wp13c; Wp24; Geo: Gm1; Wm24; Giles: R4; Henr: E6; S13; Wp24; Howell: E8; Hugh: Wp9; Jacob: E5; Jam: E5; H4; H6; Wp13f; Jane: Wg24; Johan: R4; S6; John: Ge12; Gm1; Gm23; R9; R26; Wg11(2); Wg24; Wg30; Wp1; Wp15; Wm5; Kath: E6; H2; Lewis: E1(2); E5(3); Wp11; Marg: S6; Wp9; Wp13e; Mary: E1; Miles: E8; Morgan: E6; Wb1; Nich: B28; Wm18; Patrick: H2; Phil: E1; E8; Rich: E6; Ge2; Ge9(2); H6; Wb21; Wg4(2); Wm18; Wm21; Rog: B27c(3); R19; Rob: R7; Wp13f; Sam: B13; Wg5; Wp4a; Thos: E4; E6; E8; H2; Wb10; Wgla; Walt: B10a; Ge3; H2; H3; Wg30; Wp10a; Wp13c; Wp24; Watkin: E6; Will: E4(2); E5(2); E8(2); Gm12; R4; R9; S6; S14; Wb7; Wb16; Wb17; Wp4a; Wp11(2); Wp29; Wm2; Wm3; Wm7; Wm13(2); Wm14b; Wm17; Wm20; Wm22.

Powles
John: R13; Rog: B4; B9.

Poytheras
Margery: Ge8f.

Preece; Prees; Preese; Prece; see Price
Alice: E6(2); Arth: B10a; David: E8; H8; S9; Jam: Gm2; Wp13e; Jane: Wg12; John: E7; Ge2; Wb17; Rich: H2; Wm21; Rog: Gm4; Sim: Wm9; Thos: Ge11a; Wb13(2); Walt: B10b; Will: B10e; E8; Wb20.

Price; Pryse; see Preece
Mr: B2(2); B7(2); B10b(2); B10c; B10e; B13; Mrs: B27c; Gm11a; Gm11b; wdw: E4; Gm11b; Abel: Wb12; Anne: S14; Arth: Gm21; S10; David: H8; Edm: E1; Elin: Gm3; Felice: Gm21; Fran: S1; Geo: Wb1; Griffith: H5; Henr: E3; Jam: H6(2); Wg7; Wg26; Wp19a; Johan: E5; John: B10b; B12; B27c; E3; E4; E5; E8; Gm11a; Gm16; S6; S14; Wb21; Wg23(2); Wg30; Wm18; Josias: Wb10; Math: H6; Morgan: Gm7; S11a; Phil: E3; E6; Rich: Wb12; Wp4b; Thos: E3; E4; Ge8a; Ge8f; Gm18; H6; Wb1; Wb25; Wg12; Wp25c; Wm18; Will: E5(2); S1; Wb12(2); Wm9.

Pridith; Priddith
Edwd: Wm21; Thos: Wm21; Walt: Wm18; Wm21.

Prince
John: Wg24; Wg27.

Prior
Bennett: Wp18.

Pritchett; Pritchard; Prichard
Mr: Ge15; Wp16b; Mrs: R9; wdw: Gm23; Anne: Ge2; David: H2; Edwd: B14a; Eliz: E3; Fran: Wm8; Gabriel: Wb10; Geo: E5; Gronow: E3; Henr: E8; Howell: E6; Hugh: E5; E8; Jam: Wb2; Wb17; Jane: E3(2); Jeremy: E7; John: E4; E6; E8; Wm2; Wm20; Kath: E5; Lewis: E6; Wg24; Mary: E8; Phil: E3(2); Ge11a; Wm5; Rees: E5; Rich: E3; Ro: Wm2; Thos: E5; H1; Wp9; Will: E5; Ge11a; R8; R9; Wb2; Wb13; Wm4.

Probert; Probart; Probarts
Mrs: B19; Jam: E6(2); John: Gm1; Gm13; H5(2); Wb10; Rich: E2; Gm9; H3; Wb12; Rob: H6; Thos: Gm2; Will: Wp3.

Probin
Jam: Wm25; Rich: Wb18.

Prodger
Edwd: Wp26.

Rodd—*continued.*
Wg23; Hugh: Gm11a; Jam: B18; Gm3;
Gm13; Gm23; H6; R20(2); Wb6;
Wg12; Wg22a; Wm7; Wm19; Rich:
Wg7; Wg22a; Wg26(5); Ro: Gm17;
Gm23; Thos: Ge11a; R20; Wg22a;
Will: Wg25.

Rogers
Mr: B10b; Wb19; Wb26; Wm18; Ch:
Wm17; Edwd: Ge8g(2); Geo: S8;
Henr: Gm7; Gm21; H3; James: R19;
John: B2; E5; Gm7; H5; H6; S8;
Wm17; Wm18; Rich: Wp7; Wm14a;
W16(2); Wm17; Thos: E1; S8; Wb18;
Wg24; Walt: Ge8e; H6; Will: Wm7;
Wm16.

Romsall
Phil: Gm23.

Ropier
Will: R18.

Rose
Roses: Ge8g.

Rosse
Jam: H3; Wp14; Wp29; Thos: S3.

Rosser; ? see **Rosse**
Jam: H3.

Rowbery
John: Wp13e; Rich: Wp13f.

Rowdon
Rowdon: H6; Anne: B3; Anth: B1;
B3; B4; B22; B26; Rog: H4.

Rowell
John: S8(3).

Rowland; Rouland; Roulands
John: H1(2); H4(2); Will: Wb10.

Rowse
Mr: B19.

Ruckell
Will: Wm20.

Rudd
Fran: Wg24; Henr: Wg4; Stannardine:
Wg24; Thos: Wg24.

Rudge
Anth: Ge1; wdw: Ge11a; Henr: Ge15;
John: Ge1(2); Ge7b; Ge15(4); Kath:
Ge15; Mary: Ge7b; Thos: Ge11a;
Ge15; Will: Ge1; Ge15.

Rudhall
Mrs: Ge7a; Ge15; Mary: Ge13;
Wm2.

Rumney
Paul: B9; R4.

Rusbach
Edm: Wg9; John: Wg27.

Russell
Mr: Wb23; Edm: R7; Edw: B17;
Wp13d; Hugh: Wb1; Wb23(2); Wm9;
John: B28; Ro: Wm9.

Sabin
Will: H6.

Saise; Sayse; Sayce; Saice
Saises: Gm22; Anne: S2; John: S14;
Wb15; Wp14; Ro: Wg15; Walt: S12;
Will: S14(2).

Salisbury
Earl of: E8.

Salloway; Salway
Mr: B20; Wg2; John: Wp21; Rich:
Wp21.

Sampson
Wdw: Wb1; Henr: Wb14(2).

Sandford; Sanford
Ro: R11; Thos: B2(2).

Sands; Sandes
Edwd: Ge9(2); Mr: Ge8g.

Sandy
Will: E5.

Sansum
Johan: Wb23.

Santt
Rich: S5a.

Saunders; Sanders
John: B3; B9; E3; Will: E3.

Savaker
Alex: E7; H2; Jam: H2(2); John:
Wm5(2); Rich: Gm1; Wp7.

Sawyer
Geo: Gm8; Will: R5.

Sayer
Charles: H6; Fran: B2; Geo: Wb18;
John: H6; Thos: H6.

Scandrett; Scandret; Scaundrett
Edwd: H6; S8; John: Gm1; H6; S10;
Oliver: H6; Rich: H6(2); Wg12; Steph:
H6; Walt: H6; Will: H6; Wg25.

Scarlett
Geo: Gm8; Thos: Wp13c.

Stepple; see Staple
Will: Wp20.

Stilling
John: Gm6; Wb4.

Stinton; Steenton
John: Wg20.

Stitch; Stich; Stych
Mr: B1; Henr: B16; Thos: Wg4; Wg5;
Wg27(4).

Stock; Stocke
Charles: Ge1; Ge11a.

Stockton
Anne: R9.

Stodart
John: R23.

Stokes; Stoakes
Rich: R9(2); Thos: R9.

Stone
John: R15a; Rob: R15a; R28b; Thos:
Ge7b; Ge15; R15c; Will: R26.

Storr; Storre; see Starre
Johan: Wg3; John: Wg3(3).

Strafford
John: B11.

Strangwell
Rich: Wg30.

Stratford
Fortune: Ge14; Rob: Ge14(2).

Streater
Benjamin: Wg4.

Streete; see Stritt
John: Ge2; Wp13a; Will: Wm7.

Strettalls
Ralph: Wg5.

Stritt; see Streete
John: Ge5.

Stroud
Mr: B16; John: R9.

Such; see Souch
John: B9.

Sucker
Will: Wp7.

Suett; Suatt; Shuat; Shuett
Fran: S14; Thos: S7.

Sugar
Will: S6.

Suter
Rich: Gm11a; Thos: H6.

Sutton
Miles: Ge5; Thos: B10a.

Swayne
Thos: Ge15.

Swift
Mrs: Wm15; Eliz: Wm5.

Sybrance
John: Ge14.

Sych
Will: B4.

Syllies; Syly
Mrs: Gm2; Hugh: Gm8; Phil: Gm8;
Rich: Gm8; Thos: Gm8(2).

Symes
Anth: Wp4a; Will: Wg26.

**Symons; Simons; Simmons; Symmons;
Symmonds; Simonds; Simmonds;
Symonds**
Mr: B10b; Wp19b; Alice: Gm3; John:
E5; Wb12; Wb28; Wm1b; Phil: Gm11a;
Wb4; Wb19; Wb22; Wm7; Rich: B2;
Wb19; Rog: Wb28; Thos: Gm21; Wb1;
Will: R26.

Syncock; Sinock; Synnock
Wdw: B2; Edwd: S14; Jam: S14; Walt:
B2.

Tanty
Thos: Ge16.

Tarbox
Thos: B11(2).

Tart
Thos: Wp5.

Taylor; Tayler; Tailor; see Thylor
Anth: Ge11a; wdw: R12; Brian: Wg15;
Edm: B6; Edwd: B12; Geo: Ge5(2);
Henr: S10; S11a; Wg20; Hump: B27a;
B27d; R30(2); Johan: Ge6; S11a; John:
Ge2; Ge11a; Ge11b; Ge13; Gm13;
Gm23; H6(2); R15f; Wb20(3); Wm11;
Wm25; Joseph: Ge11a; Marg: Wm24;
Nich: Gm7; Rich: B12; Gm11a; S11a;
R27; Wb16; Ro: Wg31; Wm25; Rog:
B10f; E1; Rowl: B12; B27a; R31; Wb2;
Sam: Wp13c; Silvanus: Wp16a; Thos:
B1; B6(2); B18; B27d; B28; Ge7a;
Ge11a; R1; R6; S3; S7; Wg1a; Wg16(2);
Wg17; Wp13a; Wm11; Walt: Gm7;
Will: Ge7a(2); Gm5; H4; H6; S6;
Wp13f.

Teagy; Teguy; Teague
John: Ge7a; Ge7b; Thos: Wb12.

Thomas
Wdw: R8; Charles: E4; David: E4;
E5(2); H6; Edm: E6; Gm13; H6; S8;
R9; Wg25; Eustance: E2; Gwyn:
E4(2); Howell: E3; Hugh: E5; Wb1(2);
Jam: Wg20; Johan: E8; John: E1;
E4(2); E8; Wm5; Licence: Gm7; Marg:
Wg18; Meredith: S9; Mich: E6; E7;
E8; Miles: Wg20; Paul: E5; Phil: E5;
Rachel: E7; Wb2; Rich: Wm15; Sam:
Gm7; Wm9; Will: E4; E7.

Thorne
Mr: Wb15.

Thylor; see Taylor
Arth: Gm8.

Tier
Thos: Ge5.

Tinker
Sam: R15f.

Tirpin
Thos: Wg16; Wg29.

Toffey
Thos: B2.

Toldervey; Toldervie
Eliz: Wp13c; Jane: S6; Will: Wp13d.

Tombes; Tomes
Mr: Wp16b; Jam: Ge13; John:
Ge13(2); Wp13a; Wm11; Rich; Ge11a.

Tomkins; Tomkyns; Tomkin; Tompkins
Mr: B12; B26; Mrs: B26; wdw: Wb19;
Anne: R1; S2; Audrey: Wp10b; Edwd:
R3; Eliz: R1; Fran: R31; Jam: Wp21;
Johan: B27a; John: B4; B15; B24;
B27d; R25; Wb20; Wg3(2); Wp10b;
Wp13c; Miles: S7; Nath: R13; Sim:
S1; Thos: B27c; Gm2; Gm15; S10;
S14; R11; Wp10b; Wp13d; Wp21.

Tomlins; Tomblyns
Edm: R8; R28b; Edw: R11; Tho:
Gm7; R28b.

Tomy
John: Wm2; Wm10; Rob: Wm19(2);
Wm25; Will: Wm19(2).

Torre
Tho: Wb8(2).

Tovey
John: Wm11; Wm21; Wm23; Thos:
B23.

Tower
Giles: Ge5.

Towne
John: Gm7; Gm21; Wp21; Joyce:
Wp10a; Thos: Wp21; Will: B10c;
Gm21.

Townsend
Ro: Wg2.

Toy; see Foy

Tracy
Sam: H1; H3.

Traunter
Mrs: Ge4; Barnaby: S8(2); Fran:
Gm13; John: H6; S8(2); E2; Wg25;
Sim: S8; Thos: H6(2); S8(2); Wg25.

Travell
Joseph: B6.

Treaven
Will: Ge13.

Treherne; Traherne; Treyherne
John: R19; Tho: Gm9; R19; R26; Will:
Wb13; Wm4.

Tringham
Will: Wm5.

Trippett
Wdw: Ge1.

Trumper
Geo: Wp2; John: S4; Thos: S4; Will:
S1; S4.

Tryon; Tryan
Sam: H4.

Tudor; Tuder; Tydor
Ch: Wm24; John: Ge11a; Wm2; Rich:
Wm24.

Tuflin; Tuffling
Anne: S3; Rich: S3(2); S14.

Tullie; Tully
Tullie's: B19; John: Gm11a; Will:
Gm12(2); R19.

Turbervile
Will: Wp3.

Turbill
John: Ge8d.

Turner
Anne: B19; R9; Jam: R9; John: Gm17;
R7; R9; Joyce: Wp1; Kath: R25; Rich:
B13; Ge8d; Ge8f; R8; R28b; Rob: R8;
Susan: R9; Theodosia: Wb8; Thos:
B10b; Ge7a; Gm2; Will: R9.

Tuthill
Tuthill: H6.

Tyler; Tiler
Edwd: B26; Flory: Wg30; Henr: Wg31;
John: Wb16; Wg21; Wg31; Rich: Ge6;
Wm5; Thos: Wg26; Wp4a; Wp18; Will:
R6(2); R26; Wg8; Wg21.

Tyrer
Tyrer: Wm8; Thos: Wm15; Wm22.

Uncles
John: B14a.

Underhill
Hercules: Wp1.

Underwood
Wdw: Wm7; Thos: B9; Walt: Wm8;
Wm13; Wm14c.

Unett; Unitt
Mr: R2; Eliz: Ge10; Fran: R5; Geo:
B16; B25; Rich: Ge10.

Vale
Rich: Wp4a; Ro: Wp11.

Valentine
Hugh: E3.

Valiance
John: Wg1a; Thos: Wg4.

Vaston; Waston
Charles: Gm16; Henr: Wp25a(2); John:
B8; Wp6b(2); Wp25a; Will: Wp6b;
Wp13f.

Vaughan; Vaugham
Mr: Wm11; Mrs: Gm12; Anne: S8;
S10; Edwd: H8; Eliz: Wb12; Henr:
Wb20; Jam: Wb21(2); John: Ge1; Ge2;
Ge5; Ge9; Ge11b; Ge13; H6; Wg30;
Wm2; Wm8; Wm20; Wm25; Kath:
Wm17; Phil: Wb2; Wm5; Wm15;
Wm25(2); Rich: Wm5; Wm20; Wm23;
Rob: H8; Wm20; Wm22; Rog: H1; H3;
Wb4; Wb10; Rowl: Wb3; Thos: Gm22;
H2; H5; S6; Wm5(2); Wm7; Wm15;
Walt: E1; H6; S8; S10; Wm5; Will: E5;
Gm12; Gm20; Wb12; Wm5.

Venmore
John: Wp29; Thos: Wp29(2).

Vernall
John: Wp6b(2); Thos: Wp6b(2); Wp11;
Will: Wp13b.

Viccares; Vickeres; Viccarrs
John: S9;   Sibbill: Wp24;   Thos:
R25.

Vie; Vye
Rob: B23(2); Thos: Wp10b.

Vinall;? Winall
Will: Wb17.

Viner
John: S5a.

Vines
Alice: R25.

Voare
Rich: H6.

Vobe
Anth: R8; R28; Will: R27(2); R28.

Voile
Mr: Wm14c.

Voyce
Jam: Ge7b.

Wackline; Walkley
John: Wm17.

Wade
Ro: Wb27.

Walcroft
Jam: R15a(2).

Walker
Mr: Wg6; Hump: B19; John: Wm4;
Wm21; Rich: Gm11a; Gm16; Gm18(2);
Thos: Wb12; Wb27; Will: Wg6.

Wallbeef; Wallbeefe; Walbeefe
Mrs: E4; Eliz: E4; E5; Kath: E4(2);
E5.

Wallis
Phil: Gm11a.

Walls; Wall
Mr: R2; wdw: Gm11a; Barthol: S6(2);
Fran: Ge12; Henr: S6; Wp29; Hump:
Wp11; Wp20; John: Wp29; Rog:
B25(2); Thos: S8; S10; Wp29; Will: E3;
R17; S8; S10(2); Wg20.

Walsh
John: Gm11a; Gm11b.

Walsham
Barbara: Wg12; John: Wg12; Marg:
Wg12.

Walter
Wdw: Wb1; Henr: Gm5(2); Rog: Gm7.

Walton
Christ: Ge1; Ge7b(2); Herb: Wp25c(2);
John: S9; Wp13d; Rich: Gm21; S9(2);
Thos: S6; S9; Wp9; Wp10a; Will:
Wp25a.

Q

Yapp
Johan: Wg17; Wp20; John: Wp25a; Wp29; Thos: Wp18(2).

Yarrett
Thos: Wm21.

Ychan; Ycan
Howell: E4(5); Maud: E4; E5.

Yeame
Thos: Ge14.

Yeareworth
Thos: Wm19(3).

Yeates; Yates
Eliz: B4; Thos: Wg1a.

Yeomans; Yeomons
Phil: Gm8(2); Rich: Wp3; Rog: Wp3; Thos: Wp13d; Will: Gm7; Wp11(2).

Young
Fran: Wg17(2); Johan: R9; John: Ge11b; Ro: Wg23.

Younger; Yonger
John: Wb12(2).

INDEX OF PLACES

Each township or parish for which an entry or entries exist and each place within those lists is here identified by the alpha-numerical symbol of the particular list (printed on p. 189). Each parish or township for which a list is present is printed in bold.

Wonton: S1
Wood: Wg19
Woodfields: R17
Woolhope: Ge16
Wormbridge: Wb28
Wormsley: Gm22
Wootton: S7

Wyett: B19
Yarkhill: R31
Yarpole: Wp29
Yatton: Ge9
Yazor: Gm23
Yetton: Wg31

INDEX OF EDITORIAL MATTER

This includes all references to persons and places and subjects apart from those in the text of the valuations themselves, that is in the Introduction and footnotes. The parish symbols indicate that the reference is to a footnote to a parish schedule. Symbols Ii, Iii, etc., indicate that the reference is to a particular section of the Introduction.